Rethinking Geographical Explorations in Extreme Environments

Focusing on extreme environments, from Umberto Nobile's expedition to the Arctic to the commercialisation of Mt Everest, this volume examines global environmental margins, how they are conceived, and how perceptions have changed. Mountaintops and Arctic environments are the settings of social encounters, political strategies, individual enterprises, geopolitical tensions, decolonial practices, and scientific experiments.

Concentrating on mountaineering and Arctic exploration between 1880 and 1960, contributors to this volume show how environmental marginalisation has been discursively implemented and materially generated by foreign and local actors. It examines to what extent the status and identity of extreme environments has changed during modern times, moving them from periphery to the centre and discarding their marginality. The first section looks at ways in which societies have framed remoteness, through the lens of commercialisation, colonialism, knowledge production, and sport, while the second examines the reverse transfer, focusing on how extreme nature has influenced societies through international network creation, political consensus, and identity building. This collection enriches the historical understanding of exploration by adopting a critical approach and offering multidimensional and multi-gaze reconstructions.

This book is essential reading for students and scholars interested in environmental history, geography, colonial studies, and the environmental humanities.

Marco Armiero is Research Director at the Institute for the Studies on the Mediterranean at the Italian National Research Council in Naples, Italy, and Director of the Environmental Humanities Laboratory at the Royal Institute of Technology, Stockholm, Sweden. Since 2019, he has been the President of the European Society for Environmental History.

Roberta Biasillo is Assistant Professor of Contemporary Political History at the Department of History and Art History at Utrecht University, the Netherlands, and visiting Max Weber Fellow at the Robert Schuman Centre for Advanced Studies at the European University Institute in Florence, Italy.

Stefano Morosini is Adjunct Professor of Environmental History at the University of Bergamo, Italy, and is Senior Associate Researcher at the Centre for the History of the Alps (LabiSAlp) – Italian-Swiss University in Mendrisio. He is also the Scientific Coordinator of the Heritage projects at the Stelvio National Park, Italy.

Routledge Explorations in Environmental Studies

Environmental Defenders
Deadly Struggles for Land and Territory
Edited by Mary Menton and Philippe Le Billon

Globalization, Environmental Law and Sustainable Development in the Global South
Challenges for Implementation
Edited by Kirk W. Junker and Paolo Davide Farah

The Political Ecology of Austerity
Crisis, Social Movements, and the Environment
Edited by Rita Calvário, Maria Kaika and Giorgos Velegrakis

Sociology Saves the Planet
An Introduction to Socioecological Thinking and Practice
Thomas Macias

Polluting Textiles
The Problem with Microfibres
Edited by Judith S. Weis, Francesca De Falco and Mariacristina Cocca

Biocultural Rights, Indigenous Peoples and Local Communities
Protecting Culture and the Environment
Edited by Fabien Girard, Ingrid Hall and Christine Frison

Rethinking Geographical Explorations in Extreme Environments
From the Arctic to the Mountaintops
Edited by Marco Armiero, Roberta Biasillo, and Stefano Morosini

Governance Networks for Sustainable Cities
Connecting Theory and Practice in Europe
Katherine Maxwell

For more information about this series, please visit: www.routledge.com/Routledge-Explorations-in-Environmental-Studies/book-series/REES

Rethinking Geographical Explorations in Extreme Environments

From the Arctic to the Mountaintops

Edited by Marco Armiero,
Roberta Biasillo, and
Stefano Morosini

First published 2023
by Routledge
4 Park Square, Milton Park, Abingdon, Oxon OX14 4RN

and by Routledge
605 Third Avenue, New York, NY 10158

Routledge is an imprint of the Taylor & Francis Group, an informa business

© 2023 selection and editorial matter, Marco Armiero, Roberta Biasillo, and Stefano Morosini; individual chapters, the contributors

The right of Marco Armiero, Roberta Biasillo, and Stefano Morosini to be identified as the authors of the editorial material, and of the authors for their individual chapters, has been asserted in accordance with sections 77 and 78 of the Copyright, Designs and Patents Act 1988.

All rights reserved. No part of this book may be reprinted or reproduced or utilised in any form or by any electronic, mechanical, or other means, now known or hereafter invented, including photocopying and recording, or in any information storage or retrieval system, without permission in writing from the publishers.

Trademark notice: Product or corporate names may be trademarks or registered trademarks, and are used only for identification and explanation without intent to infringe.

British Library Cataloguing-in-Publication Data
A catalogue record for this book is available from the British Library

Library of Congress Cataloging-in-Publication Data
A catalog record has been requested for this book

ISBN: 978-0-367-55983-0 (hbk)
ISBN: 978-0-367-55984-7 (pbk)
ISBN: 978-1-003-09596-5 (ebk)

DOI: 10.4324/9781003095965

Typeset in Times New Roman
by Apex CoVantage, LLC

Contents

List of Figures	vii
List of Contributors	viii
Acknowledgements	xii
Introduction: A world that is losing its margins	1
MARCO ARMIERO, ROBERTA BIASILLO, AND STEFANO MOROSINI	

1 **Emotions and mountaineering for internationalist purposes: The case of the Union Internationale des Associations d'Alpinisme (UIAA), 1939–1951**   9
 ILARIA SCAGLIA

2 **Power, politics and exploration in fascist Italy: The 1928 watershed**   22
 MARCO CUZZI

3 **Roald Amundsen *vs* Umberto Nobile: The role of the newspapers in the age of nationalism and polar imperialism**   34
 STEINAR AAS

4 **Umberto Nobile between two totalitarianisms**   56
 LUCIANO ZANI

5 **Imperialist Italian geography currents in the work of Roberto Almagià and his ambiguous relationship with the fascist regime**   72
 SANDRO RINAURO

6 **Walter Wood and the legacies of science and alpinism in the St Elias Mountains**   90
 PEDER ROBERTS

7 **Physiology and biomedicine on high-altitude expeditions (c. 1880–1980)** 106
   VANESSA HEGGIE

8 **Italian geographers, scientists, travellers and mountaineers in the Karakoram (1890–1954)** 124
   STEFANO MOROSINI

9 **Commercialisation and Mount Everest in the twentieth century** 144
   PETER H. HANSEN

10 **Geographical exploration via the environmental humanities: Decolonising approaches to space** 157
   ROBERTA BIASILLO

   Appendix: The rediscovery of two files relating to the Karakoram (1928–1929) and North Pole (1928) expeditions conserved at the Municipal Archives in Milan 176
   STEFANO TWARDZIK

   Index of names and places 196

Figures

3.1	Facsimile of the first page of the newspaper *Tidens Tegn* on 27 May 1931.	35
3.2	Incidence of the name 'Umberto Nobile' in Norwegian press from September 1925 to October 1926.	39
3.3	The last photo of the main protagonists of the Amundsen-Ellsworth-Nobile transpolar flight together in Seattle.	41
3.4	Incidence of 'Roald Amundsen' and 'Umberto Nobile' in Norwegian newspapers 1925–1930.	48
6.1	The St Elias Mountains, showing Kluane Lake and other sites mentioned in the text.	91
10.1	Chiaiano Neighbourhood, Naples (Italy).	161
10.2	Marrickville Maps: Tropical Imaginaries of Abundance (2018).	162
10.3	*New York City Climate Change Displacement Map* (2020).	163
10.4	First plan of Addis Ababa as capital of the Italian Empire (1938).	167
11.1	Examples of subfiles folders of the two dossiers.	179
11.2	Cover of the box which contained negatives of the Karakoram expedition's photos.	185
11.3	Titles and notes marked on bundle 12.	189

Contributors

Steinar Aas is Professor of Modern History at Nord University, Norway. He has been studying the adventures of Italian polar explorers seen from a Norwegian perspective. He is also interested in modernisation processes in Norway and, in particular, political, social, and cultural change in the twentieth century. He has published extensively in urban history, the development of mass democracy, memory history, and cultural history, as well as regional and local history.

Marco Armiero is Director of the Environmental Humanities Laboratory at the Royal Institute of Technology, Stockholm (Sweden), and Researcher Director at the Institute for the Studies on the Mediterranean of the Italian National Research Council (Italy). His research has contributed to bridging the fields of environmental history, political ecology, and the environmental humanities. He has recently published *Wasteocene: Stories from the Global Dump* (2021), also available in Italian translation *L'era degli scarti. Cronache dal Wasteocene, la discarica globale* (2021).

Roberta Biasillo is Assistant Professor of Contemporary Political History at Utrecht University and visiting Max Weber Fellow at the Robert Schuman Centre for Advanced Studies at the European University Institute in Florence. Roberta started exploring Italian colonialism and imperialism when she was a fellow at the LMU – Rachel Carson Center for Environment and Society in Munich and at the Italian Institute for Social Security. She has a longstanding collaboration with and has worked at the Environmental Humanities Laboratory of the KTH Royal Institute of Technology in Stockholm. Her main areas of expertise are territorial and forest issues in modern Italy and colonial environmental history with a focus on north and east Africa. She is also interested in historical theory and environmental humanities research methodologies.

Marco Cuzzi is Associate Professor of Contemporary History at the University of Milan. His research interests concern the history of fascism from domestic and international perspectives and the history of Italy's eastern border and Italian freemasonry. He has published widely on WW2, fascist regimes, and Italian military and political history. He is member of the University Network for the Day of Remembrance and sits on various scientific committees (Craxi Foundation, Center for Studies on the Historical Period of the Italian Social Republic, Jewish Center for Contemporary Documentation, Center for Studies and Documentation on Freemasonry, Dante Alighieri Society of Berlin, *Historical Magazine of Socialism*, *Hiram* magazine). He is the Co-Director of the series "History, Politics and Society" and "Chaos Kai Kosmos" for Biblion Press.

Peter H. Hansen is Professor of History and Director of International and Global Studies at Worcester Polytechnic Institute. *The Summits of Modern Man: Mountaineering after the Enlightenment* (2013) examined the intertwined histories of mountaineering and modernity since the eighteenth century. He has also written about yaks, colonialism, documentary films, climber's biographies, and the Alps and Himalayas. Hansen has been a Fulbright Scholar and a visiting fellow at Durham, Harvard, Cambridge, and the Australian National University. He has reached wider audiences as a lecturer at libraries and museums and commentator for several BBC television programs. He is currently writing a book on commercialisation and Mt Everest.

Vanessa Heggie is Senior Lecturer in the History of Science and Medicine at the University of Birmingham (UK). She gained her PhD in 2004 researching the history of degeneration in Victorian and Edwardian Manchester and since then has published widely on a range of topics relating to health, medicine, and affiliated sciences in the nineteenth and twentieth centuries; this includes papers on the history of district nursing, the role of exploration in modern science, and the development of sex testing in sports. She is the author of *A History of British Sports Medicine* (2011) and *Higher and Colder: A History of Extreme Physiology and Exploration* (2019), also available in Italian translation *In alto e al gelo. Storie di fisiologia estrema e di esplorazioni* (2021).

Stefano Morosini is Adjunct Professor of Environmental History at the University of Bergamo (Italy) and is Associate Researcher at the Centre for the History of the Alps (LabiSAlp) – Italian-Swiss University in Mendrisio (Switzerland). He is currently the scientific coordinator of a European project on the historical heritage of Stelvio National Park (Italy). He has been researcher at the Polytechnic of Milan, and in 2017 he was a visiting scholar at the Environmental Humanities Laboratory at the KTH Royal Institute of Technology in Stockholm. His research focuses on the Alpine area: his works analyse the history of mountaineering and tourism, WW1, the contested identities of South Tyrol, industrial development in Northern Italy, and protected areas. He is currently working on a history of the Stelvio National Park.

Sandro Rinauro is Associate Professor in Economic and Political Geography at the University of Milan. His works focus on Italian migrations in past and in present time and more in general on contemporary population movements, with a special focus on irregular migration and related border politics in Europe.

From a methodological perspective, he is interested in the use of public opinion surveys in social research applied to the geographic imagery of migrants, the history of human geography during the nineteenth and twentieth centuries, and the spread of illegal work among immigrants in present-day Italy. He has extensively contributed to the fields of geography and historical demography.

Peder Roberts is Associate Professor of Modern History at the University of Stavanger and a researcher at KTH Royal Institute of Technology. He has published widely on the history of science, politics, and the environment in the polar regions and the deep oceans, including the monograph *The European Antarctic: Science and Strategy in Scandinavia and the British Empire* (2011) and three edited volumes. Peder's current projects include a history of the Arctic Institute of North America and (with Adrian Howkins), editing the *Cambridge History of the Polar Regions* (to be published in 2022). He is currently Principal Investigator of the European Research Council-funded project "Greening the Poles: Science, the Environment, and the Creation of the Modern Arctic and Antarctic."

Ilaria Scaglia is Senior Lecturer at Aston University in Birmingham, UK. She was previously Assistant Professor in the Department of History and Geography at Columbus State University, USA (2013–2018) and a Volkswagen-Mellon post-doctoral research fellow in Germany (Free University Berlin)/Visiting Researcher at the Centre "History of Emotions" at the Max Planck Institute for Human Development in Berlin (2016–17). She works on twentieth-century international history with a special focus on culture, aesthetics, and emotions. She is the author of *The Emotions of Internationalism: Feeling International Cooperation in the Alps in the Interwar Period* (2020). Her previous publications dealt with the interplay of art and performative politics, nation branding and international cooperation, and the moral economy of internationalism.

Stefano Twardzik is Researcher of Archival Studies at the History Department of the University of Milan. He has dealt with the following topics: municipal archives in the nineteenth and twentieth centuries; the evolution of the Italian archival administration; and higher education institutions operating in Milan during the nineteenth and twentieth centuries, including the University of Milan and the former Royal School of Veterinary Medicine. He has rearranged the fonds of both these institutes and prepared their inventories. He has also worked on Aldo Moro's writings after being kidnapped by the Red Brigades (1978), and he edited, together with a working group coordinated by Michele Di Sivo (State Archives of Rome), a recent edition of Moro's "memoir." He is currently completing the inventory of the files of expeditions to Karakorum and the North Pole preserved at the Cittadella degli archivi of Milan Municipality.

Luciano Zani has been Full Professor in Contemporary History at the Social and Economic Science Department at "Sapienza" University of Rome until 2020.

Luciano has taught at the University of Camerino and spent a period at the University of Wisconsin-Madison as Fulbright Visiting Professor in 1983. Currently, he sits on the editorial board of the Italian scientific journal *Mondo contemporaneo* and is a member of the scientific committee of the Italian foundation Paolo Murialdi for media study.

Acknowledgements

This book is the outcome of a conference held in Milan in November 2018 titled "From the Arctic to the 8000. Scientific research, mountaineering, geography and imperialism from an international perspective (1880–1964)".

As editors, we would like to express our gratitude to the Department of History of the University of Milan and the Environmental Humanities Laboratory at the KTH Royal Institute of Technology in Stockholm, which have generously supported our project.

The Cittadella degli Archivi of Milan Municipality, International Association for Alpine History, and Laboratory of Alpine History of the University of Italian Switzerland have also been patrons of the project.

We would also like to thank the Fondazione AEM – a2a Group and PFU (EMEA) Ltd – A Fujitsu Company for the contribution gave to the project.

Finally, a special thanks to the authors who have contributed to this book.

In the long process of turning a manuscript into a book, we have appreciated the support and the patience of the series editors Rosie Anderson, Grace Harrison, and Matthew Shobbrook. We are in debt to all the anonymous reviewers for the valuable comments we received in the peer-review process.

We are also grateful for the journey this volume has provided to us, reinforcing our friendship and intellectual collaboration.

Marco Armiero, Roberta Biasillo, and Stefano Morosini

Introduction

A world that is losing its margins

*Marco Armiero, Roberta Biasillo, and
Stefano Morosini*

The making and unmaking of margins

We live in a world that is losing its margins, and every place on earth is connected or potentially connectable. From the Himalayas to Arctic Siberia, from Point Nemo in Antarctica to Vale do Javari in the Brazilian Amazon rainforest, no place can be considered radically secluded from external influences and from other social and ecological systems. From an Earth system science point of view, the entire planet has now entered into the so-called Anthropocene: in an age in which environmental changes consist of planetary-scale and systemic changes and in an era when humans are able to affect the entire bio-geo-chemical cycles of the planet, it does not make much sense to speak of isolated places. Inescapable global and globalising networks do not limit themselves to climate change dynamics; the testing of nuclear weapons, for instance, has also left its traces in remote areas of the planet, including Antarctica.[1]

However, looking at the reduction, or even the erasure, of the margins through their incorporation in the global socio-ecosystem, more than the Anthropocene, we will see other '-cenes,' less reticent to uncover unequal power relationships, making the global look like an empire rather than an interdependent community. Call it Plantationocene,[2] Capitalocene,[3] or Wasteocene:[4] whatever label we use, it appears clear that this is a story of appropriation and extraction, of mining and dumping, of enslavement and genocide. The continuous expansion of capitalism into the extreme frontiers does not erase the margins but produces them. It is via the incorporation into the global market economy that some places, communities, humans, and more-than-humans have become marginals, that is, subalterns to some political, economic, and cultural centres. It is not physical geography but power that makes something or someone marginal. And, obviously, connecting them to the centre does not solve their alleged marginality; we might argue that without connections, those would be autonomous rather than marginal spaces. As history tells us, marginal areas – jungles, mountains, marshes, steppes – have often been the fluid strongholds of any kind of rebels, undisciplined subjects immersed in untamed environments. For empires, states, or capitalist corporations, the path has always been clear: remote areas must be transformed into marginal areas;

DOI: 10.4324/9781003095965-1

nature and people must be disciplined; subordination rather than connection is the ordering principle of this process.

Margins are shape-shifting constructions, historically and culturally in the making. In this production of margins, a key process has always been that of exploration. The very act of exploring implies a complex set of material and intellectual *dispositifs*. As the contributors of this volume clearly explain, exploring requires conspicuous support, be it a financial commitment from public or private sponsors or political and ideological support stemming from a colonial project of 'othering' and a nationalistic celebration of the 'us'. Exploring is often seasoned with scientific aims, which are generally well intertwined with nationalistic and colonial ambitions. The invisibilisation of local people, the erasure of their knowledge and even skills – one can think of alpine guides and Sherpas, both concealed in any narrative about the 'exploration' of high mountains – and the vilification of Indigenous environmental practises all conjure to produce the cultural ecosystem of explorations: an empty space waiting for the explorer to give sense to it through the national flag, a barometer, the right seeds, or perhaps a brand of some expensive wrist watches. Because the exploration of margins was not only about incorporating them into a network of global commodities and empires; it also meant to create them, in a subaltern conceptual relationship to the centre, which, for its part, was affected by that very exploration. We believe that this mutual reinforcement can be considered part of what several scholars have conceptualised as environment-building.[5]

Politicising the margins

Missions reached the South Pole for the first time in 1911 and the North Pole in 1926;[6] between 1950 and 1964, the 14 eight-thousanders have been climbed. In the last ten years, the 'conquests' of these 'fallen giants', quoting Maurice Isserman and Stewart Weaver,[7] have attracted the interest of scholars from different fields and countries.[8] Quite recently, in January 2021, ten Nepalese mountaineers made the first winter ascent of K2,[9] and the achievement of one of the last great climbing challenges brought up new questions and controversies.[10] From a postcolonial perspective, we should underline that nine of the ten Nepali climbers were Sherpas, and their achievement on K2 was the culmination of long training and research practices on Everest and other peaks across the twentieth century in a context characterised by an intense commercialisation of mountaineering.[11] Sherpas' successful ascent shared some common elements of previous ascents. For instance, when they neared the top, the whole team sang the Nepalese national anthem, stressing the political meaning and national – if not nationalistic – relevance of such events.

The environment and the human-environment relationship are, thus, inherently political, and when the 'conquest' of nature occurs, environment-building and state-building emerge as interconnected processes, material and symbolic at the same time and able to produce material and immaterial infrastructures. States and environments are not only made of railroads, cities, plantations, factories, and dams; the infrastructure making them is also a narrative one that gives meaning and identity to places and people. We must refuse the simplistic idea that the state is the space of history and politics and the environment is that of nature. Nature and history are packed together in both environing and state-building. The science of governing people – which lies at the very root of the state project – and the science of governing the environment – the pillar of any environmental project – are not only tools of knowledge but also performative practices producing the object of study. As the chapters in this volume make clear, those are two sides of the same coin. This does not mean, though, that the process of producing margins through explorations and appropriation occurred without contradictions.

These contradictions question the relationship between national and local dimensions, or even between order and rebellion. Here we would like to spark a discussion about the Alps with James C. Scott's book *The Art of Not Being Governed* in mind.[12] In the book, Scott analyses the mountainous region of Southeast Asia known as Zomia. For Scott, this is a non-state area, where the lowland nations have failed to enforce their order. However, Scott does not propose a model based on some authenticity, in the sense of isolated, indigenous, rebellious nature groups. Scott writes that, more than just rebels, they are fugitives, people who have escaped the state rather than fighting against it. How does the Zomia model interact with the Alps? Can the Alps be considered a European Zomia? On the one hand, European empires and then nation-states are stronger and more articulated than those explored by Scott. On the other hand, the Alps are also much more open and at the centre of constant exchanges and flows, although we would also like to underline the symbolic passage. When, with World War I, mountaineers became Alpine soldiers in Austria, as in Italy, the discussion on the rebellious or wild mountain could not continue,[13] and the rebellious spirit of the mountaineer – alleged or real – became raw material for the construction of the nation. It seems that a European Zomia could not survive this national biopolitical project. World War I as the furnace of the Great Nationalist Factory burned all illusions of mountain rebellion. Even more than with repression, the attractive force of the plain weakened the European Zomia and emptied it of its inhabitants. Wars, nationalism, and the Alps are three major actors of this volume.

A new approach for the study of exploration

The objectives of this volume are to explore the vast array of geographical exploration dimensions, anthropological, historical, scientific, medical, political, and social, and offer new theoretical tools based on post-colonial studies and environmental humanities perspectives. Focusing on the bond between geographical explorations and the state(s), the chapters gathered in this volume analyse them as claims over lands in order to exercise control over communities and natures.[14] The expansion of state authority into novel and peripheral areas is both conceptual and physical, and "national landscape" creation embodies specific national values and fosters the formation of national identities and knowledge.[15] We will adopt David Forgacs's margins conceptual tool and look at margins from

4 *Armiero, Biasillo, and Morosini*

an environmental rather than social perspective. However, what he defines as marginal is extremely valuable in our context. For Forgacs, marginality is a fact or a state of deviance and disadvantage, and 'marginal' means distant from and unfamiliar to a given society. If margins are social constructs, then what is marginal is defined according to societal core values, and marginality is therefore always negotiated between times and spaces.[16] All these theoretical references share a strong bond between historical transformation, nation- and state-building processes, and physical spaces. Methodologically, this book offers an interdisciplinary framework approach to diverse geographical explorations around the globe and combines case-study methodology with more theoretical chapters.

The authors examine ways in which various players have supported political and social definition of exclusion and, consequently, the inclusion and appropriation of extreme environments via strategies such as commercialisation, colonialism, knowledge production, and sport. Conversely, contributors have also examined the way in which marginal communities and spaces have challenged and transformed society's centres through, for example, the creation of international networks, political consensus and identity building, and the individual and collective sense of grandeur. The volume shows how environmental marginalisation is discursively implemented and materially generated by political and social stakeholders and to what extent the status and identity of extreme environments have changed during modern times, moving them from periphery to the centre and discarding their marginality. The book consciously links up with the ongoing debate on energy and climate emergencies and aims to enrich the public debate and understanding of exploration practises. Moreover, it combines the Poles and the earth's highest mountains, which represent the main interests of the existing competition, in a multidisciplinary approach and an attempt to offer a post-colonial and environmental humanities perspective reading of such phenomena, a view of geographical exploration as two-sided historical dynamics and multi-layered and all-encompassing processes. The chapters gathered in this volume reveal, for instance, the tension between international collaborations and nationalistic drivers. This regards not only the explorers but even the very objects of exploration. In some cases, the margins were literally at the borders between nations, for instance, with the Alps and the Himalaya. Nowadays, with the incumbent effects of climate change and their geopolitical implications, the Arctic is the region where the frictions between international collaborations and nationalist interests have become extremely evident, even dramatic.

Exploring explorations in eleven chapters

The chapters gathered in this volume offer a wide panoramic on geographical explorations, blending research on fascist nationalism, touristification of mountaineering, science and war, and alpine associationism between nationalism and internationalism, to mention some broader themes crosscutting the entire volume.

In her chapter, Ilaria Scaglia analyses the case of the International Mountaineering and Climbing Federation (also known as Union Internationale des Associations d'Alpinisme, or UIAA) in order to demonstrate that the individuals, institutions (i.e. Alpine clubs), and governments involved in it used it to achieve internationalist goals, presenting mountains as a quintessential international cooperation space, resorting to contemporary emotions to downplay their own contradictions and organising emotionalised international encounters in the Alps, contending that these had the potential to improve international relations.

In the specific context of Italian scientific, sportive, archaeological, and geographical enterprises during the 1920s and 1930s, Marco Cuzzi's chapter considers these experiences in relation to the emergence of a fascist politics of power and the Italian foreign political agenda. Ambiguous plans to integrate Italy into a set of European agreements and negotiations coexisted with the idea of alleged Italian difference and its disruptive role in the Old Continent's economic-social and political-diplomatic equilibria.

Steinar Aas's chapter analyses the peculiar 'polar imperialism', recreating the rivalry between Roald Amundsen and his Italian counterpart, Umberto Nobile, starting from the 1920s. The chapter highlights the role of the printed press in contributing to nationalism and xenophobia in the 1926 transpolar flight and in the dramatic 1928 rescue mission after the Italia airship accident, when Amundsen disappeared.

Luciano Zani's chapter focuses on another side of this question, in particular Umberto Nobile's long stay in the Soviet Union from 1931 to 1936, giving a fundamental contribution to the Soviet airship industry. Nobile's personal experiences are placed against the backdrop of the epic battle for the domination of the sky between the aeroplane and the airship, as well as within the context of the competition/confrontation between two totalitarian regimes that frequently displayed contradictory characteristics of collaboration and rivalry, affinity, and animosity.

Sandro Rinauro's chapter analyses the influence of imperialist ideas of several Italian geographers in the liberal and fascist eras and in particular focuses on the geographer Roberto Almagià's academic and theoretical studies dedicated to African colonies, especially Libya after its Italian conquest (1911–1912) and then during the fascist era. The racial persecution he suffered after 1938, and his taking refuge in the Vatican to escape the Nazi roundups, helped history forget his cultural collaboration with the expansion policies of the fascist regime.

Peder Roberts's chapter investigates how the American mountaineer and geographer Walter Abbott Wood built a personal and institutional legacy in the St Elias Mountains between Yukon and Alaska. Wood participated in cold weather warfare research during World War II, followed by a research program in glaciology (Operation Snow Cornice) under the auspices of the Arctic Institute of North America (AINA). The chapter examines how Wood's personal attachment to the region mapped onto contemporary military imperatives, particularly for knowledge of human physiological reactions at high altitudes, and why this prompted speculation in Canada about connections to US military plans in south and east Asia.

Vanessa Heggie's chapter reconstructs how physiologists, doctors, and other biomedical scientists organised and participated in mountaineering expeditions to try to understand, and predict, the effects of high altitude on the human body and design technology – from oxygen systems to ration packs – to enable human bodies to climb into what was colloquially known as the 'death zone'. The chapter demonstrates how this research was reframed into crucial sites for making scientific truth; how it was leveraged to highlight the difference between White bodies and those of Native and Indigenous peoples; and how these scientists managed to justify their apparently niche, expensive, and often dangerous research practises.

Stefano Morosini's chapter offers an overview of the role played by Italian geographers, scientists, travellers, and mountaineers in the exploration of the Karakoram region from the late nineteenth century to 1954, year of the well-known first ascent of K2. Moreover, the chapter reflects on the domestic and geopolitical contexts intertwining geographical and political enterprises with world wars and the decolonisation process and on the great press and media coverage that such expeditions had in Italy and elsewhere.

Peter H. Hansen's chapter examines how the commercialisation of Mt Everest began with its mapping and naming in the nineteenth century and the earliest climbing expeditions in the 1920s and how the prominent role of scientific research, geography, and imperialism has often obscured the multiple forms taken by Mt Everest mountaineering commercialisation prior to the 1970s. Its unique status as the world's highest mountain has transformed debates over the commercialisation of the peak into proxies for broader discussion of the legacies of colonialism and globalisation.

Roberta Biasillo's concluding chapter analyses landscapes as products of geography by adopting emerging approaches in the environmental humanities. Combining environment and humanities entails a mutual transformation that offers the interpretative space and analytical tools to read (and re-write) the complex text of landscape. Given that power relations shape cultural and historical aspects of representations, which is to say geography, reassessments of geographical texts through the environmental humanities can take on the status of a decolonising practice.

The volume is enriched by Stefano Twardzik's appendix presenting the discovery of two files relating to the Italian Karakoram (1928–1929) and North Pole (1928) expeditions conserved at Milan Municipal Archives. The appendix describes the potential of this archival discovery, which will shed light on various aspects of the two events, especially their organisational, financial, publishing rights management, and legal dispute implications.

Between a global pandemic and wildfires, 2021 will also be remembered for the first space trips funded and experienced by billionaires. Was this the beginning of a new trend in space exploration? Someone has written that the space might become the new playground for the super-rich;[17] for those working on the Alps, that expression should sound extremely familiar. Nothing can represent the aim of global capitalism to force the planetary boundaries and expand the frontier of extractivism and exploitation better than these 'astrorich'. Perhaps in their exploration there is also the less optimistic plan of some kind of escape route from the planetary mess, but this 'escaptivist' approach is also not uncommon to all explorations. A national flag or a brand logo is looming somewhere in a space to be conquered. It is time to ask ourselves what those flags – and their cargo of science, nationalism, and colonialism – do to the conquered space as well as to the space left. And it would be useful to remember that 2021 was also the year when so many monuments to colonialism, slavery, and racism were taken down.

Notes

1. Margaret Jolly, "Blue Pacific, Polluted Ocean", *International Journal of Society Science* 13, no. 3 (2021): 241–257; David D. Caron and Harry N. Scheiber, eds., *The Oceans in the Nuclear Age: Legacies and Risks* (Leiden-Boston: Martinus Nijhoff, 2010); Henning Dahlgaard, "Transfer of European Coastal Pollution to the Arctic: Radioactive Tracers", *Marine Pollution Bulletin* 31, no. 1–3 (1995): 3–7; Eric Wolff, "The Influence of Global and Local Atmospheric Pollution on the Chemistry of Antarctic Snow and Ice", *Marine Pollution Bulletin* 25, no. 9–12 (1992): 274–280.
2. Wendy Wolford, "The Plantationocene: A Lusotropical Contribution to the Theory", *Annals of the American Association of Geographers* 111, no. 6 (2021): 1622–1639.
3. Donna Haraway, "Anthropocene, Capitalocene, Plantationocene, Chthulucene: Making Kin", *Environmental Humanities* 6, no. 1 (2015): 159–165.
4. Marco Armiero, *Wasteocene: Stories from the Global Dump* (Cambridge: Cambridge University Press, 2021).
5. Sverker Sörlin and Nina Wormbs, "Environing Technologies: A Theory of Making Environment", *History and Technology. An International Journal* 34, no. 2 (2018): 101–125; Sverker Sörlin and Paul Warde, "Making the Environment Historical: An Introduction", in *Nature's End*, eds. Sverker Sörlin and Paul Warde (London: Palgrave Macmillan, 2009), 1–19.
6. Matti Lainema and Juha Nurminen, *A History of Arctic Exploration: Discovery, Adventure and Endurance at the Top of the World* (London: Conway Maritime Press, 2010).
7. Maurice Isserman and Stewart Weaver, *Fallen Giants: A History of Himalayan Mountaineering from the Age of Empire to the Age of Extremes* (New Haven: Yale University Press, 2008).
8. Hester Blum, *The News at the Ends of the Earth: The Print Culture of Polar Exploration by Hester* (Durham: Duke University Press, 2019); Vanessa Heggie, *Higher and Colder: A History of Extreme Physiology and Exploration* (Chicago: The University of Chicago Press, 2019); Ilaria Scaglia, *The Emotions of Internationalism Feeling International Cooperation in the Alps in the Interwar Period* (New York: Oxford University Press, 2019); Philip W. Clements, *Science in an Extreme Environment: The American Mount Everest Expedition* (Pittsburgh: University of Pittsburgh Press, 2018); Edward J. Larson, *To the Edges of the Earth: 1909, the Race for the Three Poles, and the Climax of the Age of Exploration* (New York: William Morrow, 2018); Peder Roberts, Lize-Marié van der Watt, and Adrian Howkins, eds., *Antarctica and the Humanities* (London: Palgrave Macmillan, 2016); Peter H. Hansen, *The Summits of Modern Man: Mountaineering after the Enlightenment* (Cambridge: Harvard University Press, 2013).
9. Adam Skolnick and Bhadra Sharma, "How Climbers Reached the Summit of K2 in Winter for the First Time", *The New York Times*, 19 January 2021.
10. Robert K. Szymczak, Michał Marosz, Tomasz Grzywacz, Magdalena Sawicka, and Marta Naczyk, "Death Zone Weather Extremes Mountaineers Have Experienced in Successful Ascents", *Frontiers in Physiology*, 5 July 2021, https://doi.org/10.3389/fphys.2021.696335, last access 10 December 2021.
11. Nico Mastropietro, "Esploratori, alpinisti e Sherpa: l'avventura himalayana dalle prime esplorazioni ai viaggi di Fosco Maraini", *Antologia Vieusseux* 33 (2006): 1–32.
12. James C. Scott, *The Art of Not Being Governed: An Anarchist History of Upland Southeast Asia* (New Haven: Yale University Press, 2009).

13 Tait Keller, "The Mountains Roar: The Alps during the Great War", *Environmental History* 14, no. 2 (2009): 253–274.
14 Wilko Graf von Hardenberg, Matthew Kelly, Claudia Leal, and Emily Wakild, eds., *The Nature State: Rethinking the History of Conservation* (London and New York: Routledge, 2017).
15 Environment and Nature, Vol. 20, No. 1, February 2014 special issue *Nature and Nation* Marco Armiero and Wilko Graf von Hardenberg, eds.
16 David Forgacs, *Italy's Margins: Social Exclusion and Nation Formation since 1861* (Cambridge: Cambridge University Press, 2014).
17 Shannon Stirone, "Space Billionaires", *The Atlantic*, 8 July 2021, www.theatlantic.com/science/archive/2021/07/space-billionaires-jeff-bezos-richard-branson/619383/ Shannon Stirone, last access 10 December 2021.

1 Emotions and mountaineering for internationalist purposes

The case of the Union Internationale des Associations d'Alpinisme (UIAA), 1939–1951*

Ilaria Scaglia

The Alps as a political, emotionalised space

The Alps have long been an international region and also a highly emotionalised one.[1] Since the nineteenth century, and especially after World War I, the Alps have been site and symbol of recent conflict and equally of the various utopias that many aspired to build in its aftermath. Catholics, socialists, communists, fascists and nationalists from various countries chose the Alps as a space in which to experiment with alternative political solutions and promote what they deemed healthy recreational activities (such as hiking and climbing). As scholars such as Ellis, Weaver, Isserman and Keller have demonstrated, they sometimes pursued imperialist and extreme-nationalist agendas.[2] Yet, in contrast with – or sometimes alongside – these agendas, they also used mountains as a way of building emotional bonds of 'international friendship' they believed crucial to their success.[3] For this reason, in this study, they are treated as a group and referred to as 'internationalists'.[4]

This chapter argues that emotions played a central role in shaping these internationalist activities in the Alps,[5] imbuing their rhetoric, framing relations between nations as affective bonds, and attributing moral value to specific emotional expressions, values and behaviours.[6] Emotions such as amity and friendship also served as imagined goals, which individuals and groups worked hard to attain.[7] To do so, they engaged in a broad range of what Monique Scheer has called "emotional practices", which did not simply reflect, accompany or follow through on other forms of doing but rather had a dynamic function per se: internationalists talked about feelings, expressed them publicly, staged events and took in mountain landscapes to pursue their own specific emotions and instil these in other people, thus triggering feelings in the process.[8] They thus engaged in a form of physical, metaphorical and sentimental environment-building in the Alps that shaped internationalist rhetoric and practices – such as staging in-person encounters – in the interwar period and beyond.

This chapter focuses specifically on the case of the Union Internationale des Associations d'Alpinisme (UIAA, or International Mountaineering and Climbing Federation) to explain the form this took. It examines a broad range of materials,

DOI: 10.4324/9781003095965-2

including minutes, correspondence and media coverage, to gain an understanding of how this group constructed the Alps as *the* quintessential milieu for international cooperation, a place in which to work together in a broad range of fields from avalanche response to joint art exhibitions. It also considers how the UIAA drew on contemporary emotional references (e.g. 'Alpine friendship') to further its agenda and downplay its own contradictions and how it organised and emotionalised international encounters in the Alps, contending that these could improve international relations. It thus demonstrates that such action formed the substance of international cooperation in the field of mountaineering and beyond and influences internationalism to this day.

Internationalism and 'Alpine friendship' at the UIAA

The UIAA originated from a set of internationalist ideas and practices that had developed in the mid-nineteenth century. As mountain climbing grew in popularity, so too did the notion of an international association designed to unite people with an interest in the mountains. Twenty years after the first Alpine Club was set up in England in 1857, international gatherings of mountaineers were organised in various places in the Alps. International congresses were held in Annecy and Aix-les-Bains in 1876 and in Grenoble-Uriage and Ivrea in 1877. In 1879, an International Conference of Alpine Clubs took place in Geneva. Participants came from Austria, England, France, Germany, Spain, the United States and, of course, Switzerland. Although plans for an international organisation were discussed at these gatherings, no international body was established at that time. It was only in 1930 that the Polish Tatra Society organised the First International Alpine Congress in Zakopane, Poland. This was followed by a Second International Alpine Congress in Budapest in 1931 and a Third Alpine Congress in Chamonix in 1932. It was in Chamonix that the UIAA was set up at the behest of the president of the French Alpine Club, Jean Escarra. Shortly thereafter, Swiss journalist and mountaineer Charles Egmond d'Arcis (1887–1971) was appointed president.[9]

From its inception, the UIAA mirrored the League of Nations in both structure and emotional rhetoric. Like the League, the UIAA argued that it would unite people across borders through international friendship. Its assembly included representatives from all member associations, a permanent office with executive functions similar to the League's secretariat and an executive committee akin to the League's council, comprising the president – a representative of the Swiss Alpine Club – and seven members elected at the third congress in Chamonix.[10] The names of its representatives changed over time, but its general structure remained the same, and the UIAA effectively became a mountaineering league of nations.

The UIAA faced setbacks when some of its members left and others remained despite the fact that the countries they represented openly challenged the values embodied by the League of Nations. Feelings – and the rhetoric that described them – served as important tools for the negotiation of each member's position within the organisation and protected the UIAA's reputation by averting any association with either appeasement – especially after World War II – or empty idealism.

The case of the Alpine Club of Great Britain (AC) illustrates how framing disagreements as emotions enabled Egmond d'Arcis to mitigate the effects of losing one of the UIAA's greatest assets. The AC was the oldest of all the Alpine clubs and a founding member of the organisation. It was therefore quite a shock when it left, effective 3 October 1933, soon after its first formal meeting. The reason given for this decision was that

> unlike the great Foreign Societies, the AC possesses no territorial rights or Club huts in the Alps. It considers that the privileges of its members are guaranteed sufficiently by their membership in several or all of the great said Alpine Societies. Consequently . . . participation as a club . . . would be both assertive and redundant.[11]

Such a line of reasoning must not have sounded very convincing at the time, as the AC had enthusiastically taken part in all the international gatherings that had preceded the founding of the UIAA. Although the real reasons for the AC's departure are not clear, it is relevant that d'Arcis reassured the UIAA that there was "no bad intention in this withdrawal". He pointed out that 'the pain that the English feel when engaging in new enterprises and new ways is well known' and expressed hope that their involvement could soon be resumed.[12] Explaining the AC's withdrawal in terms of individual feelings – rather than institutional policies and deliberate decisions – effectively mitigated this setback to the UIAA as a fledgling organisation.

The case of Italy, whose chronology and set of dynamics were very different, demonstrates the way in which emotions served to rationalise relations with countries and people openly at odds with the UIAA's internationalist mission while leaving the UIAA's reputation untarnished. As one of the UIAA founding members, the Italian Alpine Club (CAI) remained active throughout the 1930s, even after Italy withdrew from the League of Nations in December 1937.[13] No fewer than two Italian representatives, Eugenio Ferreri and Vittorio Frisinghelli, attended the general assembly in Zermatt on 20 August 1939, only a few days prior to the outbreak of World War II.[14] This was not because the CAI had resisted the influence of Mussolini's fascist regime.[15] In fact, as Alessandro Pastore pointed out, "the moral atmosphere" in this Alpine club was "impregnated with a constant and pervasive patriotic vision, a vision still marked by the idea of the sacred union between mountains and war, cemented by the sacrifice of fallen soldiers and the blood shed by combatants".[16] Moreover, its head, Angelo Manaresi, was a zealous party member and wore his fascist uniform even when performing his duties as president of the Centro Alpinistico Italiano – as the CAI had been renamed in 1938, in line with the fascist policy of Italianisation and language purity.[17] Writing on a letterhead adorned with Mussolini citations (and ostentatiously stamped across with red ink to highlight the organisation's new, fully Italian name), Manaresi never failed to challenge the UIAA. As early as 1933, he took exception to the

UIAA's rejection of medals and competitions and, in 1934, suspended the CAI's reciprocity agreements for the use of Alpine huts which allowed foreigners' access to many Italian shelters (*rifugi*).[18] Such an attitude, however, did not prevent the Italian delegation from showing openness to international cooperation throughout the 1930s. In fact, in August 1939, Ferreri and Frisinghelli asked for "the honour of hosting the UIAA in 1942 in Rome", when and where an international exhibition was scheduled to take place.[19] The outbreak of war meant that this gathering never occurred, but the CAI was one of the first to resume contact with d'Arcis after the end of the conflict.[20]

Many of those involved in this relationship justified its continuation on the grounds that personal bonds were stronger than national or political distinctions. In September 1945, Eugenio Ferreri – now general secretary of the CAI – wrote to d'Arcis. He vividly recalled their last meeting at Zermatt in 1939 and also updated him on Manaresi, who was safe despite his many "misadventures" (*disavventure*) after 25 July 1943, when "with the first fall of Fascism everything had changed". Ferreri noted that "the tragedy of war has hit many of our friends, we all have felt the liveliest emotions (*emozioni vivissime*) and witnessed tragedy and pain". He also mentioned reading "with *emozione*" the news contained in a bulletin d'Arcis had sent him and ended his letter by conveying his "unchanged feelings of sincere mountaineering friendship (*immutato senso di sincera amicizia alpinistica*)". He enclosed a summary of the CAI's activities during the war, expressing much optimism regarding the future of what was now once again the Club Alpino Italiano (the stationery had now been stamped across again to highlight the significance of this change).[21]

In his reply, d'Arcis rejoiced to learn that his friend Manaresi had survived: having read in Swiss papers that the neo-Fascist government had arrested him, he had feared for his fate.[22] D'Arcis's words implied that – despite his allegiance to the Italian Fascist Party and the obstacles that he had placed in the UIAA's path – Manaresi remained an *alpiniste*. To be sure, the war was still very much present in d'Arcis's mind. In this same letter, he referred to the fact that he was working without the UIAA Archives, "which had been put in a safe place, since the Germans wanted to get their hands on them" and had yet to be returned.[23] But, in his rhetoric, these stark political differences strengthened rather than weakened the argument that the UIAA could connect people across boundaries, and the mountaineering friendship that united UIAA's members was ultimately stronger than all other feelings. A few months after this exchange, d'Arcis and Ferreri met near the Swiss-Italian border. Shortly thereafter, the relationship between the CAI and the UIAA returned to its pre-war normalcy.

A new urgency and symbolic value gave the UIAA renewed strength and amplified its emotional rhetoric, making it an indispensable tool in international communication. In 1949, the CAI asked the UIAA to intervene to allocate huts disputed by the Italian and the French Alpine clubs. Count Ugo di Vallepiana of the CAI – a long-standing mountaineer who had been removed by the fascist regime on the grounds that he was Jewish – asked d'Arcis for help: "in the face of the European federal ideal," which represented "European civilisation's only chance of salvation," he argued that "it is not a bad idea . . . to eliminate those causes of friction whose effects and damage are disproportionate, especially when compared to the immensity of the forces that might one day be at stake".[24] D'Arcis replied, promising to do his best to solve this "very delicate question", reassuring Ugo di Vallepiana that "it did not seem impossible [to him] to find a satisfying solution".[25] Never had the UIAA's mediation role been so critical. On 23 March 1950, Ugo di Vallepiana contacted d'Arcis on behalf of CAI president Bartolomeo Figari. When discussing candidates for non-permanent membership in the UIAA's executive committee, he expressed the CAI's wish to nominate the Slovenian Alpine Society, and to "make public (*rendere noto*)" that "it really is us [the CAI] that wishes for its nomination". He explained that

> whilst today, for political reasons, contacts between this club and the CAI are limited, we remain hopeful that this special situation will evolve in such a way as to allow greater co-operation with our neighbours and colleagues on our eastern border in the mountaineering field.[26]

Two months later, in preparation for the Annual UIAA Congress that was to take place in Milan in 1950, d'Arcis asked the CAI for documentation allowing the Slovenian delegation to enter Italian territory.[27] The CAI promptly responded by soliciting the Italian foreign ministry to ensure smooth passage for their friends. Certainly, scepticism remained. A handwritten note from Ugo di Vallepiana read: "*entre nous*, I am convinced that the difficulties regarding their entry into Italy came not from Rome but Belgrade".[28] However, the anti-communist edge to this remark notwithstanding, the CAI, the Alpine Association of Slovenia and the UIAA interacted across one of Europe's most contested borders.[29] World War II had strengthened the UIAA's hand in its mediation work. Issues such as in-person participation in international congresses had come to represent broader political questions – especially after fighting to determine a mountain border in a setting in which resentments were very much alive – and thus expressions of Alpine courtesy and friendship constituted elements of great symbolic value. After much violence, Italians and Slovenians would now be meeting in the Alps in a spirit of co-operation and peace.

Shared and visible emotional expressions

The UIAA devoted much energy and significant resources to organising a series of annual congresses geared towards strengthening emotional ties across borders. These were held in the Italian resort town of Cortina d'Ampezzo (1933); Pontresina, Switzerland (1934); Barcelona, Spain (1935); Geneva, Switzerland (1936); Paris, France (1937); Prague, Czechoslovakia (1938); and Zermatt, Switzerland (1939).[30] After World War II ended, on 5–6 September 1946, the UIAA organised a "friendly reunion (*reunion amicale*)" in Zermatt, which was followed by a formal congress in Geneva in 1947. After that, yearly congresses resumed in Geneva (1948); Chamonix, France (1949); Milan (1950); and Bled, Slovenia

(1951).³¹ The UIAA staged these international gatherings with the explicit purpose of fostering friendship among participants, including members of the wider public who would later read about these events either in UIAA publications or in the general press. An overall trust in the bond between *alpinistes* underlay many of its activities. As early as 1931, the president of the French Alpine Club, Jean Escarra, argued that "the common sentiment that unites us must counterbalance the political and economic differences that can divide people". He then added that it was in the light of "this rapprochement work" that he was inviting all national representatives to take part in the third International Alpine Congress in Chamonix.³² The setting up of the UIAA only reinforced his contention that such bonds could take institutional form and play an active part in modifying relations between people and groups from various countries.

The UIAA's message was that, for *alpinistes*, mountain landscapes possessed a unifying power which derived not only from their beauty but also from the feelings they inspired in those who visited them. In 1933, at the Cortina d'Ampezzo congress, Egmond d'Arcis remarked that despite the fact that it was a cloudy day, "we find [the sun] in the warmth of the friendship demonstrated by our Italian colleagues". Thus, in the mountains, "we feel . . . like in our own home, the mountaineers' home". If bad weather had diminished the beauty and overall experience of being together in the Dolomites, the set of emotions inherent with spending time together in the mountains remained strong nonetheless. Moreover, *alpinistes* knew from experience that co-operation was essential in the mountains. As d'Arcis explained, implicitly evoking the image of climbing partners roped together, "international cooperation, which is at the foundation of the UIAA, is not an empty word among mountaineers because the spirit of mutual help is a form of devotion that knows neither frontiers nor obstacles".³³ He argued that these emotional expressions and shared emotional experiences were not simply formal or sentimental talk but the cornerstone of the internationalist project uniting peoples and nations.

At a time when the League of Nations' management of emotions was disappointing many of its supporters, the UIAA responded by staging events whose specific goal was exposing peoples from various countries to a broad range of aesthetic and sensorial experiences. At each congress, participants engaged in joint excursions and expeditions, admired Alpine photographs and art; and enjoyed picnics, dinners and banquets together. The seventh International Alpine Congress, held jointly with the UIAA's third general assembly in Geneva from 27 August to 6 September 1936, is an ideal case study in this respect, since it included the broadest range of UIAA activities geared towards making people feel emotions deemed conducive to international cooperation and peace. Representatives from twenty associations from fourteen different countries gathered in Geneva for the occasion. Working from its strongest – and from an internationalist point of view, its most symbolic – location, the UIAA seized the opportunity to fully implement its vision, and it thus organised a great many events designed not only to entertain its guests but also to meet the association's goal of creating opportunities for international exchange and mutual understanding. In this context, emotions – both as a set of feelings expressed via multiple means and the sensorial experiences that nurtured them – were the most important element in this gathering. From 22 August to 2 September 1936, the UIAA organised two exhibitions that employed images and rhetoric to elicit shared emotions in audiences: one of mountain rescue materials and one of Alpine photographs, both held in the Salles du Conservatoire de Musique facing the elegant Place de Neuve in central Geneva.[34] Spurred on by a rise in the number of accidents stemming from the growing interest in mountains, this "Exhibition of materials for mountain rescue (*Exposition de matériel de sauvetage en montagne*)" displayed the tools that people in various countries had devised in order to save as many lives as possible. It presented the latest innovations in the field of mountain rescue, from pharmaceutical products to lamps and various kinds of stretchers (some professionally crafted and some made on the spot, with sticks and other fortuitous objects). This event illustrated the UIAA's efforts to standardise Alpine maps, as well as safety and rescue procedures. It also brought out the human aspect of this work. By showing the concrete objects involved in such endeavours, the exhibition gave audiences an insight into the people who benefitted from them, thereby triggering strong feelings of empathy.[35] As an article in the *Journal de Genève* observed, this exhibition was a "demonstration of human solidarity" prompting people not just to learn about but also to *feel* international cooperation in the mountains.[36]

By way of aesthetic and sensorial experiences, visitors were given an instant insight into the universal appeal and national peculiarities of the mountain experience. The *First International Exhibition of Alpine Photographs* featured 518 pictures of the Alps and mountains all over the world.[37] Numerous newspaper articles pointed out that the exhibition's photographs provided audiences with a shared emotional experience. Like painters, these photographers created art whose "power of suggestion is extraordinary (*puissance de suggestion est extraordinaire*)", to cite one description published in *La Suisse*. People "would be moved (*on est ému*)", to cite another passage from the same article, as much by nature as by a work of art, not only viewing it but also experiencing mountains on a deeper level.[38] The *Swiss Exhibition of Alpine Art*, organised by the Geneva section of the Swiss Alpine Club in the same period, was also conceived and described as an emotional event.[39] As art critic L. Florentin pointed out in a review published in *La Suisse*, realism had given way to "a romantic or decorative impressionism . . . and an architectural vision of shapes in their relationship with space". The result was an exhibition whose works "proposed fuller pleasures to our whole sensibility and imaginations".[40] Certainly, doing justice to the mountains required "exceptional acuity of vision and power of touch (*une acuité de vision et une vigueur de touche exceptionelles*)", which few people and works demonstrated; yet the show still offered a multitude of powerful moments for all visitors to appreciate, regardless of their provenance.[41]

Even outside the formal exhibition space, the UIAA made full use of the beauty and emotional power of the mountains to achieve its internationalist goals. In addition to the exhibitions cited previously, the association organised many opportunities enabling participants to live and feel their mountain passion. On

30 August, all those who had convened in Geneva for the UIAA Congress took a scenic boat tour across Lake Geneva to admire its Alpine views in all their grandeur. The choir of the Swiss Alpine Club's Geneva section provided a suggestive soundtrack, and a banquet at exclusive Hotel des Bergues followed. This lavish venue on the Geneva lakefront was expressly decorated with the colours of all the countries represented at the international gathering. Participants addressed each other in both French and their native tongues, providing a concrete example of the way the UIAA, like the League of Nations, fostered international exchange while also respecting national identities. According to those who took part, cordiality and good cheer were the order of the day.[42]

The following week, three excursions to the mountains were organised for people of all mountaineering levels to allow participants to experience the most powerful emotions the Alps could offer.[43] 'Tourists' went on a three-day tour of the region by car, crossing the Petit St. Bernard, first to the Italian resort town of Courmayeur and then Aosta. The next day, they crossed the Grand St. Bernard and followed the road all the way to Bulle, at the foot of the Fribourg Alpine foothills. They then spent the last day visiting the quaint town of Gruyère and the medieval Castle of Chillon. *Bon marcheurs* (literally, 'good walkers'), on the other hand, embarked on a seven-day tour to Interlaken, Reichenbach, Sion and Zermatt, with guided hikes along the way as well as an easy climb of the Mettelhorn (3,410 metres above sea level). Expert *alpinistes* were based in Zermatt, from which they climbed some of the most famous Alpine peaks, including the Matterhorn/Cervino (4,482 m).[44] For this occasion, the Alps had been opened up to all those wanting to enjoy them. By all accounts, the atmosphere was one of inclusion, relaxation and shared enjoyment. As Roussy noted in a report published in *Les Alpes*, in the evening, *alpinistes* met with people in the second group, "drank the cup of friendship and danced".[45] A set of shared sensorial experiences sealed the event in the memories of those present and was later described in their accounts. Nearby hotels welcomed all guests, and comfortable Alpine huts (or *cabanes*, as they were called) awaited those venturing into the Alpine peaks. *Bon marcheurs* stayed at *Cabane Hohtürli* (2,781 m), while *alpinistes* slept at *Cabane Britannia* (3,031 m), which had been built in 1912 with funds from a few English members and was the jewel in the crown of the Swiss Alpine Club. Writing in *La Tribune de Genève* at the time of the UIAA Congress in Geneva, John Michel (president of the Swiss Association of Ski Clubs and also a member of the UIAA permanent office) explained that it "left nothing to be desired" in terms of comfort. Even in the middle of winter, up to eighty people found "a welcoming, well-heated home" complete with metal-frame beds, gas lamps and stewards to ensure its perfect maintenance. "What joyous gatherings up there with our English colleagues, and what genuine international intermingling," Michel commented in his article while describing the friendly atmosphere of the place.[46] Descriptions of the mountains and their artistic depiction, the sounds of the Alps and their musical renditions, the cold of the mountain glaciers and the warmth of their huts all conveyed a deep feeling of camaraderie. These sensorial experiences came to be associated with a set of emotions which defined internationalism in this period and reverberated across the years to come.

Both concretely and metaphorically, in the 1930s, the UIAA and the internationalists who represented it and engaged with it made the Alps a symbol of the struggle against war, cynicism and destruction. When World War II began, the pages of the *Bulletin* of the Swiss Alpine Club acknowledged this fact and were punctuated with nostalgic articles speaking of "the Alps" – whatever its national sovereignty – as the embodiment of peace. In 1940, L. Gianoli, who helped to stage the 1936 *Exhibition of Alpine Art*, wrote a short piece entitled '*Notre Paix, là-haut!*' ('Our Peace, Up High') in which he explained that "in the anguish (*angoisse*) of current times it is on the peaks that we find the necessary remedy that calms our nerves and allows us to endure the dreadful calamity to which Europe has fallen victim".[47] In 1941, Swiss author Eugène Rambert celebrated the Alps as a powerful barrier protecting Switzerland from the war raging all around it, allowing for a space where

> a German majority respects a French-speaking minority, a Protestant majority respects a Catholic minority, and a number of relatively populous and strong states, launched at full speed in the current of modern life, respect the slow pace of those old pastoral democracies for which centuries could be years.[48]

In February 1942, the president of the Geneva section of the Swiss Alpine Club, C. Vernet, explained that mountaineers remained a much-needed resource for a chaotic world: "The harder the journey, the narrower the path which perhaps soon turns into a thin edge that only mountaineers can cross with a steady pace, the more our people will need steady men to guide its steps and provide an example".[49] Taken out of context, this and other messages of its kind read like caricatures of interwar idealism. Indeed, they have been interpreted as such by historians for some time. Yet, set against the background of the emotions that had generated them and accompanied them throughout their history, they were a meaningful expression of the complex process of emotional environment-building that defined internationalism during and after World War II.

Conclusion

Though UIAA rhetoric and use of emotions did not succeed in securing peace, it shaped internationalism in important ways, and emotions played a key role in making this happen. While operating in one of the period's most symbolic and emotionalised political environments, the Alps, UIAA officers emphasised national differences and strengthened the notion that these existed and needed to be taken into account. Using rhetoric engaging specific emotions (such as 'friendship') and attributing a positive value to these, they justified their relationships with extreme nationalists, thereby legitimising the regimes (e.g. fascist Italy) they represented. By engaging in specific emotional practices – such as discussing feelings, representing and displaying them through art and music and exhibitions and congresses – they felt and triggered feelings in others and remembered them later on.

By trying to affect what people felt about each other – and also about internationalism as a whole – in this period, the UIAA presented itself as a proactive agent of internationalist experimentation and change. UIAA officers continuously engaged feelings by either overtly expressing emotions or describing physical sensations associated with them. Most importantly, they accompanied this rhetoric with arguments that connected these emotions with their potential effects on relationships among peoples and nations. The bond connecting all *alpinistes* was believed to be stronger than any potentially dividing factors, and the Alpine landscape – with the unique sensorial and emotional experiences it engendered – were seen as having a unifying effect on people enjoying it as a group. Moreover, the collaborative side of mountaineering and the mutual dependency it entailed predisposed *alpinistes* to international cooperation. Contending that for such dynamics to be triggered, people needed to appreciate the beauty of the Alps by taking in mountain sights and sounds in the right settings, no effort was spared to ensure that all participants accumulated a set of experiences and memories that would convince them of the unifying power of the Alps. Newspaper articles, magazines and written memoirs guided people's interpretation of these moments, making their internationalist character explicit and arguing for their potential for a positive impact on international relations.

Indeed, after 1945, the practices promoted by the UIAA became the norm in foreign and international policy (e.g., in-person encounters became essential tools for peace-building and soft power) and also in 'non-political' realms ranging from education to corporate team-building activities. Furthermore, the UIAA's decision to place a great deal of currency on visible emotional expression contributed to providing international cooperation with an aesthetic that is still dominant in the mass and social media age we live in today.

Notes

* An extended version of this research was published in Ilaria Scaglia, *The Emotions of Internationalism: Feeling International Cooperation in the Alps in the Interwar Period* (Oxford: Oxford University Press, 2020). I would like to thank Steven Gill, Stefano Morosini, Roberta Biasillo, and the anonymous reviewers for the feedback their provided as I crafted this chapter for publication.
1 Andrew Beattie, *The Alps: A Cultural History* (Oxford: Oxford University Press, 2006); Jon Mathieu, *The Alps: An Environmental History* (Cambridge: Polity Press, 2019) and *History of the Alps, 1500–1900: Environment, Development, and Society* (Morgantown: West Virginia University Press, 2009).
2 Reuben Ellis, *Vertical Margins: Mountaineering and the Landscapes of Neoimperialism* (Madison: University of Wisconsin Press, 2001) and Maurice Isserman and Stewart Weaver, *Fallen Giants: A History of Himalayan Mountaineering from the Age of Empire to the Age of Extremes* (New Haven: Yale University Press, 2008). On nationalist appropriations, see Tait Keller, *Apostles of the Alps: Mountaineering and Nation Building in Germany and Austria, 1860–1939* (Chapel Hill: University of North Carolina Press, 2016). This list is not meant to be complete.

3 Luciano Senatori, *Compagni di cordata: associazionismo proletario, alpine sovversivi, sport popolare in Italia* (Roma: Ediesse, 2010); Andrea Zannini, *Tonache e piccozze: il clero e la nascita dell'alpinismo* (Torino: CDA & VIVALDA, 2004); Alessandro Pastore, *Alpinismo e storia d'Italia. Dall'Unità alla Resistenza* (Bologna: Il Mulino, 2003).
4 The term 'internationalists' refers here to individuals, institutions and governments of varying political persuasions who nonetheless shared the notion that achieving their goals required getting people from other countries involved. This is not to contrast them with nationalists: as recent literature has shown, internationalists accepted principles of national difference, often labelled themselves and others according to nation of provenance and sometimes also included representatives of the Nazi and Fascist regimes. See Glenda Sluga and Patricia Clavin, eds., *Internationalisms: A Twentieth Century History* (New York: Cambridge University Press, 2016); Glenda Sluga, *Internationalism in the Age of Nationalism* (Philadelphia: University of Pennsylvania Press, 2013).
5 The literature on emotions is too extensive to be summarised here. For a complete review, definition, and theorisation, see Scaglia, *The Emotions of Internationalism*, Introduction.
6 On this point, see Ilaria Scaglia, "The 'Hydrologist's Weapons': Emotions and the Moral Economy of Internationalism, 1921–1952", in *New Interdisciplinary Landscapes in Morality and Emotion*, ed. Sara Graça Da Silva (London: Routledge, 2018), 140–152.
7 On the limits of language and individual terms as the basis for historical inquiry, see Ute Frevert et al., *Emotional Lexicons: Continuity and Change in the Vocabulary of Feeling 1700–2000* (Oxford: Oxford University Press, 2014).
8 Monique Scheer, "Are Emotions a Kind of Practice (and Is That What Makes Them Have a History)? A Bourdieuian Approach to Understanding Emotion", *History and Theory* 51, no. 2 (May 2012): 193–220. On emotions as "emotives" that at once describe and trigger feelings, see William M. Reddy, *The Navigation of Feeling: A Framework for the History of Emotions* (New York: Cambridge University Press, 2001).
9 UIAA Archives, Anciennes Circulaires, Circulaire n. I, 5 January 1933. It is worth noting that mountain- and mountaineering-related international organisations proliferated in this period. The 1936 League's *Handbook of International Organizations* (*Repertoire des organizations internationales*) listed the Boy Scouts (founded in London, in 1920), the International Ski Association (Chamonix, 1924), the International Committee of Open-Air Schools and Preventoria (Paris, 1928), the World Association of Girl Guides and Girl Scouts (London, 1928), the International Office for the Protection of Nature (Brussels, 1928) and the International Federation of Camping Clubs (London, 1932). See *Répertoire des organizations internationales* (Genève: Série des publications de la Société des Nations, XII, 1936).
10 UIAA Archives, Assemblée Générale, 1932–1935, IIIème Congrès International d'Alpinisme, Voeux Adoptés & Décisions Prises par le Congrès dans la Dernière Séance Plénière, 27 August 1932, 1–3.
11 *Alpine Journal* 44, no. 245 (November 1932): 340; *Alpine Journal* 45, no. 247 (November 1933): 403. The Archives of the English Alpine Club provide no further explanation in this regard.
12 UIAA Archives, Comité Exécutif, Procès-verbal de la Séance du Comité Exécutif de l'Union International des Associations d'Alpinisme, Pontresina, 6 September 1934, 2.
13 On Italy's contradictory with the League of Nations, see Elisabetta Tollardo, *Fascist Italy and the League of Nations, 1922–1935* (Basingstoke: Palgrave Macmillan, 2016).
14 UIAA Archives, Comité Exécutif, Procès-verbal de la Séance du Comité Exécutif de l'Union International des Associations d'Alpinisme, Zermatt, 20 August 1939, 1.
15 The Italian representatives at the UIAA changed several times throughout the 1930s: Giovanni Bobba served on the first executive committee, followed by Angelo Manaresi (1933), Dr. V. Frisinghelli (1934–1935; 1939), Ardito Desio (1936) and Eugenio Ferreri (1937; 1939).

20 *Ilaria Scaglia*

16 Pastore, 106.
17 This detail is cited in the history section of CAI Turin section's website. CAI, accessed 25 July 2016, www.caitorino.it/centro-alpinistico/. For a thorough examination of Manaresi's role in the 'fascistizzazione dell'alpinismo' see Pastore, 145–181.
18 See correspondence on this topic in UIAA Archives, binder Club Alpino Italiano, AVST, FISI.
19 UIAA Archives, Comité Exécutif, Procès-verbal de la Séance du Comité Exécutif de l'Union International des Associations d'Alpinisme, Zermatt, 20 August 1939, 8.
20 Alessandro Pastore noted the way Manaresi used the UIAA for his own internal propaganda purposes, describing its meetings, and the 1933 annual congress in particular, as celebratory of the Fascist regime. Pastore, 179–180.
21 UIAA Archives, Club Alpino Italiano, AVST, FISI, letter dated 1 September [1945], from Eugenio Ferreri to Egmond d'Arcis.
22 Ibid. letter dated 14 November 1945, from Egmond d'Arcis to Eugenio Ferreri. After the collapse of Mussolini's rule, Manaresi swore allegiance to Marshal Pietro Badoglio. He was later arrested by Fascist supporters of the Repubblica di Salò and remained in prison until the end of 1943, when Mussolini himself intervened to ensure his liberation. Pastore, 209–210.
23 UIAA Archives, Club Alpino Italiano, AVST, FISI, letter dated 14 November 1945, from Egmond d'Arcis to Eugenio Ferreri.
24 Ibid., letter dated 5 March 1949, from Ugo di Vallepiana to Egmond d'Arcis.
25 Ibid., letter dated 20 March 1949, from Egmond d'Arcis to Ugo di Vallepiana.
26 Ibid., letter dated 23 March 1950, from Ugo di Vallepiana to Egmond d'Arcis.
27 Ibid., letter dated 7 May 1950, from Egmond d'Arcis to the CAI president.
28 Ibid., letter dated 11 May 1950, from Bartolomeo Figari to Egmond d'Arcis.
29 This area in particular witnessed first Fascist violence and later anti-Italian retaliation, most famously with the mass killing of civilians who were thrown alive into deep sinkholes, known as *foibe*.
30 In Zermatt on 22 August 1939, a few days before World War II broke out, representatives of only ten countries were present (Belgium, Czechoslovakia, France, Greece, Hungary, Italy, the Netherlands, Poland, Switzerland and Yugoslavia. Tonella, *50 anni di alpinismo senza frontiere*, 20.
31 I ended this list in 1951, as this was the year that Germany and Austria were readmitted, the association's priorities changed somewhat and an important chapter closed for the UIAA and its members. Details about congresses in the following periods can be found in the work by Tonella and Bossus cited previously.
32 Cited in Tonella, *50 anni di alpinismo senza frontiere*, 14.
33 Ibid., 17.
34 The first was curated by Dr. E. A. Robert and the second by Albert Roussy, both of whom were members of the UIAA Permanent Bureau.
35 Photographs of this show were published on the front page of *La Suisse* on 24 August 1936, and also in the *L'illustré*, 27 August 1936, 1103, and *La Patrie Suisse*, 29 August 1936, 824, magazines.
36 *Journal de Genève*, 25 August, 1936, 4.
37 For a full list of the work on display, see the exhibition catalogue, *Première exposition internationale de photographies alpines* (Genève, 1936). A copy is conserved at the Bibliothèque de Genève (Br 1544). Although other photographic exhibitions previously organised by various Alpine clubs had included work from authors from different countries, this was the first exhibition to call itself 'international'.
38 *La Suisse*, 25 August 1936, 5. The fact that both exhibitions were very successful was reported by *La Tribune de Genève* in a note informing the public that they would not be extended. See *La Tribune de Genève*, 2 September 1936, 3.

39 The *Exhibition of Swiss Alpine Art* opened on 19 August and closed on 19 September 1936. The organising committee was presided over by Paul Naville. For details on the rest of the committee, see Archives de la Ville de Genève, Section genevoise du Club alpin suisse, CASG.B.13.4/1 C.A.S. Section genevoise/Exposition d'art alpin 1936/Procès-verbaux/20 December 1935. An undated entry in the minutes of the organising committee provided the figure of 6,018 spectators, accompanied by comments that the exhibition had been "well attended". Archives de la Ville de Genève, Section genevoise du Club alpin suisse, CASG.B.13.4/1 C.A.S. Section genevoise/Exposition d'art alpin 1936/Procès-verbaux/undated comments at the end.
40 *La Suisse*, 1 September 1936, 5.
41 See review by W. Matthey-Claudet, *La Tribune de Genève*, 29 August 1936, 5.
42 *La Suisse*, 30 August 1936, 9.
43 Archives de la Ville de Genève, Section genevoise du Club alpin suisse, CASG.B.13.4/2: Expositions d'Art alpin/Documents administratifs (1933–1936), folder 1936. Brochure advertising events held in conjunction with the UIAA Congress. See also *Bulletin du Club Alpin Suisse, Section Genevoise* (June 1936), 88–89. A detailed description of these trips was published on *Die Alpen/Les Alps/Le Alpi* (1936), 311–313.
44 The first group (tourists) numbered six participants (four men and two women). The second group (*bon marcheurs*) numbered fourteen people, six of whom were women. The third group comprised eight men of five different nationalities. *Die Alpen/Les Alps/Le Alpi* (1936), 311–313.
45 *Die Alpen/Les Alps/Le Alpi*, 1936, 313.
46 *La Tribune de Genève*, 30–31 August 1936, 7.
47 *Bulletin du Club Alpin Suisse, Section Genevoise*, September 1940, 133.
48 Ibid., August 1941, 124.
49 Ibid., February 1942, 28–30.

2 Power, politics and exploration in fascist Italy

The 1928 watershed

Marco Cuzzi

The roots of Italian imperial ambitions

In an essay published in 2008 in the *Laboratoire politique* on the subject of the fifteenth- and sixteenth-century explorations, Mario Pozzi wrote:

> The new journeys fired imaginations, conjured up ancient fables in the popular imagination, inspired adventurous ideals and hopes of rapid enrichment and social advancement. Real life and fantasy melded; tangible scenes got confused with what could or should be according to this or that book or legend. But great geographic discoveries were not solely events worthy of epic poetry. They also implied much fewer romantic deeds, which offered a more realistic appraisal of the great personalities. I am referring, then, to many facets of political power: monarchs, ambassadors, functionaries with various names and titles, state councillors, etc.[1]

In the early modern era, the explorations of navigators were inspired by the less epic and more practical motives of extending European power and extending the borders of the Old Continent in length and breadth. Explorers were thus generally followed by missionaries and traders under military protection and then the earliest stable outposts, the colonies, governorates and merchant communities – the *fondaci* – and the imposition of the home country's socio-economic and cultural frameworks. The industrial era further reinforced the instrumental nature of newly explored lands, and there is certainly nothing accidental about the fact that the European colonisation of Africa, and the appropriation of its immense underground riches, took place in conjunction with the second industrial revolution from the seventeenth century onwards.[2] With the affirmation of the nation state and the beginning of the age of imperialism, when the possibility to acquire colonies was almost gone, exploration gradually lost, at least superficially, its former political penetration character.[3]

As the last of the European powers to take up the colonial gauntlet, Italy used the exploration tool to prepare the way for the cashing in of its belated bounty. In the second half of the nineteenth century, the myth of the *Third Rome*, celebrated by the Italian poet Giosuè Carducci and taken up by the majority of Italian

DOI: 10.4324/9781003095965-3

politicians, was revived, partly in view of a New Risorgimento designed to break out of the existing national borders, so laboriously conquered in the nation's long independence struggle.[4]

As Alfredo Oriani, the bard of Italian imperialism and one of the first twentieth-century Italian nationalists, wrote:

> Imperialism appears as a dream only to the weak and as a vice only to those incapables of command. Our last heroes were all great adventurers, our recent travellers saw the outlines of empire in all adventures. . . . What would the Italy of the future do within its narrow borders? The future of Europe is in other continents; it is only there that the greatness of its soul will be proven.[5]

The celebration of Italian explorers as the prototypes of national heroism was not something new. In 1874, Pietro Amat di San Filippo, one of the founders of the Italian Geographical Society, published a prosopographical collection of Italian explorers and travellers who had, since the far-off past, left the frontiers of their known world. The volume presented these figures as living models to emulate rather than distant memories of remote eras.[6]

The proliferation of new travellers and explorers coincided with the end of the nineteenth and the beginning of the twentieth century. Some of those travels explicitly seemed to be acting as tools of a concrete and brutal colonialism. On some occasions, they appeared to be oriented towards a more disinterested achievement of scientific goals that, nonetheless, were not devoid of racist assumption. It is, for example, difficult to see figures such as Giacomo Doria and Enrico Alberto D'Albertis as straightforward pre-colonialists, with the latter being a zealous traveller; great navigator; and also anthropologist, botanist, palaeontologist and photographer who succeeded in travelling around the world no fewer than three times, from 1882 to 1910, like a Jules Verne character. Moreover, for Manfredo Camperio, who was both politician and explorer,[7] Africa was the primary destination, followed by the Middle East. Asia attracted less interest; only a few Italians travelled to the far-off Pacific, most of them as fugitives of some kind.[8]

Besides scientific and commercial official purposes, another recurring driving factor was sport. Whether there were political interests behind enterprises that would seem to have been purely scientific and sporting is a legitimate question, although clearly sport played a significant part in the national political discourse.[9] This theme would take us too far away from the scope of this brief chapter. The first great mountaineering era of the nineteenth century, for instance, embedded the nationalistic and even imperial spirit of the time with roped parties on every peak climbing under the aegis of the various European nations, those same nations which were soon to lead their soldiers into World War I.[10]

National prestige was certainly the main motivation behind the extraordinary exploits examined here: both in the case of Umberto Nobile's 1928 Italia airship and the Karakoram expedition of Aimone di Savoia-Aosta in the following year, the desire to heighten the prestige of the *new* fascist and mussolinian Italy was certainly the primary trigger. This is what historian Emilio Gentile has effectively christened *Italianism*, namely the "belief that Italy had to play a centre stage role in twentieth century events and be the avant-garde in the creation of a new civilisation, both national and universal".[11] *Italianism* was a combination of an inferiority complex (in comparison to other European nations, and primarily France and Great Britain) and a 'superiority complex' which had come to the fore at the turn of the century and in particular in the wake of the fiftieth anniversary of the Italian unification in 1911. Italianism was not a fascist invention. Already in 1908, the *Corriere della Sera* newspaper reported the triumphs of Arturo Toscanini in New York and took the opportunity to pay homage to the nation. The journalist wrote:

> intellectual and vigorous, artistic and industrious, young in mind and body with that luminous tradition of genius and strength as an added advantage, a new Italy which is forcing luckier, richer and more powerful nations to revise judgements which have held it back for too long. . . . The Italian man challenges anyone to better him.[12]

Another article published on 1 June 1909 by the national-syndicalist Turin-based monarchist newspaper *Il Tricolore* is even more illuminating. According to the journal, "Italy cannot and must not hold back. It must compete with the great nations and not succumb tomorrow. Averting this requires a policy of strength, *of great exploits* [my italics] and expansionism".[13] This reasoning culminated in statements conjuring up Italian primacy in all fields: "The nation . . . constitutes and represents the mighty and solid collective unity on which are based at this current time global struggles *in all fields of human activity*".[14] In this context, Enrico Corradini became the herald and first theorist of imperialist nationalism, a line of thought considering imperialism as an outcome of modern nation-states. Italy, a recently unified country found itself in a crucial moment: it was high time to abandon its democratic patriotism and progressive liberalism – that had featured in the Risorgimento period – and to embrace a more aggressive imperialistic stance in order to develop its deep expansionist ambitions. According to Corradini, such a shift was not only necessary to enhance the nation formation but was necessary to global progress. The universal mission of the great nations, such as Italy, was to export their civilisation. "When the empire exists, nations enter the service of world civilisation".[15]

Mutilated Victory notwithstanding, World War I marked Italy's entry into the "great world history", as Giovanni Gentile, the Italian philosopher who would become the fascist minister of education, confirmed.[16]

A new fascist Italy and the world

Benito Mussolini soon took stock of this rhetoric and, as early as 1920 – in a still fluid and as yet incomplete phase in his political creation – envisioned his "new Italy" as marching towards world primacy:

> The first pillar of Fascism is Italianism, that is, we are proud to be Italians and expect, even in Siberia, to be able to shout out loud: 'We are Italians'. . . . Now

we lay claim to the honour of being Italians because, it is in our wonderful and adorable peninsula – adorable despite the fact that some of its people are not always adorable – that the most prodigious and marvellous history of the human race has played out.[17]

These are the ideological foundations for a new season of explorations that began in 1928. The fact that Umberto Nobile's North Pole journey and Aimone di Savoia-Aosta Karakoram expedition took place that year, after nearly twenty years of virtual stasis in Italian explorations, was not entirely random or fortuitous. 1928 was the year of the first fascist regime's turning point. Having come to power in 1922 and getting rid of the opposition in 1925–1926, in 1928, Mussolini focused on the twofold goal of the "fascistisation" of the state and institutionalisation of fascism whose outcomes were the overlapping of state and fascism and the transformation of fascism into *the* governmental body.[18] 1928 was also the year of the major economic and social Labour Charter reform that pushed the nation in a corporatist direction. It was also the year when the "fascist liturgy" was initiated.[19] Anniversaries and ceremonies were established, for instance, the fascist Epiphany, on 6 January, when gifts and money were handed out to poor families, and the celebration of the foundation of the fascist movement in Milan on 23 March. Similarly, this was the year in which the fascist conscription was introduced and children were obliged to join the party's youth organisations (*Figli della Lupa, Balilla, Avanguardisti, Giovani Fascisti* for boys; *Piccole italiane* and *Giovani italiane* for girls). In 1928, the regime also started its so-called demographic campaign aimed at increasing the birth rate and therefore strengthening the Italian nation. That very year, the regime launched a "wholesale land reclamation programme" to reclaim a third of the nation's agricultural land for farming.[20] Other important milestones occurred in 1928, such as a fascist intervention in education[21] and the implementation of a new electoral law, marking the definitive shift to a single-party system. Negotiations with the Vatican went on and culminated with the Lateran Pacts and the Concordat in the following year, reinforcing Mussolini's power even more.

The attempt on King Vittorio Emanuele III's life in Milan on 12 April 1928 (three days before Nobile's departure for the North Pole) triggered the first wave of arrests and repression directed against the anti-Fascist movement. The apex of the repression was the June trial against the Italian Communist Party's high command that ended with a twenty-year sentence for Antonio Gramsci. If the offensive had begun on the internal front, the same was true for the colonies.

In January, General Rodolfo Graziani launched the military campaign to reconquer Tripolitania, while his fellow commander Ottorino Mezzetti was to do the same in Cyrenaica. The regime represented Graziani and Mezzetti as the heroes of the new army that was supposed to emerge from the fascistisation of the country. This project, though, was not entirely successful, and some of the high commanders remained stubbornly loyal to the king. However, 1928 was a propitious year for this attempt to clothe the Savoy army in black shirts, and the occasion was served by the deaths of the two symbols of the old monarchic militarism, Armando

Diaz and Luigi Cadorna. The two World War I chiefs of staff died on 28 February and 21 December, respectively.

With the inauguration of the Farnesina Male Fascist Academy in February, the regime's sporting and gymnastic efforts began. The first sporting radio transmission of the public broadcaster in Fascist Italy – Ente italiano per le audizioni radiofoniche – was lunched under the state supervision and regulated by the Sport Charter, which was also issued in 1928.[22] That year's sporting triumphs seemed paradigmatic: the cyclist Alfredo Binda's three Tour of Italy victories; Major Mario De Bernardi breaking the seaplane speed record twice and reaching speeds of 512 kilometres per hour; aviators Arturo Ferrarin and Carlo Del Prete, who set three world records with a Savoia-Marchetti 64 aircraft flying for 58 hours and 37 minutes. Even the fascist hierarchs set to work immediately, and Roberto Farinacci, former party secretary, enrolled in the Mille Miglia historic amateur car race with a Ceirano 1500. Italo Balbo's initiative, as undersecretary at the Aeronautics Ministry, was more prestigious. From 26 May to 2 June 1928, he organised the Western Mediterranean Air Crusade from Italy to Spain with 61 aircraft and a grand total of 200 men commanded by General Francesco De Pinedo.[23] Even more prestigious was the trans-oceanic flight that Italo Balbo accomplished in June 1927, completing a two-fold flight from Europe to South America and North America to Europe. Next came the Eastern Mediterranean Air Crusade in 1929, passing through Greece, Turkey, Romania and the Soviet Union and, in 1930–1931 and 1933, the two trans-Atlantic crossings in SIAI-Marchetti S.55X seaplanes commanded by Balbo himself, now aeronautics minister.[24] These enterprises were more geo-political than sporting in nature, and their purpose was to launch Mussolini's Italy into the great international scene.

Scientific interests and geopolitical ambitions in the Italian explorations in Asia

Until the late 1920s, Fascist Italy's foreign policy was aligned overall with its traditional alliance with France and Great Britain, with no rupture taking place, as historian Enzo Collotti noted, with "a few differences in language, perhaps even of style, but nothing immediately new or radical".[25] In 1928, however, a first important signal of imminent and disruptive upcoming choices was visible. In this shift, a role, though not yet a central one, was played by the so-called *Ventottisti*, namely the around 70 young fascists incorporated into the various sections of the Foreign Ministry and foreign embassies, who won diplomatic selections precisely in 1928.[26] This injection of youthful forces distant from the legacies of the Italian liberal governments was the first step in the direction of a new approach to diplomacy, an aggressive cultural diplomacy aimed at propagandising the 'new' Italy around the world.[27]

Already in October 1928, an article by Bruno Spampanato in *Il Popolo d'Italia* seemed to be the harbinger of a new Mussolini watershed. After comparing the Fascist message to the Christian-Catholic *urbi et orbi* formula and the transnational nature of the French revolution of 1789 with the October 1922 fascist revolution, the journalist concluded by eulogising the *duce* as explicitly conjuring up a desire for political and cultural hegemony of transnational and transcontinental, virtually global, scope:

> With its order Fascism has created this state. Our state is the backbone of Fascist Italy in its preparations for the empire. But the first imperial phase is moving in parallel with the October revolution. Fascism as not simply an Italian regime, but the advent of an European political civilisation is spreading fast. Or rather, its idea is spreading fast to revive the old concept of civilisation, or replace it, as we have said of every revolution. If the face of the civilisation of the century will be Italian, Rome will live again. After the Bastille, [it will be] the Campidoglio [to bring] light to the people. Fascism, from Rome, is universal. It already belongs to the civilisation of peoples. And as all the leaders of a revolution, founders of a regime, initiators of a new civilisation belong not to their country but to the world, also Mussolini is everyone's leader. The civilisation of the century will be named after him.[28]

Roberto Ducci, in an article written five years later, summed up the shift from the transformation of the nation to nation's rebirth abroad. According to Ducci, once fascism had restored the authority of the state within the nation, it was time to look beyond the national borders.[29] As journalist Giorgio Pini noted in the early 1930s, "what is needed is to contribute to the formation of a clear Italian international conscience because the scope of the Italian fascist struggle is now shifting from inside to outside".[30]

Hence, as historian Pietro Pastorelli has argued, 1928 was also a remarkable year in terms of the revision of the Italian foreign policy[31] with the revival of the myth of the 'Third Rome' so beloved by pre-war nationalists. Two books published in 1928 were emblematic of this new global ambition: the one written by the idealist and traditionalist philosopher Antonio Bruers on "Italy's world mission"[32] and the collection of speeches and writing of Pietro Foscari, cofounder of the nationalist association in 1910 and enthusiastic supporter of Italian colonialism.[33]

My argument is that this new diplomatic orientation led to full support for competitive sporting and scientific exploration initiatives. Although not always directly connected to colonial ambitions, the Italian explorations of those years were nonetheless expressions of the new fascist nation and its renewed energies. Clearly neither the Karakorum nor, to an even greater extent, the Arctic fitted into fascist Italy's geopolitical spheres of action, which were limited to the Mediterranean, dominated by the *mare nostrum* ideal and for the most part projected towards the Danube. There were, though, pushes towards a more global sphere of action for the fascist regime. Giorgio Pini, journalist and biographer of Mussolini, argued that the "international struggle" of fascism could in no way be constrained geographically, at least eastwards. According to Pini, only a fascist Rome, with its historical legacy of a truly global empire, could "show the way and march into the future".[34] And more: "The Italian Fascist echo, which has already made its

28 *Marco Cuzzi*

way into the darkest recesses of the world, is also making itself repeatedly felt in distant Asia".[35]

In strictly geopolitical terms, there was to be, as we will see, an even shrewder interest in central Asia, bordering on the Roof of the World, while the troubled Arctic adventure fitted more fully into the framework of scientific and prestige-winning exploits for the *new Italy*. This is confirmed by the party declaration on the occasion of celebrations for the birth of Rome (namely the anniversary of the founding of the city) following on from the departure of the Italia airship (21 April 1928):

> The Polar lands, which have already witnessed Italy's bold hearts with the expeditions of the Duca degli Abruzzi and Umberto Nobile, will be seeing the nation's flag fly once again. Milanese Fascists, with noble national sentiment, wanted the first studies and research into the Arctic seas to be by Italian scientists and generously gathered together the necessary funds.... The Fascism, which inspires all bold material exploits, adventures like these whose aim is to secure precious scientific material for all humanity, salutes all aviators and follows the safe flight of the airship which bears Italy's name and hearts with ardent interest.[36]

On the occasion of these celebrations, the party secretary, Augusto Turati, spoke of "Italian presence all over the world" with reference to both communities and travellers, "veritable itinerant ambassadors of Fascism at all four corners of the earth".[37]

This kind of interpretation of geographical explorations as fascist propaganda clearly appears in the writings of the entomologist Lodovico di Caporiacco, a member of Aimone's Karakoram expedition. While lamenting the xenophilia of too many Italians, di Caporiacco argued that those Italian expeditions clearly proved the popularity of the fascist regime abroad. Writing about his experience in India, he argued that the English people he met there were quite jealous of the fascist achievements. According to di Caporiacco, not only the English people were in admiration of the fascist regime.

> [W]hat struck me more than anything else was when, in Gurcis, in a small and remote mountain village, at over 2500 metres, the manager of the post office, a pure blood Indian, having seen a photograph of our Duce in a magazine, asked me if this was Mussolini. When I replied affirmatively and showed our amazement at his recognition of our Duce, he commented: "A great man and yours is a great people! Under his guidance Italy, which has ruled the whole of Europe including England, will once again rule Europe including England."

When di Caporiacco, some weeks after, met the Italian consul in Mumbai and told him about this meeting in Gurcis, the consul replied:

> Italy and Il Duce are well known here! Among the Indians who would like to see the current state of affairs change ..., it is commonly said that only a

war will change their fate and among the nations they believe will replace the English rule in the country, one of the most popular is Italy.[38]

These quotes contain some of the most relevant themes connected to geographical exploration during the fascist regime, including the exporting of Mussolini's image, the presentation of the new Italy born with the 1922 revolution and the propaganda of regime's achievements. The passage also hints to the geopolitical dimension of these explorations, with India's desire to overthrow the British rule and Italy's ambition to replace Britain in colonial dominance. We will soon see how much of these explorations were designed to serve geopolitical purposes.

The interest in Tibet and Central Asia was to take on the characteristics of a more marked political penetration in the next decade. When Mussolini himself took the lead of the Ministry of Foreign Affairs after Dino Grandi's service,[39] in 1932, a renewed interest in the region, testified to by the Tucci expedition in Tibet in 1933, became evident. Giuseppe Tucci, Italian anthropologist, Orientalist and academic, founder of the Italian Middle Eastern and Far East Institute (Istituto Italiano per il Medio ed Estremo Oriente), had explored Indian Darjeeling, Nepal and Ladakh in the second half of the 1920s at his own expense. Having remained in India, in 1930, he proposed a new expedition to the Italian government with the aim of studying Buddhism's penetration into Tibet.[40] The foreign ministry, who had appreciated Tucci's "illustrious work" in the British colony, approved his request, supporting the explorer's "scientific propaganda abroad" purpose.[41] Although apparently Tucci's intentions, and those of his colleague Carlo Formichi who accompanied him, seemed scientific, perhaps esoteric, nonetheless, at the end of the expedition in 1934, both asked to report to Mussolini on the results of the expedition, including some "specific information on the Nepalese government's friendly intentions towards Italy".[42] This interlocking of national prestige-related interests ("scientific propaganda abroad") and geopolitical requirements is tangible here, too. In fact, the time for this was even riper than in 1928.

The attention of the military intelligence service for these expeditions confirmed the interlocking of scientific prestige and geopolitical ambitions. The entire Central Asia region had been subject to diplomatic attention since the early post-WWI years: the revolt of the new monarch of Afghanistan, Amannullah Khan, against the British Empire (May 1919) had been followed closely by the Italian ambassador in Istanbul, Carlo Sforza. Subsequently the Italian foreign minister, now Sforza himself, handed out a 'symbolic loan' to the Kabul government.[43] On 30 June 1921, Italy was the first country in the world to recognise Afghan independence, reinforcing the bond between the two countries with trade, economic and even military exchanges, including supplying aircraft for the embryonic Afghan air force.[44] Relations continued with Amannullah's two successors and rivals, Nadir and Zahir.[45]

The signing of the Asian Pact between Turkey, Persia, Iraq and Afghanistan in July 1937, which aimed at finding some independent space of manoeuvre between the cumbersome presence of the Soviets and the British, was viewed with special sympathy in Rome. Military agreements with the subsequent Afghan Zahir Shah government demonstrated Italy's special interest in an area which was a potential pawn – perhaps of secondary importance but not entirely marginal – and ally against Great Britain and the Soviet Union, as first the alliance with Kabul and Teheran and then the Baghdad putsch of 1941 demonstrate.

For this reason, Rome offered concrete institutional support to the latest expeditions to Karakorum while keeping a close eye on them. Tucci, the Italian Heinrich Harrer,[46] returned to Tibet in 1939, this time accompanied by Alpini captain (expert rock climber and, above all, Italian military intelligence agent) Felice Boffa-Ballaran, with whom he traversed northern India and Nepal, an adventure which was followed closely by Rome's intelligence agencies.[47]

The new war was to shuffle the deck once again and effectively brought this kind of activity to an end, at least for some time.

Conclusions

In this chapter, I have argued that there is a deep connection linking a series of Italian explorations, occurring in the late 1920s and 1930s, and the ideological and political contest from which they emerged. In particular, I have traced the genealogy connecting the discourse of the 'Third Rome' and Italian grandeur to the fascist universal ambitions and their translations into imperial dreams. The geographical explorations occurred under the fascist regime concurred to reinforce the narrative of the rebirth of ancient Rome and its global, if not power, at least cultural prestige.

It is true that the politics of geographical explorations did not belong to the fascist regime. Liberal Italy, fascist Italy and republican Italy all invested somehow in this worldwide game, and I believe that understanding the ruptures and continuities throughout this history is still a challenge for historians.

Notes

1 Mario Pozzi, "Politica e grandi scoperte geografiche", *Laboratoire Italien*, no. 8 (2008): 15.
2 See: John R. Ward, "The Industrial Revolution and British Imperialism, 1750–1850", *Economic History Review*, 47, no. 1 (1994): 44–65; Wolfgang Reihard, *A Short History of Colonialism* (Manchester: Manchester University Press, 2011); Deyna Parvanova, "The Industrial Revolution Was the Force Behind the New Imperialism", *ESSAI*, 15 (2017): Article 30, https://dc.cod.edu/essai/vol15/iss1/30, last access 11 December 2021. More in general: Eric Hobsbawm, *The Age of Empire* (London: Weidenfeld and Nicolson, 1987).
3 Ester Capuzzo, "La proiezione oltremare della nazione: Volpe e il colonialismo italiano", *Clio* 3 (2004): 447–471.
4 The term 'Third Rome' (*Terza Roma* in Italian) traces back to a far past of Italian history. First, the ancient Roman empire – the Ceasars' Rome – had taken over large regions of the world; second, the popes' Rome had built a spiritual empire that encompassed political, cultural and economic spheres, across the Medieval and Early Modern times; finally, the fascist Rome stemmed from the Risorgimento's battles and was ready to inherit the grand legacies of the previous two Romes.

5 Alfredo Oriani, *La rivolta ideale* (Roma: Edizioni di Libero, 2003), 208–209.
6 Pietro Amat di San Filippo, *Viaggiatori italiani* (Roma: Salviucci, 1874).
7 Mariachiara Fugazza and Ada Gigli Marchetti, eds., *Manfredo Camperio. Tra politica, esplorazioni e commercio* (Milano: FrancoAngeli, 2002).
8 Marco Cuzzi and Guido Carlo Pigliasco, eds., *Storie straordinarie di italiani nel Pacifico* (Bologna: Odoya, 2016).
9 Apart from the classics by Hobsbawm and Mosse, see also: Norbert Elias and Eric Dunning, *Sport e aggressività. La ricerca di eccitamento nel loisir* (Bologna: Il Mulino, 1989).
10 On mountaineering, an apparently apolitical discipline contaminated by nationalism, see: Stefano Morosini, *Sulle vette della patria. Politica, guerra e nazione nel Club alpino italiano 1863–1922* (Milano: FrancoAngeli, 2009).
11 Emilio Gentile, *La Grande Italia. Il mito della nazione nel XX secolo* (Roma-Bari: Laterza, 2006), 102.
12 [no author], "Verso la più forte Italia", *Il Corriere della Sera*, 28 November 1908.
13 Gentile, *La Grande Italia*, 115.
14 [no author], "Principi e direttive del nazionalismo", *La Grande Italia*, 12 May 1912.
15 Enrico Corradini, *Scritti e discorsi 1901–1914*, ed. Lucia Strappini (Torino: Einaudi, 1980), 261.
16 Giovanni Gentile, *Guerra e fede: frammenti politici* (Napoli: Ricciardi, 1919), 119. Gabriele D'Annunzio coined the expression 'mutilated victory' (in Italian *Vittoria Mutilata*) in October 1918, a few days before the end of World War I. The Italian poet used the term to convey his disappointment concerning territorial rewards in favor of Italy at the end of the conflict. This feeling turned into a political myth and a key point in the propaganda of fascist Italy.
17 Speech held in Trieste on 20 September 1920, in Benito Mussolini, *Opera Omnia*, eds. Edoardo and Duilio Susmel, vol. 15 (Firenze: La Fenice, 1957), 214 and subsequent.
18 Arnaldo Mussolini, il duce's brother, came up with this new phase in articles published in the newspaper *Il Popolo d'Italia* directed by himself. According to Arnaldo Mussolini, fascism articulated in three phases: after the initial time period of the conquest of power and the second phase devoted to the building of a regime, the third time has arrived. It was the right moment to "overcome the Party in the State, historic configuration of Italian unity, and to put the Party at the service of the State" and to "fascistisise the Italian people". Quotes from: Arnaldo Mussolini, "Terzo tempo", *Il Popolo d'Italia*, 16 August 1930.
19 Emilio Gentile, *Il culto del littorio. La sacralizzazione della politica nell'Italia fascista* (Roma-Bari: Laterza, 2003), 151.
20 Elisabetta Novello, *La bonifica in Italia: Legislazione, credito e lotta alla malaria dall'Unità al fascismo* (Milano: FrancoAngeli, 2003), 279. On this see also: Federico Caprotti and Maria Kaika, "Landscape: Nature, Materiality and the Cinematic Representation of Land Reclamationin the Pontine Marshes", *Social and Cultural Geography* 9, no. 6 (2008): 613–634.
21 Renzo De Felice, *Mussolini il Duce. Gli anni del consenso. 1929–1936* (Torino: Einaudi, 1996), 188.
22 See: Maria Canella and Sergio Giuntini, eds., *Sport e fascismo* (Milano: FrancoAngeli, 2009).
23 See: Igino Mercarelli, *Francesco De Pinedo* (Roma: Ufficio storico dell'Aeronautica Militare, 1987).
24 See: Ranieri Cupini, *Cieli e mari* (Mursia: Milano, 1973); Blaine Taylor, *Fascist eagle: Italy's Air Marshal Italo Balbo* (Missoula: Pictorial Histories Pub. Co, 1996); Italo Balbo, *La centuria alata* (Montepulciano: Editrice Le Balze, 2005).
25 Enzo Collotti, *Fascismo e politica di potenza. Politica estera. 1922–1939* (Firenze: La Nuova Italia, 2000), 7.

26 Patrizia Dogliani, *Il fascismo degli italiani: una storia sociale* (Torino: UTET, 2008), 64.
27 On the global spread of the fascist model, see: Roger Griffin, ed., *International Fascism: Theories, Causes and the New Consensus* (London: Arnold, 1998); Gert Sørensen and Robert Mallet, eds., *International Fascism 1919–45* (London-Portland: Frank Cass, 2002); Marco Cuzzi, *Antieuropa. Il fascismo universale di Mussolini* (Milano: M&B Publishing, 2006); Marco Cuzzi, *L'internazionale delle Camicie nere. I CAUR (1933–1939)* (Milano: Milano, 2005); Constantin Iordachi, ed., *Comparative Fascist Studies: New Perspectives* (London: Routledge, 2010); Arnd Bauerkämper, "Transnational Fascism: Cross-Border Relations Between Regimes and Movements in Europe, 1922–1939", *East Central Europe* 37 (2010): 214–246; Aristotele Kallis, "From CAUR to EUR: Italian Fascism, the 'Myth of Rome' and the Pursuit of International Primacy", *Patterns of Prejudice*, 50, no. 4–5 (2016): 359–377; Federico Finchelstein, *From Fascism to Populism in History* (Oakland: University of California Press, 2017); Antonio Costa Pinto, *Corporatism and Fascism: The Corporatist Wave in Europe* (London: Routledge, 2017).
28 [no author], "Universalità della Rivoluzione", *Il Popolo d'Italia*, 23 October 1928.
29 Roberto Ducci, "La diffusione del fascismo", *Politica* 109–110 (June–August 1933): 24.
30 Giorgio Pini, *La civiltà di Mussolini tra l'Oriente e l'Occidente* (Roma: Edizioni della Critica Fascista, 1930), 10.
31 Pietro Pastorelli, "Il revisionismo fascista verso la Francia", *Aspetti e problemi delle relazioni tra l'Italia e la Francia*, ed. Romain H. Rainero (Milano: Unicopli-CUESP, 2005), 241–245.
32 Antonio Bruers, *La missione d'Italia nel mondo* (Foligno: Franco Campitelli, 1928).
33 Pietro Foscari, *Per l'Italia più grande* (Roma: Edizioni della Rassegna Italiana, 1928).
34 Pini, *La civiltà di Mussolini tra l'Oriente e l'Occidente*, 12.
35 Ibid., 131.
36 Partito Nazionale Fascista, "Il Foglio d'Ordini", *Il Popolo d'Italia*, 21 April 1928.
37 [no author], "Le grandiose cerimonie romane", *Il Popolo d'Italia*, 22 April 1928; Arnaldo Mussolini, "Terzo Tempo", *Il Popolo d'Italia*, 16 August 1930.
38 Pini, *La civiltà di Mussolini tra l'Oriente e l'Occidente*, 131–133.
39 Ruggero Moscati, "Locarno-Il revisionismo fascista-Il periodo Grandi e la nuova fase della politica estera", in *La politica estera italiana dal 1914 al 1943*, eds. Augusto Torre et al. (Roma: Eri, 1963), 115.
40 Archivio Centrale dello Stato (hereafter ACS), Presidenza del Consiglio dei Ministri (hereafter PCM), 1934–36, Busta 1874, Fascicolo 3–2–4–7540 prot. 110, Lettera di Giuseppe Tucci al Direttore generale delle Scuole Italiane all'estero, Calcutta, 29 January 1930. About Giuseppe Tucci see Enrica Garzilli, *L'esploratore del duce. Le avventure di Giuseppe Tucci e la politica italiana in Oriente da Mussolini a Andreotti* (Roma: Memori, 2012).
41 ACS, PCM 1934–36, Busta 1874, Fascicolo 3–2–4–7540 prot. 110, Telespresso no. 10386 del ministro degli Esteri al Gabinetto del ministro, 24 February 1930.
42 Ibid., Reale Accademia d'Italia – Nota firmata di Carlo Formichi, 25 January 1934.
43 Andrea Vento, *Storia dei servizi segreti italiani dal Risorgimento alla Guerra fredda* (Milano: Il Saggiatore, 2010), 242.
44 Mario Ungaro, "Ricordi Afghani", *Affari Esteri* 46 (1980): 229–234.
45 Vento, *In silenzio gioite e soffrite*, 242 and subsequent.
46 See: Heinrich Harrer, *Sieben Jahre in Tibet: Mein Leben am Hofe des Dalai Lama* (Berlin: Ulstein, 2011).

47 Ufficio Storico dello Stato maggiore dell'Esercito (hereafter USSME) – Fondo SIM H-3, Busta 26, Spedizione Tucci 1939. Boffa-Ballaran became a SIM agent of the Southern Italian Kingdom (1944–45) in which capacity he infiltrated the Salò armed forces (see: USSME – Fondo SIM H-3, 11ma Divisione – Busta 161 Boffa Ballaran). See also: Oscar Nalesini, "Felice Boffa Ballaran, Diarist, Photographer and Map Maker for the Italian Expedition to Tibet in 1939", *Miscellanea di Storia delle Esplorazioni* 38 (2013): 267–309.

3 Roald Amundsen *vs* Umberto Nobile

The role of the newspapers in the age of nationalism and polar imperialism

Steinar Aas

An introduction to Norwegian hostility towards 'the other' in the age of polar imperialism

On 25 May 1928, dirigible *Italia*, with Italian navigator and constructor Umberto Nobile and his crew aboard, crashed in the polar ice North of Svalbard. Not only did this accident trigger the most extensive rescue operation ever undertaken to date, it also culminated in collective mourning in Norway when national hero Roald Amundsen vanished in the sea on his way from Norway to Svalbard. Amundsen was flying North to help rescue his former companion. With Amundsen's disappearance, the Norwegian attitude to Nobile and his fellow Italians went from bad to worse. This unkind attitude was further reinforced when Nobile emerged from the ice safe and sound a month later. One Norwegian communist paper called Nobile "a goldgallooned fascist fool" whose "insane venture had caused the whole tragedy".[1] Bitterness and hostility culminated when Nobile returned to Italy via Norway.

This chapter addresses events from 1925 to 1928 and places them in historical context with a special focus on polar exploration's place as a halfway house between international cooperation and national rivalry. In addition, this chapter also shows that this rivalry lived on in later public opinion. The role played by the Norwegian media is the focus in both the period of cooperation (1925–1926) and later years. It pays special attention to the use of the history in later commemorations of the events as well.

International cooperation in the age of Norwegian polar imperialism

One distinct reason for the antagonism towards a foreign partner, later to become bitter rival, was xenophobia and nationalism, strongly bound up with early twentieth-century nation-state formation shaped by a distinctive Norwegian polar imperialism.[2] By the time of Norwegian independence from Sweden after nearly a 100-year long union, the Arctic and Antarctic regions were both *terra nullius* – no human's land.[3] But by the 1930s, the matter of ownership of these areas needed

DOI: 10.4324/9781003095965-4

to be settled. As was the case with imperialist national rivalry for colonies, Norway had ambitions into the white expanses of the world. By 1940, Norway had gained sovereignty over Svalbard (with the 1920 Svalbard Treaty), Jan Mayen (1930) and Bear Island (1920) in the Arctic North.[4] The foreign policy of this young nation was an ambitious one, and the next step was gaining control over parts of Greenland, an attempt which failed. In the Antarctic region, however, Norway annexed Bouvet Island (1928), Peter I Island (1931) and Queen Maud Land (1939).[5] Some of the arguments behind these acquisitions were, of course, Norway's ambitious foreign policy as well as the nation's tangible presence in the region, in both research, science and exploration and commercial activities such as mining, fishing, whaling and sealing (Figure 3.1). This polar imperialism was heavily invested in polar heroes like Roald Amundsen, not to mention Fridtjof Nansen, a pioneer in polar areas as both skier and scientist.[6] These two men put Norway on the map as a polar nation.

Figure 3.1 Facsimile of the first page of the newspaper *Tidens Tegn* on 27 May 1931. The paper addresses the case of the disputed area of East Greenland where Norwegian polar imperialists intended to occupy the region under Danish rule. The Permanent Court of International Justice in the Haag dismissed the claims and put an end to the 1931–1933 Norwegian occupation of the territory.

There is no doubt that polar exploration was interconnected with nationalism and nation-state formation in the Norwegian case in particular. Einar-Arne Drivenes and Harald Dag Jølle edited a three-volume polar history of Norway – *Norsk polarhistorie* (2004)[7] – published as a single-volume English version entitled *Into the Ice*[8] to espouse this perspective. Consequently, studying this perspective's rhetoric and semantics and the way it established vital narratives during the intense years of the 1920s more thoroughly is of some interest. In Norway's polar history, the semiotic 'us' and 'them' (Norwegians' rivals) system was vital. Examining the way 'others' were spoken of – in this case potentially partners, financers, potential competitors, enemies, rivals or simply foreigners, that is, non-Norwegians – is of interest.

This way of seeing 'others' was not limited to the interwar years in Norway. During the post-war period, too, the commemoration of polar heroism played a major part in the creation of a collective memory to which polar heroes and polar expeditions were central. Anne Eriksen, a Norwegian ethnologist, has argued that Norway's sense of connection to the polar regions is kept alive by modern-day polar races but also "certain icons and cultural monuments", which "embody the collective memory of a national, heroic polar history".[9] She counts Amundsen and Nansen as two such icons whose use in Norwegian identity creation draws attention to the fact that half Norwegian territory is north of the Arctic Circle. In addition, it emphasises the "distinctive significance ascribed to things polar", qualities such as "hardiness, endurance, adaptability, and the ability to confront nature's most extreme challenges".[10]

Eriksen has drawn attention to the various commemoration practices inviting continuous collective participation, keeping collective memory alive and topical.[11] As this chapter shows, newspapers played a part in this process, commemorating occasions like the 1926 Amundsen expedition and his disappearance in 1928, not to mention South Pole Day on 14 December 1911.

The Norwegian press and polar exploration

The Norwegian press and media in general played an important part in shaping national opinion around the famous Norwegian polar explorers. The polar explorers often signed up to exclusive publishing rights with newspapers and publishing houses as part of the funding of expeditions. The thirst for stories about the polar regions and its heroes seemed insatiable in both Norway and abroad. Geographical societies, touring clubs and explorer associations worldwide paid substantial fees for explorers' presence or lectures by them.[12] Photos and films became vital elements in the demand for news of expeditions, and polar explorers soon played a leading role in the use of new technology to portray their adventures. Amundsen, for instance, "showed moving images from his South Pole expedition" at the Cirkus Verdensteatret in Kristiania (Oslo) in November 1912.[13] Before the planned expedition of 1926, the *New York Times* was one of the newspapers with exclusive rights to be supplied with telegrams giving the latest news from the airship during the flight.[14]

The 1920s were also marked by emerging nationalist movements. Nationalism was seen as a response to the menace of economic collapse, social poverty, unemployment, political unrest and polarisation.[15] The nationalist forces and their papers seemed more interested in the polar explorers and their achievements than the radical left. Before explaining the role of the Norwegian press in public coverage of polar exploration, it is worthy to take a detour into the history of the Norwegian press in the interwar period. Norway was sparsely populated and counted only 2.8 million people in 1930.[16] The population was scattered over a wide territory, with the northeasternmost and southernmost towns being around 2,000 kilometres apart.

Modern newspapers began expanding in around 1880, and during the interwar period, they continued to grow – in line with political polarisation and the development of the modern rotation press – passing from 265 in 1920 to 289 in 1930.[17] The press developed in scope into multifaceted political newspapers representing even marginalised political currents, such as the small Soviet-oriented communist party. Prior to the setting up of the Norwegian Communist Party (1923), the Labour Party was the only Scandinavian member of the Comintern, the Communist Internationals, until its break with the Comintern in 1923. However, the interwar period was a consolidation period during which the existence of a political press became a Norwegian hallmark.[18] Even small towns sometimes had a vast variety of political papers representing the three most prevalent and dominant trends in Norwegian political life: liberals (left), conservatives (right) and socialists/social democrats (Labour Party).[19] In addition, there were also papers representing the less mainstream political parties, such as the Free-Minded Liberal Party and the Communists. Some historians have seen Norway as a "a realm of media", where the various local papers were connected in a national public sphere, often borrowing articles from each other, preferably from papers with the same political leaning.[20]

Most Norwegian papers were principally centre-right oriented and anti-socialist/anti-communist. Regarding fascism, there seems to have been a tendency in the right-wing press towards curiosity where Italian fascism was concerned. One of the main papers, *Aftenposten* (conservative), marked fascist Italy's five-year anniversary in October 1927 by printing a chronicle written by Benito Mussolini and published through the United Press Association of America.[21] Five years earlier, the same paper had published an article from Bavaria about a "violent outbreak" of fascism there in a comparative article on Hitler and Mussolini.[22] Its author, Sven Elvestad, prophetically concluded that, young people in Germany "saw their country's existence threatened every day" and that they no longer would accept seeing "their future as part of unpredictable political manoeuvre" nor "the political parties". They rather would be focused on "the men, the man".[23] Elvestad is famous for publishing the first interview with Adolf Hitler in a Norwegian paper, as early as 9 April 1923 in *Tidens Tegn*, stating that Hitler's political programme was an example of "German Fascism".[24] Elvestad later moved to fascist Italy, where he lived from 1925 to 1933, more or less.[25]

Nobile and the Norwegian press

The Norwegian press was first introduced to Nobile in 1925 on the occasion, of course, of the new daring Arctic expedition. First of all, Roald Amundsen was presenting to Norwegian public opinion his planned expedition by airship – the new Amundsen-expedition – to take place in 1926. The focus was, as always by Norwegian media, on Norwegian heroes, but in this case, by introducing readers to Nobile, a novel element emerged. Indeed, the attention seemed to be more on the foreigner volunteering to help Amundsen and willing to become part of Amundsen's future records, that is, a simple Italian airship constructor rather than the well-known Nobile. In September 1925, 59 news items and articles focused on Nobile in the Norwegian press, meaning that the Norwegian public learned a great deal about the new Italian apprentice.

Today, Norwegian publications, including newspapers, can be consulted in the digitalised database of the National library of Norway, called *bokhylla.no*. Some newspapers are absent from the database, and others are only partially covered, but most papers are there, and the numbers we will present later can illustrate tendencies rather than exact numbers.[26] Central keyword searches give an impression of the interest in topics or individuals involved in certain topics. Searching for 'Roald Amundsen' or 'Umberto Nobile', for example, gives an impression of the quantitative distribution of media interest, and the intention here is to illustrate findings later and analyse and discuss hit outcomes.

The information on Nobile was formulated as a press release published identically in all types of Norwegian papers: the big national papers, smaller daily regional papers and small local papers. The information concerned those taking part in the next Amundsen flight, plans for the expedition and the building of a hangar and mooring masts along the airship's planned route.[27] The name of the airship was also an indication of the nationality of the mission: the airship was to be named *Norge*, Norway. The airship's constructor, Nobile, was appointed as managing engineer "in charge of one of the watch".[28] Another paper, *Hamar Arbeiderblad*,[29] of social democratic orientation, announced that the airship had been donated by Mussolini and that additional cheap gas was being made available from the same source. The social democrat, socialist and communist papers seemed reluctant to write anything about Nobile's role. The radical-left papers made no mention, in their news items and articles, of Nobile in October (17 news items), November (19 news items) and December (81 news items). Figure 3.2, showing the incidence of 'Umberto Nobile' in the Norwegian press in the autumn of 1925 and 1926, shows that the Norwegian press lost interest in him in the autumn of 1926. Because the airship stopped over twice in Norway in April (Oslo) and May (Vadsø), his name was naturally often mentioned by the papers in these two months.

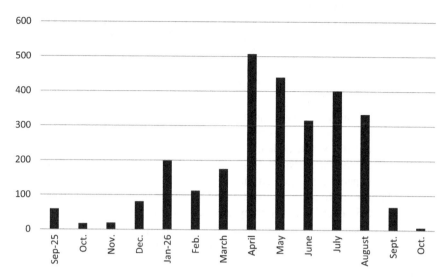

Figure 3.2 Incidence of the name 'Umberto Nobile' in Norwegian press from September 1925 to October 1926.

Tidens Tegn and Rolf Thommesen in the firing line

Tidens Tegn, one of Norway's most prominent newspapers during the interwar period, was the one Sven Elvestad published in. It voiced a more outspoken fascination with Italian culture and history and the new political direction it had taken in the 1920s.[30] It also played a specific part in connection with the 1925–1926 flight as well, because its owner – Rolf Thommesen – was the director of the Norwegian Aviation Club.[31] He thus occasionally acted as intermediary between Amundsen and his men and Italian airship constructor Nobile during the planning, preparation and building of the Amundsen-Ellsworth-Nobile transpolar flight. Consequently, *Tidens Tegn* was the Norwegian paper primarily involved in reducing damage and found itself in the firing line when conflict emerged in late 1925. Rumours of a conflict of interest between Amundsen and Nobile in connection with preparations were circulating. However, a conservative paper in Trondheim stated that these rumours were "completely groundless", quoting another of Thommesen's papers – offshoot *Oslo Aftenavis* – which spoke to Nobile in Rome.[32] During the planning and running of the expedition, this seemed to change. Initially, the Norwegian press paid no particular attention to the fact that Nobile wanted recognition for its role in the expedition of 1926.

Until Nobile suddenly raised a number of vital issues and objections regarding Amundsen's plans, the main narrative had been that this was Amundsen's expedition. Such interference would normally have been unacceptable in Amundsen's world. He usually demanded complete loyalty from his crew members.[33] The first rumours of tensions between Thommesen and Amundsen emerged in December 1925. One of the reasons for this was the lack of direct contact between Nobile and the Norwegian polar explorer. Nobile was not involved in Amundsen's plans for the flight from Rome to Svalbard. But he had now decided to intervene to change Amundsen's plans.[34] Both the Italians and Thommesen sought desperately to downplay these differences: "there has never been any disagreement between Amundsen and me", one paper quoted Nobile as saying, and there had always been "absolute agreement on everything". The alleged disagreements were "completely unfounded", Nobile added.[35]

Tidens Tegn supported Nobile regarding the choice of route from Rome to Svalbard. The paper published an interview with Nobile in which he explained that the flight from Rome to Svalbard would be extremely difficult. From Pulham in England to Svalbard was a journey of around 3,100 kilometres, and it was to take place in bad weather conditions in March and April, risking rough winds along the Norwegian coast and fog in the Arctic Ocean.[36] Nobile was more worried about this than Amundsen, and planning precautions were not random, with all places along the airship's route needing a ground crew.

This difference of opinion resulted in a change of planned route, in line with Nobile's opinion. Instead of flying along the Norwegian coast, as Amundsen had planned, the airship was to navigate via Stolp in Germany to Leningrad in the newly established communist republic of the Soviet Union. This was to the Norwegian radical-left newspapers' satisfaction and immediately attracted the interest of *Nordlys* (labour) on 19 January 19 1926, *1ste Mai* (labour) on 19 January 1926, *Arbeidet* (communist) on 27 January 1926 and *Norsk Kommunistblad* (communist) on 19 January 1926. In contrast to the right-wing papers, these four papers demonstratively used the new socialist name Leningrad instead of Petrograd.

The culmination in tensions

However, this part of the expedition was of minor importance for Amundsen, and, in fact, he and his fellow Norwegians travelled up to Spitsbergen by ship from mainland Norway. Amundsen's focus was the North Pole, since he and his crew would be the first humans to reach both the North and South Poles. Consequently, preparing this initial stretch was Nobile's task. The main Norwegian goal was the polar region, and thus the Norwegian press seemed to be of the opinion that Nobile would have a secondary role. Amundsen was successful, flying over the North Pole, and bad weather conditions did not prevent the party from successfully landing in Teller, Alaska, on 14 May 1926.[37] This was to have been the end of Amundsen's career as a polar explorer, as he saw himself as having achieved what he had set out to do.[38] When Nobile reluctantly tried to steal some of the limelight in the early stages, it was still of minor importance to the record-focused Norwegians. However, tensions came out into the open when Nobile presented himself as an equal participant on the airship at the time

Roald Amundsen vs *Umberto Nobile* 41

Figure 3.3 The last photo of the main protagonists of the Amundsen-Ellsworth-Nobile transpolar flight together in Seattle. From then on, the cooperation was over. Source: H. C. Davidson/National Library of Norway.

of the landing in the US city of Seattle (Figure 3.3). Amundsen later wrote about the occasion:

> Imagine, then, our astonishment when, as the vessel drew up toward the pier, Nobile appeared from below apparelled in the most resplendent dress uniform of a colonel in the Italian army. . . . My anger was increased when it became apparent that he had carefully calculated the spot at which the gangplank would be let down from the deck, and had stationed himself at a point beside it where he could thrust himself forward and seem to lead the expedition off the vessel. . . . Certainly, it was beneath my dignity to enter a competition for the moment's precedence with this strutting upstart.[39]

Since Nobile had stolen some of the limelight, the impression given was that he had played an important part in this noble undertaking. Not only was such behaviour impertinent, it was also completely unacceptable, as Amundsen's biographer Tor Bomann-Larsen has made clear.[40] During the subsequent tribute trip through the American continent in the spring and summer of 1926, this struggle for credit between the different groups emerged. While Amundsen planned to meet colonies of Norwegian immigrants along his west-to-east train journey in the United States, Nobile was also met by fellow countrymen in almost every corner of the United States. The Norwegians realised that the reception given him was celebratory, giving people the mistaken impression that he had played a starring role in the expedition. Amundsen was extremely annoyed, and the Norwegian press noticed that there was something wrong.[41] However, in the context of the overwhelming mood of triumph, the Norwegian press seems to have highlighted the great Norwegian polar explorer's success rather than any disruptions to it by the celebrations of other participants. From July to November 1926, the number of news items and press articles in which Nobile's name appeared fell from 401 a month to just 6. For Roald Amundsen, however, the press attention seemed never ending. Between May and December 1926 almost 4,000 news items and articles mentioned his name in the Norwegian printed press.

Political views in the age of nationalism

Given the profile of the Italian expedition, with its dubious links to the fascist regime and Mussolini, the social democrats and communists understandably cast Amundsen's Italian counterpart in a negative light. This view was especially clear after the two parties – the Norwegians and the Italians – departed Seattle. From then on, a great deal of suspicion was directed towards the Italians in Norwegian media, especially as Nobile had already struggled to explain to the Norwegian press in December 1925 that there had been no tensions between him and Amundsen.[42]

Amundsen, on the other hand, was aware of the connection between the expedition and the fascist regime but does not seem initially to have responded to it. In fact, it was "thanks to Mussolini's great interest in the matter" that the expedition was so efficiently organised and, according to Amundsen, on "excellent terms".[43] The reason behind the warm welcome given by Amundsen to Italian participation was obvious. Mussolini had contributed to the funding of the project, covering more than 40% of its expenditure. Given this, Amundsen was not especially eager to make moral considerations. Quite the contrary: "For me it is only about reaching the objective", he said.[44]

The apex of Amundsen's heroism was his return home to Oslo in 1926. At a reception at the Honnørbrygga in Norway's capital city, Amundsen displayed all his rhetorical skills in a solemn but simple act, taking the flag from airship N-1 – *Norge* – unfolding it and delivering a short speech:

> I have been asked so many times what it was that impelled me, what I was working for. It was this. [Holding up the flag to the spectators, film crew, and photographers] The flag is worn out and in tatters. But I can assure you: it is pure. May God protect it, and all Norwegian people. Long live Norway.[45]

The Norwegian press has always emphasised the connection between Nobile and Amundsen. The fact that Amundsen and Nobile were rivals was due to the character of polar exploration in nationalist Norway and fascist Italy. On the day after Amundsen's homecoming, on his birthday, 16 July 1926, he was invited to a rally which was arranged by nationalist political organisation Fedrelandslaget (The Fatherland League), and one of its founding fathers was Thommesen of *Tidens Tegn*. The organisation revolved around a leading figure – the other Norwegian polar hero – Nansen. The rally naturally directed attention to Amundsen's most recent polar record, the flight over the North Pole to Alaska from Svalbard. Nansen mobilised spectators during his speech, addressing it to Amundsen in a tangibly patriotic way:

> We need a national uprising. We yearn for a cleaner atmosphere, and it is there your deed turns up as a release. There are indeed men still left in Norway! . . . your example, shining and glittering as it stands out, will build the future of Norway.[46]

Nobile's exclusion in 1926–1927

All the negative publicity in Norwegian papers before, during and after the trip seems to have led to Nobile becoming a persona non grata in Norwegian public life in 1926. Even though he had been contracted to publish a book together with Lincoln Ellsworth and Amundsen after the trip, he was not included in the Norwegian publication in 1926. Its title was *Den første flukt over polhavet*,[47] later published in English under the title *The First Flight across the Polar Sea* a year later.[48] Conflicting views meant that the book became a joint project between loyal friends of the great Norwegian polar hero Amundsen. This exclusion – tacitly understood by most Norwegians – meant that Nobile and his Italian crew were denied the chance to give their views on what was considered a great accomplishment in the 1920s, an airship flight from Rome to Nome in Alaska.

Interest in Nobile almost entirely petered out in 1926, and no one seems to have taken an interest in his opinion on events. Time went by, and it was not until 1976 that Nobile was given a chance to publish his Amundsen-Ellsworth-Nobile transpolar flight story in Norwegian. The occasion for the book was the fiftieth anniversary of the expedition in 1926.

Back in Norway, Amundsen threw restraint to the winds and began one of the most extensive smear campaigns in polar history, attacking Umberto Nobile in every way.[49] In Amundsen's autobiography, Nobile was mentioned as many as 256 times, most relating to Amundsen's compulsion to criticise the Italian fellow in some way or other. Nobile was pompous, uniform obsessed, highly strung, haughty, arrogant and a conceited braggart. Amundsen did not spare the invectives, adding that Nobile was a foolish dreamer with vulgar taste and that he had acted to the great detriment of the expedition on multiple occasions.[50] Luckily Nobile did not live in Norway, but he was denied the opportunity to respond to Amundsen's claims. Consequently, his views on Nobile and the Italians gained a foothold in Norway which survived for years to come. Although some Norwegian papers, such as Liberal Party paper *Dagbladet*, did question Amundsen's attack, the great hero was untouchable in the Norwegian public.[51] The fallout of the attack was that Amundsen fell out with more than just the Italians and Nobile. Amundsen's biographer Bomann-Larsen claims that Amundsen attacked many people in his autobiography, including British and Americans. Amundsen's editor disliked this "literary suicide", believing that it would be difficult to send Amundsen to the National Geographic Society, the Explorers Club in the United States or the Royal Geographical Society in London.[52] Lectures at prominent clubs and salons around the world were an important part of polar explorers' funding, hence the importance of his tour across the United States after the reception in Seattle in the summer of 1926.[53]

The *Italia* crash and messianic rhetoric

Amundsen lived a retired life in the months after his provocative book. Ironically, it was the search-and-rescue operation for Nobile and his shipwreck in 1928 that became Amundsen's lifeline. A twist of fate meant that Amundsen disappeared on his way to Svalbard, and his body was never found, and thus his posthumous reputation was "knight of the ice" rather than the grumpy, isolated old man who fell out with everyone.[54] According to Bomann-Larsen, Amundsen's triumph lay in his defeat.[55] Eriksen claims that "many Norwegians actually refused to accept that he was dead and continued to gaze expectantly out over the Northern seas".[56] Even though he was lost, people still expected wonders from him, almost like after the death of the Messiah. The event was something of a replay of 1925, when Amundsen crash-landed on the ice in his Dornier Val plane. He was expected to reappear, and the Norwegian public were confident that he would. Bomann-Larsen characterised the 1925 event as 'the resurrection', with clear biblical connotations. Amundsen disappeared for days, but he came back.

The role of the "knight of the ice" sanctified Amundsen, and the Norwegian press contributed to this poetic narrative, with the commemoration and mourning process beginning in the summer and autumn of 1928. Eriksen described the national grief: "Public commemorations of Amundsen's passing could therefore function in a more uncomplicated manner, as an expression of farewell by people and state to one of the nation's great men".[57] The Norwegian government then elevated him to an even higher level. They marked the so-called South Pole Day – 14 December – as a national memorial day. Some called this day Amundsen Day because it coincided with the day Amundsen reached the South Pole in 1911. Solemn ceremonies in 1928 laid the foundations for an almost messianic cult around the polar hero.[58] Amundsen and Nansen had led Norway to grandeur through their polar achievements and made Norway famous worldwide. Now Amundsen had died a noble death while on his way to save his enemies. Now was not the time to address his shortcomings or criticise his behaviour or personality. One can imagine the sorrow felt by his fellow Norwegians when all hope was lost and Amundsen was declared dead. The people let the "swell of emotions" related to the death of Amundsen flow freely.

The combination of anger towards the Italians was combined with national grievance, not to mention forgiveness towards Amundsen. The old eagle was pardoned. Now the commemoration could go on in a respectful matter, and the main ceremonies took place on 14th December all over Norway, ending in a silent mediation at noon[59]

The grieving process now was put on national footing. Nothing was left to chance. In Oslo, the King, the Crown Prince and Nansen were the front rank figures in the main commemoration ceremony. One indication of Amundsen's popularity was the amount of money raised to support the memorial fund set up in his name in December 1928. The semiotics and iconography of the advertisement material were simple, and they produced results. The flyers and posters simply used Amundsen's profile portrait. The slogan read: "By deed he honoured his country. By deeds we will honour his memory". People were urged to make a "donation of honour" to the Roald Amundsen Memorial Fund.[60]

These events strengthened the sacralisation of Amundsen and made him, together with Nansen, part of the "narratives of national heroes". Amundsen personified not only a quest for heroic deeds but also "shared group values", performing universally admired deeds. According to Eriksen, the "good man and the good Norwegian" became "two sides of the same coin".[61]

The Bible and Jesus rhetoric was directed towards the shipwrecked Italians when they landed in the harbour town of Narvik in Nordland in July 1928. It began during the search for Amundsen in the Arctic Ocean when the Norwegian press compared Nobile to Judas: "After Judas had betrayed his Lord and master he still had enough honour intact so that he managed to hang himself", the socialist paper *Fremover* wrote.[62] The article was written by Henry Harm,[63] editor of the Labour Party paper *Telemark Arbeiderblad*, and spread to all corners of Norway through the party's press.[64] Despite being published by socialist papers, it was to non-socialist papers' taste, like *Eidsiva*[65] and *Andøy Avis*.[66]

Rumours and negative publicity for Nobile and Italy in 1927–1928

Little mention was made of Nobile in the Norwegian press between 1926 and 1928, but when the *Italia* crashed in 1928, attacks on Nobile began. It had all started when news of the *Italia* expedition was announced in 1927, but it was with the crash landing, and the subsequent disappearance of Amundsen and his flight crew, that it exploded. From then on, Norwegian papers played a vital role in disseminating all kinds of information about the Italian crew in the Arctic Ocean not only in Norway but also internationally.

One observer and friend of Amundsen in Tromsø, Peter Wessel Zappfe, set the summer of 1928 scene to illustrate the madness of the media:

> The whole polar basin was full of swarming search and rescue expeditions, in the sea, in the ice and in the air. A surf of journalists and photographers

flushed northwards from the boiling cosmopolitan cities where the rotary press stood as insatiable lizards of steel, hissing out of impatience.[67]

One example was rumours around the disappearance of Swedish meteorologist Finn Malmgren. These were repeated and circulated as early as 1928, when a number of Norwegian papers published them, and they rapidly spread worldwide. Even distant papers such as the *Barrier Miner* in New South Wales, Australia, published an article about "Cannibalism alleged against Italians" on July 25 1928, quoting British paper *The Daily Mail*.[68] The gossip snowball reportedly began with Norwegian paper *Folkets Avis* (The Peoples Paper) in a telegram from Copenhagen which told the story of the surviving Italians onboard the Soviet ice breaker *Krassin*. Various suspicious behaviours were attached to the two survivors. One was the "mystery surrounding the trek across the ice".[69] The other was that when one of them was asked where Malmgren was, he simply pointed in the direction of the ice breaker, where Malmgren was supposed to be. The Australian paper then informed its readers that Malmgren was not to be found near the ship. The source behind this information was the physician onboard the ice breaker. Another source was the Soviet search-and-rescue pilot, but most of the news stemmed from rumours and was reported with no source at all.

Nevertheless, the readers of the Australian *Barrier Miner* took the news at face value. Only the most well-informed Australians knew that there was no such paper as *Folkets Avis* in Norway in 1928. However, the news about the story spread like wildfire from a fictional Norwegian paper to Copenhagen, via London and down under to Australia.

The radical newspapers pay homage to Amundsen in 1928

If we study the content of the incidence of 'Umberto Nobile' and 'Roald Amundsen' during this intense period, there were indeed political views behind the criticism of Nobile and his polar expeditions. The Norwegian communist papers were not surprisingly critical of the Italians in general on the basis of anti-fascist sentiments in the 1920s. Norwegian communists knew how Mussolini had treated Italian socialists and communists during the fascist takeover of 1922 and subsequently, and they portrayed the expedition in 1928 as fascist propaganda exercise. *Friheten* (The Freedom), one of northern Norway's communist newspapers, highlighted that all types of exploration and polar expeditions were based on "imperialist colonisation politics" and Nobile's expedition was no exception. The main goal for the Italians was to "mark the prestige of Italian imperialism". Coal exploration at Spitsbergen had demonstrated the area's economic potential. There was also possibly oil in the sea around Svalbard.[70]

There seemed to be an intentional or unintentional international campaign among European communist newspapers to cast events of the summer of 1928 in an anti-Italian and anti-fascist light. French communist paper *L'Humanité* sent a journalist all the way from Paris to Stavanger to cover the triumph of the Soviet ice breaker *Krassin* being received in the harbour for repairs prompted by its search-and-rescue work in the Arctic Ocean in 1928. During its stay in Stavanger, journalist Maurice Donzel, alias Maurice Parijanine, was able to talk to the crew and get first-hand information about events in the ice (Biblioteque National de France, "Maurice Donzel"). Donzel was known as a translator from Russian to French and a fervent supporter of the Soviet communist project until he disassociated himself from Josef Stalin and the USSR in the 1930s and became a Trotskyite.[71]

Even Conservative papers such as *Aust-Agder Blad*, based in the small town of Risør, published communist quotes taken from Donzel's writings, despite not being the least in favour of radical socialism. In fact, they had even warned against the Social Democrats before the 1928 parliamentary election, fomenting fears of revolution.[72] Readers would expect first-hand witness stories from the *Krassin* to be true, such as the most important story involving Lieutenant Zappi alleging cannibalism. His guilt could not be proved, Parijanine concluded, but "everything pointed to the fact" that Zappi was guilty of "one if not two attempted murders".[73] The paper added that, "Zappi is a murderer", quoting Parijanine, who wrote about the events in French, *Le "Krassine" au secours de L'"Italia"* (1928), and English, *The Krassin*.[74]

Another Norwegian paper, *Østlendingen*, elaborated on this same rumour, quoting a Russian paper via Germany and finding it strange that Zappi was wearing three pairs of socks, three pairs of shoes and three suits when he was rescued, whereas his colleague, Adalberto Mariano, had only one pair of socks on. This was considered a clear sign that Zappi planned to wait for Mariano's death and then eat him.[75] No Norwegian paper seems to have been interested in talking to polar scientist Adolf Hoel, who was invited by the Soviets to take part in the search-and-rescue onboard *Krassin* in 1928 and rejected the rumours. They were not commented on or investigated properly before Hoel's contribution in Gunnar Hovdenak's book regarding the search-and-rescue operations onboard Krassin, *Roald Amundsens siste ferd*, in which Hoel concluded that the allegations were "unfounded" and "foolish".[76] We will see that these stories survived to the late 1950s.

Norway's political papers were walking a tightrope. The nature of polar exploration was such that a balancing act between the anti-fascism of the left-wing papers and Norwegian patriotism, nationalism and even racism was difficult. For example, communist newspaper *Arbeidet* in Bergen spewed out invectives against Nobile and his fellow Italians on Amundsen Day on 14 December 1928.

Anti-fascism played an important part in the approach of the communist paper. Nobile and the Italians were once again the anti-heroes, in contrast to Amundsen, who was truly a "man of the working class", and there was no doubt about Amundsen's popularity among common Norwegians, it argued. Praise of Amundsen was unanimous. Even communists found a basis for the tribute to Amundsen, who was seen as having had qualities that the working class admired, such as fulfilling his aims and working for success.[77]

Ironically, the radical papers were not especially attentive to Norwegian polar imperialism. Amundsen's death and the treatment of Nobile in connection with it is an example of the role nationalism can play in uniting different political and social groups in Norwegian society during a turbulent period in the nation's history. The idea that Amundsen was "a first among equals" seems to have been deep rooted, even among the radical left, in Norwegian political life. His martyrdom was both an example of good Christian values for the radical left as well as nationalists, with men such as Amundsen being seen as having sacrificed their lives for a noble cause.[78]

The Amundsen fiftieth anniversary in 1976

The one-sided Norwegian perspective is that Nobile was used as a nationalist propaganda tool. There is no doubt that both Roald Amundsen and Umberto Nobile were nationalist tools, and neither seems to have had issues with being used in this way. Polar achievements were a matter of national glory and prestige as well.

Whenever an article featured Amundsen, his rival was never far away, in the background. Figure 3.4 shows the link between Nobile and Amundsen in Norwegian media. This interconnection between the two survived for years to come. Although Nobile seems to have been forgotten by the Norwegian press in 1926, the attention he was paid in 1927 was enormous, culminating in more than 1,000 hits in June and July 1928.

This chapter has already touched upon how the commemoration rites sponsored certain memory narratives constructed through rituals and ceremonies, and the press certainly played a part in this memory creation process. Other "memory agents" – that is to say small groups of men and women acting as "social agents" of memory[79] – were potentially politicians, association members, historians and so on. Whoever they were, Nobile seems to have been commonly deployed to draw attention away from Amundsen, highlighting the myths and rumours revolving around Nobile and his fellow Italians. Nobile was to be Amundsen's counterpart for the foreseeable future.

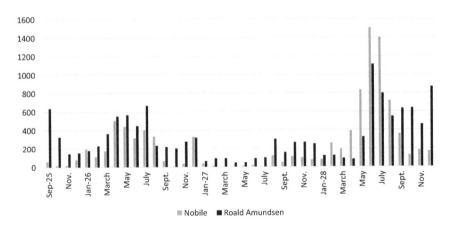

Figure 3.4 Incidence of 'Roald Amundsen' and 'Umberto Nobile' in Norwegian newspapers 1925–1930.

Nevertheless, the two were interconnected in the years to come. Amundsen deliberately strengthened the connection between them, first in his autobiography, when he highlighted the connection with Nobile by criticising him, and second during the search-and-rescue operation when Amundsen disappeared on his way to help Nobile, strengthening the bond between them even further. The power of the drama was undeniable. Instead of earning a reputation as an isolated, grumpy elderly hero on the verge of bankruptcy, with enemies both in Norway and abroad, Amundsen emerged as a "knight of the ice" on the basis of his gallant act in trying to help Nobile, his rival. Consequently, the way the two were remembered was marked by this in subsequent years.

When Nobile finally published his version of the *Norge* expedition in 1976 in Norwegian, some of the most influential Norwegian papers predictably responded extremely negatively, directing a barrage of abuse at him. This was the reason behind the reaction of the editor of weekly *Dag og Tid*, Tor Gabrielsen, on 14 May 1976, triggered by an article by Asbjørn Omberg on Nobile in *Aftenposten*, still one of the most influential Conservative papers in Norway in the 1970s. In 1976, news of Nobile's presence at the Amundsen-Ellsworth-Nobile transpolar flight of 1926 commemoration ceremony caused confusion.[80] So who was this Italian? Omberg was happy to tell the story, or, more precisely, the planned book was not reliable, as it was based on undocumented fragments of his life after the *Italia* accident. He was born under the "hot sun outside Naples" and knew nothing about snow and ice. However, he was the first to become a polar explorer, Omberg ironically argued.[81]

Gabrielsen refused to accept the idea that a person – in this case Nobile – could be solely evil. "We hardly know anything about Umberto Nobile", Gabrielsen explained, adding,

> We certainly do not know more after reading the big article in the culture section of *Aftenposten*. But we know one thing: no human created by God, not even the most detestable creature, not to mention swarthy southerners who go into the icescape, can be only evil, only self-righteous.[82]

Gabrielsen underlined, in 1976, that Norwegian primary school text books and fictional and factual prose for children and adolescents had been imbued with the narrative of the evil Italian.[83] It was not the whole story to be told, just one perspective, which he later felt obliged to react to. He clearly stated from the *Aftenposten*:

> It is the Norwegians who are self-righteous. We are eager to consider ourselves as a nation of daredevils, born with skis on, a people of courage, strong and intelligent. The Southerners drink wine and have siestas when not chasing women. This is just simple, stupid and well known. But we think this is how simple, stupid and well known the core in the conflict between Amundsen and Nobile is – in Asbjørn Omberg's and all other "good" Norwegian's understanding.[84]

The thirtieth anniversary of Amundsen's death in 1958

The mindset illustrated by Gabrielsen in 1976 seems to have been part of a certain memory culture in Norway, an Amundsen heritage in which he and Nobile were two sides of the same coin. This narrative fitted into a shared mindset, in which Norwegians mostly connected memory ceremonies for the *Norge* expedition and Amundsen's death with constant attacks on Nobile. Only a few people, such as Gabrielsen, spoke up to defend Nobile in the 1970s.

In 1958, a thirty-year anniversary of Amundsen's disappearance was held at which the abovementioned Hoel took the same stance as Gabrielsen in 1976, protesting against the then-accepted narrative.[85] Hoel found the Norwegian reaction over the loss of Amundsen incomprehensible. The campaign against Nobile had, in some countries, such as Germany, been rather harsh, but nowhere to the same extent as in Norway.[86] With the thirtieth anniversary of Amundsen's disappearance and death marked by the Norwegian press in late 1958, the campaign against Nobile seemed to be being kept alive by the Norwegian press. Hoel claimed that, "Nobile and his companions' tragic faith" was judged "in a more understanding way" abroad, but this change of atmosphere did not seem to have reached Norway.[87] Hoel was familiar with Norway's polar heritage, as one of the founders of the Norwegian Polar Institute and having taken part in the search and rescue onboard *Krassin* in 1928. The prevailing version was still based on "harsh assaults from the press against General Nobile in Norway".[88] Hoel was referring, in particular, to Georg Svendsen's *Kooperatøren* and accusations of "foolishness" on Nobile's part leading to the "death of 14 men".[89] The allegations regarding Nobile's treason on the ice were also repeated and used as part of the Amundsen commemoration. Nobile ran on board the airplane when Swedish aviator Einar Lundborg landed on the ice during the search-and-rescue operation, "before anybody else reacted", Svendsen claimed.[90] This was, of course, a mortal sin for a captain of a wrecked ship and was used in Norway to underline his lack of leadership qualities, confirming earlier criticisms by Amundsen. Even though eyewitnesses such as Lundborg and Czech scientist František Běhounek had very different accounts of this part of the rescue operation,[91] Svendsen ignored these, claiming that Nobile acted according to Italian orders. He was the first Italian out of the ice because he was to lead the rescue operation from Kings Bay, Spitsbergen.[92]

The alleged cannibalism story was still alive in 1958 Norwegian papers. Svendsen charged Nobile with "the death of fourteen men" in support of Amundsen,[93] who had rightly attacked Nobile in 1927. Nobile was a bad navigator, a front rank fascist and an ice sea imperialist wanting to create a "small Italian empire in the Arctic", Svendsen concluded in 1958, taking Amundsen's side.[94] Amundsen's absence was laid at Nobile's door, and Hoel was one of the few Norwegians, with Gabrielsen in 1976, to address this narrative critically already in 1958–1959. Hoel completely dismissed the cannibalism rumours as "a web of lies", adding that he had still not met the man behind the rumours.[95] He attacked the smears directed not only at Nobile but also at Italians in general, and his critique accorded with Gabrielsen's in 1976: "There has to be something wrong with the Norwegian mentality, every now and then running down the Italians" or, as one Norwegian paper called the Italians after the crash in 1928: "those blackish orange pickers".[96]

The widespread opinion seemed to be that the *Italia* expedition was a waste of time and that Nobile was blind to this fact. The old accusations, familiar from years earlier, were stressed both in 1958 and in 1976. Why was Nobile doing the same flight as Amundsen? The question was implicitly critical of the motives behind the flight, which was seen as a waste of time and money.[97] Hoel's counterargument was that no polar expeditions, strictly speaking, were absolutely necessary, except search-and-rescue operations. Nevertheless, Hoel fully certified the scientific aims of the *Italia* flights. Some reputable international scientific journals even published its results.[98] Hoel was supported by another Norwegian who also took part in the search-and-rescue operations after Nobile and Amundsen in 1928, Rolf S. Tandberg. The latter also reacted negatively to the common Norwegian narrative, adding that the *Italia* expedition had contributed "new geographical knowledge" and "useful scientific results".[99]

A national collective narrative ritualised

The *Aftenposten* article in 1976 was definitely not the last article containing the narrative criticised by Gabrielsen and Hoel. Conservative newspaper *Nordlandsposten* (24 July 1978) from Bodø published another feature article arguing for the same views on the *Italia* crash as those of 1958 and 1976.[100] The article was connected to the fiftieth anniversary of the Italia tragedy and Amundsen's death. The old smear campaign was reiterated; thus, one can definitely speak of a commemoration tradition in Norway connected to Amundsen. It can also be argued that a critical image of Nobile was becoming part of the commemoration ritual with the focus being on the non-scientific approach of Nobile's expedition and the expedition being presented as motivated by Nobile's quest for "personal prestige, national ambitions" in addition to "a great deal of vanity". The entire project was driven by "the national ambitions of the fascist regime". Finally, the *Italia* flight's only "aim was to strengthen the Italian fascist regime towards the rest of the world", and this led to the death of many good men, like Amundsen.[101]

Tandberg, Hoel and Gabrielsen have all illustrated the existence of a Norwegian narrative, and the trio represents the handful of critical voices speaking out against this narrative. We can definitely conclude that these counter voices were not the dominant ones. The national narrative was rooted in a collective memory, the commemoration of the polar hero Amundsen, a collective narrative revolving around a dichotomy between good Norwegians and bad 'others' – Southerners, Mediterraneans. Unfortunately for Nobile, he was cast as the antagonist and became the whipping boy of Norwegian collective memory.

This chapter demonstrates that, in the Norwegian case, the polar heroes were important cross-party actors in Norwegian nation-state building. They acted to bind together various social and political groups in Norway, creating a common understanding of the national importance of polar achievements and heroes. One cornerstone in the development of this fellowship was the importance of the foreign antagonist. The part the press played in creating this antagonism was a crucial one, with the one-sidedness of the Norwegian press seeming to set aside critical reflection. Political differences within the Norwegian press were forgotten for a time as they acted as a tool for nationalist-oriented commemoration of Norwegian polar heroes.

Notes

1 "Den hvite stillhet er stadig ubrutt. Tragedien i Ishavet synes nu aa være en kjendsgjerning. Intet livstegn", *Friheten*, 8 June 1928. Translation of quotes from Norwegian papers are my own.
2 Einar Arne Drivenes, "The Conquerors", in *Into the Ice: The History of Norway and the Polar Regions*, eds. Einar Arne Drivenes and Harald Dag Jølle (Oslo: Gyldendal, 2006), 281.
3 Odd-Bjørn Fure, *Mellomkrigstid 1920–1940* (Oslo: Universitetsforlaget, 1996), 109–112.
4 Ibid., 18–20.
5 Ibid., 18.
6 Einar Arne Drivenes and Harald Dag Jølle, "The History of Norway in the Polar Regions", in *Into the Ice: The History of Norway and the Polar Regions*, eds. Einar Arne Drivenes and Harald Dag Jølle (Oslo: Gyldendal, 2006), 9.
7 Einar-Arne Drivenes and Harald Dag Jølle, eds., *Norsk polarhistorie* (Oslo: Gyldendal Norsk Forlag, 2004).
8 Drivenes and Jølle, eds., *Into the Ice*.
9 Anne Eriksen, "Memories", in *Into the Ice*, 475.
10 Eriksen, "Memories", in *Into the Ice*, 475.
11 Ibid., 475, 477.
12 Tor Bomann-Larsen, *Roald Amundsen, en biografi* (Oslo: Cappelen Damm, 1995), 488.
13 Jan Anders Diesen, "A Century of Polar Expedition Films: From Roald Amundsen to Børge Ousland", in *Small Country, Long Journeys*, eds. Eirik Frisvold Hanssen and Maria Fosheim Lund (Oslo: Nasjonalbiblioteket, 2017), 85.
14 Roald Berg, "Amundsen og hans Aeronauter", in *Norsk polarhistorie, bind 3, Ekspedisjonene*, eds. Drivenes and Jølle (Oslo: Gyldendal, 2004), 260.
15 Berge Furre, *Norsk historie 1914–2000: industrisamfunnet – frå vokstervisse til framtidstvil* (Oslo: Samlaget, 2000), 59.
16 SSB, "Folketellingen 1930", www.ssb.no/a/folketellinger/fob1930.html, last access 10 December 2021.
17 Helge Østbye, "Spredningens mønster", in *Norsk presses historie, Bind 2, parti, presse og publikum 1880–1945*, ed. Rune Ottosen (Oslo: Universitetsforlaget, 2010), 24.
18 Henrik G. Bastiansen, "Partipressen konsolideres (1920–1940)", in *Norsk presses historie, Bind 2, parti, presse og publikum 1880–1945*, ed. Rune Ottosen (Oslo: Universitetsforlaget, 2010), 37.
19 Østbye, "Spredningens mønster", in *Norsk presses historie*, 34.
20 Jan Eivind Myhre, *Norsk historie 1814–1905. Å byggje ein stat og skape ein nasjon* (Oslo: Samlaget, 2012), 174–175.
21 Benito Mussolini, "Hvorledes vi kom til makten", *Aftenposten*, 27 October 1927.

22 Sven Elvestad, "Fascismen i Bayern I voldsomt frembrudd", *Aftenposten*, 21 December 1922.
23 Ibid.
24 Rune Ottosen, "1905–1945: Pressen i den store verden", *Norsk presses historie, Bind 2, parti, presse og publikum 1880–1945*, ed. Rune Ottosen (Oslo: Universitetsforlaget, 2010), 360.
25 Odd Magnar Syversen, "Sven Elvestad", *Norsk Biografisk Leksikon, utgitt 1999–2015* (13 February 2009), https://nbl.snl.no/Sven_Elvestad, last access 10 December 2021.
26 The database is not accessible from servers outside Norway.
27 "Naar Amundsen næste gang skal avsted", *Norges Handels og Sjøfartstidene*, 10 September 1925.
28 Ibid.
29 "Amundsens nye polferd", *Hamar Arbeiderblad*, 11 September 1925.
30 Bomann-Larsen, *Roald Amundsen*, 442.
31 Rune Ottosen, "Rolf Thommessen", *Norsk Biografisk Leksikon, utgitt 1999–2015* (13 February 2009), https://nbl.snl.no/Rolf_Thommessen, last access 10 December 2021.
32 "Rygterne om uoverenstemmelse mellem Nobile og Amundsen helt ugrundede", *Trondhjems Adresseavis*, 8 December 1925.
33 Ragnar Kvam Jr., *De fire store* (Oslo: Gyldendal, 2000), 114.
34 "Rygterne om uoverenstemmelse mellem Nobile og Amundsen helt ugrundede", *Trondhjems Adresseavis*, 8 December 1925.
35 "Amundsen-Ellsworth-ekspeditionen", *Bergens Tidende*, 8 December 1925.
36 "Luftskipet 'Norge 1' vil faa en haard prøve underveis til Svalbard", *Fædrelandsvennen*, 5 December 1925.
37 Roald Amundsen and Lincoln Ellsworth, *Den først flukt over polhavet* (Oslo: Gyldendal, 1926), 120–121.
38 Roald Amundsen, *My Life as an Explorer* (New York: Doubleday, 1927), 224.
39 Ibid., 212.
40 Bomann-Larsen, *Roald Amundsen*, 461–472.
41 Steinar Aas, *Tragedien Umberto Nobile, polarhelt eller svikar?* (Oslo: Samlaget, 2002), 54–57.
42 *Bergens Tidende*, 8 December 1925.
43 Bomann-Larsen, *Roald Amundsen*, 422.
44 Ibid., 438–439.
45 Eriksen, "Memories", in *Into the Ice*, 454.
46 Bomann-Larsen, *Roald Amundsen*, 474.
47 Amundsen and Ellsworth, *Den først flukt over polhavet*.
48 Roald Amundsen and Lincoln Ellsworth, *The First Flight across the Polar Sea* (London: Hutchinson & Co, 1927).
49 See Amundsen's autobiography: Roald Amundsen, *Mitt liv som polarforsker* (Oslo: Gyldendal, 1927). Available also in English translation: Roald Amundsen, *My Life as an Explorer* (New York: Doubleday, 1927).
50 Steinar Aas, "'One Man's Foolishness Led to the Death of 14 Men': Norwegian Reactions to Umberto Nobile and the 'Italia' Disaster", *Acta Borealia* 20, no. 2 (2003): 172.
51 A. Spørck, "Amundsens nye bok", *Dagbladet*, 5 October 1927.
52 Bomann-Larsen, *Roald Amundsen*, 477, 487–488.
53 Aas, *Tragedien Umberto Nobile*, 54–58.
54 Bomann-Larsen, *Roald Amundsen*, 512.
55 Bomann-Larsen, *Roald Amundsen*, 535.

56 Eriksen, "Memories", in *Into the Ice*, 452.
57 Ibid., 452–453.
58 Ibid., 452.
59 Ibid., 252.
60 Ibid.
61 Ibid., 253.
62 Henry Harm, "La latteren runge . . .!", *Fremover*, 7 July 1927.
63 Kristian Dons Kirkvaag, *Arbeiderpressen i Norge, kort historikk* (Oslo: Det Norske Arbeiderpartis forlag, 1935), 47.
64 Henry Harm, "La latteren runge . . .!", *Vestfold Fremtid*, 7 July 1928; Henry Harm, "La latteren runge . . .!", *Haugesunds Arbeiderblad*, 9 July 1928; Henry Harm, "La latteren runge . . .!", *Kongsvinger Arbeiderblad*, 10 July 1928.
65 Henry Harm, "La latteren runge . . .!", *Eidsiva*, 13 July 1928.
66 *Andøy Avis*, 13 July 1928.
67 Aas, *Tragedien Umberto Nobile*, 116.
68 "Cannibalism Alleged against Italians", *Barrier Miner*, 25 July 1928, https://trove.nla.gov.au/newspaper/article/46027364, last access 10 December 2021.
69 Ibid., 25 July 1928.
70 "Hvorfor Nordpolsflyvning?", *Friheten*, 8 June 1928.
71 Leonid Livak, *Russian Émigrés in the Intellectual and Literary Life of Interwar France* (Québec: McGill-Queens University Press, 2010), 22.
72 Odd Munksgaard, "Et kuppert politisk terreng", in *De satte det på trykk. Sørlandske pressefolk i liv og trengsel gjennom 100 år*, ed. Egil Remi Jensen (Kristiansand: IJ-forlaget, 2003), 95.
73 "Zappi beskyldes for mord", *Aust-Agder Blad*, 31 August 1928.
74 Maurice Pirijanin, *The Krassin* (New York: Macaulay Company, 1929).
75 "Russiske uttalelser om Malmgrens død", *Østlendingen*, 31 July 1928.
76 Adolf Hoel, "«Krassin»-ferden", in *Roald Amundsens siste ferd*, ed. Gunnar Hovdenak (Oslo: Gyldendal, 1934), 249–254.
77 "Roald Amundsen", *Arbeidet*, December 14, 1928, 3.
78 Eriksen, "Memories", in *Into the Ice*, 456–457.
79 Jay Winter, *Remembering War: The Great War between Memory and History in the Twentieth Century* (New Haven and London: Yale University Press, 2006), 136.
80 Omberg, "Perpetuum Nobile", *Aftenposten*, 4 May 1976.
81 Omberg, *Aftenposten*, 4 May 1976.
82 Tor Gabrielsen, "Umberto Nobile og nordmennene", *Dag og Tid*, 14 May 1976.
83 Jan Østbye, *Roald Amundsen. Hans liv og ferder. Fortalt for ungdommen* (Oslo: Gyldendal, 1950); Bernt Balchen, *Kom nord med meg* (Oslo: Gyldendal forlag, 1958).
84 Gabrielsen, *Dag og Tid*, 14 May 1976.
85 Aas, "One Man's Foolishness Led to the Death of 14 Men", 188.
86 Einar Lundborg, *När Nobile Räddades: Mina Upplevelser Under Den Svenska Spetsbergs Expeditionen 1928* (Stockholm: Hugop Gerbers Förlag, 1928), 211–212; Elisabeth Dithmer, *Andrèe – Nobile* (København: Kihls bogtrykkeri, 1930), 11; Willy Meyer, *Der Kampf um Nobile, Versuch einer objektiven Darstellung und Wertung der Leistungen des italienischen Luftschiffers* (Berlin: Verlag Gebr. Radetzki, 1931); Steinar, "One Man's Foolishness Led to the Death of 14 Men", 188.
87 Hoel, "Amundsen – 'Latham' – Nobile", *Aftenposten aften*, 19 July 1958.
88 *Nationen*, 22 January 1959.
89 Georg Svendsen, "En manns dumhet førte til fjorten manns død", *Kooperatøren* 6 (1958).
90 Ibid.
91 František Běhounek, *Männen på isflaket* (Uppsala: Lindblads, 1929); Lundborg, *När Nobile Räddades*.

92 Aas, *Tragedien Umberto Nobile*, 146–148.
93 Amundsen, *Mitt liv som polarforsker*.
94 Svendsen, "En manns dumhet førte til fjorten manns død", *Kooperatøren* 6 (1958).
95 Hoel, *Aftenposten aften*, 19 July 1958.
96 Ibid.
97 Ibid.
98 Hoel, "Roald Amundsen, 'Latham' og Nobile", *Aftenposten aften*, 26 June 1958; Hoel, "Roald Amundsen – 'Latham' – og Nobile", *Aftenposten aften*, 4 July, 1958; Hoel, "Amundsen – 'Latham' – Nobile", *Aftenposten aften*, 19 July 1958.
99 Rolf S. Tandberg, "Roald Amundsen, 'Latham' og Nobile", *Aftenposten aften*, 3 July 1958.
100 Aas, "One Man's Foolishness Led to the Death of 14 Men", 188.
101 Arne Svendsen, "50 år siden luftskipet 'Italias's tragedie i Polhavet", *Nordlandsposten*, 24 July 1978.

4 Umberto Nobile between two totalitarianisms

Luciano Zani

Exchange of expertise across regimes

Using the word *totalitarianism* for both fascism and bolshevism does not mean to rigidly adopt a theory that forces the affinities and similarities between the regimes while overlooking their profound differences so as to arrive to the conclusion that they are essentially the same. Fascism and communism are considered genetically, culturally and historically different. While they may mirror and understand each other in many ways, and may have used many similar tactical means, they were destined for irreducible hostility and were completely antagonistic to each other from a strategic point of view.[1] They are new, modern and totalitarian experiments in the political domination of mass society in the twentieth century. Indeed, their most important common characteristic, their declarations to be new and modern political religions, "integralist and intolerant", that claim to define the meaning and final purpose of individual and collective existence by imposing a mandatory belief system of myths, rituals and symbols, contained within it the seed of an irremediable conflict: two giants in a deadly struggle, "antagonistic experiments of totalitarian modernity".[2] The two were thus destined to collide once their common democratic capitalist enemy would have been defeated, because they were divided by their mutual aversion and rivalry more than they were united by their common totalitarian faith. To quote the French historian François Furet, "the total political investment that they require and celebrate makes the battle they fight for succession over bourgeois values – along incompatible paths – even more horrific. The traits they have in common exacerbate those that divide them".[3]

Within this context, the professional, personal and political trajectory of Umberto Nobile can illuminate the relationship between the two regimes.[4] Nobile was a well-known Italian airship designer and pilot during the 1920s, a fascist hero until 1929, who joined the Soviet regime from 1931 to 1936 to contribute to the building of the Soviet airship industry from the ground up. Nobile owed most of his popularity to his spectacular flight over the North Pole in the airship *Norge* in 1926. Unexpectedly, only two years later, in 1928, his reputation was destroyed by the tragedy of the airship *Italia*, which crashed on the ice pack in an attempt to replicate the *Norge*'s successful flight.

DOI: 10.4324/9781003095965-5

After the 1928 big crash, the reciprocal interest between fascism and bolshevism grew. First, the Soviet Union and its Five Year Plan attracted many fascist observers, and the Soviet planning was studied so extensively that the myth of the plan can be hardly considered a mere marginal component of corporative ideology.[5] Second, trade agreements between the two countries were renewed annually from 1930 on, and a pact of friendship, neutrality and non-aggression was signed in 1933.[6] Third, Italian engineer Angelo Omodeo and his colleagues were entrusted with consulting on and then directing programmes to create irrigation systems, reclaim lands and produce hydroelectric energy in the USSR between 1931 and 1936[7] (about which Mussolini made much to-do in public).[8] Finally, FIAT, the main Italian car producer firm, and its engineers Ugo Gobbato, Secondo Marocco and Gaetano Ciocca built a ball bearing factory in Moscow.[9] Given these solid exchanges of expertise between Italy and Soviet Union, it should be no surprise that the most famous aeronautical engineer in Italy was asked to build the Soviet airship industry from scratch. But, while other collaborative enterprises were completely commercial in nature even though they implied the existence of a certain political approval, Nobile's collaboration involved more subtle implications inherent in the competitive and contiguous relationship between the two totalitarian regimes. Not only did the Soviet regime aim at demonstrating its capability and determination in a sector which was crucial for the fascist regime; more relevantly, Russians demonstrated their superior ability to make use even of an ex-meritorious fascist by making him their own poster child after he had been abandoned by his original totalitarian regime. For the fascist regime, though, Nobile's migration to the Soviet Union was not a great loss; it offered the possibility to confirm the regime's choice to invest in the airplane rather than airship industry while getting rid of a former hero who had become a political burden. Even without Nobile, Mussolini's regime was certain it would not lose the challenge of modernity against the Soviet Union.

Everything possible to return to that pack ice

Thanks to the sensational success of the 1926 flight over the North Pole by the airship *Norge*,[10] designed and built by Nobile but sold to the Norwegian Roald Amundsen, Nobile became one of the symbols of fascist boldness. The expedition was carried out under the personal direction of Nobile and the Norwegian Aeroclub, without the direct involvement of the Italian government. After the undertaking, Mussolini made it his own and ordered Nobile and his crew to make a triumphal voyage among Italian emigrants to the United States. Upon his return to Italy, Nobile continued his triumphal march, first to Naples then to Rome, accompanied by Mussolini and engulfed by applauding crowds. Popular enthusiasm continued for many days, promoted by a long series of official ceremonies. In a congratulatory speech to the Senate on May 18, 1926, Mussolini stated that the government was putting "Colonel Umberto Nobile – inventor, builder, commander of airships on the national agenda, for having given a new, indisputable glory to our Air Force and to our flag". Nobile was then awarded the Military Order of Savoy, was given a reception at the Capitol in Rome and at the Geographical Society, was granted a conference in the presence of the king in Pisa and received public honours in many Italian cities. As one of the opposition newspapers put it, fascism made Nobile "a sort of Fascist champion". He was promoted to the rank of general at only 41 years of age, and on 15 September 1926, in a ceremony at Palazzo Vidoni in Rome, in Mussolini's presence, he was presented with an honorary membership of the National Fascist Party.[11]

Two years later, another attempt to fly over the pole with a dirigible that was all Italian, the *Italia*, ended in tragedy. The airship crashed into the pack ice, eight crew members died (nine others would die in relief operations, including Amundsen) and Nobile and the other survivors were saved in an eventful rescue effort.[12] The *Italia* disaster had severe consequences for Nobile. The commission of inquiry that was ordered to discover the causes of the disaster and the rescue of Nobile and the other survivors placed the ultimate responsibility for the tragedy on an incorrect manoeuvre made by Nobile. Moreover, the commission concluded that Nobile's decision to save himself by being the first to leave on the Swedish airplane of Einar Lundborg, which had reached the survivors on the pack ice, was unjustifiable. Nobile, indignant over the accusations and the plot that was formed against him, renounced the rank of general and resigned from the Air Force.[13]

With his honour humiliated and his professional ambitions crushed, Nobile soon had to consider the possibility of leaving Italy to build a future for himself. Nobile dreamt of a place, a country, from where he could attempt to relocate traces of the men lost on the pack ice three years earlier and where he could get a taste once again for extreme ventures and fulfil his desire to lose himself on the pack ice again while discovering his inner self in the utterly cold and eternal ice. Above all, he longed for a country where he could reaffirm his professional expertise and rebuild a future for the airship. Italian institutions and authorities neither held him back nor did Mussolini himself oppose the removal of a cumbersome individual. While he did not intend to compensate Nobile for damages, Mussolini had no intention of adding insult to injury by refusing him the freedom to remake a life for himself elsewhere. This personal attention mixed with distance is the key to interpreting the relationship between Mussolini and Nobile. Mussolini did not try to save the North Pole aviator from the disgrace following the *Italia* disaster. However, Mussolini did not seem to be hostile to Nobile, consenting to all his demands as long as they did not interfere with the regime's political objectives or the institutional balance. As for himself, until the fall of the fascist regime, Nobile never severed the tie that gave him direct and privileged access to Mussolini. Nobile remained sincerely devoted and faithful to Mussolini and was genuinely convinced that the leader's decisions were based only on reasons of state. He always held the hope that sooner or later, history and the duce would have supported his version of the story.

Nobile received an unexpected invitation from his friend Professor Rudolph L. Samoilovitch to join the "*pleasure* cruise" on board the icebreaker *Malyghin* that was departing from Archangel harbour in July 1931. The invitation was music to Nobile's frustrated ears for several reasons. It brought him immediately back to the climate of three years before, when the *Malyghin* itself, together with the *Krassin*, another icebreaker, had assisted the survivors of the *Italia*'s crash sheltered in the "red tent". Although this was like reopening a painful wound, it was almost a flashback to the scene of the unsolved mystery. It also offered Nobile, echoing his own words, the opportunity to "return to my profession" at the end of the cruise, even if only for a short time, by assisting the Soviets in the construction of an airship. Finally, the invitation also provided him with the opportunity to return to Franz Joseph Land (part of the Arctic Archipelagos), where the Soviets hoped to find traces of Amundsen (Nobile felt the Barents Sea was a more likely location for this search). Nonetheless, that was the area where Nobile hoped that the remains of the victims of the *Italia* might be, even though he thought the possibility was "extremely remote".[14]

The *Malyghin* set sail on 19 July 1931. Nobile socialized with the scientists and journalists who were on board with him and appeared very satisfied with the experience. In the diary he kept on board, his only recurring criticism addressed the unwarranted cruelty displayed by his travelling companions, who passed time killing the birds and polar bears that unsuspectingly came near the ship. Nobile expressed his "indignation" towards those who killed "unnecessarily, merely for the pleasure of killing".[15] He compared the gratuitous brutality of these episodes with the "terrible need" that three years ago had forced the *Italia* shipwreck victims to kill a bear for food.[16]

This is not the only reminiscence of the *Italia* disaster noted in Nobile's diary; these memories are a leitmotiv that added an introspective dimension to Nobile's voyage.[17] For instance, they were also aroused by an encounter in the Bay of Tranquillity between the *Malyghin* and the *Graf Zeppelin* in flight over the Arctic[18] and were intensified by the traces and graves of past expeditions that were passed during many stages of the voyage. It was almost like a pilgrimage through what he perceived as symbols of courage and sacrifice. For him, that voyage was mostly a quest to find traces of his friends who were lost three years earlier when the *Italia* was split in two and crashed onto the pack ice.

Nobile was extremely disappointed when, on 6 August, the director of the *Malyghin* expedition Vladimir Julevich Wiese told him they would not be able to reach Alexandra Land due to the thickness of the ice, lack of time and insufficient coal supplies. "A hope and a dream have vanished",[19] Nobile wrote. He dedicated an entire chapter, under the telling title *Disappointment*, to describe his "tormented angst" while awaiting the "most important destination of the voyage", his "fixation over the past month", his absurdly inflated hope.[20] He wrote of fantasies, daydreams and rudely interrupted dreams that left in their place a "sad return" from which "all the attractions of an Arctic voyage disappeared" and the "magical fascination" of a return to the pack ice was dispelled:

> For three years I burned with the desire to return, and to have fulfilled that desire brought me indescribable happiness. All this was gone. My memory

of these strong emotions faded and almost disappeared. I felt I had failed my objective. I even felt humiliated.[21]

Anyway, Nobile accepted the invitation to remain in the Soviet Union. The real reason that was keeping him in the Soviet Union was the possibility, no longer realistic in Italy, to fulfil his profession goals (and to settle a score) and his continuing fascination with the exploration of the Arctic:

> You see. I am still not well. I thought that this time I would be cured of my illness. I believed that my memories of those solemn solitary lands would have been overshadowed by the memories of the people who surrounded me. I thought that the profanation of the desert in the *Malygin* would have broken the spell. But no. People are not in the memory. They are gone. I was alone up there on the pack ice. In deeply moving moments I sought solitude, and was alone. It was cold, but I did not feel the cold. I was intoxicated by the extremely pure, freezing air. My eyes rested with deep joy on the immaculate purity of the snow that was broken up only by azure patches of ice.[22]

The myth of the solitary hero, who overcomes the physical sensation of extreme cold and crowding, was woven into the obsession with the mystery that surrounded the comrades who disappeared three years earlier. Returning to the pack ice: that was the driving force that led Nobile to leave his family and sick wife. After Carlotta's death, he confessed these feelings to a friend with a mixture of regret and guilt: "I drove myself crazy searching for a way to return up there for the third time. She didn't suspect it, but for this reason I abandoned her in her sickbed to go to Russia".[23] To "go back up there" was an absolute necessity, which places Nobile in the wake of the classical narratives of Polar expeditions:

> For those who have been there once, the attraction of the Polar Regions is irresistible. That feeling of absolute liberty; that separation from all material things except that which is indispensable for survival; that loss of value in ideas, principles, feelings that seem essential and important in the civil world; money, gold, precious objects that become totally useless, to be thrown away with no regret whatsoever; man's laws that no longer exist but yield to nature's laws; that immense solitude where every person feels like he is king of himself; all this, once experienced, cannot be forgotten, and holds a lure that is impossible to resist.[24]

From commander to engineer: Nobile's stay in the Soviet Union

When he visited the Soviet Union in the summer of 1931, Nobile's psychological mindset was probably unusual with respect to the numerous other Italians who were living there. Compared to many other communist and socialist workers and technicians, some of whom collaborated with him in the airship industry, Nobile's motives for being in the Soviet Union were not based on ideological solidarity. On the contrary, until his fall, his story was closely interconnected with the realm of fascism. Because of his traumatic break with fascism, he was emotionally (more than rationally) estranged from his own co-nationals. Paradoxically, this condition gave him more in common with the Anglo-Saxon intellectuals studied by the sociologist Paul Hollander[25] rather than with Italian journalists and travellers who were curious but guarded in their approach to the Soviet Union. He shared with the English-speaking community the experience of the "id massage" – a hospitality technique the Soviets used to win the trust and respect of their guests, which they methodically gauged to the rank and receptivity of the visitor.

In addition, the close collaboration between Italy and the USSR in economic and military matters made Nobile's decision less unorthodox than his paradoxical circumstances might have made it appear: that is, a man who, after having been promoted to general and presented with an *honorary* party membership card by the fascists, fell from their grace and went to build airships for the bolsheviks, bringing glory to them and their revolution.[26] That the foreign press wrote of an "odd project" that had many "vague" characteristics was not surprising. A Czech daily paper wrote, "with this contract the Fascist general is obligated to serve a communist state for a number of years". Perhaps the duce had agreed to Nobile's transfer to the Soviet Union because it was the easiest – and softest – way to get rid of an individual who was a source of embarrassment for the Italian Air Force and the regime, but "unintentionally, it almost seemed that he surrendered him willingly to the Russians because he was an untrustworthy individual".[27] Although in exile, Nobile was still hoping to be redeemed and appreciated for his merits, perceiving his experience in the Soviet Union more as an occasion for his rehabilitation rather than as a permanent rupture of relationships with this own country.

Why did the Soviet Union focus on Nobile? Antonio Piccin, a FIAT engineer who worked in Russia from 1924 to 1937, passed on a "Soviet individual's" opinion of Nobile:

> He is a great engineer, perhaps the best in the world with regards to airships. But it was an error to believe that a good engineer must also be a good commander. They are two different things. Italy repeated the same error after he revealed that he was not a great commander or that he was unlucky, and decided to ruin the engineer, the general, and the man, thereby harming its own reputation.[28]

These events take on a less personal and more epic meaning when they are couched in the golden age of great aviation pioneers, and the race – by now at its final stages – between the airship, which was "lighter than air" with its bizarre and grandiose shape and its fearless non-stop flights, and the airplane with its adaptability and its extraordinarily rapid technological advances, daring pilots, speed records, air competitions and long-distance flights. In spite of numerous and spectacular American and German airships accidents, the Soviets – as Piccin noted – believed that the airship industry made sense and had a future because of the "flat configuration of the entire Russian territory where cyclones were rare" and because "airships did not need specially prepared large landing fields, could be tied down easily, and could be used for transportation and as auxiliary relief vehicles in large forests where airplanes could not land."[29]

Nobile wrote Mussolini to inform him that he had signed, "after having obtained your general approval", a four-year agreement with the Panunionist Civil Air Corporation, which was already registered with the People's Labour Commissariat. The agreement called for the opening of "an initial construction site for airships" near Moscow, which would have a technical department for research and development, a number of workshops, two large hangars and a pilot's school. All employees would be under Nobile's direct supervision, constituting "a new development in the USSR's relations with foreign specialists". Nobile would be responsible for selecting crews, directing test flights and commanding flights. At first, they would build type N airships, with a small cubic capacity.[30]

Nobile's adventure began in May of 1932. This was the beginning of a long period of hard work in difficult conditions, especially because of the harsh winter of 1932–1933. The offices of the Dirigiablestroi firm were in Moscow but were moved a number of times. The base of operations was twenty-five kilometres from the city in Dolgaprudnaja, an area that had just been deforested. "Everything had to be done, everything had to be organized".[31] Even the most essential things for work were missing, from drafting tables, which Nobile ordered from Germany, to drawing paper. The only thing available in abundance was engineers. With the end of summer, the first disagreements began, above all with engineer Felice Trojani, a comrade in the unfortunate *Italia* endeavour. Further reasons for disappointment arose in the months to come. After a while, Nobile realized that Nastia, the servant he had been assigned, "had among her duties that of spying on me and referring everything",[32] forcing him to fire her. In summer 1932, the polar expedition he was so looking forward to was cancelled: "This year things seem to be going very badly. The polar expedition was a real necessity for me; a moral and physical need".[33] The presence of his daughter Maria, who joined him in Moscow for October and November, was his only relief from fatigue and these initial problems. An unexpected event complicated things even further. In late February 1933, Nobile suddenly fell ill. Appendicitis developed into peritonitis. It seemed too late for surgery, and Nobile was presumed dead. News of his death and obituaries were printed in American and European newspapers.[34] In fact, his condition so worsened that Nobile asked Ambassador Bernardo Attolico, who had hurried to his bedside, that Monsignor Pie Eugène Neveu, the apostolic administrator of Moscow, administer him the last sacraments. Attolico also informed the Ministry of Foreign Affairs of the seriousness of Nobile's situation. He cited a telegram from Nobile to Mussolini: "If God wants me to die my last thoughts go to my family, my country, and to You. I commend to you the only precious things I leave behind, my wife and my daughter".[35] Nobile, however, recovered unexpectedly.

His personal misfortune; the less-than-brilliant outcome of nearly a year's work; and the "very bad day for airships" when the *Akron*, the biggest airship in the world, fell in flames in the United States and provided yet another chance to heap criticism on the future of the airship – these difficulties caused his homesickness to re-emerge with great intensity. This was clearly apparent from his reaction to the news he received of the airplane cruise led by the Italian fascist hero of airships and Nobile's great enemy Italo Balbo:

> Although of course I cannot feel any sympathy towards Balbo personally, since I received news of his cruise I have sincerely wished him great success, and I am glad everything has gone well so far. One truly needs to be away from one's own country in order to be proud of all its beautiful and brave ventures, like this one.[36]

At the same time, the charm of the Soviet Union started fading. On a train from Berlin to Moscow in March 1934, he confided in his daughter Maria: "It always feels somewhat like entering a prison – a really big one".[37] However, eleven years later, in 1945, recalling his Soviet experience, the "great prison" seemed to be forgotten, swept away by the renewed Soviet myth. Nobile wrote about leaving Russia and entering Poland:

> I missed the pure and ardent atmosphere of Moscow. In Germany, the spectacle in the streets of Berlin, with all its signs of corruption, contrasted to the modesty and decency of the busy crowd that flowed like a river on the sidewalks of Moscow, and disgusted me deeply.[38]

When he was in this fragile state of mind, drifting between despondency and the anticipation of attaining his first successes, he was hit with the unexpected news that Carlotta, his wife, had died. Nobile rushed to Rome "with the hope of holding her in my arms while still alive. Instead, I held a corpse that had been dead for two days!" He wrote these bitter words to Mussolini to tell him, "with deep, long-time devotion", about the "immense misfortune" that had befallen himself.[39]

All that remained left to him was to plunge headlong into his work with even more haste and determination than before. The project took form, and the lift-off time for the first flight drew near. This was the only antidote for the problems and painful ordeals he had been through. The balm sustained him, and its beneficial effects increased when the first results of two years of hard work materialized. Nobile conducted the first two flights with the 18,500-cubic-metre V6 between the end of October and the beginning of November 1934. The entire ship was built in fourteen months by Russian workers with the help of only three Italians: Giacomo Garutti, Attilio Villa and Natale Di Bernardino. "Its shape was even nicer than the *Italia*, and I think it will perform just as well. The Russians are very happy, and I am even happier than they are".[40]

Nobile stayed in Russia two more years, until November 1936. During this time, he battled with conflicting drives. On the one hand, he dedicated great effort to gathering the fruits of his labour, as if the success of his personal mission in the USSR could outweigh, perhaps even remove, the bitterness and injustices he had undergone in Italy. He also hoped to be able to return to fly over the North Pole at the command of an airship.[41] On the other hand, he wanted to return to Italy, the daring and victorious Italy that was conquering an empire. To his daughter, he observed: "If I had something to do in this war [the Ethiopian war] (which I would happily do), this would be a good reason to leave everything".[42]

But at that moment in Russia, "things were going much better"; flights continued for the entire second half of 1935, while at the same time Nobile was busy writing a book on airships that was to be translated and published in Russia. Lessons to prepare Soviet pilots for flight were also in progress. His invigorated outlook was evident in a letter to Mussolini on July. He began enthusiastically by telling the duce about "the satisfaction in seeing the *Italia* live again, and to bring her to the threshold of the polar region on Rome's birthday, 21 April of this year". It was as if these successes cancelled certain distances, reopening the possibilities for a proper rehabilitation. He asked to be received by Mussolini and wrote that "in times like this I am, as always, awaiting Your orders" to be utilized "wherever the risk is greatest and the responsibility is most pressing".[43] In November 1936, Nobile decided to go back to Italy. Despite what he wrote shortly before, in his last letter to his daughter Maria from Russia, he justified his decision in this way: "Generally, an unpleasant wind is blowing here for most foreigners, but particularly for Italians. So it really is time to return".[44]

Nobile's most important and successful undertaking in Russia was the construction of the V6 airship. From September to October 1937, it established a new world record for flight length: 130 hours and 27 minutes.[45] But during a flight that was challenging because of low clouds and snow, the V6 flew into dense fog and exploded against the side of a mountain.[46] The Russian Air Force's adventure with airships ended here.

Nobile's totalitarian seduction

The last tile in the mosaic that this chapter has tried to reassemble comes from the memoirs that Nobile wrote after the war, which reflected the traits of the *totalitarian seduction*, the fascination with totalitarian power and the men who embodied it that was deep and widespread in Western culture between the two wars. This fascination undoubtedly played a role, if only a complementary one, in Nobile's journey from dependence on Mussolini to dependence on Stalin. Nobile was not a politician, nor was he an intellectual or a career soldier. He was basically a scientist and an impassioned explorer who let his instincts guide him. He had little familiarity with subtleties, detailed analyses or the use of tactics. While these traits led the political establishment to become hostile toward him, these same characteristics endeared him to common people, who in fact felt this and recompensed Nobile by showering him with unexpected and extraordinary popularity. Totalitarian seduction, in Nobile as in many others, was given form in the aspiration to perform individual heroic deeds as expressions of a higher collective entity, within fascism as well as bolshevism. To Nobile, the Soviet Union appeared as a great construction site, full of faith and enthusiasm directed toward a common objective, in which the most daring explorer and the humblest servant could feel part of a whole, in a climate of permanent mobilization that was fed by totalitarian pedagogy.

In the new post-World War II climate that emerged after the Allied victory over nazi-fascism, Nobile recast his own stay in the Soviet Union in line with the more classic and characteristic canons of reconstructed myth. I use the term "recast" not so much because he remembered his long sojourn in Moscow as "one of the happiest periods in the past twenty tormented years of my life",[47] since he could not have *not* felt gratitude towards the Soviets, but rather because he redefined the actual reality he had experienced in the first person. When describing his experience in the Soviet Union, Nobile, like many others,[48] asserted that he wanted to provide objective and dispassionate information. But there was more, he claimed it to be "precise", given his long experience of direct contact with that reality. Rather than precision and objective information, what he provided us with, instead, was an exemplary product of a concentrated double myth – the Soviet Union of the Five-Year Plan and the Soviet Union as a winner of World War II – after which Nobile wrote his memoirs.[49] Five-Year Plan Soviet Union seemed like

> a huge construction site, where millions of people worked at an enormous task with unequalled faith and enthusiasm, rapidly, without a moment's pause, without any indulgence in vice. Compared to the petty daily lives of western Europeans, the lives of Russian people seemed almost heroic. Their youth had the impression they were participating in a grandiose creation. They discussed universal issues. They breathed an atmosphere burning with ideas. Their individual lives were greatly enriched by intense participation in the collective.

Nobile was also convinced that individual freedom was "guaranteed" and in some cases "even excessive"; even freedom of speech and political expression were guaranteed. The only "important limitation" was forbidding discussion of decisions taken by the majority and not being able to criticize outside the Party. These "restrictions" were justified by the continual climate of war which never ended after the revolution.[50]

Nobile, too, saw poverty, famine, fake cheese forms in shop windows, peasants who were forced to barter, beggars who rummaged through garbage, yet he was not moved to doubt or criticise. He, too, saw the people who worked with him disappear and then die, but he managed to casually disregard this reality.[51] Or, better still, criticism and public self-criticism in the workplace seemed to him "an enormous stimulation for all intelligence". He was enthused by the idea that it could involve the private and family life of the "accused" and even include the fault of having a peasant father who was "impenetrable to Communist ideas". In this way, purging could almost be seen tenderly, like a pure and simple household task, with Stalin acting as the diligent housewife.

> Even in the most orderly households in which you try to keep everything perfectly clean, inevitably a bit of dirt gathers here and there. Every now and

then you have to decide to do a thorough cleaning. In Russia, the Communist Party did a thorough cleansing every now and then – whenever Stalin deemed it was necessary.[52]

When compulsory discipline coincides with pure freedom, then reality is completely overturned to the paradoxical point where belonging to the party is no longer a privilege but becomes a heavy burden:

> whoever wanted the freedom to choose an occupation or a residence to his liking, whoever wanted to be free to rest when he chose to, whoever wanted to live a peaceful existence without problems, had to forego belonging to the party.[53]

All the conditions were there for another communist party, the Italian one, to offer Nobile a place in the electoral list as an independent candidate in the election for the national Constituent Assembly. The Christian Democrats offered Nobile a place as well, but after pondering many doubts, he decided to accept the proposal of Palmiro Togliatti, secretary of the Italian Communist Party.[54] The Soviet myth was stronger than his devotion to the Pope and the gratitude owed to the Vatican, which tried in vain to convince him to renounce his candidacy. Nobile was elected, and a two-year political parliamentary parenthesis began in his life. On 18 April 1946, when Nobile accepted his candidacy, Togliatti wrote him this letter:

> Dear General, I did not want to intervene until now in the issue of your candidacy because I feared that it might have pressured you. I am very pleased about your decision that shows You have been able to overcome prejudices that, unfortunately, still exist in our Country and which are so harmful to its rebirth and its political and moral unity. We are proud to include in our electoral list the name of a man who has honoured this Country with his inventiveness, his work, and his courage, and from whom we are certain we can expect much more. I am pleased that You are adhering to our lists in Rome and Salerno and, if you will agree, to our national list. I am all the more pleased because your participation will reinforce bonds between the more advanced workers who are active in our Party, and those groups of intellectuals and members of the scientific and cultural communities whose contribution is indispensable to rebuilding the economy, political system, and morale of our Country.[55]

Among the more than 200 workers employed by Dirigiablestroi before the war, there were a number of Italian communists who had sought refuge in the Soviet Union.[56] Factory 207 in Dolgaprudnaja was obviously considered a safe refuge, and Nobile had no difficulties giving them a job. For at least five of them – Gaetano Marcolin, Luigi Vanoli, Lino Manservigi, Robusto Biancani and Mario Menotti – employment there was the beginning of a tragic journey. In April of 1935, Vanoli, Menotti, Manservigi and Biancani were publicly accused within the party of conspiring with Italian technicians from Nobile's group. Manservigi and Biancani were expelled from the party, and the other two were severely censured. Three years later, the evidence against them resurfaced. It was manipulated and used to condemn them to death, with the full collusion of the Italian Communist Party leaders in Moscow, Togliatti in particular. All five men were shot to death in 1938, victims of the Stalinist purges.[57]

The myth of an anti-fascist and pro-Soviet Nobile was built after World War II, by Nobile himself, with the goal of a never-obtained real rehabilitation and in view of his political positioning. The real facts lie not only in Nobile's harsh words about the Soviet prison, forgotten after the war, but above all in the documented bond of trust and loyalty to the duce – and the hope of being called by him to fight in Ethiopia – which never failed until the fall of fascism on 25 July 1943. In the same way, Balbo's role as a bitter enemy, also functional to the image of an anti-fascist Nobile, must be revised: certainly the two did not have sympathy for each other, but Balbo's hostility was due to a different assessment of the future of the aeronautics and to not unfounded doubts about Nobile's reliability.[58]

But Nobile's myth goes far beyond the boundaries drawn from time to time by himself. In November 1944, a military chaplain from the Italian Social Republic, Don Antonio Ledda, suggested Mussolini which arguments and words to use to regain the over 650,000 Italian soldiers captured by the Germans after the armistice of 8 September 1943 and deported in the internment camps in the Reich:

> The Cross stands on Churches, on the peaks of our mountains, on Cemeteries. With the living and the dead. On the top of the world, on the North pole, with the Flag of our Homeland, the Cross of Christ has been raised, dropped by an airship named *Italy*.[59]

At the same time that Nobile worked frantically, in the Southern Kingdom, to build his image as "victim of fascism", the Republic of Salò, the "occupied ally" of the Reich,[60] deprived of autonomy and sovereignty, tried to find, in the murky twilight of the last fascism, values and myths on which to re-found a dying idea of homeland – without mentioning Nobile, of course, but reasserting that the myth of the *Italy*'s enterprise remains a cornerstone of the collective memory of the fascists, perhaps also because that tragic episode was well suited to the atmosphere of dissolution and death of those months.

Notes

1 Emilio Gentile, *Il mito dello Stato nuovo. Dal radicalismo nazionale al fascismo* (Rome-Bari: Laterza, 1999), XVII–XVIII; Emilio Gentile, *Fascismo. Storia e interpretazione* (Rome-Bari: Laterza, 2002), 57–58.
2 Emilio Gentile, *Le origini dell'ideologia fascista (1918–1925)* (Bologna: Il Mulino, 1996), 44.
3 François Furet, *Le passé d'une illusion* (Paris: Robert Laffont, 1995). In Italian translation, *Il passato di un'illusione. L'idea comunista nel XX secolo* (Milan: Mondadori, 1995), 185.

4 Gertrude Nobile Stolp, *Bibliografia di Umberto Nobile* (Florence: Olschki, 1984). The most complete biography is the two-volume Ovidio Ferrante, *Umberto Nobile* (Rome: Tatangelo, 1985), in which the Soviet part begins on page 159. Other relevant publications are Luciano Zani, "Between Two Totalitarian Regimes: Umberto Nobile and the Soviet Union (1931–36)", *Totalitarian Movements and Political Religions* 4, no. 2 (2003): 63–112; Luciano Zani, *Fra due totalitarismi. Umberto Nobile e l'Unione Sovietica (1931–1936)* (Roma: Aracne, 2005). Umberto Nobile, born in Lauro (Avellino) on 21 January 1885, must be placed in the context of the history of Polar explorations: Monica Kristensen, *L'ultimo viaggio di Amundsen* (Milano: Iperborea, 2019); Garth Cameron, *Umberto Nobile and the Arctic Search of the Airship Italia* (Oxford: Fonthill Media, 2017); Giuseppe Nencioni, *The Italians in the Arctic Explorations: A Critique of the Reinterpretation of Nationalism* (Umeå: Umeå University and the Royal Skyttean Society, 2010) [in Italian translation: Giuseppe Nencioni, *Gli Italiani e le esplorazioni artiche. Per una critica delle reinterpretazioni del nazionalismo* (Roma: Aracne, 2018)]; Robert Ruby, *The Unknown Shore: The Lost History of England's Arctic Colony* (New York: H. Holt, 2001); John McCannon, *Red Arctic: Polar Exploration & the Myth of the North in the Soviet Union, 1932–1939* (New York and Oxford: Oxford University Press, 1998); Clive Holland, *Arctic Exploration and Development c. 500 B.C. to 1915: An Encyclopedia* (New York and London: Garland, 1994); Nancy Fogelson, *Arctic Exploration and International Relations, 1900–1932: A Period of Expanding National Interests* (Fairbanks: University of Alaska Press, 1992); George Simmons, *Target: Arctic* (Philadelphia: Chilton, 1965); Giotto Dainelli, *La gara verso il Polo Nord* (Torino: UTET, 1960). The making of Nobile a national hero suggests a comparison with analogous processes in other countries: Huw Lewis-Jones, *Imagining the Arctic* (London and New York: I. B. Taurich, 2017); Charles Officer and Jake Page, *A Fabulous Kingdom: The Exploration of the Arctic* (Oxford and New York: Oxford University Press, 2012); Robert G. David, *The Arctic in the British Imagination, 1818–1914* (Manchester and New York: Manchester University Press, 2000); Francis Spufford, *I May Be Some Time: Ice and the English Imagination* (London: Faber&Faber, 1996).

5 For an overview, see: Giorgio Petracchi, "Roma e/o Mosca? Il fascismo di fronte allo specchio", *Nuova Storia contemporanea* 6, no. 1 (2002): 69–92. See also Luciano Zani, "L'immagine dell'Urss nell'Italia degli anni trenta: i viaggiatori", *Storia contemporanea* 21, no. 6 (1990): 1197–1223.

6 J. Calvitt Clarke III, *Russia and Italy against Hitler: The Bolshevik-Fascist Rapprochement of the 1930s* (New York: Greenwood Press, 1991), 29–32. For the preceding period, see G. Petracchi, *La Russia rivoluzionaria nella politica italiana, 1917–25* (Rome-Bari: Laterza, 1982). On diplomatic aspects, see: Giorgio Petracchi, *Da San Pietroburgo a Mosca. La diplomazia italiana in Russia, 1861–1941* (Rome: Bonacci, 1993).

7 Marcella Cecchini, "Due missioni tecniche italiane in Urss 1930–1936", *Storia contemporanea* XVIII, no. 4 (1987): 731–765.

8 Emil Ludwig, *Colloqui con Mussolini* (Verona: Mondadori, 1932), 150.

9 Gaetano Ciocca, *Giudizio sul bolscevismo. Come è finito il Piano Quinquennale* (Milan: Bompiani, 1933).

10 Umberto Nobile, *In volo alla conquista del segreto polare* (Milan: Mondadori, 1928); Centro Documentazione Umberto Nobile [hereafter CDUN], Category "Norge N 1", Envelopes 1–8.

11 Umberto Nobile, *Posso dire la verità* (Rome: Mondadori, 1945), 3–23.

12 Claudio Sicolo, *Umberto Nobile e l'"Italia" al Polo Nord. Politica e storia nelle carte inedite, 1928–1978* (Rome: Aracne, 2020); Steinar Aas, *Tragedien Umberto Nobile. Polarhelt Eller Svikar?* (Oslo: Det Norske Samlaget, 2002); Umberto Nobile, *L'Italia al Polo Nord* (Milan: Mondadori, 1930). See also archival sources: CDUN, Category

'Italia N4', Envelopes 1–23; ACS, Special Secretariat of the duce [hereafter SPD], Reserved Papers [herafter CR] (1922–1943), Envelope 54 (on the flights of the *Norge* in 1926 and the *Italia* in 1928); Archivio Centrale dello Stato [herafter ACS], Presidency of the Council of Ministries [hereafter PCM], 1928–1930, File 3/2–4, No. 1830 (all the phases of the rescue in telegraph dispatches from the ship *Città di Milano*). A reconstruction of the expedition that presents Nobile in a positive way is Wilburn Cross, *Disaster at the Pole: The Tragedy of the Airship Italia and the 1928 Nobile Expedition to the North Pole* (Guilford, CT: The Lyons Press, 2000).

13 Sicolo, *Umberto Nobile*, 141–302. The Acts of the Commission are preserved in ACS, SPD, CR, Envelopes 55, 56, 57, 58, 59; see also ACS, PCM, 1928–30, File 3/2–4, N. 1830 (with a memoir by Nobile with his version of Lundborg's rescue). Regarding the defence of Nobile, featuring various memoirs used after WWII as the basis for his petition for riabilitation, see ACS, Ministry of Aviation, Cabinet, Variuos series – Secret, Envelope 1, Files 1-S, 7; Nobile, *Posso dire la verità;* Umberto Nobile, *La verità in fondo al pozzo* (Milano: Mondadori, 1978).

14 Umberto Nobile, *Addio, 'Malyghin'!* (Verona: Mondadori, 1948). The manuscript of the diary is in the CDUN library. Maria Nobile Archives [hereafter AMN], "Russia 1931", Umberto to his wife Carlotta, July 1931.

15 Nobile, *Addio, 'Malyghin'!*, 94.
16 Ibid., 101–103.
17 Ibid., 90, 96.
18 Ibid., 60–63.
19 Ibid., 111.
20 Ibid., 114–118.
21 Ibid., 118.
22 AMN, Nobile to Carlotta, 28 August 1931, from Moscow.
23 AMN, Nobile to a friend, no date, but after 25 July 1934.
24 Nobile, *Posso dire la verità*, xiii.
25 Paul Hollander, *Pellegrini politici. Intellettuali occidentali in Unione Sovietica, Cina e Cuba* (Bologna: Il Mulino, 1988); originally published as *Political Pilgrims* (Oxford: Oxford University Press, 1981).
26 Guy Launay commented ironically in the French *Le Matin* on 22 April 1932 when he reported about the role Nobile would play in the Soviet Union. See ACS, MI, PS, Political Police, Envelope 905, *Nobile Umberto – Generale*, 7 May 1932.
27 *Aussiger Tagblatt*, 23 Februray 1932, in ACS, MI, PS, Div. AAGGR, Category A1, 1941, Envelope 75, *Nobile prof. Umberto, ex generale aeronautica*.
28 Antonio Piccin, *La Russia sovietica vista dall'uomo della strada* (Rome: Editoriale Romana, 1945), 439. For a complete overview, see Zani, "L'immagine dell'Urss nell'Italia degli anni trenta"; Pier Luigi Bassignana, *Fascisti nel paese dei Soviet* (Torino: Bollati Boringhieri, 2000); Loreto di Nucci, "I pellegrinaggi politici degli intellettuali italiani", in *Pellegrini politici*, ed. Hollander, 621–677; Italians are mentioned in Marcello Flores, *L'immagine dell'URSS. L'Occidente e la Russia di Stalin (1927–1956)* (Milano: Mondadori, 1990).
29 Piccin, *La Russia sovietica*, 149.
30 ACS, PCM, 1931–33, File 15/2–2, n. 4597 *Russia: costruzione dirigibili*, Nobile to Mussolini, 29 February 1932.
31 Umberto Nobile, *Quello che ho visto nella Russia sovietica* (Rome: Atlantica, 1945), 242.
32 AMN, Nobile to Carlotta, from Moscow, 10 December 1932.
33 AMN, Nobile to Carlotta, from Leningrad, 22 August 1932.
34 Nobile, *Quello che ho visto nella Russia sovietica*, 17; see ACS, MI, PS, Political Police, Envelope 905, File *Nobile Umberto – Generale*, reports dated 6 March and 26 April 1933.

35 Diplomatic Archive of the Italian Foreign Ministry in Rome [hereafter ASMAE], Political Affairs, USSR 1931–1945, Envelope 15, File 9.
36 AMN, Nobile to Carlotta, from Moscow, 19 July 1933.
37 AMN, Nobile to Maria, from Berlin, 10 March 1934.
38 Nobile, *Quello che ho visto nella Russia sovietica*, 9.
39 ACS, SPD, CR, Envelope 59, File Nobile Umberto, Sub-folder 4 Atti diversi, Nobile to Mussolini, 28 July 1934.
40 AMN, Nobile to his daughter Maria from Moscow, 9 November 1934; ASMAE, Political Affairs, URSS 1931–1945, Envelope 15, File 14.
41 ACS, MI, PS, Political Police, Envelope 905, File *Nobile Umberto – Generale*, 10 February 1935, according to which Nobile was "organizing a large polar expedition from Russia to Japan by way of the North Pole", with Mussolini's seal of approval.
42 AMN, Nobile to Maria, from Moscow, 9 March 1935.
43 ACS, SPD, CR, Envelope 59, File 'Nobile Umberto', Sub-folder 4 Atti diversi, Nobile to Mussolini, 22 July 1935. The letter was delivered to Mussolini, who was in Riccione, by his special secretary Osvaldo Sebastiani.
44 AMN, Nobile to Maria, from Moscow, 26 November 1936.
45 Umberto Nobile, *My Five Years with Soviet Airships* (Akron: LTA, 1987), 141–143.
46 Nobile, *My Five Years with Soviet Airships*, 145–148.
47 Nobile, *Posso dire la verità*, 107.
48 Zani, "L'immagine dell'Urss nell'Italia degli anni trenta", 1200–1223.
49 Nobile, *Quello che ho visto nella Russia sovietica*; see also *My Five Years with Soviet Airships*. In CDUN, there is also the text of a manuscript entitled *Dieci anni di contatto con i russi, 1926–1936*, which does not provide any additional information than the volumes that have been cited.
50 Nobile, *Quello che ho visto nella Russia sovietica*, XX–XXII.
51 Ibid., 169.
52 Ibid., 14, 29.
53 Ibid., 36.
54 Umberto Nobile, *La tenda rossa, memorie di neve e di fuoco* (Milano: Mondadori, 1969), 420.
55 CDUN, 'Documenti vari', Envelope 16.
56 The engineer Felice Trojani, in Russia with Nobile, remembers other three men: the communists Benservigi (actually Lino Manservigi), foreman of the mechanics shop at Dolgaprudnaja; the Bolognese Bertoni (almost certainly Giovanni Bertoni, one of the communists who was given the task of killing "comrades who made mistakes"); and the anarchist Otello Gaggi: Felice Trojani, *La coda di Minosse. Vita di un uomo, storia di un'impresa* (Milano: Mursia, 1964), 607–608 and 615–616. See Giancarlo Lehner, *La tragedia dei comunisti italiani. Le vittime del Pci in Unione Sovietica* (Milano: Mondadori, 2000). Actually, there were more Italian communists who either worked in Nobile's workshops or were directed to the Dirigiablestroi by Dante Corneli. On this last point, see Dante Corneli, *Il redivivo tiburtino* (Milano: La Pietra, 1977) and other volumes that were self-published in Tivoli between the 1970s and 1980s. All these communists met the same fate: they were arrested, tried and shot in 1938; see Romolo Caccavale, *Comunisti italiani in Unione Sovietica. Proscritti da Mussolini, soppressi da Stalin* (Milano: Mursia, 1995); Francesco Bigazzi and Giancarlo Lehner, *Dialoghi del terrore. I processi ai comunisti italiani in Unione Sovietica* (Florence: Ponte alle Grazie, 1991); Gianni Corbi, *Togliatti a Mosca. Storia di un legame di ferro* (Milano: Rizzoli, 1991), 212–229; Giorgio Fabre, *Roma a Mosca. Lo spionaggio fascista in Urss e il caso Guarnaschelli* (Bari: Dedalo, 1990).
57 Elena Dundovich, *Tra esilio e castigo. Il Komintern, il Pci e la repressione degli antifascisti italiani in URSS (1936–38)* (Rome: Carocci, 1998), 162–166.

58 Luciano Zani, *Cronaca di una tragedia annunciata*, preface in Sicolo, *Umberto Nobile e l'"Italia" al Polo Nord*.
59 ASMAE, RSI, Gabailg, b. 4, fasc. 24.
60 Lutz Klinkhammer, *L'occupazione tedesca in Italia 1943–1945* (Torino: Bollati Boringhieri, 1993).

5 Imperialist Italian geography currents in the work of Roberto Almagià and his ambiguous relationship with the fascist regime

Sandro Rinauro

The image of Roberto Almagià in the Italian geographic thought

Geographer Roberto Almagià's (1884–1962) attitude to Italian imperialism and the fascist regime fits into the nineteenth- and twentieth-century debate on the nexus of geography and imperialism.[1] Geographers and historians have extensively reconstructed the pioneering role that the first Italian geography institutions, and the Italian Geographical Society (1867) in particular, played in stirring up early expansionist aims. They also illustrated national academic geography's cultural, epistemological and political inspirations, which were often conservative and reactionary. However, they demonstrated that the geography-imperialism alliance was never total or uniform. In fact, first of all, they highlight that, for many decades, the Italian Geographical Society was directed and animated by politicians, diplomats and soldiers to a much greater extent than geography scholars. Second, they show that Italy's African colonies were a rather marginal subject of study for professional geographers, even during the fascist regime's most belligerent years.

Within this diverse panorama, Roberto Almagià emerges as one of the most precocious of the radically aligned scholars in a pro-imperialist sense, and this automatically aligned him with the cultural and imperial politics of the fascist regime. However, doubts and misunderstandings regarding his political loyalty led to progressive suspicion of him by the regime, and anti-Semitic persecution placed him definitively on society's sidelines, helping to safeguard his reputation after World War II. Illustrating his relationship with imperialism and Fascism is therefore necessary not only for the purposes of finding out more about one of the twentieth century's most prestigious geographers but also to contribute to the debate around the diversified Italian geography-imperialism relationship.

Almagià's obituaries make no mention of his compromise with imperialism, and his pupil Lucio Gambi also treats him indulgently, despite the latter's profound criticism of the reactionary inspirations behind part of the Italian geographical tradition.[2] In fact, Gambi repudiated his teacher's epistemological approach – the so-called "integral geography"[3] – but was verging on reticent about his attitude to imperialism and the fascist regime. In his 1970 essay *Uno schizzo di storia della*

DOI: 10.4324/9781003095965-6

geografia in Italia, Gambi described Almagià as the best exponent of the scholarly line of historical cartography and exploration history, stating that these arguments "were weapons well-suited to averting government instrumentation and, therefore, a decline [in support for the regime], in many cases".[4] Even with regard to the most blatantly propagandistic pro-fascist imperialism, *L'Africa orientale* (1935), Gambi stated that, although Almagià endorsed the attack on Ethiopia, he marked himself out scientifically from other similar purely propaganda-based geography studies.[5] It was only in relation to the emergence, at the end of the thirties, of the most markedly imperialist Italian academic geography current, German-inspired geopolitics, that Gambi made no allowances for Almagià, that is, the latter's demographic justification of Italian expansionism in Africa and the Eastern Mediterranean and adherence to the concept of "vital space".[6]

The whitewashing of this episode in the volume that the Institute of Human Geography at the University of Milan dedicated to Almagià in 1988 was even more radical: while nothing was said of his numerous writings on the Italian colonies, his studies on Albania were judged by all to have been extraneous to Italy's imperialist ambitions.[7] Costantino Caldo, illustrating Italian geography during the 'ventennio', argued that Almagià's was a "contradictory" position which, although of imperialist inspiration, did not "consciously align the aims of his work with those of the government".[8] In actual fact, Almagià's Balkan and Africa writings show that his support for Italy's imperial expansion had been precocious and very determined. This chapter analyses the most significant of these writings.

Almagià's early imperialistic infatuation: his Albanian studies

It was the need to eradicate foreign influence from the Adriatic Sea which had prompted Italy's ambitions to control the Albanian side of the Otranto Canal since unification. Albanian independence radicalised these ambitions and ushered in a more intense interest on the part of Italian geographers in the country.[9]

Almagià's interest in the eastern Mediterranean and African regions coveted by Italy emerged well before the advent of the fascist regime, in accordance with a not-insignificant proportion of post-unification Italian geographers.[10] His family origins also played a part in his fervent nationalism, as his was one of Ancona's most prominent Sephardi-origin Jewish families, and an ancestor of the same name had volunteered with Garibaldi during the Austrian siege of Ancona in 1849 when he was still underage before volunteering for the civic guard in 1860, while his brother, Vito Almagià, had taken part in the conquest of Rome in 1870.[11] The geographer's brothers, Corrado and Guido, were respectively awarded the war cross and two medals for valour, and Guido became an admiral.[12]

Almagià's cousin was famous mathematician and physicist Vito Volterra, senator of the Kingdom of Italy, democratic interventionist and World War I volunteer, hostile to Italian colonialism, early anti-fascist, an opponent of Giovanni Gentile's education reform and one of twelve university professors who were stripped of their posts for refusing to swear allegiance to the fascist regime. It is from Volterra's letters that we learn that the outbreak of the Libyan war in 1911 inflamed the young Almagià's colonial enthusiasm and led to him becoming a learned and assiduous propagandist.[13]

After organising an exploration expedition to Eritrea in 1912, the Italian Society for the Progress of Sciences (SIPS) in 1913 (not surprisingly, a few months after the declaration of Albanian independence) organised a mission to Albania in which Almagià took part, beginning a long-lasting interest in a country to which he devoted twenty essays prior to 1944. Almagià's contribution to the mission's report volume was purely scientific in purpose.[14] However, the mission was promoted by one of the most fiercely nationalist of the era's scientific forums, SIPS, which had been re-founded in 1906 by Vito Volterra. Heading the expedition was geographer and army major Silvio Egidi, while, at the behest of the Ministry of War and with the help of the Ministry of Foreign Affairs, captain Giovanni Magrini also took part. Proof of Almagià's identification with the most fervently nationalist cultural circles is supplied by the fact that starting from 1921, he sat on the SIPS scientific board and, from 1923 onwards, the President's Office, acting as its secretary several times until the racial laws later led to him being dismissed. Then, from 1949, he acted as "perpetual secretary".[15]

In any event, as early as May 1917, during the Italian occupation of southern Albania, Almagià lauded the action carried out by the army and Italian civilian agents in published work. In the rhetorical style characteristic of his writings on the colonies and the Balkans, Almagià blamed the alleged inefficiency of the previous administration (Ottoman in Albania's case) and contrasted it with "the fervour of restorative activity" ushered in by Italy's "enlightened civilisation".[16] Furthermore, in accordance with his equally recurrent ethnic and civil hierarchy theme regarding the peoples of Western Europe and those of the Balkans and Africa, his work was replete with demeaning paternalistic judgments on local peoples, stating, for example, that the backwardness of Albanian agriculture derived from the "natural indolence of its inhabitants".[17] He argued that Italian occupation was generating progress, especially in public education and infrastructure, that is, the sectors most subject to Italian influence. Almagià applauded the fact that, alongside Albanian, the teaching of Italian had been made compulsory by means of teachers from Albanian villages in the south of Italy, noting with approval that these schools were counteracting Athens's attempts to Hellenise the south of the country and that they served "to awaken in the younger generations an awareness of Albanian nationality and the bonds of ancient and fraternal friendship with which it is linked with Italian nationality".[18] As for Italian achievements in the field of communications, for Almagià, they made Albania "another strip of Italy" and, above all, they would ultimately make it possible to cross the Balkans from West to East, thus opening up ample commercial traffic with the Middle East to Italy.[19]

Albania in the Treccani *Encyclopaedia* and Almagia's ambiguous attitude to fascism

Almagià's involvement as director of the geographical section of the Treccani *Encyclopaedia* probably stemmed from his scientific reputation alone: Almagià had not initially applied for fascist party membership, and he had joined the cultural institutions he was then part of – Istituto Coloniale Italiano, SIPS and the Istituto per l'Europa Orientale – before the regime came to power.[20] However, having joined Gentile's encyclopaedia, Almagià behaved with great political and human ease.

It is well known that the decision to compile a great Italian encyclopaedia had been taken in 1919 by Modenese publisher Angelo Fortunato Formiggini, who accompanied the project with a new journal, *L'Italia che scrive*. Initially, both Volterra and Almagià (a childhood friend of Formiggini's) signed up to both the publisher's initiatives. However, Formiggini's cultural and political openness led to Giovanni Gentile sabotaging the planned encyclopaedia and taking it over for the purposes of creating a work responding to Italy's cultural aims and directions as dictated by the nascent fascist regime, from 1925, together with Treccani. As a counterpart to Formiggini's journal, Gentile set up a journal entitled *Leonardo* (1924) and entrusted it to the journalist Giuseppe Prezzolini, who began to draw in several *L'Italia che scrive* contributors.[21] Whilst, in keeping with his hostility to the regime and to Gentile, Volterra refused to work with either Treccani or *Leonardo*, Almagià accepted both proposals. Formiggini complained of his friend's betrayal, but Almagià wrote only two reviews of geographical texts for *Leonardo*.[22] In any case, the two friends kept in touch until 1938, when, in protest against the racial laws, Formiggini committed suicide by throwing himself from Modena cathedral's bell tower.[23]

In 1925, the Leonardo Foundation was absorbed into the Istituto nazionale fascista di cultura and, consequently, Almagià's continued contributions to the *Leonardo* journal involved a conscious adherence to Gentile's cultural policies and those of the regime. However, this does not itself equate participation in Treccani with support for fascism. In addition to being the year the *Encyclopaedia* was founded and of the so-called '*fascistissime*' laws, 1925 was also the year of Gentile's *Manifesto degli intellettuali fascisti agli intellettuali di tutte le Nazioni* (21 April 1925) and, in response, of the *Manifesto degli intellettuali antifascisti* (1 May 1925) promoted by Croce. Almagià did not subscribe to either of these two manifestos (of the geographers, only Paolo Revelli signed the Gentile *Manifesto*; Carlo Maranelli, Arrigo Lorenzi, Assunto Mori, Giuseppe Ricchieri and geography historian Cesare De Lollis signed Croce's). After all, he could hardly have signed an anti-Gentile manifesto, since he had just joined Treccani at the minister's invitation.[24] However, on 26 June 1925, Almagià signed an *Indirizzo di simpatia a Gaetano Salvemini* on the occasion of the latter's arrest, a choice that, as we will see, was to backfire tragically, especially with the advent of the racial laws.[25]

Alongside his support for Salvemini and his enduring non-membership of the National Fascist Party, there is, however, also another indication of the distance that still separated the geographer from the regime between 1922 and the early 1930s, namely the February 1926 letter in which he notified Formiggini of the death of geographer and mutual friend Giuseppe Ricchieri, an occasion in which Almagià disconsolately blamed the present climate and expressed his hopes for "a different future" if not a "better" one. Ricchieri, wrote Almagià, was "one of the most genuine gentlemen I have ever met, a race that is, unfortunately, dying out quickly – How sad! We hope for a different future (I no longer dare to write better)". Telling words when we consider that Ricchieri was of radical political orientation, an anti-colonialist, hostile to the Libyan war, a Socialist interventionist, friend of Leonida Bissolati and Salvemini and advocate of the anti-nationalist stance of Carlo Maranelli and Salvemini on the eastern border, as well as one of the signatories of the Croce *Manifesto* and, like Almagià, of the *Indirizzo di simpatia a Gaetano Salvemini*.[26]

In any event, Almagià was fully aware that the Treccani *Encyclopaedia* was Fascism's central tool in its planned Italian cultural renewal. In 1930, he wrote that it was the product of the "resurrected civil conscience of our country" and that, for this conscience, it should be "a truly Italian Encyclopaedia in conception, content, execution".[27] Illustrating the role that he himself, as director of the geographical section, attributed to geography in the work as a whole, he specified that the *Encyclopaedia* should not be the sum of the individual disciplines but "an organism" whose purpose was to express "a certain moment in the life of the nation's cultural heritage". Consequently, its geographical entries had to be in tune with "the supreme requirements of an Encyclopaedia considered as a work of the whole nation". Therefore, the geographical items had been chosen in accordance "with *Italian* criteria, and a very large part was made up of Italy" [Almagià's italics]. "Special attention was naturally paid to the geography of Italy and its colonies": "One of the most important entries in the entire Encyclopaedia in the geographical field", he argued, "is the one on the Alps" and the problem of their partitions and borders, "which are not only of formal importance". Similarly, in the items relating to Italian places and foreign countries, any illustration of their history had to deal "extensively" with "the Roman period" and, in the case of colonial countries, the "colonial problems of our time". As far as the thirty pages devoted to the Albania entry are concerned, he argued that it was "certainly not too much space, in relation to the importance that this country has today for Italy". The entry on Argentina, for example, also included a paragraph entitled *Gli Italiani nell'Argentina*.[28] The same concepts were reiterated in 1933 in a paper published, significantly, in *Educazione fascista*, the Istituto Nazionale Fascista di Cultura's official journal. Here, the main merit of the Touring Club's International Atlas – the *Italian Encyclopaedia*'s reference maps – noted that, rather than the usual two sheets of maps for each country, four sheets had been dedicated to Italy "in compliance with the wishes of many" to accord "Italy pre-eminent importance". Furthermore, not only for Italy but also for Albania, the scale of the maps was larger than those used for other nations, as the latter was "a country that is now very close to us, and not only spatially".[29] In short, for Almagià, the *Encyclopaedia* had to make geography's role in the context of the Italian culture of the moment explicit to readers, as a discipline which exalted the mother country and its borders, the glories of Rome in the ancient world and its legacies in the present, Italy's colonised territories and those it coveted.

Consistent with these premises, the 1929 Treccani Albania entry, written with five other scholars, emphasised what it presented as the legacies of the Roman era, the progress made in all eras and in all fields by Italians and the issue of territorial mutilation enacted by the Slavs. This entry also suggested making Albania the "transit country for Balkan trade", building a special railway there. Furthermore, with reluctance and partiality, he presented the Italian military occupation as aimed exclusively at Albanian independence.[30]

Alignment to the fascist regime's Albanian policy

The largest text dedicated to Albania by the Florentine geographer was a 1930 monograph. In it, Almagià insisted on the presumed persistence of the ancient Romanisation of the country, re-reading its history as a precursor to present Italian influence, underlining that the pre-unification states had always defended Albanian independence when it was threatened by the Slavs and Greeks. The country's decline was the result of Ottoman domination, and the sole purpose of Italian occupation since 1914 was to prevent Austrian control of the Otranto Canal and guarantee Italy's territorial integrity. His reconstruction of the tumultuous post-war period was a masterpiece of mystification and discretion which tried to conceal Italian attempts to control Albania by passing it off as aid against the annexationist ambitions of neighbouring countries.

He therefore praised the alliance between President Zog and Mussolini and, in line with the contemporary fascist policy of supporting Albanian territorial expansion at the expense of Yugoslavia, he regretted that many Albanians were living in the territories of neighbouring states, an "unredeemed Albania" that presented it as "unfortunately seriously mutilated". Even more blatant was Almagià's lauding of Italian economic influence and his belief that the regime should hinder the economic influence of other nations in Albania. He extolled the new vehicle access roads and the first sections of railway built by Italian companies, infrastructure that he hoped would favour less an intensification of Italian exports to Albania, a market that Almagià realistically considered poor, than an intensification of exports to the rest of the Balkans and the Near East. He therefore concluded his study by trumpeting the potential reconstitution by the Italians of the ancient Roman Via Ignazia in the form of a railway along the Shkumbini river.[31]

Writings on Italy's African colonies

In any event, Almagià's main pro-imperialist focus was on Italian Africa, particularly if his commitment to it is compared with that of the other academic geographers of his time: after a great deal of attention being paid to Africa in the last decades of the nineteenth century, in the fascist period, the African colonies were a secondary and little-studied research subject until the mid-1930s. This was less a matter of hostility or indifference towards fascist politics in Africa than of an awareness of geography's unpreparedness as a discipline to tackle such a complex and relatively new topic.[32]

By contrast, Almagià's writings on Italian Africa dating to shortly before the Great War were prompted by his colonialist infatuation on the occasion of the Libyan war, which intensified from the early 1920s, appearing, in particular, in *Rivista coloniale*, official journal of the Istituto Coloniale Italiano, since 1928 Istituto Coloniale Fascista. Almagià's 'conversion' to colonialism took the form of a public commitment from June–July 1917 at the latest, when he joined the Istituto Coloniale's Central Council.[33] From at least 1921, Almagià also contributed to the institute's courses in "colonial education".[34]

The *Cyrenaica* lecture of February 1912 argued that Italy's agricultural and economic decline in the aftermath of the collapse of the Roman Empire did not derive from a worsening of the climate but from later "careless or uncivilised rulers", namely the Arabs and Turks. Consequently, the region would recover "if the new Italy is inspired by the example of Rome". Almagià then quoted a verse from the *Canzone d'oltremare* with which D'Annunzio greeted the war in Libya, arguing, on the basis of very little documentation, that the country was capable of hosting "a certain number" of Italian settlers.[35]

The 1921 *Prolusione* to the courses in colonial education was even more revealing of the politicised character of Almagià's studies, since his intention was to understand whether Libya's soil and climate resources could justify Italian occupation. On the basis of the few studies carried out, in particular, by the Italian army, he concluded that several Tripolitania coastal territories had potential for agricultural and livestock development and, therefore, could host "our settlers".[36] With its "colonial attitudes," then, Italy proved to the world that it was "up to the task of civilisation begun ten years ago with the occupation of Libya and which it satisfies to an extent not unworthy of its glorious traditions".[37] In short, this text illustrates the structure of his later studies on the Italian colonies: using geography to evaluate the soundness of the Italian colonial wars, to arouse "colonial consciousness" in Italians and to "orient" colonial government policy.[38]

It was, however, with the war in Ethiopia that the focus in his colonial studies on justifying the colonial policy of the fascist regime on a pseudo-scientific level culminated. The 1935 book *L'Africa orientale* is the clearest example of this. Written by three academic geographers – Almagià, Attilio Mori (Almagià's father-in-law) and Giotto Dainelli – and a regime figure, colonial governor Corrado Zoli, on the occasion of the military attack, the book intended to "participate in Italy's great African enterprise of the year XIV" and was:

> Dedicated to the officers, soldiers, Black Shirts and loyal colonial units which, with their new generous blood, are preparing to bring to fruition the patriotic dream of their precursors; to the technicians, industrialists and Italian farmers who will be called to bring the precious benefits of our civilisation to these new African lands.[39]

Almagià wrote the chapter *Geografia antropica ed economica* on the basis of the same argument used for his other writings on the Balkans and the colonies. In line with the racist anthropology of the time, he affirmed that its human population was high quality since it was mostly "Hamitic" and secondarily "Semitic", while the "lower" coloured element was in the minority. Furthermore, he was careful to affirm that "Hamites and Semites are very similar to each other, indeed, according to many anthropologists, they represent differentiations occurring in a not very remote age, from the same original type", a statement that sheds light on Jewish Almagià's hierarchical perspective in racial terms. Its population was limited, however, due to bad Ethiopian government, and only the Italian occupation of Eritrea and Somalia, according to Almagià, had increased the number of inhabitants. He therefore concluded that a low population and its climate meant that the Ethiopian plateau offered "ample space for settlement by the people of our continent", calculating that there was space for as many as seven million European settlers.[40] However, at the time, Italian businesses, communications and the exploitation of its soil and subsoil were being held back by limited concessions by Hailé Selassié. His conclusion was, therefore, obvious: "With a fair and stable administration, the production of this part of Abyssinia could be multiplied several times".[41] Moreover, according to Almagià, the real and potential agricultural production of the most fertile area of Eritrea showed what the Italians could achieve in the much more fertile Ethiopia.[42] His conclusion was, therefore, that "for the general advantage ... colonisation from Europe is a necessity".[43] Almagià also hoped that "a preponderant power" would come to the fore, to put an end to the European rivalry that he saw as hindering a more coherent exploitation of hydroelectric and fossil fuel resources.[44] In conclusion, the rational economic enhancement of East Africa as a whole appeared to Almagià to be dependent on the "broad contribution of white colonisation", and Italy was the "European state most naturally suited to addressing and solving this problem: it is a highly exalted mission, of enormous benefit to humanity, in which Italy's action will win the consensus and support of the entire civilised world".[45]

Suspicions of anti-Fascism

Having now been recognised as an authority on the Balkans, from 1931 to 1936, Almagià managed the *Studi Albanesi* journal with the high *commis d'état* Amedeo Giannini.[46] In 1932, he was made a member of the Accademia dei Lincei, while in 1934, Volterra was ousted for not having sworn allegiance to the regime.

Despite his cultural association with eminent regime authorities since the end of the 1920s, the regime's distrust of Almagià was growing, mindful of his 1925 solidarity with Salvemini. As a member of the National Research Council (CNR) geography committee, in 1928, Almagià tried to defend himself in a grovelling letter to Guglielmo Marconi, then president of the CNR. In the letter, he argued that his feelings of "loyalty" "towards the National Government and Fascism" had been "marked, and for some time, with great devotion". As for his signing of the Salvemini support letter, he claimed that he had done so in homage to the latter's cultural value as a historian and, above all, because, at the time of the signature, Salvemini "had not yet publicly expressed that anti-national sentiment that later cast him in such a light that all good Italians cannot fail to deplore in the most fervent way". Indeed, he claimed to have signed in the hope that such an "appeal" would serve "to bring Salvemini back to a more righteous path". He also added that, as secretary of SIPS, he had always "contributed to channelling Italian science in the direction of the directives issued by the National Government and, over the last three years, to the wishes personally expressed by HE the Head of Government, whom I have had the honour of being received by several times" together with the other SIPS directors. He added that he had joined the Fascist Syndicate of University Professors in 1924 and then the Fascist Syndicate of Authors and Writers and above all that for years he had been accorded "the task of holding colonial conferences at the Istituto Coloniale Fascista". He apologised, therefore, for not having been able to take part in the 1926 Colonial Day, despite being appointed to do so by the Partito Nazionale Fascista (PNF), as he had been simultaneously tasked with leading the Third Interuniversity Geographic Day. But, of course, he said nothing of his failure to join the fascist party.[47]

This self-defence was noteworthy. In 1933, Mussolini had his secretary Alessandro Chiavolini write to Gentile, complaining that several of Treccani's staff were "anti-fascists". Gentile defended Almagià, reminding il duce that he had urged those of his staff who had not yet done so to join the party, that he had twice told him about "the vicissitudes of Prof. Almagià" and that he had ascertained that the "geographer was to be accepted into the Party".[48] Therefore, at Gentile's request, Almagià finally agreed to join the party, under threat of exclusion from Treccani. Gentile's intervention was necessary above all because the Parioli section of the PNF had initially (April 1933) refused Almagià a party card, accusing him of wanting it for opportunism, not conviction.[49]

From 1936, Almagià's situation deteriorated further due to an ill-omened bureaucratic error: he had applied for a new passport to travel to Basel and Zurich to hold propaganda conferences in favour of the fascist reclamation of the Pontine marshes, and the Rome police headquarters carried out a brief investigation to this end in which Almagià's signing of the *Indirizzo di simpatia* for Salvemini (real) was confused with the Croce *Manifesto* (which he did not sign). It was, above all, this error that sealed his fate, since, from then on, all official documentation replicated this misunderstanding.[50]

On this occasion, the Ministry of the Interior granted Almagià a passport, given the propaganda value of the Swiss mission but, in the meantime, the Rome police had begun systematically spying on him in February 1936 and continued to do so until December 1943, when Almagià disappeared to escape the nazi-fascist roundups of the Jews in Rome.[51] By then, this enthusiastic scholarly supporter of Italian imperial conquests had been marked down by the police as "a subversive", a "political suspect". The aforementioned police report of 30 January 1936 claimed that in previous years "his attitude had not appeared to be favourable to the regime", but "currently, at least apparently, his attitude to the Regime is respectful". In November 1937, the Piazza d'Armi police commissioner reported that "his attitude to the Regime had not been favourable in recent years", while a confidential report dated March 1941 went as far as to define him a "Jew, profound anti-Fascist" and described him as "carrying out anti-Fascist propaganda, spreading harmful news and salacious comments on the conduct of the war and the person of Il Duce". The secret police opened a file in his name but found nothing to confirm all this, believing it to be unfounded rumours and noting deferential conduct towards the regime.[52]

Almagià's political geography and geopolitics

While his colonial studies were becoming so pro-government, Almagià's theoretical discourse explicitly justified fascist imperialism by recourse to organicist geopolitics of Ratzelian derivation. In this, too, his argument followed a more generalised Italian geography trajectory exemplified, in particular, by Roletto and Massi's *Geopolitica* journal.[53] In his 1936 manual of economic and political geography, Almagià's chapter on *Le basi della geografia politica* was entitled *Lo Stato come organismo* and referred to Friedrich Ratzel and Rudolf Kjellén but, above all, to Alfredo Rocco's fascist theory of the state.[54] In it, Almagià argued that states naturally tend towards demographic development, ethnic homogeneity, economic autarchy, colonisation and emigration. He also justified colonialism by means of geographical determinism, arguing that "real state organisms" can only be born in temperate climate regions and that, for this reason, peoples living in other climates are naturally destined to subjugation to temperate-climate states.[55]

Another "natural" tendency was conquering an opposite sea shore: for Almagià, this was the cause of Italy's expansion in Libya, Japan's in the Far East, and so on.[56] Finally, the population growth typical of "vital states" determined their *"right to life"* and, therefore, also their right to secure the essential and fundamental bases of life" through the colonies [Almagià's italics].[57] For these reasons, colonialism in non-European nations, where demographic and civil development was advanced, such as India, Indonesia and Indochina (note his adherence to Mussolini's propaganda against the colonialism of the Western democratic nations), was no longer justified, whilst it was still justified in African regions, where Europeans had the "moral" right to mitigate civil, economic, demographic and racial backwardness. These were the aims that Almagià believed to correspond

> to the most genuine concept of colony in the ancient Roman meaning of the word which the colonial expansion of civilised peoples should now be inspired by. Italy, heir to Rome, constitutes a magnificent example of this in the African territories in its sphere of influence.[58]

Studies on the colonies and the Balkans as a defence against the racial laws

All this meant nothing to the regime: when, in July 1938, Almagià was preparing to take part in the International Geography Congress in Amsterdam, the regime refused him a passport. The historian Renzo De Felice attributed this to the imminent racial laws (September 1938),[59] but it is possible that the Croce *Manifesto* signing misunderstanding also played a part.

Almagià decided to defend himself against the racial laws and, also urged on by his friend and colleague, economist Alberto De Stefani (also marginalised by the regime in the meantime), applied for exemption, replying to the latter: "I am calm because my conscience is entirely clear: few can have a feeling of Italianness as profound as mine as, for thirty years now I have been travelling and studying every nook and cranny of Italy".[60] As is well known, exemption was foreseen for exceptional military and civil merit (Article 14 of the Royal Decree-Law No. 1728 of 1938) but only slightly attenuated the far-reaching limitations placed on the civil rights of Jewish people. Thus, even had he been granted it, he would, in any case, have been stripped of his professorship and expelled from the cultural institutions he worked with. It was thus essentially a defence of his own feeling of Italianness: in requesting Gentile's help, Almagià stated that he hoped for exemption in order to "be considered on a par with all Italian citizens. . . . Basically I believe that I have dedicated my whole life exclusively to the homeland and to studies for the benefit of the nation".[61]

So, he attached a memorandum on his claim to "exceptional merit" to his application and sent it to Gentile, who was asked to support him with the National Ministry of Education. In this, he highlighted what he saw as best demonstrating his contribution to the regime's politics in his scientific work: his studies on landslides, given their "particular and exceptional importance for Italy"; his 1913 trip to and subsequent studies on Albania; his history of geography studies "aimed at demonstrating Italian primacy in the field of cartography, often contested abroad"; his direction of Treccani's geography section; his affirmation of "Italian primacy in the great geographical discoveries" at the Congress of Americanists in Seville (1935) on mandate by the Ministry of National Education; his management, for the CNR's National Geography Committee, of the *Geographical Studies on the redeemed Lands* series; his publication of *L'Africa orientale* (1935), which earned him "the very high honour of being received, together with other staff, by HE the Head of Government, who deigned to express his satisfaction with the work done"; having "raised awareness internationally of the achievements of the fascist regime where geography (integral reclamation and its repercussions) is concerned"; having "contributed to the autarchic renewal of Italian cartography"; having held "a series of conferences on fascist culture for the officers of the Royal Navy" in 1935, with the latter "then praising the patriotic work done on that occasion"; his work on the geographical part of the "Dictionary of Politics being developed by the National Fascist Party"; and having directed the Commission on the Teaching of Geography in Middle and High Schools under the aegis of the Ministry of National Education.[62]

At this point, a number of judgments decided the outcome of his request for exemption. Meanwhile, he was required to rewrite his racial sheet (he had initially not answered the question regarding his parents' "race"), declaring that he was Jewish through both mother and father and part of the Jewish community but professed no faith.[63] The vice-quaestor of Rome judged his application negatively both because Almagià had not fought but simply worked in an office in World War I and on the grounds that he had shown himself to be "indifferent" to the regime; had joined the PNF "for reasons of expediency" only; and, above all, for the Croce *Manifesto* misunderstanding.[64] It was only Giuseppe Bottai at the Ministry of National Education who, after examining Almagià's memo, declared that, despite the Croce *Manifesto* issue, Almagià's cultural merits at the service of Italy and the regime deserved exemption. In short, Bottai confirmed Almagià's imperialist inspiration.[65] But it was not enough, judging by his expulsion from all the forums he sat on and the difficulty he had in keeping his "Aryan" maid, and it would seem that he was not awarded exemption.[66] His cousin Volterra, on the other hand, did obtain exemption, despite open anti-Fascism and a refusal to swear allegiance to the regime, remaining senator and earning a war cross as World War I volunteer.

Threatened by nazi-fascist roundups of the Jews in Rome, in the autumn of 1943, Almagià managed to take refuge at the Pontifical Roman Major Seminary at the Lateran, on intercession by eminent figures. I do not know who interceded on his behalf, but it may have been his influential friend Amedeo Giannini, who, as Arturo Carlo Jemolo testified during his purge trial, did his utmost to rescue the Roman Jews. Giannini was close to the Vatican, especially since his involvement in the Concordat negotiations in 1929, and he himself took refuge at the Roman Major Seminary.[67]

In June 1944, Rome was liberated, and while several Italian geographers were purged and removed from teaching for periods of various lengths, as a victim of the regime, Almagià was appointed Extraordinary Commissioner of the Italian Geographic Society by the Ministry of Education in August, drawing up its new statute, which, in addition to eliminating the exclusion of Jews from the assembly, made all its offices elective. He did not participate in the Geographic Society conferences held from July to November 1945 in defence of Italy's eastern borders. Indeed, on 12 October 1944, he inaugurated its new post-Liberation conference cycle, with a lecture dedicated to the discovery of America, in relation to his studies on Columbus but, evidently, also in honour of, and in gratitude to, the Allies (*Bollettino della Società Geografica Italiana*, 1946).[68] In August 1945, he resigned from the post of commissioner, citing his many academic commitments.

After World War II, Almagià almost immediately abandoned his studies on Italian Africa and the Balkans, and what little he subsequently wrote focused primarily on morphology, the history of cartography and exploration. His academic influence and leading role in Italian geography culminated in these years. Probably some bitter memories remained with him of the Italian geography of the years of imperialism and fascism, one of whose exponents he had been. When, in 1954, the Italian Geographic Society awarded Giotto Dainelli a gold medal for eminent scientific merits and for fifty years of membership, only Almagià and Renato Biasutti, and their respective students, Migliorini and Nice, voted against such an award.[69] It is not clear why, in Almagià's case, though clear regarding Biasutti: when the GAP partisans killed Giovanni Gentile in April 1944, Biasutti was considered one of the alleged moral agents of this murder, and it was only thanks to the intercession

84 Sandro Rinauro

of Gentile's widow and son that the prefect of Florence, Raffaele Manganiello, saved him from execution. Giotto Dainelli was mayor of Florence at the time, but it was not thanks to him that Biasutti's life was saved.[70]

Notes

1 Morag Bell, Robin Butlin, and Michael Heffernan, eds., *Geography and Imperialism 1820–1940* (Manchester: Manchester University Press, 1995); David Atkinson, "Constructing Italian Africa: Geography and Geopolitics", in *Italian Colonialism*, eds. Ruth Ben-Ghiat and Mia Fuller (New York: Palgrave Macmillan, 2005), 15–26.
2 Lucio Gambi, *Problemi di contenuto scientifico e di vitalità culturale (discorso ad un geografo)*, in Lucio Gambi, *Una geografia per la storia* (Torino: Einaudi, 1973), 79–108.
3 Lucio Gambi, *Geografia fisica e geografia umana di fronte ai concetti di valore*, 1956, in Lucio Gambi, *Questioni di geografia* (Napoli: Esi, 1964), 20, 29, 48.
4 Gambi, *Problemi di contenuto scientifico e di vitalità culturale*, 28.
5 Lucio Gambi, *Geografia e imperialismo in Italia* (Bologna: Patron, 1992), 17.
6 Gambi, *Geografia e imperialismo in Italia*, 31–32.
7 Michele Dean, "Roberto Almagià e l'Albania", in *Roberto Almagià e la geografia italiana nella prima metà del secolo. Una rassegna scientifica e una antologia degli scritti*, ed. Giaocmo Corna Pellegrini (Milano: Unicopli, 1988), 183–202.
8 Costantino Caldo, *Il territorio come dominio. La geografia italiana durante il fascismo* (Napoli: Loffredo, 1982), 53.
9 Massimo Borgogni, *Tra continuità e incertezza. Italia e Albania (1914–1939): la strategia politico-militare dell'Italia in Albania fino all'operazione 'Oltre Mare Tirana'* (Milano: FrancoAngeli, 2007); Alessandro Roselli, *Italia e Albania. Relazioni finanziarie nel ventennio fascista* (Bologna: Il Mulino, 1986); Pietro Pastorelli, *Italia e Albania, 1924–1927. Origini diplomatiche del trattato di Tirana del 22 novembre 1927* (Firenze: Poligrafico toscano, 1967); Pietro Pastorelli, "La questione albanese nel 1924. Dal patto di Roma al 'Trionfo della legalità'", *Rivista di studi politici internazionali* 35, no. 3 (1965): 330–408. Prior to Albanian independence, Italian botanist and geographer Antonio Baldacci, together with other scholars, had played an important part in supporting Italy's imperialist gazes towards Albania since the late nineteenth century. On the role of Baldacci, see: Francesco Martelloni, "La 'questione italo-albanese' al congresso geografico del 1898 (A. Baldacci e la costruzione dell'espansione italiana in Adriatico", *Itinerari di ricerca storica* 28, no. 2 (2014): 121–144; Maria Grazia Bollini, ed., *Una passione balcanica tra affari, botanica e politica coloniale. Il fondo Antonio Baldacci nella Biblioteca dell'Archiginnasio (1884–1950)* (Bologna: Comune di Bologna, 2005).
10 Daniele Natili, *Un programma coloniale. La Società geografica italiana e le origini dell'espansione in Etiopia (1867–1884)* (Roma: Roma, 2008); Claudio Cerreti, *Della Società geografica italiana e della sua vicenda storica, 1867–1997* (Roma: Società Geografica Italiana, 2000); Costantino Caldo, *Il territorio come dominio; Lucio Gambi, Geografia e imperialismo in Italia* (Bologna: Patron, 1992); Luigi Gaffuri, "Ideologia e geografia: l'Africa coloniale nel contributo dei geografi italiani ai Congressi specializzati (1871–1898)", *Terra d'Africa* 1 (1992): 61–109; Ilaria Luzzana Caraci, *La geografia italiana tra '800 e '900 (dall'Unità a Olinto Marinelli)* (Genova: Università degli Studi di Genova, 1982); Anna Milanini Kemeny, *La Società di esplorazione commerciale in Africa e la politica coloniale (1879–1914)* (Firenze: La Nuova Italia, 1973); Maria Carazzi, *La Società geografica italiana e l'esplorazione coloniale in Africa, 1867–1900* (Firenze: La Nuova Italia, 1972). Andrea Perrone, "*Mare Nostrum* e «Geopolitica». Il mito imperiale dei geografi italiani", *Diacronie. Studi di storia contemporanea*, 25, no. 1 (2016): 1–20; Sandro Rinauro, "La conoscenza del territorio

nazionale", in *Storia d'Italia. Annali 26. Scienze e cultura dell'Italia Unita* (Torino: Einaudi, 2011), 497–524; Anna Maria Vinci, "'Geopolitica' e Balcani: l'esperienza di un gruppo di intellettuali in un ateneo di confine", *Società e Storia* 13, no. 47 (1990): 87–127.

11 Italian Central State Archives [herafter ACS], Ministry of the Interior, General direction for demography and race (1938–1944), b. 203, dossiers about Clelia, Clotilde and Clara Almagià. David and Saul Almagià (his great-uncle) had taken part in the defense of Ancona in 1849: Marco Severini, *I grandi assedi del 1849* (Ancona-Fermo: Zefiro Books, 2016). The cousin of Almagià's father, Edoardo (1841–1921), founder of a well-known port infrastructure company active especially in Egypt, had been a Garibaldi volunteer during the liberation of Trentino (1866). For the Jewish community of Ancona and the Almagià family, see: Ercole Sori, ed., *La comunità ebraica ad Ancona: la storia, le tradizioni, l'evoluzione sociale, i personaggi* (Ancona: Comune di Ancona, 1995); Ercole Sori, "Una 'comunità crepuscolare'. Ancona tra Otto e Novecento", *Proposte e ricerche*, 14 (1993): 189–278, special issue edited by Sergio Anselmi and Viviana Bonazzoli, *La presenza ebraica nelle Marche, secoli XIII-XX*.

12 Archives of Fondazione Giovanni Gentile, Rome (AFGG), Corrispondenza (1882–1945), Letters to Gentile, fasc. 113 "Almagià, Roberto", Letter from Almagià to Giovanni Gentile, Rome 10 October 1938.

13 Judith R. Goodstein, *Vito Volterra. Biografia di un matematico straordinario* (Bologna: Zanichelli, 2009), 244–245.

14 On the photographs collected and taken by Almagià during the mission, see: Sandra Leonardi, *Le lastre fotografiche. Valorizzazione e interpretazione delle fonti geo-fotografiche* (Roma: Ed. Nuova Cultura, 2017).

15 Società Italiana per il Progresso delle Scienze, *Indice generale storico cronologico alfabetico e analitico. Lavori, contributi e quadri direttivi (1839–2005)* (Roma: SIPS, 2005). On the SIPS and its imperialist and fascist trajectory, see: Antonio Casella, "Di un acerbo progresso. La Sips da Volterra a Bottai", in *Una difficile modernità. Tradizioni di ricerca e comunità scientifiche in Italia (1890–1940)*, eds. Antonio Casella, Alessandra Ferraresi, Giuseppe Giuliani, and Elisa Signori (Pavia: La Goliardica pavese, 2000), 37–89; Sandra Linguerri, "La Società italiana per il progresso delle scienze, 1907–1930", *Nuncius. Annali di Storia della Scienza* 15, no 1 (2000): 51–78.

16 Roberto Almagià, "Il territorio d'occupazione italiana in Albania e l'opera dell'Italia", *Rivista coloniale* 13, no. 5 (1918): 189.

17 Almagià, "Il territorio d'occupazione italiana in Albania", 189. Regarding Almagià's ethnic prejudices towards non-Western nations, see: Gianluca Gabrielli, *Il curricolo "razziale". La costruzione dell'alterità di "razza" e coloniale nella scuola italiana (1860–1950)* (Macerata: Edizioni Università di Macerata, 2015).

18 Almagià, "Il territorio d'occupazione italiana in Albania", 192.

19 Ibid., 195.

20 Almagià joined the Istituto per l'Europa Orientale since its foundation in 1921. Gentile, Prezzolini and Amedeo Giannini were some of the Institute's main personalities; see G. Mazzitelli, *Le pubblicazioni dell'Istituto per l'Europa orientale. Catalogo storico (1921–1944)* (Firenze: Firenze University Press, 2016).

21 Gabriele Turi, *Il mecenate, il filosofo e il gesuita. L'"Enciclopedia italiana" specchio della nazione* (Bologna: Il Mulino, 2002); Gabriele Turi, *Il fascismo e il consenso degli intellettuali* (Bologna: Il Mulino, 1980).

22 Angelo Fortunato Formiggini, *La ficozza filosofica del fascismo e la marcia sulla Leonardo, libro edificante e sollazzevole* (Roma: Angelo Fortunato Formiggini, 1923), 144; "Un indirizzo di simpatia a Gaetano Salvemini", *La Voce Repubblicana*, 26 giugno 1925; "Un indirizzo di simpatia a Gaetano Salvemini", *Corriere della Sera*, 27 giugno 1925; Roberto Almagià, "Ashby Thomas: *Some Italian scens and festivals*,

with 26 illustr. London, Methien 1929, 8° pp. 15, 175", *Leonardo. Rassegna mensile della cultura italiana* 5, no. 5–6 (1929): 159–160. See also the correspondence between Almagià and Formiggini in 1924–1926: Editorial Archives of A. F. Formiggini, Biblioteca Estense Modena [hereafter AEF], b. 2, fasc. 7 (available online at http://bibliotecaestense.beniculturali.it/info/img/mss/i-mo-beu-aef.almagia.roberto.html, last access 10 December 2021). Giovanni Gentile (1875–1944), an important intellectual and neo-idealist philosopher, was minister of public education in 1923–1924 and launched the public education reforms in 1923. In 1943, he joined the Italian Social Republic and was killed in Florence in 1944 by communist partisans.

23 Formiggini had been Almagia's friend since childhood, and in 1918, he was baptismal witness for Almagià's daughter, Fiorenza. On this, see: Formiggini, *La ficozza filosofica del fascismo*, 144; Fiorenza's birth certificate is in ACS, Ministry of Public Education, General direction on higher education, folders on academic professors, III series (1940–1970), b. 9, f. "Almagià Roberto"). Regarding Formiggini, see: Gabriele Turi, *Storia di Angelo Fortunato Formiggini e della sua casa editrice* (Modena: Il Dondolo, 2018) (reprint from 1978); Nanzia Manicardi, *Formiggini. L'editore ebreo che si suicidò per restare italiano* (Modena: Gueraldi, 2001); Gianfranco Tortorelli, *L'Italia che scrive, 1918–1938: l'editoria nell'esperienza di A. F. Formiggini* (Milano: FrancoAngeli, 1996).

24 Roberto Almagià, "Osservazioni morfologiche sull'Albania centrale", in *Relazione della Commissione per lo studio dell'Albania. Studi geografici*, eds. Roberto Almagià, Giorgio Dal Piaz, and Antonio De Toni (Roma: SIPS, Roma, 1915), 53–62; Roberto Almagià, "Intorno al carattere ed alla distribuzione dei centri abitati nell'Albania centrale", in *Relazione della Commissione per lo studio dell'Albania*, 63–81. For Almagià's invitation from Gentile to take part in the Treccani project, see: AFGG, Correspondence (1882–1945), Letters to Gentile, fasc. 113 "Almagià, Roberto", Almagià's letter to Gentile, Cortina d'Ampezzo 26 December 1938; Roberto Almagià, "La Geografia nell'Enciclopedia Italiana", *Bollettino della Società Geografica Italian*, s. V, 7, no. 4 (1930): 303. For the two manifestos, see: Gabriele Turi, *Il fascismo e il consenso degli intellettuali* (Bologna: Il Mulino, 1980); Mario Isnenghi, *Intellettuali militanti e intellettuali funzionari. Appunti sulla cultura fascista* (Torino: Einaudi, 1979); Emilio Raffaele Papa, *Storia di due manifesti. Il fascismo e la cultura italiana* (Milano: Feltrinelli, 1958).

25 "Un indirizzo di simpatia a Gaetano Salvemini", *La Voce Repubblicana*, 26 June 1925; "Un indirizzo di simpatia a Gaetano Salvemini", *Corriere della Sera*, 27 June 1925. Geographers Ferdinando Milone and Giuseppe Ricchieri also signed the manifesto expressing solidarity with Salvemini. Foreign readers are reminded that Benedetto Croce (1866–1952) was one of the greatest Italian intellectuals of his time, neo-idealist philosopher, historian, literary critic, liberal politician and one of the most prestigious anti-Fascist intellectuals. Gaetano Salvemini (1873–1957) was an Italian historian and politician of socialist reformist inspiration. His fierce opposition to Fascism led to him being forced to take refuge in the United States.

26 AEF, b. 2, fasc. 7, Letter from Almagià to Formiggini, Rome 11 February 1926; letter from Formiggini to Almagià. Rome, 12 February 1926 (available online at http://bibliotecaestense.beniculturali.it/info/img/mss/i-mo-beu-aef.almagia.roberto.html, last access 10 Deecember 2021). On Ricchieri, see: Francesco Micelli and Giuseppe Ricchieri, "Dizionario Biografico degli Italiani", *Treccani* 87 (2016), www.treccani.it/enciclopedia/giuseppe-ricchieri_%28Dizionario-Biografico%29, last access 10 December 2021.

27 Almagià, "La Geografia nell'Enciclopedia Italiana", 301.
28 Ibid., 301.
29 Roberto Almagià, "Una grande opera italiana di cultura", *Educazione Fascista* 11, no. 7 (1933): 613–618.

30 Carlo Tagliavini, Paolo Emilio Pavolini, Roberto Almagià, Mario Berti, Luigi M. Ugolini, Francesco Jacomoni, and Cirillo Korolevskij, *Albania*, Enciclopedia Treccani (1929). www.treccani.it/enciclopedia/albania_%28Enciclopedia-Italiana%29/, last access 10 December 2021.
30 Roberto Almagià, *L'Albania* (Roma: Cremonese, 1930).
31 Ibid.
32 Fabio Lando, "Geografie di casa altrui: l'Africa negli studi geografici italiani durante il ventennio fascista", *Terra d'Africa* 2 (1993): 73–124; Luigi Gaffuri, "Ideologia e geografia: l'Africa coloniale nel contributo dei geografi italiani ai Congressi specializzati (1871–1898), *Terre d'Africa* (1992): 61–109.
33 *Rivista coloniale* 12 (June–July 1917): 6.
34 Roberto Almagià, "Un decennio di studi italiani in Libia. Prolusione del prof. Almagià alla inaugurazione dei corsi di istruzione coloniale. Anno 4", *Rivista coloniale* 10 (1921): 545. On the role of geographers in the creation of the Italian Colonial Institute, see: Giancarlo Monina, *Il consenso coloniale. Le società geografiche e l'Istituto coloniale italiano (1896–1914)* (Roma: Carocci, 2002); D. Grange, "Peut-on parler au début du XX siècle d'un parti colonial italien?", in *Fonti e problemi della politica coloniale italiana. Atti del convegno Taormina-Messina, 23–29 ottobre 1989*, vol. 1 (Roma: Ministero per i Beni Culturali e Ambientali, 1996), 547–559; Alberto Aquarone, "Politica estera e organizzazione del consenso in età giolittiana: il Congresso dell'Asmara e la fondazione dell'Istituto coloniale italiano", *Storia contemporanea* 3, no. 1–2 (1977).
Italian colonialism in Africa began with the acquisition by the Italian state of the bay of Assab (1882) and the port of Massawa (1885), the first bases in the colonies-to-be of Eritrea and Somalia. The initial aims were, on the one hand, to control trade through the Suez Canal and, on the other, to respond to the frustration caused by the French occupation of Tunisia (1881), where the majority of European inhabitants were then of Italian origin. In 1911, Italy took over Libya from the Ottoman Empire, and from 1935 to 1941, the Fascist regime occupied Ethiopia. For an overview on Italian colonialism, see: Gian Paolo Calchi Novati, *L'Africa d'Italia. Una storia coloniale e postcoloniale* (Roma: Carocci, 2011); Nicola Labanca, *Oltremare. Storia dell'espansione coloniale italiana* (Bologna: Il Mulino, 2007); Jean-Louis Miège, *L'imperialismo coloniale italiano dal 1870 ai nostri giorni* (Milano: Rizzoli, 1976); Angelo Del Boca, *L'Africa nella coscienza degli italiani. Miti, memorie, errori, sconfitte* (Roma-Bari: Laterza, 1992); Anna Milanini Kemeny, *La Società di esplorazione commerciale in Africa e la politica coloniale (1879–1914)* (Firenze: La Nuova Italia, 1973).
35 Roberto Almagià, "La Cirenaica: il paese ed i suoi aspetti nel passato e nel presente", *Bollettino della Società Geografica Italiana* 5 (1912): 479–504.
36 Almagià, "Un decennio di studi italiani in Libia", 545.
37 Ibid.
38 Roberto Almagià, "Pubblicazioni coloniali italiane. Somalia", *Rivista coloniale* 5 (1926): 407–413.
39 Roberto Almagià, Attilio Mori, Giotto Dainelli, and Corrado Zoli, *L'Africa orientale* (Bologna: Zanichelli, 1935).
40 Almagià, Mori, Dainelli, and Zoli, *L'Africa orientale*, 237–238.
41 Ibid., 249.
42 Ibid., 259.
43 Ibid., 266.
44 Ibid., 268.
45 Ibid., 283.
46 Roberto Almagià, "Progressi e lacune nella conoscenza geografica dell'Albania", *Studi albanesi* 2, no. 1 (1932): 128–139.
47 ACS, CNR, Presidenza e Consiglio di Presidenza, Presidenza Guglielmo Marconi (1927–1937), b. 23, f. 416. Almagià to Guglielmo Marconi, Rome 6 December 1928.

88 *Sandro Rinauro*

48 AFGG, Corrispondenza (1882–1945), Carteggi principali, fasc. 21 "Benito Mussolini (1922–1944)", Gentile to Mussolini, Rome 8 July 1933.
49 ACS, Mininistry of Interior, Divisione Generale di Pubblica Sicurezza, Divisione Affari Generali e Riservati, Sez. II, Rome, cat. A1, 1938, b. 14, f. "Almagià prof. Roberto fu Alfonso", Quaestor of Rome to the ministry of Interior, *Almagià Roberto – conferenza*, 30 January 1936; State Archives of the City of Rome [hereafter ASR], Questura di Roma – Ebrei 1938–1944, b. 1, fasc. 10 "Almagià Roberto fu Alfonso – sospetto politico – schedato" (1937–1943), Vice-quaestor of Rome to the quaestor, *Domanda di discriminazione per benemerenze eccezionali*, Rome 12 March 1939.
50 ACS, Mininistry of Interior, Divisione Affari Generali e Riservati, Sez. II, Rome, cat. A1, 1938, b. 14, f. "Almagià prof. Roberto fu Alfonso", Quaestor of Rome to the ministry of Interior, *Almagià Roberto – conferenza*, 30 January 1936.
51 ASR, Questura di Roma – Ebrei 1938–1944, b. 1, fasc. 10 "Almagià Roberto fu Alfonso – sospetto politico – schedato" (1937–1943).
52 ACS, Ministero dell'Interno, Direzione generale di Pubblica sicurezza, Divisione Polizia politica, Fascicoli personali, b. 23, fasc. "Almagià Roberto fu Alfonso"; ASR, Questura di Roma – Ebrei 1938–1944, b. 1, fasc. 10 "Almagià Roberto fu Alfonso – sospetto politico – schedato" (1937–1943).
53 Perrone, *"Mare Nostrum* e «Geopolitica»"; Marco Antonsich, "*Geopolitica*: 'The Geographical and Imperial Consciousness' of Fascist Italy", *Geopolitics* 14, no. 2 (2009): 256–277; Anna Vinci, "'Geopolitica' e Balcani: l'esperienza di un gruppo di intellettuali in un ateneo di confine", *Società e Storia* 13, no. 47 (1990): 87–127.
54 Roberto Almagià, *Elementi di geografia economica e politica*, Parte I, *Geografia economica e politica generale* (Giuffré: Milano, 1936), 195.
55 Almagià, *Elementi di geografia economica e politica*, 196–197.
56 Ibid., 202.
57 Ibid., 206.
58 Ibid., 221–223.
59 Renzo De Felice, *Storia degli ebrei italiani sotto il fascismo* (Torino: Einaudi, 1993), 278.
60 Banca d'Italia historical archives [hereafter ASBI], De Stefani papers, b. 65, fasc. 4, letter quoted in: Anna Rita Rigano, "Alberto De' Stefani: un politico 'accademico'", in *La cultura economica tra le due guerre*, eds. Piero Barucci, Simone Misiani, and Manuela Mosca (Milano: FrancoAngeli: 2015), 464–490.
61 AFGG, Corrispondenza (1882–1945), Letters to Gentile, fasc. 113 "Almagià, Roberto". I am grateful to Dr. Cecilia Castellani, head of the Giovanni Gentile Foundation Archives, for providing me with the two memos of 20 September and 10 October 1938.
62 The quotations are taken from the two memos in AFGG, Corrispondenza (1882–1945), fasc. 113 "Almagià, Roberto", letters sent to Gentile.
63 ACS, Ministry of Public Education, General direction of Higher Education, folders on academic professors, III series (1940–1970), b. 9, f. "Almagià Roberto", R. Università degli Studi di Roma, Ufficio del Personale, *Scheda personale*, signed by Almagià.
64 Vice-Quaestor of Rome to the Questura, Rome, March 15, 1939, "Domanda di discriminazione di Almagià Roberto fu Alfonso", in ASR, fondo Questura di Roma – Ebrei 1938–1944, fasc. 10 "Almagià Roberto fu Alfonso – sospetto politico – schedato" (1937–1943).
65 Ministero dell'Educazione nazionale, Dir. Gen. Istruzione Superiore, to Ministero dell'Interno, Direzione generale per la demografia e Razza, Rome, November 9, 1940, "Ebreo Prof. Roberto Almagià – Discriminazione", in ACS, Min. Pubblica Istruzione, Dir. Gen. Istruzione universitaria, fascicoli professori universitari, III serie (1940–1970), b. 9, f. "Almagià Roberto".
66 ASR, Questura di Roma – Ebrei 1938–1944, b. 1, fasc. 10 "Almagià Roberto fu Alfonso – sospetto politico – schedato" (1937–1943); ACS, Mininistry of Interior,

Divisione Generale di Pubblica Sicurezza, Divisione Affari Generali e Riservati, Sez. II, Rome, cat. A1, 1938, b. 14, f. "Almagià prof. Roberto fu Alfonso", *Promemoria per L'Ecc. il Capo della Polizia*, Rome 28 October 1940 (which shows that Gentile supported Almagià's request for a maid).

67 For Almagià's scientific work during the years of the racial laws, see: Annalisa Capristo, "Sei anni di dolorosa parentesi". Roberto Almagià e le leggi antiebraiche", in *L'integrazione degli ebrei: una tenace illusione? Scritti per Fabio Levi* (Torino: Zamorani, 2019), 89–122.
For Almagià's presence at the Lateran, see Andrea Riccardi, *L'inverno più lungo 1943–1944: Pio XII, gli ebrei e i nazisti a Roma* (Roma-Bari: Laterza, 2012); Carlo Badalà, "La scelta di accogliere. I rifugiati al Laterano: l'attività del Pontificio Seminario romano maggiore e il ruolo della Santa Sede", *Ricerche per la storia religiosa di Roma* 12 (2009): 287–360; Elio Venier, "Il clero romano durante la Resistenza. Colloqui con i protagonisti di venticinque anni fa", *Rivista diocesana di Roma* 11, no. 1–2 (1970): 142–156; Elio Venier, "Il clero romano durante la Resistenza. Colloqui con i protagonisti di venticinque anni fa", *Rivista diocesana di Roma* 10, no. 11–12 (1969): 1320–1327. For Jemolo's testimony in favour of Giannini, see Stefano Santoro, "La diplomazia italiana di fronte all'epurazione. Il caso di Amedeo Giannini", *Italia contemporanea* 216 (1999): 529–540.

68 Giotto Dainelli (geologist), Pietro and Ferdinando Gribaudi, Goffredo Jaja, Ardito Desio (geologist) and Ernesto Massi were purged, while Giorgio Roletto obtained an act of clemency due to his precarious psycho-physical state. See: Mattia Flamigni, *Professori e università di fronte all'epurazione. Dalle ordinanze alleate alla pacificazione (1943–1948)* (Bologna: Il Mulino, 2019).

69 Giuseppe Vedovato, "Giotto Dainelli tra scienza e politica", *Rivista di studi di politica internazionale*, no. 3 (2009): 413–414.

70 On Gentile's death, see Gabriele Turi, *Giovanni Gentile. Una biografia* (Firenze: Giunti, 1995).

6 Walter Wood and the legacies of science and alpinism in the St Elias Mountains

Peder Roberts

Introduction

At the southern end of the eastern shore of Kluane Lake, nestled just beyond the St Elias Mountains in Yukon, Canada, stands a small research facility operated by the Arctic Institute of North America (AINA). Among the houses is the Walter A. Wood building. This chapter considers how the man whose name stands on this structure, a patrician veteran of the golden age of Alaskan mountaineering, helped build a research programme in glaciology that grew to encompass broader studies of alpine environments – including as analogues to the Himalayas. In so doing, I hope to also say something about the changing structural conditions for alpine research in North America without losing sight of the relations that were made and eventually (to a point) unmade within the specific site of Kluane Lake.

This is not a paean to a great individual. Nor is it a story of linear progress from adventure to research or a history of the many research programmes that have been based at the Kluane Lake facility.[1] Rather, this is a study of how Wood strove to build a set of infrastructures for alpine research (material and intellectual) that made and cemented his own connection to a landscape while also reflecting the wider political and scientific contours of his time. The chapter is built largely on the archival records of AINA held at Libraries and Archives Canada, which reveal much about how Wood built his legacy in the mountains and a good deal – though not quite as much – about the place that it held in his heart.

Wood helped define how the mountains were known and engaged with, and his particular set of ambitions and anxieties is not simply ornamental to a story of research in Kluane Lake. The legacies included a range of research projects – some world-leading – but also the erasure of Indigenous presence. My hope is therefore that in putting the analytic focus on Wood as well as on the research that took place within the structures that he built, I will stimulate some broader reflection on contingency and agency in alpine research.

DOI: 10.4324/9781003095965-7

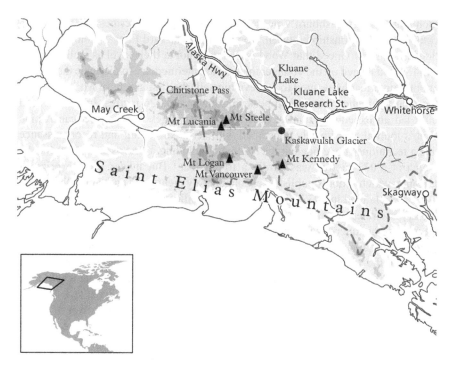

Figure 6.1 The St Elias Mountains, showing Kluane Lake and other sites mentioned in the text. Map made by Red Geographics.

Mountaineering from adventure to the military

Walter Abbott Wood was born in 1907, scion of a prominent family in the state of New York.[2] He was introduced to the Alps during four years of study in Zürich, after which he attended Harvard University and moved in the same circles as the celebrated "Harvard Five" – Charles Houston, Bob Bates, Adams Carter, Terris Moore, and Bradford Washburn, who between them conquered a slew of Alaskan peaks and ventured into the Himalayas and central Asia.[3] Wood subsequently climbed in Greenland with Noel Odell, the last man to see George Mallory and Andrew Irvine alive on their 1924 attempt at Mt Everest. Blessed with independent wealth, Wood threw his energies into the American Geographical Society (AGS), where he helped establish a Department of Field Exploration and Research focused on assisting expeditions with their preparation and the working up of their results.[4]

Wood was nevertheless a marginal figure in the golden age of North American mountaineering.[5] Washburn's biographer David Roberts describes a courteous but competitive relationship between Wood and the Harvard Five, Washburn in particular being convinced that Wood was simply not at their level as a climber.[6] In 1934, Wood leaned on the younger men via an intermediary to dissuade them from attempting a feat he wanted to achieve himself, the first ascent of Mt Lucania, at the time the highest unclimbed peak in Canada at 5,226 metres. In 1935, Wood duly led an expedition that he described in the pages of the American Alpine Club's journal as primarily concerned with aerial surveying and reconnaissance using techniques developed at the AGS and including a first ascent of Mt Steele, which at 5,073 metres was hardly a trivial feat.[7] But it was not the prize of Lucania, which Wood's published account barely mentioned and which Washburn and Bates claimed in 1937.[8] The story was an indication of Wood's weight within the upper circles of American mountaineering and of a sense that the mountains were his to conquer.[9] Nevertheless, it would be a mistake to view Wood as holding a view of either the mountains or their conquest as exclusively possessive. His claim that the 1935 expedition had as its aim "to carry out a piece of research in photographic mapping" in an unmapped region was true also, and he would later work together with both Bates and Houston from the Harvard Five.[10]

Wood's career took a turn of sorts with World War II. The Winter War of 1939–40, in which well-trained Finnish troops proved surprisingly effective at slowing the invading Soviet forces, pointed to the importance of adapting to and ideally mastering the challenges of combat in specific environments.[11] The US Army had already inaugurated a relationship with the National Ski Patrol, a volunteer alpine safety organization founded in Vermont in 1938. From an initial token investment of $6,500 for equipment testing, this flourished to cover more specialized ventures such as the Tenth Mountain Division, trained for combat in alpine and wintery theatres.[12] Wood was initially seconded as a civilian to the equipment testing programme, in which he and many others – including Washburn – tested gear while climbing in Alaska. Wood combined business with pleasure by recording two new first ascents.[13] In 1944, Wood was brought into the military at the rank of colonel, evaluating the Army's alpine training program, and advising recruits at the Tenth Mountain Division's Camp Hale facility in Colorado to be grateful not to be toiling in the humid swamps of Louisiana.[14] Toward the end of the war, he was appointed assistant military attaché in Ottawa, where he helped to manage the developing defence relationship between Canada and the United States.

The wartime imperative to develop environmental knowledge had another consequence that would prove vital for Wood's later career. In 1942, the Army established the Arctic, Deserts, and Tropics Information Center (ADTIC), charged with gathering environmental data with relevance to military operations. A desire to make use of the ADTIC data prompted a collection of US and Canadian figures to found the Arctic Institute of North America, a binational, non-governmental organization formally founded in 1945 to stimulate the "intelligent and orderly development" of Arctic North America.[15] Whereas its US founders were largely polar scientists with wartime experience – men such as the geologist Lawrence

Gould and the glaciologist Lincoln Washburn (no relation to Bradford) – its Canadian founders included figures such as Hugh Keenleyside and Arnold Heeney, prominent examples of what historian Jack Granatstein later termed "the Ottawa men," an elite cadre of civil servants who wielded substantial (and in Granatstein's view unprecedented) power within government.[16] Wood knew many of these individuals personally, and his initial involvement was in keeping with his status as a benevolent fixer, helping to secure Lincoln Washburn's release from the Army so he could become the Institute's executive director. In 1947, he took on the directorship of AINA's first American office from his quarters at the AGS.[17]

And finally, the war directly shaped the Kluane Lake region. Historian David Neufeld has described how the area became a game sanctuary in 1943 largely as a response to US concerns that the construction of the Alaska Highway, with its rush of new temporary residents, would lead to pressure on wildlife numbers.[18] As a later report put it, "Climbing parties took over from hunting parties and the exhilaration of conquering a mountain replaced the joy of bagging a trophy."[19] The statement erased the Indigenous residents of the region, who found themselves barred from their own traditional hunting grounds.[20] And indeed, in the years that followed, science and mountaineering – rather than hunting or the pursuit of traditional lifeways – became the privileged activities within the reserve. Wood more than anyone else embodied a sense that through regular, recurring engagement with the mountains and their environments, a sense of attachment could be created that transformed the space on a map to a place anchored in a set of institutional and personal commitments. Yet there were already people to whom those lands held a deep attachment. Anthropologist Julie Cruikshank has shown that even glaciers were intimately connected to the world of human culture, part of a living environment known and regularly traversed by the First Nations of the region.[21] Inscription was premised on erasure, from the personal level – the absence of Indigenous names and faces in the records generated by Wood's many activities in the region – to the structural – the presumption on the part of those who created the game reserve that the actors who mattered were climbers and hunters from outside. What changed was not the underlying logic of conquest but rather its form, from animal trophies to peaks.

Operation Snow Cornice

For Wood, science and climbing formed a spectrum rather than a duality. Each was a means of inscribing himself and those around him on the land. In 1948, he inaugurated Operation Snow Cornice, one of AINA's first flagship projects. Snow Cornice focused on the Seward Glacier, which flowed from Alaska over the border to Canada – a symbolically resonant field for a binational institution. Wood left overall direction in the field to the glaciologist Bob Sharp, who had worked with Wood during the war and later with ADTIC.[22] Bringing Sharp into Snow Cornice solidified rather than undermined Wood's centrality because he retained the status of benefactor and guiding spirit, the one individual without whom the program would be impossible, while taking the study of the region to a level that Wood himself could not attain – thus providing an evolving justification for ongoing presence.

Wood initially sketched the programme under the working title Operation Fairy Castle, a name that more accurately evoked his own romantic attachment to the region, but Snow Cornice proved more fitting given the latent danger associated with an overhanging snow ledge.[23] The first season acted as a trial run for some new techniques – including seismic sounding to determine glacier depths, which did not work as well as planned[24] – but the bad weather and equipment problems tested Wood's patience to the point where he threatened to give up expeditions and grow potatoes in Arizona.[25] Routines developed over the following two years, and the project continued smoothly until 1951, when a chartered bush plane carrying Wood's wife and daughter disappeared. Despite extensive searching, its final resting place remains a mystery to this day. One might speculate that the accident sacralized Wood's relationship with the mountains where his greatest previous loss had been one of pride, the failure to make the first ascent of Mt Lucania. The quest to know the mountains became linked to the quest to find his lost family.

The fact that the aircraft was carrying family members prompts another reflection. Snow Cornice was not the bastion of homosociality that most other mountaineering expeditions were but rather a space where Wood could share his love of alpine environments with those closest to him, inscribing his way of living as well as working upon the mountains. This had long been a feature of his expeditions: the 1935 venture included both his wife Foresta – remembered as a highly capable alpinist in her own right who shared her husband's love of the mountains – and his younger brother Harrison. The largesse of the benefactor permitted him to know the mountains on his own terms.

That largesse could also facilitate research beyond Wood's own competence. While the Office of Naval Research (ONR) covered Sharp's salary on Snow Cornice, much of the rest of its funding was recorded in the AINA records as being from a private source – in other words, Wood's own pocket. It did not detract from the rigour of the glaciology that others than glaciologists were present. Mountaineering was not invisible from Snow Cornice – its members made the first ascent of Mt Vancouver, at the time the highest unclimbed peak in North America at 4,812 metres – but mountaineering was neither a selling point nor an end in itself. Rather, Snow Cornice embodied a wider sense that an alpine environment could be known and understood through the languages of science. It is telling that Wood expressed disappointment about the work of Odell, whom Wood had brought to Snow Cornice for the 1949 season. Odell was a fine mountaineer and field companion, but Wood worried that he would add little to the geological observations that Sharp had already made as a sideline to his glaciological work – and thus fail to maximize the opportunity that Wood had created.[26]

The Icefield Ranges Research Project and the High Altitude Physiology Study

Snow Cornice ended after the tragedy of the 1951 season, but Wood's enthusiasm for the mountains of northwest North America remained. In 1955, he negotiated for AINA to provide most of the logistical support for the United States glaciological program in the Brooks Range of Alaska for the International Geophysical Year (IGY; 1957–58), a step that helped position the Institute as a provider of polar and alpine logistics.[27] Meanwhile Wood began working on a new project that would revive and expand Snow Cornice under the joint aegis of AINA and the AGS (Wood having become president of the latter body in 1957). The success of Snow Cornice in scientific terms, plus Wood's status as a deep-pocketed facilitator of research with a strong commitment to this specific region, led the Institute's leadership to eagerly sign off on the new project in December 1960.[28] Thus was born Wood's last baby – the Icefield Ranges Research Project (IRRP).

From its start, Wood intended the IRRP to increase both knowledge of a specific alpine environment and develop the cadre of researchers who would study glaciers as windows into the relationship between ice masses and the total environment, and how that relationship changed through time.[29] But in a letter to AINA executive director John Reed, Wood admitted perhaps the most important reason, a personal hankering to get back into the St Elias Mountains sharpened by a sense that glaciological focus of institutions and researchers in the United States was shifting worryingly strongly toward Antarctica.[30] From his base at Kluane Lake, Wood hoped to build a very different culture than that which predominated in the Antarctic, one on which his personal largesse could still be sufficient to underwrite a story of success that did not require the massive finances for military sealifts and the like.

The IRRP started in 1961 amid awful weather conditions (reportedly the worst in fifteen years).[31] Thanks to an arrangement with the Canadian Department of Transport, observations from two IRRP stations (one at the Kluane Lake base camp and another at higher altitude on the Kaskawulsh Glacier) were sent to Whitehorse, from where the IRRP in return received detailed forecasts that helped plan flights.[32] That flying was done in a Helio Courier aircraft purchased by AINA and for many years piloted by Phil Upton, who would become a legendary figure within the IRRP thanks to his remarkable flying skills and unflappable demeanour. Dick Ragle, a veteran of work in Greenland and the Ward Hunt Ice Shelf and former leader of an Antarctic deep drilling project during the IGY, oversaw a glaciology program and became particularly popular after earning a promise of steaks for the whole party as thanks for flying a local farmer to search for his stray cows.[33]

Senior figures within AINA worried about the need to train glaciologists (the IGY was finished, after all) and the lack of university partners, which they feared could lead to a situation where "the logistical tail will begin to wag and beat the scientific dog to death."[34] Their worries perhaps reflected a wider sense that glaciology was a small discipline due to its not being particularly important in the larger constellation of natural sciences rather than a consequence of its being at an early stage of disciplinary development. Wood was able to mitigate these concerns through his own resources: although the IRRP incurred a deficit of $17,000 the following year, he dipped into his pockets to keep it running.[35] After two summer seasons, Wood remained enthusiastic about the project and quite literally invested in it, but there were limits to his financial resources, and he began to argue that with more funding, it could reach a higher level of ambition – "an integrated approach to the study of a specific high mountain environment."[36] The St Elias mountains would thus became part of "man's quest for knowledge of his total environment."[37] Wood increasingly saw ecology and even human geography as viable components of a comprehensive study into the Kluane Lake region.[38]

Wood recognized that environmental research could also be attractive to military patrons. As historian Ronald E. Doel and others have argued, the US military took a strong interest in the physical sciences during the early Cold War on the grounds that understanding the earth was an important part of understanding the terrain on which the military had to operate.[39] AINA had strong connections to the ONR, one of the most prominent patrons of earth and environmental sciences during the era, and cultivated contacts among US Army research agencies.[40] The Army Quartermaster Research Facility provided meteorological instruments for the IRRP, while the Cold Regions Research and Engineering Laboratory sponsored a surveying programme, and the Atomic Energy Commission made a small grant for collecting samples that could be analyzed for radiation (apparently more as a proof of concept than to obtain specific measurements of fallout in the specific region covered by the IRRP).[41]

The connections between the IRRP and the US military deepened during the 1960s, thanks in large part to the conviction of AINA's entrepreneurial Washington office director, Robert Faylor, that the Institute could draw stronger connections to US strategic interests in other alpine regions. Faylor was the brains behind the High Mountain Environment Project (HMEP), premised on the St Elias Mountains being a viable analogue for the Himalayas in terms of the overall climatic environment, the higher latitude compensating for the lower altitude. In late 1965 successfully Faylor pitched the project to the Army Research Office.[42] China had recently defeated India in a brief war fought at the lower levels of the Himalayas, and an imaginative mind could envision an expanded conflict that dragged the United States from Vietnam into combat with China.

In the northern summer of 1966, AINA organized a reconnaissance of potential sites for the analogue study. One of the individuals Faylor invited to participate was Barry Bishop. Mountaineering royalty following his leadership of the first US expedition to successfully summit Mt Everest in 1963, Bishop was also a veteran of US Antarctic administration and sufficiently close to Wood that the IRRP leader even offered to (anonymously, as ever) subsidize Bishop's taking a year off from the National Geographic Society to complete a PhD at the University of Chicago.[43] Bishop was an obvious choice for finding a workable analogue given his Himalayan experience. But he also harboured a secret – albeit one known within the highest mountaineering circles, possibly including the well-connected Wood. In 1965, Bishop had helped organize a secret expedition with CIA support to place a listening device on the peak of Nanda Devi to monitor China's Lop Nur nuclear testing site.[44] It is tempting to speculate about the larger justifications for the HMEP that Bishop might have seen. Be that as it may, the reconnaissance was successful, identifying a promising site at May Creek on the Alaskan side of the border. Research began shortly thereafter and continued with minimal incident, quickly taking on the character of a comprehensive survey of a specific environment with reference to a range of physical geographical factors.

Nevertheless, higher latitude would struggle to compensate for the higher altitude of the Himalayas as it affected human performance, and Wood and Faylor became increasingly convinced that a high-altitude physiology study would make a logical complement to the HMEP. Mt Logan, at nearly 6,000 metres, would make a suitable site. And Wood knew the perfect candidate to lead such a study. Charles Houston, now a medical doctor on the faculty of the University of Vermont, was a veteran of the Harvard Five and had a distinguished Himalayan mountaineering career to his credit in addition to experience with high altitude physiology from World War II.[45] Houston's first attempt on K2 in 1938 was unsuccessful, but it was still unclimbed when he led a second attempt in 1953. Again, he failed to reach the summit, but the harrowing story of the attempt – particularly the near-disaster that befell the party on their descent while unsuccessfully trying to save a critically ill member – became a mountaineering classic and ensured Houston's lasting fame.[46]

Houston's biographer Bernadette McDonald describes a phone call from Wood in October 1966 with an irresistible opportunity: would Houston care to lead a high-altitude research programme on Mt Logan, which the Army Research Office had already agreed to fund?[47] The following summer, Houston, along with Bishop, identified and established a site for a base camp over 5,000 metres up the mountain with just enough space for Upton to land the Helio Courier (and, more importantly, get it back into the air). In 1968, the High Altitude Physiology Study (HAPS) began under Houston's leadership. Houston later described some of the early experiences on Mt Logan as "rather frightening."[48] Flown in directly from Kluane Lake, some of the early subjects experienced severe symptoms beyond the usual headaches and other ailments associated with mild mountain sickness. During the decade that followed HAPS proved a resounding success in terms of both research output and safety. Through a number of studies, HAPS probed the effects of oxygen deprivation on human physiology, initially using Canadian military personnel as subjects.[49] The military's hand was light: Houston was free to develop a comprehensive attack on the effects of oxygen lack on the human body and to bring in bright colleagues with their own research ideas, without specific directives about what questions he should investigate. HAPS described and named the phenomenon of high-altitude retinal haemorrhages, along with studying the effects of drugs such as Diamox on high altitude sickness, its focus gradually shifting from identifying the causes of "mountain sickness" to the physiological factors behind acclimatization to high altitudes.[50]

Wood seems to have been relatively unconcerned about the IRRP taking on a more direct alignment with the US military and its goals. In the May Creek area, HMEP was openly known as the Himalaya Project.[51] In October 1967, the *New York Times* ran a (largely positive) article on HAPS that bluntly linked it to preparing the United States for fighting China in the Himalayas.[52] The war in Vietnam was deeply unpopular in Canada, and Hugh Keenleyside, a founding member of the Institute and a prominent left-leaning member of the Canadian elite, expressed deep concern about AINA facilitating its possible expansion.[53] In 1971, the Canadian magazine *The Last Post* revived the link between HAPS and US military ambitions in a lurid story that claimed that Mt Logan was the site of classified military research.[54] The accusations never gained any traction in the United States, furthering the sense that they were essentially a manifestation of a wider Canadian panic over US dominance.[55] But the catalytic role of the India-China war in making the analogue between the Himalayas and the St Elias Mountains relevant was real. The Army was certainly satisfied both with the results and with the concept of analogue studies more generally, although they balked at continuing their investment past 1972.[56] The Mt Logan research, which was mainly sponsored by the US National Institutes of Health, continued until 1978.

Later in the decade, the Alpine Club of Canada marked the century of Canada's 1867 confederation by planning a mass of expeditions to the St Elias Mountains. Historian PearlAnn Reichwein has noted how this commemoration presented the mountains as a corner of Canada ripe for naming and climbing, a fitting site for the articulation of a vital Canadian identity – its federalist character marked by the naming of twelve hitherto unclimbed peaks for the twelve territories and provinces.[57] Fred Roots, the influential head of the Canadian government's Polar Continental Shelf Project and an AINA insider, composed a pitch that Reichwein has analyzed for its description of a "large-scale mountaineering tournament" in which teams of Canadians would conquer the unclimbed mountains.[58] To Roots, the St Elias Mountains were in part an amphitheatre where feats would be performed. This they were, and more, being also a territory that would be made quintessentially Canadian through those performances – even as their Canadian character provided helped justify them in the first place.

Wood regarded the episode with detachment. He was open to the mountains as a site where naming and climbing could express good Canadian-US relations, pushing (quietly) in the wake of John F. Kennedy's assassination that a peak be named Mt Kennedy in the late President's honour – a suggestion that ultimately led to a first ascent that included the late president's brother Robert F. Kennedy.[59] Wood was mindful of the logistical complications: the IRRP's resources were already in high demand from the project's expanding group of researchers. But his attitude also reflected his deep sense of being a guest in Canada, a visitor who did not seek to influence Canadian political matters. It would not do for an American to take a prominent role in a commemoration of Canadian federation beyond offering the quiet encouragement one might expect from a good neighbour. And perhaps it also reflected disquiet with the sporting character of the expedition. One wonders if he saw something almost undignified in the rush to name and conquer peaks that were neither the tallest nor the most challenging in the region – which Reichwein argues contributed to the expedition being regarded by many alpinists as a showy performance rather than a feat of mountaineering.[60] Wood showed little interest in mass performance tinged with nationalism, born as he was in a world where mountaineering was a genteel fraternity, the race to conquer new peaks cloaked by conventions of modesty.

Kluane Lake in the era of the national park

If the Kluane game reserve aimed at restricting hunting, the plans that emerged in the late 1960s for a national park in the region aimed at restricting extractive industry. Mining loomed large as a vested interest in Yukon given its outsized footprint on the territory's economic history.[61] A brief from the Alpine Club of Canada gave a history of the reserve that depicted conservation and mining as in conflict since the reserve's creation, a conflict that could be resolved by a core national park area that might expand in time to include adjacent areas once they were declared no longer interesting for mining.[62] It captured a prevailing sense that advocates of the national park would have to tread carefully – a delicate situation into which Wood and the IRRP became drawn.

The green winds that had begun to blow strongly across much of the world at the end of the 1960s also reached the IRRP. Thanks to a grant from the Mellon Foundation, the project grew to include a series of large mammal studies under the general direction of Ian McTaggart-Cowan, professor of wildlife biology at the University of British Columbia. But might scientific work also be inconsistent with a national park? As he explained to Alpine Club of Canada president David Fisher in September 1970, Wood liked the idea of the park as a boon for mountaineers, but he had grave reservations if it would hinder scientific work such as the large mammal studies. He reserved special criticism for "so-called 'environmentalists'" whose demands for untouched nature might prevent tagging or marking animals.[63]

The IRRP became drawn into the debate in 1971 when word reached AINA headquarters that Manfred Hoefs and Bill Benjey, IRRP researchers working respectively on Dall sheep and micrometeorology, had circulated a petition demanding that the Yukon territorial government act quickly to create the national park.[64] Wood told Benjey that he had sympathy for their cause but certainly not for their methods. The IRRP and its researchers needed to remain scrupulously above local politics in order to avoid being dragged into disputes that could threaten its continued operation.[65] Even after nearly forty years, Wood retained a sense that he was a guest, his legacy at Kluane Lake contingent upon his own ability to maintain appropriate relations with Canadian authorities.

The national park was eventually proclaimed in 1972. Wood chaired an AINA committee aimed at positioning the IRRP as an asset to the Canadian National Parks Service in its management of the park. As Wood hoped, the Service viewed the IRRP as a potential ally, a source of data to inform management and infrastructure capable of monitoring and potentially assisting mountaineering expeditions.[66] The IRRP base would not be an unwelcome intrusion into a pristine space but a forward base from which "the initial inventory assault" on the park could be launched.[67]

The interests of First Nations were given far less weight. Neufeld has argued that the concerns of Indigenous residents were essentially invisible within this process, which he links to other erasures of privileged Indigenous rights within Canada – notably the 1969 White Paper that infamously attempted to end Treaty rights for First Nations. Instead, the debate focused on "the 'rational' park issue – western protection versus western exploitation."[68] "Kluane is the story of wilderness," began the draft of a Parks Canada tourism brochure prepared around this time.[69] That invisibility extended through the written records generated by the IRRP. Formal reports and informal letters alike dwelled on the results accomplished, the atmosphere at the base camp, and Phil Upton's preternatural skill in the Helio Courier, but practically never mentioned the Indigenous residents of the region. One of the few references is itself revealing. The daughter of Jose Sias – a respected Elder of the Kluane First Nation and key local personality – worked at the Kluane Lake base camp as a cook in 1974, a task she performed so well that Wood worried about her absence being a drawback for impressing the dignitaries whom he often flew in to inspect and admire the IRRP and its facilities.[70] My personal communications with many who worked at Kluane Lake during this period indicate that informal relationships between researchers, support staff, and Indigenous residents were far more extensive and mutually respectful than the written record would suggest. Determining the extent to which Wood consciously erased First Nations from his own construction of space is impossible. But, it is tempting to speculate that their "official" invisibility was an artefact both of a more general convention – to marginalize individuals deemed non-central to the core accomplishments of field research – and of Wood's own vision, which relied upon the presumption of novelty for its significance and for the priority of his own connection.

The creation of the national park coincided with Wood's retreat from active involvement with the IRRP. Already in 1971 he had begun to scale back his personal commitment, though still dictating terms when necessary and grumbling at AINA for its refusal to match his financial contributions and improve the facilities.[71] Researchers continued to bring their families to the base camp, though Wood's patience with the antics of the children diminished with time.[72] Many of the younger participants in HAPS forged a strong sense of esprit de corps that developed into lifelong friendships. Houston could be difficult – even those who greatly liked him recalled his being nicknamed "the curmudgeon" – but reading through the documents generated by from HAPS and speaking to those who knew him, a distinct sense emerges that the combination of mountains, medicine, and fellowship produced one of the happiest periods in his life.

By 1975 Wood had largely retired from active involvement, administratively and financially, and the Institute's wider financial problems threatened the project's future. Ultimately AINA as a whole, and with it the Kluane Lake facility, became integrated with the University of Calgary. Its research profile continued to shift. Another of McTaggart-Cowan's students, Charles Krebs, led a series of long-term ecological studies that would, over the coming decades, reframe the main research profile of Kluane Lake away from glaciers and towards ecosystems, the IRRP giving way to a Boreal Forest Research Project.[73] Many of the staff from the late 1960s and early 1970s remained, including camp manager Andy Williams, but Wood faded into the background, though he returned to visit in later years.

When he died in 1993, his *New York Times* biography did not mention the IRRP at all – though it found space for other exploits such as his participation in a search for Noah's Ark on Mt Ararat in 1949.[74] I find it difficult to believe that Kluane Lake and the St Elias Mountains were relegated to a similarly marginal place in Wood's own heart and mind.

Conclusion

In his fine history of how the Kluane national park came to be, David Neufeld recalls a telling encounter with Mary Jane Johnson of the Kluane First Nation in 1992. Johnson described the erasure of Indigenous presence and knowledge in the region by holding her open left palm while referring to her people's land and stories, and then covering it with her right palm and stating "then your stories came and covered them all up."[75] Neufeld makes the important point that Canadian government officials excised Indigenous presence through new narratives of what the Kluane Lake region was, why it was important, and who had authority to regulate and police it. I contend that it was not just the stories told by Canadian officials that created new narratives of possession and authority. The career arc of Walter Wood produced stories of conquest and success within a larger narrative of personal legacy. The structural invisibility of Indigenous figures in his career was a product of how he characterized the places and spaces that he constructed. Relations between the Kluane Lake Research Station and the First Nations of the region have certainly improved in subsequent years, albeit with a long road ahead.[76]

How important was Wood's self-identification as a mountaineer? The initial impetus for his love of the region was to climb summits and to be among the glaciers of the St Elias Mountains, with Kluane Lake a base camp from which the icefields could be reached. Mountaineering, with its fetishization of priority and its codification of feats, lent itself to this view. As Wood's baby grew and broadened its horizons in the 1960s and 70s, with the large mammal studies and the later boreal forest project expanding the IRRP into something rather more omnivorous in terms of environments, Kluane Lake became more than simply a gateway to the mountains. The rise of Indigenous rights movements in the latter part of the twentieth century only confirmed that AINA's presence could no longer be regarded as a form of place-making on open space, even the glaciers recognized as known and travelled by First Nations.

Acknowledgements

This project has received funding from the European Research Council (ERC) under the European Union's Horizon 2020 research and innovation programme (grant agreement No. [716211 – GRETPOL]) and from the Swedish Research Council. The manuscript builds upon research conducted in collaboration with Lize-Marié van der Watt. Archival research in Ottawa was made possible by the generous hospitality of Janet and Richard Martin-Nielsen. I benefited considerably from the detailed and generous comments of two anonymous referees, who encouraged me to take it in a different and more coherent direction. Last, but certainly not least, I am grateful to the many veterans of the AINA programs at Kluane Lake who shared their memories with me off the record.

Notes

1. For an overview of this research, see Ryan K. Danby, Andrew Williams, and David S. Hik, "Fifty Years of Science at the Kluane Lake Research Station", *Arctic* 67, supplement 1 (January 2014): iii–viii and Garry K.C. Clarke, "A Short and Somewhat Personal History of Yukon Glacier Studies in the Twentieth Century", *Arctic* 67, supplement 1 (January 2014): 1–21.
2. No biography has been written of Wood, and the extant material on his personal life is slight. For an overview of his life, see, for instance, the obituary written by his son Peter Wood, "Walter Abbott Wood 1907–1993", *Arctic* 47, no. 2 (June 1994): 203–204.
3. Maurice Isserman, *Continental Divide: A History of American Mountaineering* (New York: W.W. Norton, 2016), especially 230–251.
4. Peter Lloyd, "Noel Ewart Odell 1890–1987", *The Alpine Journal* 93 (1988): 309.
5. Wood is barely mentioned in *Continental Divide*, Isserman's magisterial history of American mountaineering, something that I feel reflects Wood's status as it was perceived by his contemporaries rather than any oversight on the part of the author.
6. David Roberts, *The Last of His Kind: The Life and Adventures of Bradford Washburn, America's Boldest Mountaineer* (New York: Harper, 2010), especially pp. 66–67.
7. Water A. Wood, "The Ascent of Mt. Steele", *The American Alpine Journal* 48, no. 252 (1936): 81–85.
8. Roberts, *Last of His Kind*, 66.
9. Wood was sufficiently well respected to be charged with leading the American Alpine Club's inquiry into the ill-fated 1939 K2 expedition, a report that criticized the authoritarian leadership style of its German-born leader Fritz Wiessner. Isserman, *Continental Divide*, 259.
10. Walter A. Wood, "The Wood Yukon Expedition of 1935: An Experiment in Photographic Mapping", *Geographical Review* 26, no. 2 (1936): 228–246.
11. On the Winter War, see, for instance, William R. Trotter, *A Frozen Hell: The Russo-Finnish Winter War of 1939–40* (Chapel Hill: Algonquin Press, 1991).
12. Joshua P. Howe, *Climbing to War: The Development of Mountain Forces in the Context of U.S. Army Mobilization, 1939–1945* (Senior thesis, Middlebury College, 2002), 22; Maurice Isserman, *The Winter Army: The World War II Odyssey of the 10th Mountain Division* (New York: Houghton Mifflin Harcourt, 2019).
13. Robert H. Bates, "Walter Abbott Wood 1908–1993", *American Alpine Journal* (1994): 319–320.
14. Isserman, *Winter Army*, 60.
15. This particular phrase was included in the original press release of the Institute's aims from 1944 and nicely captured its initial direction, which faded and then was revived with vigour in the late 1960s when the Prudhoe Bay oil strike returned Arctic resources to prominence. See, for instance, "Group Here Plans Arctic Promotion", *Montreal Gazette* 9 (September 1944).
16. Granatstein, *The Ottawa Men: The Civil Service Mandarins, 1935–1957* (Oakville, ON: Rock's Mills Press, 2015).
17. AINA Board of Governors meeting minutes, 7 May 1948. Libraries and Archives Canada (hereafter LAC) MG28 I79 box 193, folder Board minutes 1944–1947.
18. David Neufeld, "Kluane National Park Reserve, 1923–1974: Modernity and Pluralism", in *A Century of Parks Canada 1911–2011*, ed. Claire Campbell (Calgary: University

of Calgary Press, 2011), 235–272, especially 243–44; Robert G. McCandless, *Yukon Wildlife: A Social History* (Edmonton: University of Alberta Press, 1985), 64–87.
19 Anonymous, "Glacier Inventory of Donjek River Hydrological Basin St. Elias Mountains, Yukon", undated (1975). Copy held in LAC MG 28 I79 box 158, folder Projects – IRRP Glacier Inventory 1975.
20 Neufeld notes that Canadian officialdom was aware of the disruption this would cause to First Nations hunters but that they argued that without the reserve, there would be no game for any hunters – Indigenous or otherwise. Neufeld, "Kluane National Park Reserve", 243.
21 Cruikshank, *Do Glaciers Listen? Local Knowledge, Colonial Encounters, and Social Imagination* (Vancouver: University of British Columbia Press, 2005).
22 Garry K.C. Clarke, "A Short and Somewhat Personal History of Yukon Glacier Studies in the Twentieth Century", *Arctic* 67, supplement 1 (2014): 2–4.
23 Board of Governors meeting minutes, 6 February 1948. LAC MG28 I79 box 193 folder Board minutes 1944–1947.
24 J.D. Salt to Baird, 24 September 1948. LAC MG28 I79 box 25 folder "Snow Cornice" Project part 2 July 1948-June 1949.
25 Wood to Lincoln Washburn, 22 July 1948. LAC MG28 I79 box 25 folder "Snow Cornice" Project part 2 July 1948–June 1949.
26 Wood to Baird, 16 August 1949. LAC MG28 I79 box 11 folder Baird, P.D. – Baffin Island expedition – miscellaneous correspondence.
27 Executive Committee meeting minutes, 4 March 1957. LAC MG28 I79 box 210 folder Executive Committee – Minutes 1945–1967.
28 Nutt to Walter Wood, 15 December 1960. LAC MG28 I79 box 9 404E to 204E.
29 Wood to Reed, 8 December 1960. LAC MG28 I79 box 70 folder Projects – IRRP – 1961.
30 Wood to Reed, 29 December 1960. LAC MG28 I79 box 70 folder Projects – IRRP – 1961.
31 IRRP 1961 newsletters 1 and 2. LAC MG28 I79 box 70 folder Projects – IRRP – 1961.
32 AINA report to NRC on 1966–67 activities. LAC MG28 I79 box 63 folder Committees – N.R.C./A.I.N.A Advisory Committee 1964–1966.
33 Wood, IRRP newsletter, 3 August 1961. LAC MG28 I79 box 70 folder Projects – Icefield Ranges Research Project – 1960–1961.
34 Faylor to Wood, 15 September 1961. LAC MG28 I79 box 70 folder Projects – IRRP – 1961.
35 Faylor to Wood, 16 March 1962. LAC MG28 I79 box 69 folder International Geophysical Year – McCall Glacier.
36 Wood to Reed, 25 October 1962. LAC MG28 I79 box 70 folder Project – Icefield Ranges Research Project – 1962. Underlined in the original text.
37 AINA and AGS, Icefield Ranges Research Project, undated brochure (1965). LAC MG28 I79 box 107 folder Article on Greenland, Col. P. Krueger 1965.
38 IRRP advisory committee report to Board of Governors, 1 May 1965. LAC MG28 I79 box 63 folder Icefield Ranges Research Project.
39 Ronald E. Doel, "Constituting the Postwar Earth Sciences: The Military's Influence on the Environmental Sciences in the USA after 1945", *Social Studies of Science*, 33, no. 5 (2003): 635–666.
40 On the ONR, see, for instance, Harvey Sapolsky, *Science and the Navy: The History of the Office of Naval Research* (Princeton, NJ: Princeton University Press, 1990); Naomi Oreskes, *Science on a Mission: How Military Funding Shaped What We Do and Don't Know about the Ocean* (Chicago: University of Chicago Press, 2020).
41 IRRP planning meeting minutes, 12 March 1963. LAC MG28 I79 box 63 folder IRRP Advisory Committee 1963–1965.
42 Faylor, to William W. Dick (Chief of R&D, Army), 4 November 1965. LAC MG28 I79 box 69, folder Project – IRRP.
43 Executive Committee meeting minutes, 30 September 1966. LAC MG28 I79 box 96, folder Miscellaneous Grants 1966–1967.

44 For a recollection of this episode written by one of the participants, see Mohan S. Kohli and Kenneth Conboy, *Spies in the Himalayas: Secret Missions and Perilous Climbs* (Lawrence: University Press of Kansas, 2002). See also Pete Takeda, *An Eye at the Top of the World: The Terrifying Legacy of the Cold War's Most Delicate CIA Operation* (New York: Thunder's Mouth Press, 2006).
45 Bernadette McDonald, *Brotherhood of the Rope: The Biography of Charles Houston* (Seattle: The Mountaineers Books, 2007), 49. On Houston's wartime work (Project Everest) and the wider context of high altitude physiology research, see Vanessa Heggie, *Higher and Colder: A History of Extreme Physiology and Exploration* (Chicago: University of Chicago Press, 2019).
46 See Charles S. Houston and Robert H. Bates, *K2: The Savage Mountain* (London: Harper Collins, 1955).
47 Bernadette McDonald, *Brotherhood of the Rope*, 198.
48 Charles S. Houston, David E. Harris, and Ellen J. Zeman, *Going Higher: Oxygen, Man, and Mountains* (Seattle: The Mountaineers Books, 2005), 183.
49 Vanessa Heggie notes that part of the reason for moving away from military subjects was that they did not show much interest in the research itself. See Heggie, *Higher and Colder*.
50 Many of the HAPS records are preserved in LAC AINA collections. See also Houston, *Going High: The Story of Man and Altitude* (Burlington, Vermont: self-published with assistance from the American Alpine Club, 1980), 151; Houston, Harris, and Zeman, *Going Higher*, 183–184.
51 H.E. Wahl (Canadian Department of Transport), memorandum on conference held at IRRP base camp 26–28 July 1966, 30 August 1966. LAC MG28 I79 box 207 folder Project – Icefield Ranges Research Project 1966–1968.
52 Anonymous, "Altitude Illness Fought on a Peak", *New York Times*, 31 October 1967.
53 Keenleyside to Lloyd, 5 December 1967. LAC MG 28 I79 box 125 folder Projects High Mountain Environmental Study – March 1967.
54 Anonymous, "And the Arctic Trails Have Their Secret Tales That Would Make Your Blood Run Cold", *The Last Post* 1, no. 8 (1971): 59–62.
55 On the wider US-Canadian relationship at this time, see, for instance, Robert Bothwell, *Alliance and Illusion: Canada and the World, 1945–1984* (Vancouver: University of British Columbia Press, 2007), 212–236. I have been struck when speaking with US veterans of the Mt Logan project by their reactions to the Canadian uproar – the dominant reactions being surprise (the issue not having at all appeared on their radars at the time) and amusement, the latter reaction certainly not shared by many in Canada.
56 Herbert Love memorandum (AINA Executive Director), 2 September 1970. LAC MG 28 I79 box 154, folder Executive Director – Memorandums for the Record 1967–1971.
57 PearlAnn Reichwein, "Expedition Yukon 1867: Centennial and the Politics of Mountaineering in Kluane", *Canadian Historical Review* 92, no. 3 (September 2011): 487–489. Nunavut became Canada's third territory in 1999.
58 Roots, quoted in Reichwein, "Expedition Yukon", 489.
59 The ascent is described by Roberts in *Last of His Kind*, 282–284.
60 Reichwein, "Expedition Yukon", 503–505.
61 See, for instance, Kenneth Coates and William R. Morrison, *Land of the Midnight Sun: A History of the Yukon*, 3rd ed. (Montreal and Kingston: McGill-Queen's University Press, 2007).
62 Alpine Club of Canada, "A National Park in the Yukon", 19 June 1970. LAC MG28 I79 box 171 folder Icefield Ranges Research Project – Kluane National Park 1970–73.
63 Wood to Fisher, 3 September 1970. LAC MG28 I79 box 171 folder Icefield Ranges Research Project – Kluane National Park 1970–73.

64 Manfred Hoefs, "Petition for Quicker Government Action in the Establishment of a National Park in the Kluane Game Reserve", undated (early 1971). LAC MG28 I79 box 171 folder Icefield Ranges Research Project – Kluane National Park 1970–73.
65 Wood to Benjey, 5 May 1971. LAC MG28 I79 box 171 folder Icefield Ranges Research Project – Kluane National Park 1970–73.
66 IRRP advisory committee report, 20 October 1973. LAC MG 28 I79 box 165 folder Committees – IRRP Advisory Committee 1971–75.
67 L.H. Robinson to de la Barre, 24 September 1973; on the role of AINA as scientific advisory experts in the IRRP, see Benjey to Ragle, 26 June 1973. LAC MG28 I79 box 171 folder Icefield Ranges Research Project – Kluane National Park 1970–73.
68 Neufeld, "Kluane National Park Reserve", 259.
69 Draft brochure text, attached to de la Barre memorandum, 20 February 1973. LAC MG28 I79 box 171 folder Icefield Ranges Research Project – Kluane National Park 1970–73.
70 Wood to Andy Williams, 18 June 1974. LAC MG28 I79 box 103 folder Wood, Walter A. 1974.
71 Wood to de la Barre, 28 October 1974. LAC MG28 I79 box 13 folder Wood, Walter A. 1974.
72 Gerry Thompson to Love, 10 September 1973. LAC MG28 I79 box 156 folder IRRP General Projects 1971–1974.
73 Charles J. Krebs, Stan Boutin, and Rudy Boonstra, eds., *Ecosystem Dynamics of the Boreal Forest: The Kluane Project* (Oxford: Oxford University Press, 2001).
74 Wolfgang Saxon, "Walter A. Wood Is Dead at 85: World Explorer and Geographer", *New York Times*, 20 May 1993.
75 Quoted in Neufeld, "Kluane National Park Reserve", 258.
76 See, for instance, Green Raven Environmental Inc., *Lhù'ààn Mân Kluane Lake Research Summit* (4–5 May 2018), Summary Report, 34, https://kfn.ca/wp-content/uploads/2020/05/Kluane-Lake-Research-Summit-2018_full-summary-report.pdf, last access 10 December 2021.

7 Physiology and biomedicine on high-altitude expeditions (c. 1880–1980)

Vanessa Heggie

Introduction

Climbing to heights over 8,000 metres and, more importantly, returning safely from them was as much a scientific as a physical challenge in the twentieth century. Even after extensive experiments in barometric chambers and repeated experiments and experiences on high mountains, it was not certain until the late 1970s whether human beings could survive this high without supplementary oxygen. Understandably, then, the history of altitude physiology has so far concentrated on research into human respiration and oxygen supply systems, although more recent work has moved away from a reductive, oxygen-focused understanding and towards a science in which many more technologies of survival, including quotidian things such as food rations and boots, are included.[1] This research topic drew scientists from a range of young, cutting-edge and often marginal disciplines, such as sports medicine or aviation physiology, and coalesced into a recognisable sub-specialism – extreme (altitude) physiology – in the middle of the twentieth century. The *marginality* of this relatively small clique of Western researchers is debatable – their work was integrated into major national and international projects, such as the space race and the International Biological Program(me) – but they were certainly working on *frontiers*.[2] These were in many cases literal: political and geographic in terms of the physical location of their research; biomedical and psychological in that they studied the limits of human performance and the spaces on earth often considered at the very edge of human survivability.

Despite their apparently exotic research topic and small number, the history of these scientists, of their work and of their human guinea pigs offers important insights into the history of science and exploration, and of course into mountain history. First, in an era of Big Science, technoscience and the rise of the laboratory and the data bank, extreme physiology remains a resolutely field-based specialism. While barometric chambers, wind tunnels, laboratory-based blood analyses and molecular biology contributed to the discipline, time and time again, it was the physical space of the mountainside that confirmed or denied the hypotheses of the laboratory worker. Although some mountaineers openly grumbled about being turned into guinea pigs or hoped to summit with the minimum of technical assistance, the reality was that in the first half of the twentieth century, every expedition

Physiology on high-altitude expeditions 107

over 8,000 m relied heavily on physiological research and frequently made space in their parties for physiologists and a programme of research. Although this sometimes led to culture clashes – particularly in expedition priorities – the principle of using science to improve the material culture and practice of high-altitude mountaineering was widely accepted by Western climbing teams.

The role of mountaineering in constructing national mythologies is outlined in several chapters in this volume; previously in accounts like these, there has been a tendency to paint the British high-altitude mountaineering culture as uniquely opposed to scientific intervention. This is a reflection of the assumed 'gentlemanly amateurism' of early twentieth-century climbers but does not reflect the reality, and it is only relatively recently that the cutting-edge physiological research conducted to support the 1953 expedition has been scrutinised.[3] This is in contrast to revisionist science-focused histories of British polar expeditions, a difference that is perhaps caused by the fact the mountaineers were successful in their sporting goal, while the 'glorious failure' of British Antarctic expeditions required a boost by emphasising their scientific credentials instead.[4] This chapter will reframe early and mid-twentieth-century British high-altitude mountaineering as part of an emerging global scientific practice; in doing so, it of course ties twentieth-century mountaineering back to its roots in earlier European 'scientific' exploration, to Alexander von Humboldt, Bénédict de Saussure, John Tyndall and others whose combination of mountaineering and science has been much more extensively studied than that of modern scientist-explorers.[5]

In this chapter, I will concentrate on the themes of this collection, namely frontiers and margins – in other words, on place. One thing extreme physiology research emphasises, particularly from a science and technology studies viewpoint, is the importance of the physical reality of the mountain to the creation of truth in science.[6] This is both in an abstract and an applied sense; as I suggested previously, the hypotheses developed in the laboratory were proved not in the lab but on the mountainside (and often found wanting), and likewise the technologies of survival produced off the mountain could only prove their real value with live testing in the high-stakes world of high-altitude climbing. However well a boot performed in a wind tunnel, it was its performance on the mountain that really mattered. It was also its performance on *different kinds of bodies* that mattered. Individual climbers had very different preferences and prejudices for and against certain kinds of technology produced by physiological research, and most notably, this was both heavily gendered and racialised. Extreme physiology worked to frame certain kinds of bodies as normal, as belonging, in certain kinds of space.

Concentrating on margins and frontiers also implies concentrating on contact zones. Unlike Antarctic exploration, high-altitude mountaineering relied on the presence of local populations. The indigenous populations of mid-altitude worked as guides, porters, cooks, informers, advisors, companions and life-saving assistants on mountaineering expeditions; less well acknowledged, they also acted as human guinea pigs, providing labour, blood and even urine samples which were analysed largely for the purposes of advancing Western understandings and Western colonial and military goals.[7] The role of indigenous peoples makes a final point about the margins and frontiers in high-altitude scientific work: these spaces were not pristine or 'undiscovered'. While it is true that the explorers and scientists were voyaging into the unknown when it came to scientific questions, particularly through their study of the limits of human performance, it was much less the case that the physical spaces through which they moved were unstudied or unexplored. Although some expeditions did pioneer new routes up familiar mountains or were exploring in spaces that had not previously received substantial Western attention, it is also the case that many others relied heavily on the work of previous visitors. The metaphorical 'standing on the shoulders of giants' turns into a literal reliance on not only the knowledge but also the material culture, and even the abandoned technology, of previous expeditions. In at least one case, a crucial experiment could only be conducted thanks to the litter of a climber who died on the mountain; in another, a scientist's life was saved by the technology left behind by other anonymous climbers. Even in some of the most isolated spaces on the earth respiratory physiologists still found passing visitors calling in to their lab and offering new scientific opportunities.

Relatively little physiological or biomedical work has been done above 8,000 metres, so I will be concentrating on the vaguer category of 'high altitude', mostly on work done in the Himalayan and Andean mountain ranges, with auxiliary work in lower mountain ranges such as the Alps and in laboratories worldwide. The dominating topics of this research have been respiration and circulation, so it is largely the study of breath and blood which is outlined here, with a little on nutrition and other survival technologies; histories of the study of psychological and stress physiology in extreme environments are still limited and remain a potent area of new research.[8] I will also be concentrating on Western exploration, predominantly European and North American activity; it is clear that other nations, particularly Russia and China, were engaging in extreme physiology work in the Himalaya, and histories of their scientific activity would be a significant addition to our understanding of these spaces. In the pages that follow, I will first outline the key expeditions and researchers in altitude physiology and biomedicine, and then I will briefly discuss the main topics of research (respiration, circulation, metabolism and psychological reactions). Next, I will make four key claims for the value of studying mountain history: demonstrating the relationship between field and laboratory, discussing the conservative as well as progressive nature of this kind of research, revealing the roles of indigenous peoples and showing how extraordinarily *crowded* these apparently marginal, frontier spaces could be.

Research at, and on, altitude

The conventions of Early Modern 'scientific' travel required its participants to gather observations, and this often included accounts of their own bodily reactions to new environments. Humboldt is usually cited as the archetype for such self-observation and self-experiment in mountainous regions, but it is important to note the contribution of non-European peoples; Western explorers also collected the observations of and about non-European travellers in mountainous regions, particularly those who lived at mid-altitude.⁹ When Paul Bert, the laboratory-bound French physiologist, published his monumental *La Pression Barometrique* in 1878, his opening chapter on "Mountain Journeys" was a collage of reports from all kinds of sources, including the folk knowledge implied by names such as "Headache Mountain" or "[high] pass disease".[10] While much of this consisted of the reports from European travellers in South America and the peaks of Europe, it included cures developed by indigenous peoples (such as the drinking of Mate tea – "l'herbe du Paraguay" – in mining camps in Chile and Peru to "moisten the lungs")[11] and accounts of the disease, in translation, by Chinese writers and surveyors.[12] Notably, Bert is reading women as well as men; in the case of the Indian Himalaya, he actually claims that the "most interesting accounts [he has] found ... are certainly those published by Mistress Hervey", who, being "a simple tourist, not heeding politics or geography, or science ... gives special attention to everything relating to her health".[13]

Whatever their origin, these accounts offered a largely overlapping series of observations about the response of the human body to altitude or, rather, the effect of mountain environments on the human and animal body. These included fatigue, breathlessness, headaches and difficulty sleeping and eating, as well as a host of other symptoms, and explanations for these varied from the spirits of the mountain to the poisonous vapours of alpine plants. Traditionally, histories of the study of these disorders concentrate on the series of European scientists who subjected these diverse symptoms to laboratory study, attempting to mimic the experience of mountain climbing with high-tech equipment and converting the complex symptoms of mountain sickness into simple, reductive, biomedical explanations. Bert, already mentioned here, is usually taken as the founder of the discipline, not least because his reductive experimental work converted the complexity of mountain sickness into the simplicity of 'altitude sickness' – a pathology caused by nothing more than the lack of oxygen at high altitude and consequently easily remedied by the application of an oxygen-rich breathing system.

Although this simple model was challenged, the consequent focus on respiration and then on blood remains central to altitude physiology until well into the twentieth century. Blood studies dominated in field work – while Bert's work was laboratory bound, he drew heavily from (and had financial relationships with) more adventurous scientists, including Denis Jourdanet and François-Gilbert Viault.[14] Viault's blood studies at altitude in the Andes demonstrated a simple, and apparently universal, response to altitude: the increasing production of red blood cells, interpreted as an attempt by the human body to increase oxygen transport in a reduced-oxygen atmosphere. While indigenous residents at altitude, including non-human mammals such as llamas, showed high concentrations of red blood cells, sea-level travellers could also gradually achieve these concentrations with time spent at altitude.[15] Note here that, of course, 'normal' red blood cell concentration was automatically assumed to be that of the sea-level born-and-bred white Europeans; 'high' is a relative term in physiology, just as it is on a mountainside.

The development of military aviation offered extra funding and significance for this research, and several of the key figures in twentieth-century respiratory physiology started or consolidated their careers doing military research during World War II. That said, planes were not always a good model for the mountain, and the experience of mountaineering was very different to the rapid, technologically enclosed ascent of the pilot, so while the technology and opportunities for research that military aviation provided were useful, mountains still functioned as crucial laboratories for the study of the human body in extreme environments. The most obvious instantiation of this is the Harvard Fatigue Laboratory (HFL), founded as a joint enterprise between Harvard's medical school and business school in 1927. The HFL was formed to investigate problems of *industrial* physiology, in part in response to the "problems" and unrest in labour in the United States, but rapidly used this remit to expand its research into fundamental questions of physiology and into areas that would later become sports and extreme physiology.[16] These included studies of fatigue and heat, both on the treadmill and during agricultural work, and high-altitude expeditions to the Andes in 1935, where Ancel Keys set a record for high-altitude blood sampling (20,140 feet) that was not broken for 74 years.[17] Keys is a clear example of how field work in 'extreme' environments could feed back into everyday science – as Tracy has argued, his work on Andean mountains inspired his later interventions into heart disease and obesity, and his work was both sponsored and used by the US military in areas such as ration design.[18]

As well as researchers from Europe and North America, the Andes also hosted autochthonous research. Key here was the founding of the Instituto de Biología y Pathología Andina in the early 1930s, headed by the physiologist Carlos Monge Medrano, who had led his own physiological expeditions into the mountains in the 1920s. The work of the Instituto had a much broader remit than that pursued by researchers from the Global North, in that as well as fundamental work on respiration and metabolism, it also studied "life at altitude" in the round, including things like fertility studies, sociological investigations and cultural inquiries.[19] This is in stark contrast to the work being done at similar heights in the Himalaya, where research was conducted by team doctors, or by physiologists who were part of primarily mountaineering-focused exploration teams, rather than as part of specifically biomedical expeditions. Although European climbing teams and mountaineering societies were certainly interested in altitude physiology and participated in, and funded, both lab and field research, it was not until the 1950s that specifically research-focused teams were sent into the Himalaya rather than the Andes. British anxieties about being 'beaten' to the summit of Everest in the 1950s inspired a route-scouting, physiology-studying and oxygen equipment-testing expedition to Cho Oyu in 1952. It was another decade before a physiology-focused expedition returned to the Himalaya, with the Silver Hut expedition of 1960–61, led by the Everest veterans (Sir) Edmund Hillary and Dr Lewis Griffith Cresswell Evans Pugh. Silver Hut was an overwintering exercise designed primarily to test whether long residence at altitude would improve acclimatisation, inspired by the two men's experiences in Antarctica in the late 1950s (it did not). But even this trip was multi-purpose, including a 'first' summit attempt on Makalu that ended in disaster and an equally unsuccessful sponsored hunt for the yeti.[20]

Physiology on high-altitude expeditions 111

This research at altitude has been dominated by blood and respiratory studies. At Silver Hut, the programme was largely dictated by the interests of Pugh – whose work had been the scientific key to the successful ascent of Everest in 1953 – and therefore consisted of a series of studies examining exercise and altitude, particularly looking at all stages of oxygen transport, including blood studies.[21] But in addition the team also studied kidney function, psychomotor skills and basal metabolism, three areas which, if overshadowed by blood and breath, had still captured the interest of researchers on mountains. Kidney function was related to the phenomenon of dehydration at altitude; researchers and those organising expeditions had long noticed that mountaineers experienced increased thirst and increased risk of dehydration at altitude, although they disagreed on the cause – was it another effect of altitude or rather the effect of increased respiration and fatigue? The cause and consequences of dehydration were also important to a question related to blood; in dehydrated human subjects, the blood becomes more concentrated, with less plasma and therefore proportionally more red blood cells. This is a confounding factor in studies of increased red blood cell production – has the body really produced more red blood cells or merely concentrated the existing blood by removing water?

Psychomotor skill studies had become more significant with the rise of military aviation – if altitude had an effect on cognition this had repercussions for safe flying, identifying targets accurately and making quick decisions in tense situations. Barometric chamber studies often included handwriting, card counting or other mathematical tests as studies of the rapid mental decline caused by lack of oxygen.[22] These were mirrored by tests on mountainsides – for example, Joseph Barcroft outlines an extensive series of mental tests used in the Chilean Andes during the 1920–1921 expedition, including identifying repeated letters in a display of the alphabet, reading a clock face with numbers reversed, handwriting tests, memorisation and mental arithmetic.[23] At lower altitudes, the Austrian physiologist Arnold Durig had attempted to measure the impact of mid-altitude (e.g. in the Alps) on reaction times, although at the heights available, up to 4,560 metres above sea level, the impact seemed minimal. Durig is probably better known for the more dramatic results he gained in his metabolic studies, demonstrating the increased energy requirement of men working at altitude.[24]

Perhaps the most intensive study of psychology at extreme altitudes was the 1963 American Mount Everest Expedition (AMEE 1963). As Clements has argued, the American expedition leant more heavily on science and biomedicine as justifications for their travels – at least when it came to funding – and the expedition leader Norman G. Dyhrenfurth explicitly recruited research scientists "the darlings of contemporary state-funding institutions" as part of a narrative that argued for the strategic value of high-altitude climbing to military and space research.[25] Two of the research team had specific psychological interests, clinical psychologist James T. Lester and the sociologist Richard M. Emerson, who between them conducted personality testing, asked climbers to keep dream and mood diaries and in Emerson's case engaged in a form of ethnographic study of stress and leadership. Unfortunately, the results of this expedition were ambiguous and incomplete: physiologist Will Siri concluded that the ability to climb Everest was more a matter of luck and subjective experience than extraordinary physiology, and the team's sociological diaries – most of Emerson's research – were accidentally left in Nepal. Most devastatingly, the death of the youngest climber, Jake Breitenbach, notably changed the mood of the expedition away from a desire to "do science" to a passion to "conquer the mountain" that had killed their friend.[26]

What AMEE 1963 demonstrates is the challenge and reward of refiguring a space like the slope of Everest as an experimental site. The pre-departure rhetoric of the expedition (again, at least as far as funders were concerned) emphasised the unique opportunities offered by this unusual research space, blurring the boundary between the specific field site and the 'universal' knowledge produced in a laboratory. The studies on AMEE 1963 were supposed to be generalisable enough to be of relevance to the US military and the space race. Instead, they found a research space with what Clements calls "emergent properties", requiring research processes that were constantly shifting to account for the unexpected. In every area of human biomedical study, it is clear that high-altitude research is as risky as it is rewarding, and so even where simulated environments were not thought accurate enough to model for the mountainside itself, they were still used to practice data collection and to trial survival technology. Barometric chambers could be used to design the *experiments*, if not to generate 'true' data about altitude. This process is most obvious when we look not at the headline survival technologies of oxygen or the study of blood and respiration but rather the more easily overlooked essential support: food.

Basal metabolism and the related issue of food supply and ration design was the subject of both experimental and observational scientific work through the nineteenth and twentieth centuries. Indeed, some of the fundamental tenets of nutritional physiology were established with a climb to mid-altitude in the Alps. In 1865, the chemist Johannes Wislicenus and the physiologist Adolph Eugen Fick used an ascent of the Faulhorn in Switzerland and a restricted paste-and-water diet to demonstrate that fats and carbohydrates could supply the body with motive energy, in contradiction of the theory, proposed by Justus von Liebig, that proteins, and proteins alone, provided the energy for human movement.[27] But actually studying nutrition at high altitude was a risky prospect, as well as dehydration one of the major challenges to the first high-altitude expeditions was undernutrition. Loss of appetite was a feature mentioned in the earliest reports of mountain sickness, and the early twentieth-century European expeditions to the Himalaya repeatedly reported similar phenomena, with mountaineers returning from their expeditions dangerously underweight in some cases.[28] Choosing effective rations could be the difference between a successful and a fatal expedition, and so there was a clear disincentive to practicing actual experimental studies once on the mountain itself; work on nutrition therefore tended to be more observational and experiential at altitude, with team doctors and attending physiologists writing up their experience of different ration packs. Extensive work was done at sea level in preparation – most expeditions' records include questionnaires about food preferences and previous expeditionary dietary experiences in an attempt to tailor specific ration packs that would suit the particular needs of a specific team.

Paradoxically, the seriousness with which European mountaineering teams took their food has led to suggestions that they were somehow 'unscientific'. In particular, the extensive packing lists for the early British expeditions of the 1920s and 1930s are cited as evidence of the 'gentlemanly amateurism' of the climbers, representing them as upper-middle-class and middle-class gentlemen who were unable to consider travelling without champagne and caviar in Fortnum & Mason hampers.[29] In fact, the packing lists were rational and often based on the best available knowledge of altitude nutrition: variety and familiarity were essential to encouraging a mountaineer suffering from shifts in his sense of taste to eat, as well as dealing with the psychological pressures of isolation and homesickness. Variety also helped to deal with the fact that the impact of altitude was unpredictable – one mountaineer might crave quite different foods to his colleagues. Given one of the first deaths on a British expedition – of a doctor researching oxygen systems – was from dysentery, a deep concern with hygiene and preference for tinned, preserved and easy-to-prepare foods drove much of the logistics. Finally, some apparently exotic food choices in fact had specific biomedical justifications: in 1952, the lead physiologist for the British Everest expeditionary team, Pugh, solicited advice from a nutrition expert, Miss MW Grant, at the London School of Hygiene and Tropical Medicine, seeking foods that would stimulate or support red blood cell production. Her advice included both foie gras and caviar (although she pointed out these could be substituted with the cheaper options of liver sausage and smoked cod roe).[30]

Exploration food is a stark warning against projecting back our current prejudices about food: it is very easy to read caviar and foie gras as archaic and luxurious rather than investigating and recognising them as evidence of scientific rationalism in ration design. Particularly in the case of British mountaineers, there has been a long tendency to pit 'gentlemanly amateurism' against scientific engagement, most obviously in the debates over the use of oxygen at high altitude. The idea that the 'oxygen debate' of the 1920s and 1930s was primarily about class has obscured for too long the rather complex debate in this period about the limits of scientific knowledge and the technical limits of contemporary oxygen equipment. The systems tried in the 1920s and 1930s were extremely problematic, and there was no scientific consensus about the effectiveness of oxygen or the best method of delivery.[31] Despite this uncertainty, every single British expedition did in fact take and use or at least try to use oxygen on their expeditions, and the most famous 'gentlemen' mountaineers – George Mallory and Andrew Irvine – climbed to their deaths on Everest wearing respirators. The main difference, then, between the failed expeditions of the 1920s and 1930s and the successful summiting in 1953 was not so much one of class or attitude but rather driven by the significant changes in oxygen technology brought on by World War II. While the experience and needs of pilots and mountaineers have many differences, the material culture of respirators changed significantly; after 1950, the newly developed British Royal Air Force (RAF) masks became the standard base model for most European climbing teams. Likewise, the funding of respiratory physiology during the war meant that by the 1950s, there was a body of expertise in many Western countries that had not previously existed – men who had trained in military laboratories and who were able to leverage their experience into mountaineering science (and getting funding for what had often previously been a personal hobby or interest).

The focus on oxygen has also obscured the research – including field research – that went into developing and testing other 'assistive technologies' to tackle altitude sickness. As well as standard oxygen and a primitive form of 'rebreather' technology (this is a system that scrubs exhaled carbon dioxide out of the breath, allowing air to be recycled and minimising the wastage of oxygen), the British Everest expedition of 1924 also took bicarbonate of soda, chlorodyne and essence of garlic as potential drugs for the treatment of altitude sickness.[32] Substances such as morphine, cocaine hydrochloride and preparations of caffeine were regular contents in the first aid kits carried by European expeditions.[33] Mallory reported to the organisers of the 1924 expedition that "young Haldane" (almost certainly JBS Haldane) recommended "a stimulant similar to caffeen [sic] and kola, but much better and absolutely innocuous".[34] The subjects of these studies were not always the white explorers themselves; in 1953, the British team 'experimentally' gave amphetamines (Benzedrine) to two of their Sherpa porters while they navigated the deadly Khumbu Icefall. No change in performance was noted, although one porter reported that it had cured his cough and the other that it made him sleepy. Other assistive technologies were more the subject of gossip than study, and rumours swirled in the 1950s that the Germans had experimented with blood transfusions as early as the 1930s, although there is no evidence this took place; in fact, blood transfusion became a sea-level doping scandal for cyclists in the 1980s, while mountaineers experimented with the opposite intervention, transfusing plasma to 'thin' the blood, before realising that it was more efficient simply to remain adequately hydrated while mountaineering.[35]

Learning from mountains

As this outline has shown, from the 1920s to the 1960s, Western scientists clustered on a few peaks in the Himalaya and the Andes as the main sites for physiological research at altitude, often chosen for ease of access, familiarity or as a side project in more conquest-oriented expeditions. There were, however, distinct differences in the style and nature of the research in the two regions. The makeup of the expeditions differed, with specifically scientific expeditions to the Andes in the first half of the twentieth century, while expeditions to the Himalaya tended to either combine science and exploration or to be preparatory and scoping expeditions in support of a later attempt on a particular peak – with Silver Hut being the first significant primarily scientific expedition to the Himalaya, an approach not repeated for another 20 years, with the American Medical Research Expedition to Everest in 1981 (AMREE 1981). Likewise, the subjects of the scientific study in each region tended to differ, with significant attention paid to indigenous mid-altitude populations in the Andes, while in the Himalaya, it was almost exclusively the bodies of white Western climbers that were studied by physiologists and doctors – why this might be the case is explored further in this section.

What all these types and places of research have in common – from blood to Benzedrine – is that work in laboratories and simulated mountain environments was always in need of validation by the 'real' mountain itself and required confirmation from mountaineering scientists. For example, while the equations produced by aviation medicine and barometric chamber studies suggested that it would be physiologically impossible for a human being to climb Everest without supplemental oxygen, mountaineering physiologists and their human subjects increasingly thought that such a climb would – given sufficient acclimatisation – be possible. Indeed, that was the motivation for the Silver Hut expedition, which was designed around a prolonged period of residence at altitude (although the results were slightly disappointing with regard to acclimatisation, showing that extended stays tended to lead to physical deterioration). Nonetheless, the optimists were only proved 'right' in 1978, when Reinhold Messner and Peter Habeler successfully climbed Everest without supplemental oxygen. It took another three years before the explanation for the divergence between the laboratory and the mountain was revealed; the first barometric air pressure measurement on the summit of Everest showed that the mathematical models were not just wrong but specifically Eurocentric – 'atmospheric pressure' was calculated based on the thickness of the atmosphere in Europe – and that local weather significantly altered the physiological climb-ability of the mountains over 8,000 meters.[36]

Whatever the relative role of the laboratory and the mountain, one thing that is clear about mountain research is that it was not always progressive. Knowledge could be lost as well as gained, and the research conducted on the mountains was not always used to equally benefit the people who risked their lives conducting it. This will come as no surprise to historians or sociologists of science, so I need not belabour the point here, but oxygen systems are a good case in point.[37] As essential pieces of survival technology, their development was intense but in essence deeply conservative. While, on the one hand, successive expeditions did draw on the knowledge of previous explorers, they did not, on the other, necessarily have the time, inclination or funding to redesign fundamental pieces of equipment – making small changes to something like a breathing mask could have significant knock-on consequences to other technology (valves, pipes, oxygen systems, harnesses, backpack).

While trying to prepare for the AMEE 1963 expedition, physiologist Dr Tom Hornbein expressed his frustration that even after four decades of development, all the sample masks he could source in 1961 – from the Swiss, French and British teams he contacted – were essentially the same 'RAF type' mask.[38] (This led him to design a new 'all-American' oxygen mask, which played a part in the nationalist rhetoric used in the funding bids, important not least because the National Geographic Society refused to fund the purchase of French oxygen tanks which were needed to work with the various European masks.)[39] Likewise, although rebreathers were considered and occasionally trialled by the British teams from the 1920s onwards, the 1953 British Everest Expedition team eventually had to

116 *Vanessa Heggie*

redirect focus onto developing a simple oxygen supply system that would work on the mountain: they could not afford to split their labour and funding on two different systems, one of which was deeply experimental. Despite occasional flurries of interest after the 1950s, rebreathers never achieved the traction in mountaineering as they did for diving.

Mask technology is also an excellent case study of the Eurocentrism of altitude physiology in the middle of the twentieth century. Offering feedback to Hornbein about the fit of the 'RAF style oxygen masks', John Cotes – who had designed these masks himself – noted that they were largely satisfactory, except in the case of the Sherpa porters, whose "flat noses . . . presented difficulty" requiring on-site alterations, mostly the use of "extra padding".[40] For 40 years, European and American teams had relied both on oxygen systems and on Sherpa porters yet had never developed a mask to fit them; further, despite registering this issue officially, and bemoaning the lack of mask diversity, the problem persisted. In 1971, the International Himalayan Expedition obviously thought it had solved the issue by taking two types of mask, both from the US Air Force, one branded 'Caucasian' and the other 'Oriental'. Apparently, to the team's surprise, the 'Oriental' model, based on Vietnamese fighter pilot's faces, did not fit the Sherpa.[41]

This neglect brings me to another insight that mountain research provides – it shines a clear light on the role of the peoples indigenous to altitude, as well as other forms of 'local' guide and expert. Again, the story of South American and South Asian populations differs significantly. In the Andean regions, a strong autochthonous research tradition built up through the middle of the twentieth century, especially in Peru, which focused on altitude physiology and in some cases did so in explicit opposition to the racialised assumptions made by visiting Northern Hemisphere scientists. These research institutions were important hosts for visiting researchers (and mountaineers) and were plugged in to complex South American networks of science and politics, which mobilised indigenous identities in various ways to represent a united or diverse national image, depending on circumstances.[42] Conversely, Sherpa and other Asian altitude populations remained almost invisible in altitude physiology, despite their superior performances being part of Western mountaineering tradition since at least the 1920s. Likewise, the founding of research institutes focusing on extreme physiology was later in the Asian nations than in South America. While South America boasted the Instituto by the 1930s, the major source of Indian altitude physiology research, the Defence Institute of Physiology and Allied Sciences (DIPAS), was formed only in 1962, in part in response to conflict with China. Its historical materials cite the Silver Hut expedition as inspiration – more, in fact, as the silver hut itself was dismantled and donated to the Indian government, becoming a regular space for DIPAS research through the 1970s, albeit in a new location at Chowri Kang (which is closer to an Alpine height, at 4,500 m above sea level, than the original Himalayan location of the hut at 5,800 m above sea level).[43]

The founding of local research institutes and the stimulation of (often military) interest in mountain physiology led to increased study of altitude-adapted peoples. It is hard to account for the apparent disinterest of Western scientists in studies of South Asian peoples prior to the 1960s, but the main reason seems to be an assumption that all altitude populations adapted in the same ways, so that studying any one stood in for any other.[44] As Western researchers often reported that Sherpa were 'less willing' to participate in medical research than comparative Andean populations, the lure of better infrastructure and apparently willing (and universally relevant) human subjects may explain the skew of study towards South American populations. This was, as it turns out, a mistake, as when efforts were made to examine Sherpa populations, the discovery was made that adaptation to altitude is *not* a homogenous process. While Andean populations and sea-level-born visitors adapt to altitude by the upregulation of red blood cell production, Sherpa and other Himalayan peoples adapt in literally the opposite way, by thinning their blood.[45]

Western mountain research did not have to make this mistake; in fact, as early as 1925, a British doctor reported on "anomalous" findings in the blood he persuaded his Sherpa porters to "donate" to his studies.[46] Taken on the 1921 British expedition to Everest, the team doctor Thomas H. Somervell pursued respiratory studies as well as doing blood work on the mountain (again belying the idea of the exploration-focused, anti-science British amateur expeditions). Unfortunately, the blood work was a sideline to the main project, which – directed by the focus on oxygen technology – concentrated on collecting and analysing the air expired by the mountaineers at mid and high altitude. This gas work was seriously compromised by the fact that Somervell collected the expired air in bladders from the insides of footballs (soccer balls), which proved porous to carbon dioxide, making the analysis conducted later at Base Camp and elsewhere almost worthless. It is unclear why Somervell's findings on Sherpa blood were apparently unnoticed by the rest of Western science, but perhaps his experimental failings distracted from the conclusion of the work, where the comparatively low red cell counts of the Sherpa are mentioned almost as an afterthought. It is also possible that the assumption of increased red blood cell production (polycythaemia) as a response to altitude was so firmly established by the 1920s that a small amount of contradictory data was not enough to redirect scientific work. The cliché that scientists stand on the shoulders of those who precede them also means that sometimes they too narrowly follow in their tracks or their footprints – as we have seen with the technology of survival, the pressures of mountainside research sometimes acted to limit research questions and avenues of investigation. High altitude-research was expensive, time limited and dangerous, and to a degree, this may have limited the innovation of research or made investigators more conservative when it came to the studies they pursued, picking only (what they believed to be) the most important studies or those most likely to produce solid results.

The 'footprints' the mountaineering physiologists trod in were literal as well as metaphorical. High-altitude studies also demonstrate how *crowded* these apparently remote and 'exotic' field sites were. While expeditions did scope and test new routes on a fairly regular basis, there is also a natural conservatism forced by the geography of mountains: from the 1920s onwards, expeditions to Everest almost always traced over a route that had at least in part been traversed by previous expeditions, and the same became true of other mountains (including the Andes) through the middle of the twentieth century. Sometimes such choices were explicit – J.S. Haldane chose Pikes Peak in Colorado, USA, as a research space in 1911 in part because there was a train running to the summit. This eased the challenge of transport (particularly getting sensitive experimental equipment up the mountain) but also allowed research opportunities, as climbers who had walked gradually up the mountain, and presumably 'acclimatised' to altitude could be compared to the train riders who experienced a rapid ascent.[47] This echoes that significant difference between Andean and Himalayan research (indeed, this could be expanded to a rough generalisation about research in the Americas versus the Asian mountains) – where the former focused on infrastructure and indigenous/local populations for study and the latter sought more remote and field-based studies.

Unpopulated mountains were not, however, unpeopled. There are plenty of accounts of 'accidental' encounters in the reports of Himalayan expeditions, and some of these have direct impacts on research practices. The research programme at Silver Hut in the early 1960s relied on the climbing and research team on the expedition as human guinea pigs, but when a Nepalese monk unexpectedly turned up at the glacier laboratory, Pugh immediately took advantage of the opportunity to study a locally born resident.[48] Even crucial logistical information could be passed "by accident" – as is the case of the physiologist John West meeting Tom Hornbein on the way back from Silver Hut and letting him know that there was a new airstrip near Everest base camp, a fact Hornbein thought was extremely "useful knowledge" in terms of getting medical and experimental supplies in to the region.[49] Whilst these personal encounters were often significant, the most frequent and possibly important forms of human contact were via material culture: the debris, rubbish, lost objects and abandoned items that mountaineers left on the mountainside itself.

Just as the accounts of the scientific work of the 1920s and 1930s belie the notion of the gentleman amateur on the mountain, so the accounts of the 1950s and 1960s give the lie to the idea of the pristine, remote or untouched research space. In reality, due to the limited safe routes on the mountains, explorers repeatedly discovered the evidence of previous human residents. Indeed, sometimes this was actively factored into the exploration and its experiments: in 1952, Pugh went to Zurich to meet with the Swiss team who had just returned from their unsuccessful attempt on Everest to discuss with them their physiological experiences and get them to "point out on photographs the approximate positions where charged oxygen cylinders had been left on the mountain" with the intention of incorporating them into the logistical planning of the 1953 British attempt on the mountain.[50] This recycling of abandoned technologies also emphasises and reinforces the conservation of technology – to use a tank, it must be compatible with your own team's respiratory technology. Other encounters were more serendipitous, such as the discovery of one of the Swiss team's abandoned food caches, unveiled by Tenzing Norgay to reveal "frozen Swiss orange juice, the most delicious of all imaginable drinks".[51]

The importance of recycled and repurposed human litter should not be underestimated – it is possible that one of the most significant physiological research moments on Everest was only possible because of abandoned technology: in 1981, Dr Chris Pizzo took the first-ever physiological measurements on the summit of the mountain, collecting his alveolar air at 8,848 metres. On the morning he was due to ascend, Pizzo discovered he had lost his ice axe – a disaster – but a few meters from his high camp, he found another, simply lying in the snow, and with this, he successfully summitted. The ice axe, it was later confirmed, had belonged to the German climber Hannelore Schmatz, who had died on a retreat from the summit two years earlier.[52] During the very same expedition, Pizzo's colleague, Peter Hackett, was saved from certain death when he found a rope fixed to the mountain by an unknown previous climber and was able to pull himself out of a dangerous position, having fallen down an ice sheet on the Western Cwm.

The impact of human remains on the mountainside – bodies as well as technologies – should rightfully be the subject of its own chapter. Through to the 1980s, almost everyone involved in high-altitude research will have experienced some form of loss in relation to the mountainside, including friends, family and colleagues, as well as the less well-acknowledged deaths of Sherpa porters and guides. Those who fell or froze to death on the mountainside like Mallory, Irvine or Schmatz are the famous cases, but explorers and scientists succumbed to illness on expeditions, like Dr Kellas dying from dysentery on the British expedition to Everest in 1921, or died in more dramatic circumstances, such as Peter Mulgrew, who survived a disastrous attempt on Makalu (led by Edmund Hillary) during the Silver Hut expedition – albeit having to have both his feet amputated – but then died in the Air New Zealand 901 crash in Antarctica in 1979, having taken Hillary's place on the trip as a commentator. While much has been written, critically in most cases, about the callousness that leads climbers to treat human corpses as way markers, or sightseeing 'must dos', such a response can be seen as a necessary form of self-protection. For many high-altitude climbers, the risk of encountering the material remains – ice axe, tent, corpse – of a dead colleague was an almost inevitable part of the experience. This is also a direct consequence of the fact that while the mountain might not have been a pristine and empty field site, it was one that contained a fairly limited, self-selecting population.

I have written elsewhere on the processes by which extreme physiologists created a tight field of practice, with limited opportunities for entry and conservative hiring practices.[53] The metaphor of 'treading in others' footsteps' does multiple work in the high Andes and Himalaya: we have seen that routes and technology could be developed only cautiously, building on previous experiences at each iteration. So too could the personnel allowed into, and, one presumes, the research questions asked in, extreme physiology research spaces. The same names, and the same institutions, crop up time after time across extreme physiology research spaces, not just at high altitude but also in the Antarctic or the Australian outback; frequently, the leading researchers of one generation were trained by the small group of elite explorer-scientists of the preceding one. It is hard to evidence a counterfactual, but it is worth speculating whether the lack of 'fresh blood' in these research spaces might also have acted as a force of conservatism: in routes, technology and research focus. This could in part explain the lack of research on Sherpa through the first two-thirds of the twentieth century.[54]

Conclusion

This chapter has offered an overview of the biomedical and physiological work conducted on, and around, the highest mountains on earth. Throughout, these researchers, usually physiologists and/or expedition doctors, have juggled two interests: first, the immediate wellbeing of the expedition, often including the support of an extreme mountaineering goal. For this purpose, they tested oxygen sets, analysed ration packs and paid close attention to the psychological wellbeing of their colleagues. But in almost all cases, the physiologists and doctors sought to bring something back from the mountain, too – a knowledge about basic physiology, about the effect of altitude, about the technology of survival that would be useful in other contexts. Often these contexts were military, but sometimes this was for other forms of frontier exploration, such as the AMEE 1963's aim to support space exploration.[55] Research was also 'basic' and has fed back into everyday human experiences, such as Ancel Key's later life interest in obesity and heart disease or more recent work on Everest that seeks to inform the treatment of seriously ill patients in intensive care units.[56] So despite the fact that these studies looked at the limits of human performance and were conducted in marginal or remote geographical spaces, they were nonetheless serious pieces of contemporary science and part of a global traffic in biomedical knowledge. The dual identity of the mountainside as both a unique field site for environment-specific research and as a potential 'natural laboratory' to produce generalisable, universalisable knowledge is a tension threaded through this research and has been examined in more detail in other works,[57] but it can be seen in this chapter that they were important sites for truth-making alongside, and sometimes instead of, laboratories.

As margins and frontiers – both of space and of knowledge – high mountains have also functioned as contact sites. This chapter has outlined how everyday technologies and even 'basic' research can reveal the colonial, racialised assumptions of modern biomedicine. This is particularly evident in the way in which mountain research has both used and neglected the bodies of populations indigenous to altitude. Racialised assumptions about adaptation to altitude and about the ability of 'primitive' populations to participate in modern Western science have clearly affected the direction of Western scientific work, and it is still unclear how much, and to what ends, mid-altitude populations benefited (or otherwise) from twentieth-century scientific exploration of altitude.[58] Finally, then, this chapter demonstrates how paradoxically well travelled and populated these frontier sites really were; although only by a limited and constrained group of travellers and researchers, they left their traces and their tracks – and sometimes their bodies – in these marginal spaces.

Notes

1 The key text here is John B. West, *High Life: A History of High-Altitude Physiology and Medicine* (New York: Published for the American Physiological Society by Oxford University Press, 1998).
2 Vanessa Heggie, *Higher and Colder: A History of Extreme Physiology and Exploration* (Chicago: University of Chicago Press, 2019).
3 Vanessa Heggie, "Experimental Physiology, Everest and Oxygen: From the Ghastly Kitchens to the Gasping Lung", *The British Journal for the History of Science* 46, no. 1 (2013): 123–147; Harriet Tuckey, *Everest: The First Ascent: The Untold Story of Griffith Pugh, the Man Who Made It Possible* (London: Rider, 2013).
4 Max Jones, *The Last Great Quest: Captain Scott's Antarctic Sacrifice* (Oxford: Oxford University Press, 2003).
5 Philipp Felsch, "Mountains of Sublimity, Mountains of Fatigue: Towards a History of Speechlessness in the Alps", *Science in Context* 22, no. 3 (2009): 341–364; Caroline Schaumann, *Peak Pursuits: The Emergence of Mountaineering in the Nineteenth Century* (New Haven: Yale University Press, 2020).
6 Vanessa Heggie, "Why Isn't Exploration a Science?", *Isis* 105, no. 2 (June 2014): 318–349.
7 Compare to the analysis of the 'use' of circumpolar peoples: Tess Lanzarotta, "Ethics in Retrospect: Biomedical Research, Colonial Violence, and Iñupiat Sovereignty in the Alaskan Arctic", *Social Studies of Science* (2020). doi: 10.1177/0306312720943678.
8 Philip W. Clements, *Science in an Extreme Environment: The 1963 American Mount Everest Expedition* (Pittsburgh: University of Pittsburgh Press, 2018); Vanessa Heggie, "Extreme Acts: Narratives of Balance and Moderation at the Limits of Human Performance", in *Balancing the Self: Medicine, Politics and the Regulation of Health in the Twentieth Century*, eds. Mark Jackson and Martin D. Moore (Manchester: Manchester University Press, 2020), 219–249.
9 Michael Dettelbach, "The Stimulations of Travel: Humboldt's Physiological Construction of the Tropics", in *Tropical Visions in an Age of Empire*, eds. Felix Driver and Luciana Martins (Chicago: University of Chicago Press, 2005), 42–58.
10 Daniel L. Gilbert, "The First Documented Report of Mountain Sickness: The China or Headache Mountain Story", *Respiration Physiology* 52, no. 3 (1983): 315–326.
11 Paul Bert, *La Pression Barométrique. Recherches De Physiologie Expérimentale, Etc* (Paris: G. Masson, 1878), 28.
12 Bert, *La Pression*, Section 8 "Asie Centrale".
13 Translation from Paul Bert, *Barometric Pressure, Researches in Experimental Physiology*, trans. Mary Alice Hitchcock and Fred A. Hitchcock (Columbus, OH: College Book Company, 1943), 147.
14 See West, *High Life* and John B West and Jean-Paul Richalet, "Denis Jourdanet (1815–1892) and the Early Recognition of the Role of Hypoxia at High Altitude", *American Journal of Physiology* 305 (2013): I.333–I.340.
15 Jeremy S. Windsor and George W. Rodway, "Heights and Haematology: The Story of Haemoglobin at Altitude", *Postgraduate Medical Journal* 83, no. 977 (2007): 148–151.
16 Robin Wolfe Scheffler, "The Fate of a Progressive Science: The Harvard Fatigue Laboratory, Athletes, the Science of Work and the Politics of Reform", *Endeavour* 35, no. 2 (2011): 48–54.
17 Steven M. Horvath and Elizabeth C. Horvath, *The Harvard Fatigue Laboratory: Its History and Contributions* (Englewood Cliffs, NJ: Prentice-Hall, 1973); Sarah W. Tracy, "The Physiology of Extremes: Ancel Keys and the International High Altitude Expedition of 1935", *Bulletin of the History of Medicine* 86, no. 4 (2012): 627–660.
18 Sarah W. Tracy, "Interdisciplinary Interprofessionalism at Mid-Century: Ancel Keys, Human Biology, and the Laboratory of Physiological Hygiene, 1940–1950", *Nursing History Review* 24, no. 1 (2016): 81–89.

19. Marcos Cueto, "Andean Biology in Peru: Scientific Styles on the Periphery", *Isis* 80, no. 4 (1989): 640–658.
20. Tuckey, *Everest – The First Ascent*.
21. James S. Milledge, "The Silver Hut Expedition, 1960–1961", *High Altitude Medicine & Biology* 11, no. 2 (2010): 93–101.
22. For an example of handwriting and other tests in chambers, see Ulrich Cameron Luft, "Höhenanpassung", *Ergebnisse Der Physiologie, Biologischen Chemie Und Experimentellen Pharmakologie* 44 (1941): 256–314.
23. J. Barcroft et al., "Observations Upon the Effect of High Altitude on the Physiological Processes of the Human Body, Carried Out in the Peruvian Andes, Chiefly at Cerro de Pasco", *Philosophical Transactions of the Royal Society of London. Series B, Containing Papers of a Biological Character* 211 (1923): 436–437.
24. Martin Burtscher et al., "Arnold Durig (1872–1961): Life and Work: An Austrian Pioneer in Exercise and High Altitude Physiology", *High Altitude Medicine & Biology* 13, no. 3 (2012): 224–231.
25. Clements, *Science in an Extreme Environment*, 18.
26. Clements, *Science in an Extreme Environment*, 18.
27. Vanessa Heggie, "Bodies, Sport and Science in the Nineteenth Century", *Past & Present* 231, no. 1 (2016): 169–200.
28. See the extensive discussion of weight loss and its cause in Hans Hartmann, Günter Hepp and Ulrich C. Luft, "Physiologische Beobachtungen am Nanga Parbat 1937/1938", *Luftfahrtmedizin* 6 (1942): 10–44.
29. See: Paul Gilchrist, "The Politics of Totemic Sporting Heroes and the Conquest of Everest", *Anthropological Notebooks* 12 (2006): 41.
30. Mandeville Special Collections Library, University of California, San Diego [henceforth: Mandeville]. Pugh Papers (MSS491), box 35, folder 1, letter, M. W. Grant to Pugh, 14 November 1952.
31. Heggie, "Experimental Physiology".
32. Royal Geographical Society Archives, London; RGS/EP EE/38/3/5/1 Everest Equipment Memorandum.
33. Wellcome Library, Archives & Manuscripts, London, UK Explorers Cuttings Book (WF/M/GB/35).
34. Royal Geographical Society Archives, London; RGS/EP EE/22/1/8 Baldrey to Colonel Bruce, 22 November 1923.
35. Vanessa Heggie, "Blood, Race and Indigenous Peoples in Twentieth Century Extreme Physiology", *History and Philosophy of the Life Sciences* 41, no. 2 (2019): 26.
36. J.B. West et al., "Barometric Pressures at Extreme Altitudes on Mt. Everest: Physiological Significance", *Journal of Applied Physiology* 54 (1983): 1188–1194.
37. See also Lanzarotta, "Ethics in Retrospect".
38. Mandeville, Hornbein Papers (MSS669), box 31, folder 7, Report by Hornbein on Development of Oxygen Masks, c. 1961.
39. Clements, *Science in an Extreme Environment*, 63. American gas and mask companies were relatively slow to respond to these exhortations to make a better "American" project; see, for example: Mandeville, Hornbein Papers (MSS668), Box 31 folder 7, Letter Hornbein to Harry L Daulton president Sierrra Engineering, 2 January 1961, & 21 January 1961; Letter Dyrehnfurth to Mr Minto Dole, Union Carbide, 9 June 1961; Letter John A. Cusimano Zep. Aero to Hornbein 7 February 1962.
40. "Mandeville, Hornbein Papers (MSS669), box 31, folder 7, letter, John Cotes to Hornbein, 11 January 1962.
41. Walt Unsworth, *Everest: The Mountaineering History*, 3rd ed. (London: Bâton Wicks, 2000), 40.
42. Marcos Cueto, "Andean Biology in Peru: Scientific Styles on the Periphery", *Isis* 80, no. 4 (1989): 640–658.

43 J.B. West, "Letter from Chowri Kang", *High Altitude Medicine & Biology* 2, no. 2 (2001): 311–313; D. Dass and G. Bhaumik, "The Silver Hut Experiment", *Science Reporter* (2012), http://nopr.niscair.res.in/bitstream/123456789/15016/1/SR%20 49%2811%29%2056-57.pdf, last access 13 September 2021.
44 Heggie, "Blood, Race and Indigenous Peoples".
45 Heggie, "Blood, Race and Indigenous Peoples".
46 T. Howard Somervell, "Note on the Composition of Alveolar Air at Extreme Heights", *The Journal of Physiology* 60, no. 4 (1925): 282–285.
47 J.S. Haldane, "Acclimatisation to High Altitude", *Physiological Reviews* 7, no. 3 (1927): 363–384.
48 L.G.C.E. Pugh, "Tolerance to Extreme Cold at Altitude in a Nepalese Pilgrim", *Journal of Applied Physiology* 18 (1963): 1236.
49 Mandeville, Hornbein Papers (MSS669), box 31, folder 6, letter, Hornbein to Dyhrenfurth, 30 July 1961.
50 John Hunt, *The Ascent of Everest* (London: Hodder & Stoughton, 1953), 51.
51 Wilfred Noyce, *South Col: The Personal Account of One Man's Adventure on Everest* (London: The Reprint Society, 1955), 87.
52 John B. West, "American Medical Research Expedition to Everest, 1981", *Himalayan Journal* 39 (1981–1982): 25.
53 Heggie, *Higher and Colder*.
54 For more on the sometimes mutually misunderstood relationship between Sherpa and western climbers, see: Sherry B. Ortner, *Life and Death on Mt. Everest: Sherpas and Himalayan Mountaineering* (Princeton, NJ: Princeton University Press, 1999).
55 Clements, *Science in an Extreme Environment*.
56 Tracy, "Interdisciplinary Interprofessionalism"; recent high-altitude expeditions, such as the Caudwell Xtreme Everest Expedition, specifically link high altitude and ICU research – although also working on 'solving' the puzzle of Sherpa performance; see James A. Horscroft et al., "Metabolic Basis to Sherpa Altitude Adaptation", *Proceedings of the National Academy of Sciences* 114, no. 24 (2017): 6382–6387.
57 Clements, *Science in an Extreme Environment*; Heggie, "Experimental Physiology, Everest and Oxygen", Felsch, "Mountains of Sublimity".
58 Heggie, "Blood, Race and Indigenous Peoples"; Ortner, *Life and Death on Mt. Everest*. The story in South America is somewhat different to that of the Himalaya: Marcos Cueto, "Andean Biology in Peru: Scientific Styles on the Periphery", *Isis* 80, no. 4 (1989): 640–658.

8 Italian geographers, scientists, travellers and mountaineers in the Karakoram (1890–1954)

Stefano Morosini

Introduction

Via an analysis of largely previously unseen archival sources and an examination of the contemporary literature, the purpose of this chapter is to reconstruct the role played by Italian geographers, scientists, travellers and mountaineers in exploration of the mountainous Karakoram region from late nineteenth century to the well-known 1954 first ascent of K2 (8,611 m).[1] Beyond Valle d'Aosta-based Roberto Lercoz's mysterious and adventurous journey to the foot of K2 in 1890 and what was probably the first ascent attempt, and explorations from 1892 onwards by English- and German-speaking travellers led by Italian mountain guides, this chapter will focus on the 1909 expedition led by Luigi Amedeo di Savoia-Aosta, Duke of Abruzzi, before continuing with that organised by Filippo De Filippi (1913–1914); the 1928–1929 expedition led by Aimone di Savoia-Aosta, Duke of Spoleto; Giotto Dainelli's 1930 geographic exploration; and the international expedition led by German Gunther Oskar Dyhrenfurth with mountaineer Piero Ghiglione as one of its members (1934). After the description of these different experiences, the main focus will be on an examination of the well-known 1954 Ardito Desio expedition which culminated in the first ascent of K2. First, the following sections will examine the personal stories of the individuals who took part in these adventures. Second, the chapter will illustrate the considerable prestige, fame and aura of heroism achieved, in particular, by those breaking altitude records and making first ascents to 6,000-, 7,000- and 8,000-metre-high peaks. As Peter Hansen observed in 1995, during the eighteenth and nineteenth centuries, "the possession of a mountaintop was a title to lordship", and "conquest transferred prestige from the mountain to the climber".[2] In addition to a concise list of participants; a description of the areas travelled to; and the most significant geographical, scientific and/or mountaineering achievements of the various expeditions, the chapter will finally analyse the great visibility enjoyed by such expeditions in Italy and elsewhere from the end of the nineteenth century to the end of the 1950s – passing through two terrible world wars and in the midst of the decolonisation process – and their resulting political and national significance. In this same period, in fact, Italians were not the only ones who explored the Karakoram region. American, Austrian, British, Dutch, French, German and Swiss expeditions also

DOI: 10.4324/9781003095965-9

had their sights set on it. With rivalry of this sort, for an international power of secondary status like Italy, Karakoram represented a significant terrain of "vertical colonialism".[3] In the specific context of Italian history, all this took place at three very different phases (liberal, Fascist and democratic/republican), featuring elements of both continuity and discontinuity.

First expeditions of Italian mountaineers, Alpine guides and topographers (1890–1912)

The little-known expedition carried out by Roberto Lercoz – traveller and mountaineer born in Gressoney, Valle d'Aosta – in 1861 constitutes the first time the Karakoram was approached with mountaineering ambitions. Of this journey, fragmentary but interesting documentary evidence exists. Lercoz was the nephew of Johann Nicolaus Vincent, owner of a gold mine at Alagna Valsesia (Vercelli) and the first to climb two peaks in the Monte Rosa massif, Piramide Vincent (4,215 m) and Punta Zumstein (4,563 m) in 1819–1820. From a wealthy Walser family (and thus a native German speaker), Lercoz had travelled extensively in Europe and the United States at his own expense. In 1887, he went to the Caucasus with Swiss Alpine guide Jakob Müller of Gsteigwiler (Berner Oberland), completing the third ascent of Mt Elbrus (5,642 m) and the second of Mt Kazbek (5,047 m) at length unclimbed on its southeast face.

In 1890, accompanied by guide Matthias Zurbriggen of Macugnaga (an Italian town located under the east face of Monte Rosa), he undertook a lengthy journey through Karakoram, the Himalayas and Tibet during which he climbed up to the Baltoro glacier and made a first mysterious attempt on K2 before adverse weather conditions and an avalanche hitting his tent forced him to turn back. On his return to Italy, the British Royal Geographical Society invited Lercoz to London to speak at a conference on his adventurous exploits, which he turned down.[4] In October 1954, the Club Alpino Italiano (hereafter CAI) journal *Lo Scarpone* devoted an article to him and attributed this refusal to attend the prestigious conference to Lercoz's personal reticence and excessive modesty, despite his being "the first European to take on the terrible mountain".[5] Effectively, with the exception of an article published in 1888 in the CAI's *Bollettino* taken from a longer, never published report on the Caucasus mountains,[6] Lercoz never published anything on his pioneering explorations at all. The only tangible proof of this mysterious journey to Karakoram is, in fact, two hunting trophies held at the Turin Museo Nazionale della Montagna and Museo Beck-Peccoz in Gressoney Saint-Jean (Aosta). These are both horns of ibex shot by Lercoz in Karakoram in June and July 1890.[7]

As previously mentioned, Lercoz was accompanied by mountain guide Matthias Zurbriggen. The presence of mountain guides, mountaineers or scientists on multiple Karakoram expeditions is an important constant in all the cases analysed here, as they were seen as having direct experience of an area remote to most Europeans. Based on the knowledge of the area acquired in 1890, Zurbriggen was also recruited by William Martin Conway for the 1892 organised expedition, which focused, however, on the Hispar, Biafo, Braldo and Baltoro glacier valleys to the glacial cirque offering wide-ranging views of K2, which Conway himself named after the Concordia circus. In continuing the Baltoro glacier ascent, Conway and Zurbriggen achieved the first ascent of Pioneer Peak (6,790 m) and, in so doing, broke the altitude record of the time.[8]

Zurbriggen merits a brief biographical description. Born in 1856 in Saas-Fee, in Valais canton, he emigrated from Switzerland to Italy in his early childhood when his cobbler father found a job as miner in Macugnaga. During his childhood, before becoming one of the most important and respected Alpine guides of his generation, he wandered across Europe and North Africa working at whatever came his way. His linguistic – he spoke German, Italian, English and French – and mountaineering skills led to Zurbriggen attracting an important, cosmopolitan mountaineering clientele who not only employed him to accompany them on Alpine ascents, especially in the Monte Rosa massif, but also paid him to come with them on explorations and pioneering ascents outside Europe. In addition to the Karakoram expedition referred to here, in 1894–1895 Zurbriggen also travelled to New Zealand where he made a number of first ascents with American mountaineer Edward Arthur FitzGerald before returning the following year with wealthy Italian hat manufacturer Giuseppe Borsalino. He then went to South America, where, in January 1897, he carried out the first ascent of Mt. Aconcagua (6,962 m), solo, and in 1900 to the Tien Shan massif with Prince Scipione Borghese, where he completed a series of ascents. After years of travelling across some of the world's extreme locations, in the last years of his life, Zurbriggen succumbed to serious personal difficulties which led to alcoholism, vagrancy and finally suicide in Geneva in 1917.[9]

Zurbriggen returned to Karakoram in 1899 to lead the American explorer couple Fanny Bullock and William Hunter Workman and German topographer Johann Wilhelm Karl Oestreich along the Biafo glacier to the Hispar pass.[10] The party then travelled the length of the Shigar valley and completed the first ascent of Koser Gunge (6,400 m). With this climb, Fanny broke the record for the highest altitude then climbed by a woman by over 1,000 metres.[11] After their ascents with Zurbriggen, the Workmans ventured into the Karakoram (getting into the mountains principally by means of bicycles!) on many other occasions, always in the company of Courmayeur Alpine guides and Cyprien Savoye first and foremost. In 1903, guides Joseph and Laurent Petigax were also present while, in 1908, carriers Adolphe Rey, Ferdinando Meliga, Cesare Chenoz and little-known Piacenza count naturalist and topographer Cesare Calciati also took part. In 1911, the Workmans were back in Karakoram again with Cesare Calciati, guide Cyprien Savoye and carriers (once again from Courmayeur) Cesare Chenoz (at his second expedition), Simeone Quaisier and Emilio Glérey and in 1912 with guide Cyprien Savoye and English topographer Grant Peterkin and carriers Cesare Chenoz (who was on his third expedition, fell into a crevasse and died), Simeone Quaisier and brothers Adolphe and Henry Rey.[12]

The expedition led by Luigi Amedeo di Savoia-Aosta, Duke of Abruzzi (1909)

The 1909 Karakoram expedition led by Luigi Amedeo di Savoia-Aosta, Duke of Abruzzi, stands out from the previously mentioned experiences for its institutional character and the huge funds required for it. Undertaken at the behest of Istituto Geografico Militare, which was the first Italian topographical expedition beyond Italy's national boundaries, the part played by explorer, mountaineer and royal family member Luigi Amedeo di Savoia-Aosta, Duke of Abruzzi, was a key one. Participants included famous mountaineer and photographer Vittorio Sella; Turinese doctor Filippo De Filippi; topographer Federico Negrotto and assistant photographer Erminio Botta; Courmayeur Alpine guides Joseph and Laurent Petigax (who, as we have seen, had already visited Karakoram in 1903 with the Workmans); brothers Alexis and Henri Brocherel; and three carriers, also from Courmayeur, Emile Brocherel, Albert Savoye and Ernest Bareux.

A considerable international limelight was shined on the expedition as a result of its ascents. First of all, the attempt on K2 reached an altitude of 6,200 metres along its southeast spur, then named Sperone Abruzzi. K2's west face was also explored for the first time after a pass had been identified at 6,666 metres on its northwestern ridge (called Savoia Pass for the occasion). The group climbed up from the Austen glacier in a northerly direction, attempting to climb Skyang Kangri (7,544 m) and reaching an altitude of 6,600 metres. The party then moved southwards and attempted to climb Chogolisa (or Bride Peak, 7,665 m), reaching an altitude of 7,498 metres, the highest altitude then ever achieved.

> Every English climber will regret that so gallant an attempt was not crowned with complete success. But as it stands, these two climbs on Bride peak and the three on weeks' bivouac on Chogolisa saddle surpass all previous achievements in the annals of in the high mountaineering.[13]

The great publicity given to Vittorio Sella's stunning photographs brought the great Karakoram mountains (and the striking and imposing K2 pyramid in particular) and its majestic glaciers to a large international audience for the first time. Filippo De Filippi's detailed report became the main reference for the knowledge of the region.[14]

The expedition led by Filippo De Filippi (1913–1914)

De Filippi's official 1909 expedition report repeatedly highlighted that various Karakoram areas remained unexplored and many aspects of the region unknown. This was the reason behind De Filippi's decision to organise a new, primarily scientific expedition in the immediately following years. He sought and obtained financial support from the Italian government and the sponsorship and patronage of prestigious Italian and international institutions such as Accademia dei Lincei,

Società Geografica Italiana, Société Internationale de Physique, the Royal Geographical Society and the Royal Society.[15] A large number of scientists involved in wide-reaching studies across Italy took part in this expedition, which lasted up to 17 months (August 1913–December 1914): Florence University's famous geographers Giotto Dainelli and Olinto Marinelli, astronomer Giorgio Abetti, geodesy scholar Alberto Alessio, meteorologists Camillo Alessandri and Nello Venturi Ginori, photographer Cesare Antilli and Alpine guide Joseph Petigax (previously in Karakoram in 1903 and 1909). The Indian trigonometry office also took part in the expedition with two representatives Henry Wood and John Alfred Spranger and topographers Jamna Pershad and Shib Lal.

The exploration model adopted by De Filippi, with smaller research groups breaking off from the main party for brief trips, enabled it to gather a huge amount of data and bring in important results: the Rima glacier was explored and the source of the river Yarcand identified; maps of the region were drawn up; and important environmental surveys took place, with a great many fossils and samples collected. A grand total of 2,600 photographs were taken and catalogued and a film camera used to make several hundreds of metres of film documented the everyday life of the local community and religious festivals in Baltistan and Ladakh. In the summer of 1914, the expedition was brought to a premature and unforeseen end by the outbreak of World War I. Considering that Italy, having declared neutrality in early August 1914, did not take a direct part in the fighting until May 1915, the expedition planned to continue into Chinese Turkmenistan (now the Xinjang region), involving suspending communications for weeks, perhaps months. At this point, three of the expedition's members (Alessandri, Alessio and Antilli) decided to return home right away through India and the Red Sea and then by rail from Port Said to Alexandria, while the others separated off into independent groups, completing the planned surveys and returning to Italy only in December 1914, after crossing southern Russia and Romania. The expedition's scientific results were published in a large series of high-quality, accurate volumes and maps from 1920 onwards.[16]

The expedition led by Aimone di Savoia-Aosta, Duke of Spoleto (1928–1929)

Plans for a new Italian expedition to Karakoram dated to 1927 and certainly stemmed from the desire for international prestige linked to enterprises, such as reaching the North Pole and the top of one of the 14 unclimbed over-8,000-metre peaks. Benito Mussolini greeted these highly ambitious goals warmly in a period in which his regime was asserting its power domestically and explorations could be used as propagandistic tools. Milanese political and entrepreneurial elites pushed for and supported the plan, aiming to get to the peak of K2 or, failing that, the lower and more accessible Broad Peak (8,047 m). Geographer Giotto Dainelli (who had taken part in the 1913–1914 De Filippi expedition) was appointed leader but soon had to stand down as a result of serious organisational delays and conflicts within the sponsorship committee. It was then, thanks to the good offices of the Società Geografica Italiana, who had, in the meantime, come on board, that the availability of young and inexperienced prince Aimone di Savoia-Aosta, Duke of Spoleto (29 years of age), was sounded out and soon obtained. The expedition documentation, recently rediscovered in the Milan Cittadella degli Archivi and inventoried in a Milan University project,[17] has enabled the project's stages to be reconstructed.

Dainelli's concerns were well founded: reaching the Karakoram region in the summer of 1928 meant leaving from Italy in early March at the very latest. The impossibility of respecting this deadline meant that it had to be put off to the following year and with only a reconnaissance expedition being undertaken that year with a purpose to transporting foodstuffs and mountaineering material to Askole, in the Shigar valley (modern-day Pakistan). This preparatory journey took Aimone di Savoia-Aosta five months (mid-May to mid-October 1928), and he was accompanied by army captain Mario Cugia and Turin magistrate and mountaineer Umberto Balestreri.

While this expedition was being prepared, on 25 May 1928, the dramatic accident of the *Italia* airship flown by Umberto Nobile occurred. *Italia* was returning from a flight over the North Pole when it crashed accidentally onto the ice pack to the north of the Svalbard islands.[18] The massive and, in turn, eventful rescue operations organised, the consequent increased costs and, above all, the serious damage to Italy's image internationally with the "inhumane and anti-Italian wave which struck the protagonists of this unfortunate enterprise"[19] led to Mussolini himself getting involved, determining that the Karakoram expedition was to give up all mountaineering ambitions and take on an exclusively (and prudently) scientific character.[20] The number of participants was thus reduced and cost estimates trimmed from 2 million lire to 1 million six hundred (a reduction, in today's money, from around €1,820,000 to €1,460,000).[21]

Twelve people took part in the second, and principal, expedition phase: its commander, Aimone di Savoia; captain Mario Cugia, in charge of its organisation; Umberto Balestreri, camp and convoy leader; lieutenant colonel Gino Allegri, doctor and surgeon and responsible for the expedition's official diary; geologist Ardito Desio, Milan University professor and responsible for geological surveys and geographical observations; Count Lodovico di Caporiacco, zoologist, who carried out nature collections; Giuseppe Chiardola, engineer and mineral expert, geological assistant and topographer; Vittorio Ponti, assistant camp and convoy leader; Angelo Anfossi, navy radio-telegraph operator; filmmaker Massimo Terzano; and two Courmayeur Alpine guides, Leone Bron and Evaristo Croux.

The expedition set off in February 1929 with the aim of reaching and studying the Baltoro glacier and exploring the north of the Shaksgam valley. A first group, made up of Aimone di Savoia, Cugia and Anfossi, set off from Genoa in February and docked in Mumbai port three weeks later for a two-day train journey to Srinagar. After getting their huge load of equipment, supplies and scientific equipment through customs, they split it up into a grand total of five hundred 25–28-kg loads to be carried by porters.

On the subject of these crucial but frequently disregarded local staff, the English word "coolies" was frequently used in the documents, an offensive term frequently bound up with racial stereotypes, such as those used by Aimone di Savoia when referring to a small group of porters recruited in Askole who "caused us no especial difficulties although they turned out to be a little lazy" or when he expresses his fear that these same porters might "desert, given the laziness of the natives, which will certainly not be lacking".[22]

The expedition continued with the second group landing in Mumbai and reaching Srinagar on 20 March. With the group now complete, the journey began which was to take 25 days to reach Askole on foot, passing through the towns of Gund and Skardu after crossing the 3,528-metre-high Zoji La pass. The group reached Askole on 22 April and broke their journey there for a few days to pick up the food and equipment supplies left there the previous year. They then crossed the Braldo valley and reached the edge of the Baltoro glacier, where the climb began. On 8 May, a base camp was set up in Urdukas, at 4,057 metres, to the left of the glacier.

The expedition's full-blown exploration and scientific work began on 14 May when Desio embarked on a series of trips on Panmah glacier before turning his attention to the upper Baltoro. On 9 June, he crossed Mustagh pass (5,422 m) and descended to the Sarpo-Lago glacial basin and then the Shaksgam valley as far as the Urdok glacier. Then a smaller group led by Balestreri and Desio climbed back up the Shaksgam valley and struggled across the challenging Singhiè glacier, returning to base camp on 14 July.[23] In the meantime, from Urdukas, Aimone led a further group which reached the Concordia circus on the upper Baltoro glacier on 27 June and set up camp there at an altitude of 4,627 metres, from which a great deal of topographical surveying took place up to altitudes of 6,400 metres.

Having gathered at base camp, the expedition's return journey began on 24 July. While Desio and Ponti surveyed the Panmah glacier one last time, Balestreri, Bron, Chiardola and Croux returned to Italy early, formally to "lighten the return convoy" but in actual fact as a result of Balesteri's "bad behaviour", consisting of a heated argument with the Duke of Spoleto.[24] The rest of the group reached Srinagar on 12 September and then travelled to Mumbai by train. Their ship reached Naples on 24 October.

A great many anthropometric, geographical, natural, topographical and zoological studies and field work had been done. In particular, lieutenant colonel Gino Allegri analysed the anthropological traits of the Baltì people, completing detailed studies on 83 individuals, "most of whom were peasants or porters",[25] classifying their physiognomical and somatic features, measuring height and limb and torso length and documenting his studies with many detailed photographs. On the basis of this field data, Florence University geographer Renato Biasutti wrote a volume entitled *I caratteri antropologici dei Baltì*, published years later in the expedition's official reports. In this work, Biasutti classified the anthropological traits of the local population in accordance with a historical-geographical methodology designed to formulate a series of somatic parallels between peoples distant in both space and time, which he explained on the grounds of ancient migrations.

This thesis, also espoused by well-known German anthropogeographer Friedrich Ratzel, fitted into a powerfully Eurocentric interpretative framework but does not appear to have been caught up in the racial stereotypes so widespread in these years. What emerges from the images and accounts is the huge difference in status between European explorers – who paid close attention to their clothing and appearance even in these remote places – and the local population, whose harsh living standards are all too evident. The markedly colonial character of this representation casts light on the impact the geographical and mountaineering expeditions were designed to have. In these remote places, expeditions such as these were people's first significant contact with Western culture and its customs and means but also a financial opportunity whose profound impact on the local population grew incrementally, with local people's role in the expeditions being primarily as porters. Renato Biasutti classified the Balti people's somatic features in this way:

> It should be borne in mind that this ethnic group speaks the Tibetan language and follows the Islamic religion while its overall physical appearance shows a prevalence of Caucasian types. It is thus the result of an encounter and fusion between diverse ethnic waves with varying impacts on its race, culture and language. Various individuals show rougher physical features (wide face, low forehead, large deep-set nose, etc.), on the other hand, demonstrating a reaction to historic southern elements which are, perhaps, not dissimilar to those which became part of the darker Indian peoples. In bodily proportions the Balti people have normal . . . legs with values similar to European averages.[26]

The Duke of Spoleto's typewritten memoirs describe the group's relationship with local people, showing a paternalistic tone suffused with the long-term 'good Italian' stereotype and frequent references to the benevolence, consideration and gratitude which the Italians showed themselves worthy of.

> In the souls of the strong, meek people who saw us at work . . . our memory will live on. For many years the good Balti people will conjure up the memory of these strange sahibs from a far-off land called Italy. They will remember our mountaineers, calm and strong in the face of danger, scientists hard at the toughest work, patient, good doctors bending over their wounds.[27]

Giotto Dainelli's and Gunther Oskar Dyhrenfurth's international expeditions (1930, 1934)

The Karakoram expedition undertaken in 1930 by Giotto Dainelli was the direct consequence of that fact that the Florentine geographer missed the chance to take part in Aimone di Savoia's expedition two years earlier. Dainelli chose to fund the expedition himself to avoid any imposition on the itinerary and staff related constraints and accepted the patronage of the Società Geografica Italiana only.[28] He also invited Ardito Desio to take part, but the latter pulled out at the last minute "as a result of certain university commitments which it was not in his interests to ignore".[29]

In addition to Dainelli, the following also took part: Elisabeth Kalau von Hofe, his faithful assistant of Swiss origin and a capable botanist; two officials from the Istituto Geografico Militare, Enrico Alfonso Cecioni and Alessandro Latini; and the governor of the trans-Himalayan region and the state of Kashmir, Hashmatullah Khan. Accompanied by a limited number of porters, this small party explored the glacial Siàcen valley and climbed up to and crossed a pass (which Dainelli called Italia pass) to gain access to the Rimu glacier. The geological, glaciological and botanical observations gathered enabled this Florentine geographer to complete

> the multi-faceted contribution I have been able to make to our knowledge of the Karakoram, both its natural and human environment, and which I consider to be the greatest of the achievements I will leave behind as a naturalist, geographer and explorer.[30]

In 1934 – after being obliged by Nazism's rise to power to abandon his university teaching post in Germany and take refuge in Switzerland[31] – German mountaineer and geologist Gunther Oskar Dyhrenfurth led an international expedition to the upper Baltoro basin. The crew included his wife Harriet Paolina Heymann; Swiss mountaineers Marcel Kurz, Hans Winzeler and Andrè Roch; Englishman James Belajeff; Germans Hans Ertl and Albrecht Höchl; and Turin engineer Piero Ghiglione. As it was funded by a Swiss film production company with a view to making a film, *Der Dämon des Himalaya* (1935), naturalised American director of Hungarian and Jewish origins Endre (alias Andrew) Marton – another post-1933 emigrant from Germany – also took part, together with his wife Jarmila Vacek, Austrian actor Wladimir Rogoschin (alias Gustav Diessel) and Swiss Richard Angst as photography director. The initial objective had been to climb Hidden Peak, or Gasherbrum I (8,068 m), where adverse weather conditions and snow led to an altitude of 6,300 metres being reached, and the expedition turned to easier-to-climb and slightly lower peaks. Pushing ski mountaineering to altitudes never previously reached, Ghiglione and his companions climbed Baltoro Kangri (7,312 m) and four peaks in the Sia Kangri massif at altitudes ranging from 7,422 to 7,680 metres.

Despite the expedition's internationalist character and the Nazi party's documented aversion to and/or persecution of many of the group's members, the expedition was presented by the CAI's president and high-ranking fascist official Angelo Manaresi as a sort of rivalry between nations in which Italy, via Ghiglione, would stand out from the others for courage and mountaineering skills. According to Manaresi, this derived from the prestige of the Italian explorers who had previously tried their hands on the Karakoram mountains. In the preface to a book by Ghiglione published in 1936, the fascist CAI president underlined the pride the Turin engineer must have felt when he saw maps by Italian explorers and mountaineers in the hands of his foreign companions – De Filippi, Dainelli, Desio – chosen because the best; proudly following in the footsteps of noble Savoy princes in exploits which live on today in the memories and admiration of all! . . . Ghiglione is priding himself on being one of the first. He has almost always with him those faithful skis which take him to never-before-reached heights.[32]

The victorious and controversial Italian ascent of K2 (1954)

The epoch-making changes of 1947 when India and Pakistan obtained independence from Great Britain and, at the same time, the advent of still unresolved bitter conflict in the Kashmir area made it impossible to get to the Karakoram mountains from the Indian town of Srinagar. Since then, a much longer and more challenging journey has been required. The departure point became the Pakistan capital Islamabad, euphemistically called the Karakoram Highway.

By examining the famous expedition which led to Italians being the first national group to get to the top of K2, this concluding section briefly presents the key phases in this ascent and the protracted controversy around what really happened at over 8,000 metres on the night of 30–31 July 1954 when Walter Bonatti and Hunza Amir Mahdi had to attempt an outside emergency bivouac at over 8,100 metres. Fifty years after the event, in 2004, a commission set up by CAI and made up of Fosco Maraini, Alberto Monticone and Luigi Zanzi re-examined the historical facts and events and acknowledged the fundamental contribution made by Bonatti and Mahdi to Lino Lacedelli and Achille Compagnoni's ascent to the peak on the basis of a great deal of documentary analysis, demonstrating that the latter (contrary to their own version of events) relied on oxygen right to the top.[33]

Whilst the matter is extremely well known and much debated internationally, too, including in recent years,[34] important archival sources which would cast additional light on our knowledge and thinking about this important expedition have remained substantially unexamined. With the brevity required by a chapter of this length, it will thus shed light on the early phases in the expedition, the political and diplomatic interactions between the Italian and Pakistani authorities for permit purposes and a series of insights into the choice of who was to take part in the climb and especially the sensational exclusion of Riccardo Cassin, first as the expedition's mountaineering leader and then from the expedition itself.

Regarding what happened in the days, months and years following on from the first K2 ascent, the sources reveal the extraordinary visibility and importance (including in commercial terms) the climb had in both Italy and around the world. For the rest of their lives, all those who took part in it and the two who reached the peak, Compagnoni and Lacedelli, and expedition leader Desio in particular became celebrities and full-blown legends. Last will be examined the various controversies which emerged in the days, months and years which followed,

Italy-Pakistan relations and the permit issue

Regarding the negotiations between the Italian and Pakistani authorities which made the expedition permits possible, the letters exchanged by Desio, Paolo Canali (special secretary to Alcide De Gasperi, prime minister from 1945 to 1954 and foreign secretary from 1951 to 1953), the cabinet secretary to the foreign secretary Zanetto Scola-Camerini and the Italian legation functionaries in Karachi are extremely interesting. On 19 June 1953, De Gasperi met Pakistani president Muhammad Ali Bogra on an official visit to Rome, and the latter granted permission for a "preliminary small expedition and at the same time . . . for the expedition to Baltoro (K2) in 1954".[35] Recalling that in this same summer (10 August 1953), an American expedition to K2 led by Charles Houston reached an altitude of 7,800 metres but had to turn back to attempt to save the life of Arthur Karr Gilkey, who was struck down by pulmonary oedema and died in an avalanche along a dramatic descent in which all seven mountaineers risked death.[36]

During Riccardo Cassin and Ardito Desio's first reconnaissance trip from 18 August to 17 October 1953, a first overview of the Italian-Pakistani exchange emerged, with Desio agreeing to assess the risks bound up with the extremely anomalous advance of the Kuthiah glacier in person. Desio's 1974 typewritten memoirs recount that, in the summer of 1953, local people were very worried about the "constant advance of the huge slide which had advanced around three kilometres from the lateral Kuthiah valley to the Stak valley, site of a great many villages and scattered with flourishing oases". The Pakistani government feared that if the glacier continued to move, not only might it push into populated areas, but it could also potentially block the course of the Indus River "with catastrophic consequences which are not difficult to imagine".[37] Desio was able to observe that, in the space of a few months, the glacier had moved over 10 kilometres (technically what is called a "surge") as the result of an enormous ice and rock slide. The following year, during scientific research linked to the mountaineering expedition, captain Francesco Lombardi carried out a thorough survey of the glacier which confirmed Desio's thesis and ruled out further advance.

In a longer timeframe and with important economic interests at stake, in 1962 the famous Italian architect Gio Ponti was commissioned to design and build part of the ministries area in Islamabad. At some points, 5,000 workers were on site at the same time, and two years later, the buildings were completed.[38] Between 1968 and 1974, the building of the Tarbela dam and hydroelectric plant with primarily Italian engineering, technology and workforce in north-western Pakistan, where the river Indus leaves the Karakoram mountains, is also relevant.[39]

These signs of good Italian-Pakistani relations reveal effective geopolitical forward thinking on Italy's part and are corroborated by the contents of a book on De Gasperi's foreign policy strategies and objectives, written by Paolo Canali, the ministerial functionary cited previously, using the pseudonym Adstans (in Latin "standing beside"):

> Its [Italy's] geographical position, current trading traditions and employment market never ceased . . . to push it in the direction of outcomes which were historically and economically natural. . . . The young Italian Republic neither hesitated nor held back at any time but rather found capital to take advantage of.[40]

In an international relations context of this sort, it is clear that the expedition was never simply a matter of mountaineering: the first 8,000-metre climbs attempted and achieved in the years immediately preceding this by American, Austrian, British, French, Polish, Swiss, German and Swedish climbers now included the Italians, "who had played no secondary part in this noble international rivalry in the past".[41] The expedition's organisers, and those who supported it on a political and economic level, were well aware that the first K2 ascent would be an extraordinary Italian national redemption opportunity. It was granted, as a *qui pro quo*, to a nation of secondary geopolitical importance brought to its knees by fascism and the military and moral tragedy of World War II, in search of opportunities for economic and national affirmation: "Italy's honour had to be rebuilt after the disaster of war and Nobile's North Pole. Other countries had to be shown that Italy was still capable of winning".[42]

The organising commission

The handwritten notebook containing the minutes of the commission which coordinated the various organisational aspects of the expedition, kept in Milan at the CAI's head offices, is a relevant document in all sorts of ways. The commission met from November 1953 to October 1954 at Milan University's Geology Institute, where Desio taught. Its work is highly revealing of the highly centralising role of the expedition head who, in a discussion on Italian newspaper reporting of indiscretions on the expedition, observed that "we should be saying as little as possible"[43] and asked that "news [be] provided by him alone".[44]

First and foremost, the notebook enables to reconstruct institutional exchanges and relations. It contains the names of various front-rank Italian political figures of the day of various origins and political affiliations. "Tissi refers to conversations with Saragat who had made contact with De Gasperi for expedition funding purposes. Saragat has also spoken to Pella who asked for a memo".[45] The notebook also provides insights into which bodies were appealed to and which of these contributed to the expedition and to what extent, with financial management in the hands of Brescia-born but now Milan-based Vittorio Lombardi, a self-made man and philanthropist who was a trusted friend of Desio's and, in a book on the latter which came out in 2014, defined as a "perfect embodiment of the unscrupulous world of Italian financial interest".[46] Moreover this source delves into the various phases in the selection process for the mountaineers who were to take part in the expedition. First, it is worthy of note that the CAI central management body's nomination of Lecco-based Riccardo Cassin was immediately withdrawn on the following grounds: "Desio underlined the need for there not to be any nominations other than that of expedition leader. After lengthy discussions Cassin declined the council's offer and Desio was nominated president of the commission."[47]

On 21 November, the commission elaborated a first list of 20 names selected on the basis of "both age (with optimal being 27 to 40) and character",[48] whose origins and dates of birth were given. Their mountaineering experience, professional skills and any knowledge of foreign languages (especially English, of use in dialogue with the Pakistani authorities) were also taken into account. In considering the candidates and making "physical and moral judgements"[49] on them, the intention was to include both a large group of French-speaking Valle d'Aosta guides and at least one exponent of the German-speaking minority with South Tyrolean Erich Abrahm.[50]

The final participant selection process took place after medical tests carried out at the Turin University physiology laboratory led by Anita Di Giorgio, a childhood friend of Desio's, "from Friuli, whom I trusted implicitly".[51] These tests sanctioned the choice of the 13 mountaineers who effectively took part in the expedition: Erich Abram, Ugo Angelino, Walter Bonatti, Achille Compagnoni, Mario Fantin, Cirillo Floreanini, Pino Gallotti, Lino Lacedelli, Doctor Guido Pagani, Mario Puchoz, Ubaldo Rey, Gino Soldà and Sergio Viotto. These same tests sanctioned the exclusion of Riccardo Cassin, Armando Da Roit, Ernesto and Oliviero Frachey, Cesare Maestri, Arturo Ottoz and Vittorio Penzo.[52]

Of these exclusions, Cassin's stands out, with clinical tests validated by the Rome University physiology lab as well and results which "advised against mountaineering at the highest altitudes".[53] Cassin learnt of his exclusion without criticism or recrimination but over subsequent years he demonstrated his skills to the full as well as his optimal state of health in the non-European expeditions he took part in.[54] Rumors wanted Desio fearing that Cassin's charisma and strong personality might have threatened his own leadership and Cassin might have taken the credit for a successful expedition.[55] Another interesting case is Cesare Maestri, whose tests found a stomach ulcer which was not confirmed in other diagnostic tests.[56] This Trentino mountaineer attributed his exclusion to his open Italian Communist party membership and his consequent political incompatibility with Desio, whose adherence to the fascist party was well known and who was nicknamed "the little Duce" by the expedition's mountaineers.[57] A paper written by Enrico Sturani, published in 1994, argued that

> the suspicion arises that the key selection criteria were less medical and scientific than "character" based. In their own opinions and those of others, Cassin and Maestri were left out on the grounds of their personalities and overly pronounced individuality.[58]

Great visibility in Italy and abroad

First and foremost, after its first ascent, the mountain's straight-to-the point name – simply the topographic initials assigned it by Henry Haversham Godwin-Austen in the Survey of India – [59] became a brand name which dozens of bars, hotels, restaurants and shops and other businesses across Italy and also abroad (with these latter being mainly businesses managed by Italian emigrants) were named after. In addition to these business aspects – which have been long term and have continued into the present – the extraordinary welcome given the mountaineers when they returned to Italy by ship is worthy of mention, with a 40,000-strong crowd turning up to greet them at Genoa port on 22 September.[60] The upper echelons of the CAI hoped that celebrations would remain "in keeping with the solemnity which the greatness of the achievement merits"[61] and thus organised an official ceremony with a highly structured programme for 25 October in Milan. It included a mass in honour of Mario Puchoz (the Valle d'Aosta guide who died from pulmonary oedema in the early stages of the expedition), an official reception at Palazzo Marino by the mayor of Milan Virgilio Ferrari, a procession in which the mountaineers crossed Milan city centre on foot to cheering crowds and a closing evening ceremony at Teatro della Scala. On 25 March the following year, an official preview of the Italia K2 film was screened in Rome and Washington simultaneously. Luigi Einaudi, the Italian president, spoke at the Rome screening and announced that the country's education secretary had issued a circular ensuring that the "memorable actions of the climbers should be brought to the attention of all school classes".[62]

Controversies and legal proceedings

The controversies whose wide-ranging resonance and public importance irremediably compromised personal relations between the expedition's members for years to come began in the first days after the K2 ascent. At the beginning of August, while the expedition's climbers were returning to base camp, the Pakistani press published a series of articles which were strongly critical of the treatment meted out to Hunza Mahdi, who had to have all his toes amputated because of his severe frostbite. Compagnoni was held especially responsible and accused of having first given Mahdi the false impression that he might in turn reach the peak and then abandoning him to the makeshift shelter referred to previously. This controversy culminated in the diplomatic intermediation of Italian ambassador Benedetto D'Acunzo and the drawing up of a memorandum signed on 1 September 1954 by all members of the expedition and Ata Ullah, the expedition liaison officer.[63]

In the months which followed, other controversies arose, resulting in protracted legal complications between CAI, Desio and the Milan Museo della Scienza e Tecnica on the subject of who Genoa city's Cristoforo Colombo – Caravella d'oro prize should rightfully be awarded to,[64] between CAI and Compagnoni on the subject of the authorship of the *Italia K2* film[65] and between CAI and Desio on the subject of the important contribution made by the Consiglio Nazionale delle

Ricerche (50 million lire, around €825,000 in 2020 values).[66] CAI won all these court cases, but in January 1956, a request for the compulsory administration of the CAI presidency and central directorate (whose origins are not revealed by the papers consulted) reached the Interior Ministry on the grounds that it had been "infiltrated by Communists".[67] After learning confidentially of the matter, the CAI deplored that "this denigration campaign . . . would certainly cause incalculable damage to the CAI's image"[68] and replied in a note to the Milan prefect to the effect that the

> political principles of the membership nucleus could not be healthier. . . . All its sections and national presidents are known to be apolitical by tradition and nurture duly patriotic sentiments. . . . The club is a disciplined and organic whole of profound national sentiment.[69]

In the weeks which followed, the upper CAI echelons found, to their relief, and once again confidentially, that the "matter of compulsory administration had been definitively set aside".[70]

These intricate and delicate matters clearly confirm the accusations of Walter Bonatti – who was certainly not *super partes* in all this – regarding both the CAI and Compagnoni and Desio. Bonatti accused CAI of being "a mountaineering club which has, for many years, turned a deaf ear to the mountaineering events of these days"[71] and Compagnoni, against whom Bonatti won a libel case in the early 1960s, of "continuing to bash his head against a glass wall of lies",[72] and, lastly, Desio was defined as:

> an aristocratic and autocratic university professor whose attitude to his underlings is shared by all the world's autocrats . . . , an egocentric figure, a bulldozer who would never have accepted any criticism of his decisions . . . an order and protocol obsessive.[73]

In conclusion, about the wider significance of an expedition which was as successful in its mountaineering achievements as it was painful, destructive and contradictory in its short- and long-term consequences demonstrated (once again in Bonatti's words) "all Italy's vices: nepotism, hiding from the truth, hoping problems will resolve themselves on their own, not taking responsibility".[74] The first ascent of K2 has gone down in history as a "national triumph. It is a claim which, over time and at payback time, was revealed to be a national scam . . . a story of confusion, betrayal and brazen hypocrisy like none other in the annals of mountaineering".[75]

Notes

1 Mario Fantin, ed., *Alpinismo italiano nel mondo* (Milano: Commissione centrale delle pubblicazioni del Club Alpino Italiano, 1972); Stefano Caciolli and Fabrizio Fallani,

Italians in the Karakoram (1890–1954) 139

"Esplorazioni e spedizioni alpinistiche nel Karakorum: il contributo dell'I.G.M", *L'Universo* no. 3 (2007): 410–446; Maurice Isserman and Stewart Weaver, *Fallen Giants: A History of Himalayan Mountaineering from the Age of Empire to the Age of Extremes* (New Heaven and London: Yale University Press, 2008); Edward J. Larson, *To the Edges of the Earth: 1909, the Race for the Three Poles, and the Climax of the Age of Exploration* (New York: Harper Collins, 2018).

2 Peter Hansen, "Albert Smith, the Alpine Club, and the Invention of Mountaineering", *Mid-Victorian Britain* no. 34 (1995): 317.

3 Simon Schama, *Landscapes and Memory* (London: Harper, 1996), 423.

4 Francesco Cavazzani, "I precursori. Roberto Lerco", *Rivista Mensile del CAI. Numero speciale dedicato al K2* no. 12 (1954): 403. In earlier decades, British explorers had visited the Karakoram region, and the first pioneering British and German geography and topography research missions had been undertaken.

5 *Lo Scarpone*, 16 October 1954, 3.

6 Roberto Lerco [sic], "Nel Caucaso. Dalla descrizione di Un viaggio in Caucasia di R. Lerco", *Bollettino del CAI* no. 55 (1888): 272–288.

7 The Beck-Peccoz Museum, Gressoney Saint-Jean (Aosta) trophy is that of an ibex killed on the slopes of Nanga Parbat on 20 June 1890. See Mario Fantin, *Alpinismo italiano nel mondo*, vol. 1 (Milano: CAI, 1972), 40. The trophy held at the Turin Museo Nazionale della Montagna (with inventory number OG – 586) was, on the other hand, shot on 31 July 1890 at Skoro La pass.

8 Matthias Zurbriggen, *From Alps to the Andes: Being the Autobiography of a Mountain Guide* (London: Fisher Unwin, 1899), 101.

9 Peter Stettler, "Matthias Zurbriggen 1856–1917", *Les Alpes*, January 2004, 26–28.

10 Karl Oestreich, "Die Täler des nordwestlichen Himalaya: Beobachtungen und Studien", *Petermanns geographische Mitteilungen* 155 (1906).

11 Oestreich, "Die Täler des nordwestlichen Himalaya", 268.

12 Fanny Bullock and William Hunter Workman, "Glaciers and passes of the Karakoram", *Geographical Journal* no. 1 (1918): 38–42. See also Michael Plint, "The Workmans: Travellers Extraordinary", *Alpine Journal* no. 97 (1992–1993): 231–237. About Cesare Calciati, see Cesare Calciati, *Al Caracorum. Diario di due esplorazioni con 100 illustrazioni, fotografie panoramiche e una carta geografica* (Firenze: Bemporad, 1930).

13 T.G.L., "Expedition of H. R. H. the Duke of the Abruzzi to the Karakoram", *The Geographical Journal* 3 (1910): 332.

14 Luigi Amedeo di Savoia-Aosta and Duca degli Abruzzi, *La spedizione nel Karakoram e nell'Imalaia occidentale (1909). Relazione del Dott. Filippo De Filippi illustrata da Vittorio Sella* (Bologna: Zanichelli, 1911). See also Laura Cassi, ed., *"La Dimora delle nevi" e le carte ritrovate. Filippo de Filippi e le spedizioni scientifiche italiane in Asia centrale (1909 e 1913–14). Atti del Convegno – Firenze 13–14 marzo 2008* (Firenze: Società di Studi Geografici, 2009).

15 Archivio Centrale dello Stato (hereafter ACS), Presidenza del Consiglio dei Ministri (hereafter PCM), Serie 431, Gabinetto Rubriche 1928–1930, f. 3/2–4, b. 1206, De Filippi's Italian expedition scientific report (1913–1914). The many direct letters exchanged between De Filippi and Prime Minister Giovanni Giolitti are interesting and demonstrate the great attention paid the expedition and the considerable funding it received.

16 Filippo De Filippi, *Storia della spedizione scientifica italiana nel Himàlaia, Caracorùm e Turchestàn cinese. (1913–1914)*. (Bologna: Zanichelli, 1924). From May to September 1913, Biella-based lawyer and businessman Mario Piacenza organised a mountaineering trip in the Zanskar valley in which doctor Lorenzo Borelli, Piacenza count Cesare Calciati (mentioned previously), photographer Erminio Botta and the two Alpine guides Cyprien Savoye and Giuseppe Gaspard took part. The twin peaks Nun and Kun (7,150 and 7,095 m) and Z3 (6,270 m) were climbed in August. See Mario

Piacenza, "Esplorazione dei monti dell'Himalaya Occidentale. Conferenza tenuta nel Teatro Vittorio Emanuele di Torino il 15 aprile 1914", *Rivista del CAI* 5 (1914): 131–148.
17 For an analytical description of this documentation, see Stefano Twardzik's appendix in this volume.
18 About these aspects, see in this book Steinar Aas's and Luciano Zani's chapters.
19 ACS, PCM, Serie 431, Gabinetto Rubriche 1928–1930, f. 3/2–4, b. 1205, ff. 1–5000, Consiglio dei Ministri extract dating to 23 July 1928. For all aspects relating to Umberto Nobile's 1928 Arctic expedition, see Steinar Aas's and Luciano Zani's papers in this volume.
20 Archivio storico del Comune di Milano (hereafter ACM), Archivio generale, 1935, fasc. 133, cart. 10, sott.fasc. 8 The Arctic Expedition Collection 59–1928 "Commendator Gabardi". Letter sent by De Capitani d'Arzago to Gabardi on the conditions Mussolini set for the Karakoram expedition (6 November 1928).
21 ACM, Archivio generale, 1935, fasc. 133, cart. 10, sott.fasc. 8, Bilancio della spedizione.
22 Aimone di Savoia-Aosta and Ardito Desio, *La spedizione geografica italiana al Karakoram (1929 – VII E. F.). Storia del viaggio e risultati geografici* (Milano-Roma: Bertarelli, 1936), 17.
23 Ardito Desio, *Sulle vie della sete dei ghiacci e dell'oro. Avventure straordinarie di un geologo* (Novara: Istituto Geografico De Agostini, 1987), 110.
24 ACS, PCM, Serie 358, f. 3/2–4, anno 1934–36, Spedizione italiana del 1929 in Karakorum.
25 Aimone and Desio, *La spedizione geografica italiana al Karakoram*, XLVI.
26 Ibid., XLV–XLVI.
27 ACM, Archivio generale, 1935, fasc. 133, cart. 10, sott.fasc. 8, Spedizione Caracorum. Contabilità.
28 Giotto Dainelli, "La mia Spedizione al ghiacciaio Siàcen nel Caracorùm Orientale", *Bollettino del Comitato Glaciologico Italiano* (1933): 39–57.
29 Giotto Dainelli, *Esploratori e alpinisti nel Caracorum* (Torino: UTET, 1959), 364. This was a Milan University chair which Desio had successfully applied for.
30 Dainelli, *Esploratori e alpinisti nel Caracorum*, 380.
31 Anders Bolinder, "Prof. G. O. Dyhrenfurth", *Le Alpi* 33 (1975): 238.
32 Piero Ghiglione, *Dalle Ande all'Himalaya* (Torino: Montes, 1936), XV.
33 Luigi Zanzi, ed., *K2 una storia finita* (Scarmagno: Priuli&Verlucca, 2007). See also Robert Marshall, *K2. Tradimenti e bugie* (Dalai, 2012). For a different point of view about this long *querelle*, see Massimo Cappon and Agostino Da Polenza, *Quattro mesi in cima al mondo. Dall'Himalaya al Karakorum, il diario della spedizione che ha riportato l'Italia in vetta al K2 cinquant'anni dopo* (Milano: Rizzoli, 2004). For new and unedited references about Bonatti, see *Walter Bonatti. Stati di grazia. Un'avventura ai confini dell'uomo. Catalogo della mostra a cura di Roberto Mantovani e Angelo Ponta* (Torino-Milano: Museo Nazionale della Montagna – Solferino, 2021).
34 Mick Conefrey, "Filming the Summit of K2", *The Alpine Journal* 121 (2017): 239–244; Eric Viola, "Walter Bonatti and the Ghosts of K2", *The Alpine Journal* 120 (2016): 216–230; Mick Conefrey, "Machiavellian Bastardy? The First Ascent of K2", *The Alpine Journal* 119 (2015): 257–265.
35 ACS, PCM, Serie 422, Ufficio del consigliere diplomatico, b. 46, Viaggi e colloqui di De Gasperi 1948–1954.
36 Charles S. Houston and Robert H. Bates, *K2, the Savage Mountain* (New York: The Lyons Press, 1954). See also Galen Rowell, *In the Throne Room of the Mountain Gods* (San Francisco: Sierra Club Books, 1977), 226–234.
37 Claudio Smiraglia's private archive (Milan), Ardito Desio, *Una visita al Ghiacciaio Kuthiah nel Central Karakorum*. Preliminary typewritten document published with the same title in the *Bollettino del Comitato Glaciologico Italiano*, no. 22 (1974): 39–44.

I would thank Claudio Smiraglia for his availability to make me consult documents and pictures on glaciological surveys in the Karakoram.
38 Derek Lovejoy, "The Design of Islamabad: New Capital City of Pakistan", *Journal of the Royal Society of Arts* 5123 (1966): 923–941.
39 Asianics Agro-Dev. International (Pvt) Ltd., *Tarbela Dam and Related Aspects of the Indus River Basin, Pakistan: A WCD Case Study Prepared as an Input to the World Commission on Dams* (Cape Town, 2000), www.dams.org, last access 10 December 2021.
40 Adstans, *Alcide De Gasperi nella politica estera italiana 1944–1953* (Milano: Mondadori, 1954), 222.
41 ACS, PCM, Serie 422, Ufficio del consigliere diplomatico, b. 49, Spedizione italiana al Karakorum K2–1954.
42 *K2 Millenovecentocinquantaquattro. Cahier Museomontagna 93* (Torino: Museo Nazionale della Montagna "Duca degli Abruzzi", 1994), 256. Many of the relevant documents are held at ACS, PCM, Serie 422, Ufficio del consigliere diplomatico, b. 49, Spedizione italiana al Karakorum K2–1954.
43 Archivio della Sede centrale del Club Alpino Italiano (Milano), Quaderno Q.11.53. Commissione tecnico-esecutiva spedizione K2–1954 (hereafter Quaderno), Verbale della riunione del 15 dicembre 1953, 15.
44 Archivio della Sede centrale del Club Alpino Italiano (Milano), Quaderno Q.11.53. Commissione tecnico-esecutiva spedizione K2–1954 (hereafter Quaderno), Verbale della riunione del 15 dicembre 1953, 15.
45 Quaderno, Verbale della riunione del 9 novembre 1953, 2.
46 Luca Trevisan and Andrea Savio, *Vittorio Lombardi. Mecenate illuminato e tesoriere della conquista italiana del K2* (Sommacampagna: Cierre, 2014), 31.
47 Quaderno, Verbale della riunione del 9 novembre 1953, 3.
48 Quaderno, Verbale della riunione del 21 novembre 1953, 6–7. These are the 20 mountaineers whose names were initially put forward: Ugo Angelino, Luigi Barmasse, Riccardo Cassin, Achille Compagnoni, Armando Da Roit, Cirillo Floreanini, Ernesto Franchey, Pino Gallotti, Luigi Ghedina, Lino Lacedelli, Giuseppe Oberto, Guido Pagani, Arturo Ottoz, Augusto Pala, Vittorio Penzo, Camillo Pelissier, Mario Puchoz, Enrico Rey, Ubaldo Rey, Eugenio Ryon. The meeting also discussed additional names – Luigi Carrel, Ezio Costantini, Ferdinando Gaspard, Antonio Gobbi, Sergio Viotto and some not otherwise specified Lecco and Monza climbers, but the decision was taken not to add these in this phase. The 15 December 1953 meeting discussed the involvement of Walter Bonatti, Luigi Oggioni and Carlo Mauri, and it was suggested that Bonatti should replace Oberto and Viotto, Barmasse and that Cesare Maestri and Erich Abrahm should be added.
49 Quaderno, Verbale della riunione del 7 febbraio 1954, 35–36. The most interesting judgements are certainly these: Bonatti "an enthusiast, Westernist and Orientalist"; Compagnoni "calm, cheerful"; Floreanini "not good on ice, trashed by his companions"; Gallotti "cultured, intelligent, physical condition needs checking"; Lino Lacedelli "undisputed rock climber, disciplined, good character"; Rey "intelligent"; Soldà: "good character, exceptional resilience, disciplined, a leader"; Viotto "mouthy and aggressive, doesn't take orders".
50 Quaderno, Verbale della riunione del 15 dicembre 1953, 11.
51 *K2 Millenovecentocinquantaquattro*, 106.
52 Quaderno, Verbale della riunione del 29 dicembre 1953, 22.
53 Quaderno, Verbale della riunione del 7 febbraio 1954, 33.
54 Think, first and foremost, of the CAI-organised Karakoram expedition of 1958 which Cassin led, with Walter Bonatti and Carlo Mauri being the first to get to the peak of Gasherbrum IV (7,925 m); the challenging first ascent of the southwest spur of Mount Denali (or McKinley, 6,190 m, in Alaska, in 1961); his organisation and leadership

of the 1975 expedition which was the first to attempt the south face of Mount Lhotze (8,516 m, in the Himalayas). See Guido Cassin and Daniele Redaelli, *Cassin. Vita di un alpinista attraverso il '900* (Torino: Vivalda, 2001).
55 Mirella Tenderini, "Riccardo Cassin: In Memoriam", *The American Alpine Journal* (8 December 2010): 375.
56 For a biography of Cesare Maestri, see Alessandro Pastore, "Laudatio per il conferimento della laurea honoris causa a Cesare Maestri", *European Society for Sports History* 6 (2013): 179–184.
57 Walter Bonatti, *K2. La verità. Storia di un caso* (Milano: Rizzoli, 2014), 118. On the fascist position of Desio, see Stefano Morosini, "L'epurazione antifascista all'Istituto Lombardo Accademia di Scienze e Lettere", *Nuova Rivista Storica* 1 (2013): 133–158.
58 *K2 Millenovecentocinquantaquattro*, 134.
59 Hubert Adams Carter, "Balti place names in the Karakoram", *The American Alpine Journal* (1975): 52.
60 Fantin, Rey, Compagnoni and Pagani had returned by plane earlier, and the mountaineers who docked in Genoa on 22 September were Abrahm, Angelino, Bonatti, Floreanini, Gallotti, Lacedelli, Soldà and Viotto. Desio returned to Italy only on 15 October, after remaining in Karakoram to finalise surveys and samples together with the expedition's scientific components (Florence University archaeologist Paolo Graziosi, previously cited IGM geodesy scholar Francesco Lombardi, Trieste University geophysicist Antonio Marussi and Padua University petrographer Bruno Zanetti). About the research done during the 1954 expedition, see the nine volumes: Ardito Desio, *Italian Expeditions to the Karakoram (K2) and Hindu Kush. Scientific Reports* (different editors: 1964–1991). See also Claudio Smiraglia, "K2 cinquant'anni dopo. Fra esplorazione, alpinismo e ricerca (qualche riflessione poco sistematica)", *Bollettino della Società Geografica Italiana* 9 (2004): 335–354.
61 Quaderno, Verbale della riunione del 26 agosto 1954, 78.
62 *K2 Millenovecentocinquantaquattro*, 133.
63 Shahzeb Jiliani, "Amir Mehdi: Left Out to Freeze on K2 and Forgotten", *BBC News* (Hasanabad, Pakistan, 7 August 2014), accessed 1 August 2021, www.bbc.com/news/magazine-28696985, last access 10 December 2021.
64 Museo Nazionale della Montagna – CAI Torino, Fondo spedizione italiana al Karakorum – 1954 (d'ora in avanti MuseoTorino), Serie 1.8, Premio "Cristoforo Colombo" – La caravella d'oro" (1954–1963).
65 MuseoTorino, Serie 1.6, Vertenza CAI-Compagnoni (1953–1956).
66 MuseoTorino, Serie 1.4, Vertenza CAI-Desio e CNR (1953–1960). The expedition's overall budget was 212,149,948 lire, equivalent to € 3,400,000 in 2020 values. On expedition accounting matters, see Archivio storico della Sezione di Bergamo del CAI, Fondo Lombardi, bundle 15, Contabilità spedizione italiana al K2. Bilancio di verifica relativa alle operazioni a tutto il 30 agosto 1954.
67 MuseoTorino, Serie 2.6, Promemoria confidenziale sul Club Alpino Italiano, 29 gennaio 1956.
68 Silvio Saglio, "La vita del CAI nei suoi primi cento anni", *1863–1963. I cento anni del Club Alpino Italiano* (Milano: CAI, 1964), 308.
69 MuseoTorino, Serie 2.6, Promemoria confidenziale sul Club Alpino Italiano, 29 gennaio 1956. The note specifies, however, that vice president Renato Chabod "stood in Aosta in 1955 as a cryptocommunist (Stella Alpina) and was elected in the minority component of the council. . . . It is right to say that he kept politics out of CAI altogether and was an extremely able mountaineer". About the political commitment of Renato Chabod, see Marco Cuaz, "Renato Chabod politico", in Renato Chabod, *La cima di Entrelor* (Milano: CAI, 2019), 29–37. Vice-president Costa was also accused of having a "Communist brother . . . who gave up his membership and is now gravely ill in

Rovereto. Costa is an important industrialist and businessman and we have seen no sign of political activity from him. We in CAI certainly never noticed this".
70 MuseoTorino, Serie 2.6, Lettera del Segretario Generale del CAI Elvezio Bozzoli Parasacchi ai vicepresidenti generali del CAI Amedeo Costa e Renato Chabod, 4 febbraio 1956.
71 Bonatti, *K2. La verità*, 201.
72 Bonatti, *K2. La verità*, 203.
73 Bonatti, *K2. La verità*, 166–169.
74 Pierangelo Melgara, "Vivere L'avventura: Intervista a Walter Bonatti", *Quaderni Valtellinesi* no. 3 (1996). See Bonatti, *K2. La verità*, 235.
75 Bonatti, *K2. La verità*, 252–293.

9 Commercialisation and Mount Everest in the twentieth century[1]

Peter H. Hansen

Mount Everest between climbing and commerce

"Everest: Climbers' Challenge or Commercial Venture?" asked the cover of the *Daily Telegraph Magazine* on 16 April 1971. The magazine was touting a story about an international Everest expedition with "thirty men and one woman" from 12 nations, a massive BBC film crew, and publishing agreements in ten countries. The *Daily Telegraph* surveyed a wide-ranging debate about Everest's commercialisation. Eric Shipton, Joe Brown, and Ian McNaught Davis criticised the introduction of publicity and "Big Business" into climbing, though some form of commercialism was considered inevitable by Don Whillans, a professional climber who made his living as a mountaineer. Chris Brasher argued that the affluence of the 1950s had enabled working-class climbers to break through a class barrier, and now climbers in the 1970s could break through a nationalist barrier. To stir the pot further, the article asked a series of rhetorical questions: "Is the International [Everest Expedition] taking risks purely in the name of climbing? Are they filming a climb – or climbing to make a film? Is it a mountaineering adventure? Or a marketing enterprise?"[2]

Climbing Mount Everest has long been *both* climbers' challenge *and* commercial venture. The either/or proposition creates a false opposition that reflects a common, though problematic, way of talking about Everest and commercialisation more generally. More recent criticism of commercialisation on Everest has followed this pattern, often influenced by Jon Krakauer's *Into Thin Air* (1996), which blamed commercial teams for deaths in a storm. Climbing and commerce have always been intertwined, and placing them in opposition has led to unattainable expectations among climbers and vacuous analyses by commentators. The conditions of geographical exploration in modern times do not involve unsullied environments set apart from commerce, society, or marketing. Simplistic narratives that either exploration or mountaineering declined with the onset of commercialisation – before a state of grace, afterwards corrupted – conceal earlier forms of commercialisation and obscure the role of Sherpas, Nepalis, Tibetans, women, and other partners throughout these years.

Imperialism and nationalism justified the risks of dying while climbing in the Himalayas during the first two-thirds of the twentieth century. If nationalism

DOI: 10.4324/9781003095965-10

no longer provided a convincing rationale for mountaineering or exploration in extreme environments, as Brasher suggested in 1971, what replaced it? Brasher had participated in international climbing expeditions, and transnational collaborations appealed to many during periods of thaw in the Cold War.[3] Some climbers, like Reinhold Messner, replaced nationalism with individualism. After climbing Everest without supplemental oxygen in an Austrian expedition in 1978, Messner, a German-speaking Italian from the south Tyrol, renounced nationalism by declaring at a rally: "I am my own homeland, and this handkerchief is my flag."[4] The financial rewards enjoyed by Messner and a few other professional mountaineers have been substantial. The temptation exists to echo the headline writers of the *Daily Telegraph* and draw a contrast between the earlier eras when brave climbers surmounted challenges with new ages of individualism and commercial ventures on Everest.

This temptation should be resisted. The commercialisation of Everest has been going on for more than a century, though recent debates have distinctive features. Since the first ascent in 1953, Everest has been climbed about 10,000 times, with 9,000 ascents since the year 2000.[5] Recent crowding on the mountain has exceeded earlier expectations. The masculine heroism of climbers has been called into question as more people, especially women and formerly underrepresented groups, climb Everest and as high-altitude workers in the Himalayas assert more control over the mountain, even cancelling ascents in some years.[6]

Games that climbers play have multiplied over the last 50 years, as new styles of climbing are preferred by one group or another. Sherry Ortner persuasively argued that twentieth-century Himalayan mountaineering was a "serious game" of competing masculinities, in which Sherpas have their own agendas and exercise their own agency. The western counterculture of the 1960s problematised the military-style hypermasculinity of the earlier Everest climbers and enabled Sherpas to press for more egalitarian relations and for women to question gender norms. Mark Liechty also notes that "what tourists view as a quest is for Nepalis an industry."[7] Commercial tourism and trekking developed rapidly in the 1970s as the result of deliberate efforts by the Nepali government to rebrand Nepal as a site for adventure tourism. Mountaineering, tourism, and the commercialisation of Everest in Nepal and China have been the result of continuing cross-cultural interactions.

The commercialisation of mountaineering should be understood along a continuum. As Ortner and Liechty suggest, some forms of commercialisation are not external imports but indigenous strategies for development, in which Sherpas or Nepalis pursue their own agendas to tap into global modernity. Ironically, some critics of commercialisation on Everest have been among its greatest beneficiaries. Yet the anarchic individualism of many elite mountaineers makes it difficult for them to locate their activity in a wider context. Debates about commercialisation on Everest also highlight disparities of risk and inequalities of wealth.[8] Everest is not alone in raising such issues, but its position as the world's highest mountain has amplified voices that are less often heard in global debates over the legacies of colonialism and the consequences of globalisation.

Mountaineering has been commercial from the beginning, no matter the starting date. In the Alps, the guides of Chamonix and other places in the Alps escorted visitors through the mountains by the mid-eighteenth century. Visitors such as Marc-Théodore Bourrit and Horace-Bénédict de Saussure collaborated with these guides to create panoramic views from the mountain top that illustrate the summit position of the autonomous individual who dominates nature.[9] The infrastructure for commercial Alpine tourism expanded rapidly throughout the nineteenth century as mountain climbing became a popular pastime. Alpine clubs across Europe were instrumental in building the network of huts, paths, and guides, often as deliberate steps in local economic and social development in the Alps, just as has happened more recently in the Himalayas.[10]

Everest's commercialisation has taken multiple forms across this longer history. This chapter highlights several episodes in Everest's commercialisation, from early mapping to expedition films of the 1920s, the commercialisation of climbing paraphernalia in the 1950s, and the mass-market commercialisation of Everest in the last 50 years. Periods of imperial exploration and nationalist mountaineering were *also* commercial and serve as examples of the continuum of commercialisation and varieties of capitalism on Everest.

The 'discovery' of Chomolungma

Chomolungma, as the peak is known in Tibet and China, was mapped for the Kang-xi emperor and appeared on Manchu and European maps during the eighteenth century.[11] A century later, British and Indian surveyors identified Peak XV as the highest in the world and assigned the name "Mount Everest" by imperial prerogative in the 1850s. Trigonometrical surveys from India are often filed under the 'discovery' of the Himalayas but are better understood as the commodification and incorporation of mountain spaces into the knowledge networks of a chartered monopoly, the East India Company. The measuring, mapping, and naming of Mt Everest are examples of commercialisation and its forms of knowledge. The surveying of mountains, taming of rivers, and study of the meteorology of the monsoon were undertaken by the company state and became instruments of imperial and later national governance in India. The record keepers of the Great Trigonometrical Survey of India laboured mightily in the nineteenth century to transform external perceptions of its role from a commercial enterprise to scientific endeavour.[12]

In the 1920s, the earliest Mount Everest expeditions were also commercial ventures. British climbers and explorers received permission to approach the mountain from Tibet as part of a commercial bargain in 1921. The government of Tibet traded access to Chomolungma-Everest in exchange for British weapons during periods of military conflicts with China. As bargaining chips in diplomacy, Everest climbing permits became a commodity, and so they have remained. British Everest expeditions in the 1920s and 1930s were funded by government subsidy, commercial endorsements, and selling the media rights. London newspapers or British filmmakers paid most of the cost in exchange for exclusive rights to publish news and official dispatches or make films about the expedition. Manufacturers donated equipment in exchange for testimonials. Subsidies came in the form of paid leave for officers or gifts-in-kind from the British military and government of India. Put another way, the Indian taxpayers of the British Raj paid part of the cost of the British expeditions in the 1920s and 1930s. The first commercial Everest expedition should be dated to 1924, when John Noel's Explorer's Films Limited paid 80% of the cost of the expedition on which George Mallory and Andrew Irvine disappeared near the summit.[13]

Why did Mallory join the first Everest expeditions and keep coming back? Mallory was persuaded by a friend to join the team because the "Everest label" would open doors beyond his career as a schoolmaster.[14] In 1923, Mallory was on a paid lecture tour through Britain and the United States when he told the *New York Times* that Everest should be climbed "because it's there." Mallory toured to pay his way and raise money for the expedition, and his remarks highlighted the rising costs to reach higher elevations much like a fundraising appeal.[15] Mallory had become a professional mountaineer, supporting himself on the lecture circuit, though he was not the first, and many more would follow.

In 1925, John Noel's film, *The Epic of Everest*, was screened in London with a group of "dancing lamas" whose performances offended officials in Tibet and caused the cancellation of Everest expeditions for nearly a decade. The commercialisation of Everest put the Tibetans in a position to critique Noel's film and stop British ascents of the mountain. The closing intertitles of *The Epic of Everest* describe the mountain as Chomolungma, Goddess Mother of the World. The continuing use of this translation is itself an artefact of the commercialisation of Everest by this film. Alternate translations exist, and the preference for this one was established by Noel's intercultural dialogue with his local informants and his choices in the editing and release of this film.

A century later, Royal Geographical Society Enterprises, the commercial arm of the society, sells reproductions of the photographs from the early Everest expeditions. This is a contemporary reminder of the continuing commercial exploitation of the geographical exploration of Everest and other extreme environments. Commercialisation through sponsorship by the Royal Geographical Society, National Geographic Society, and other societies has been severely underestimated. Rachel Gross observes of Everest expeditions that "sponsorship is, in fact, marketing," and this was true before the strategy of sponsors shifted from public relations to paid advertising in the second half of the twentieth century.[16] Continuities across the twentieth century suggest that the contrast between 'exploratory' and 'commercial' climbing has been exaggerated in the history of mountaineering and other expeditions in extreme environments.

The first ascent of Everest by a British team in 1953 took place in a national/commercial nexus at the end of empire and height of the Cold War. The iconic photograph taken by Edmund Hillary of Tenzing Norgay on the summit holding aloft the flags of Britain, India, Nepal, and the United Nations circulated widely. After intense debates over who stepped on the summit first, Tenzing and Hillary were each celebrated as national heroes in multiple nation states.

In later decades, images of Tenzing, Hillary, and Everest appeared on postage stamps and currency, with Hillary's youthful face on New Zealand's five-dollar bill. The use of these images in infinitely replicable series such as stamps or currency is a sign of the commercial exploitation of nationalism by the nation state.[17] This pattern was repeated by other national teams on Everest and other Himalayan peaks.

The Mount Everest Foundation and commercial sponsorship

For several decades after 1953, British mountaineering was underwritten by the financial success of the first ascent. Profits from Everest books, films, and lectures in 1953 were placed in a trust, the Mount Everest Foundation; reinvested; and ploughed back into later climbing expeditions. The cost of the British first ascent of Kanchenjunga in 1955 and the ascent of Annapurna in 1970 were both fully paid by the Mount Everest Foundation.[18] In other words, the commercialisation of Everest in 1953 funded British mountaineering in the Himalayas into the 1970s and has continued to subsidise climbing teams through smaller grants.

The search for commercial sponsorship expanded in the 1950s and took on increasing importance in the 1970s. Take Rolex, for example. Rolex had sponsored Himalayan expeditions since the 1930s and presented watches to the 1953 Everest team. Hillary appeared frequently in Rolex advertising, initially with Tenzing and later on his own or with Messner, as further adventures kept Hillary in the public eye. Hillary and Tenzing's sons and grandsons have continued this sponsorship into later generations.

Rolex is an example of the commercialisation of paraphernalia, to adopt the terminology of scholars of commercialisation and lifestyle sports.[19] Paraphernalia commercialisation refers to the production and marketing of climbing or sports equipment and has been distinguished from two other kinds: movement commercialisation, that is, specialty enterprises located within and dedicated to serving the climbing community, and finally mass-market commercialisation, when mainstream businesses use the aura of mountaineering to sell products to non-climbers as well as climbers. These are heuristic categories that co-exist with one another, not stages of development. By the 1960s, the movement commercialisation of climbing and the mass-market promotion of Everest were entrenched and lucrative sources of income for some climbers.[20]

The expansion of the outdoor industry, mountaineering paraphernalia, and commercial sponsorship continued to develop alongside Everest expeditions in the 1960s and 1970s. In 1963, the huge American Mount Everest Expedition (AMEE) was organised as a commercial enterprise. Jim Whittaker, the first American to reach the summit of Everest, worked for and later became the CEO of Recreational Equipment Incorporated, an excellent example of movement commercialisation of climbing and outdoor recreation.[21] The *Wall Street Journal* noted with some satisfaction that the AMEE was, literally, a corporation (tax-exempt, non-profit). Costing over $400,000, the AMEE represented the largest party to climb any mountain and combined scientific research with the climbing efforts.[22]

Commercialisation and Mount Everest 149

Mass-market commercialisation and mega-expeditions continued into the 1970s, and many of the arguments offered in later debates about the commercialisation of climbing took shape in these years. It is tempting to identify this discursive change – the development of certain kinds of critique of commercialisation – with a shift in practice from national to international, or siege to 'alpine'-style, expeditions. Once again, national expeditions were already commercial before 1970, and perhaps for that very reason, national teams remained the predominant mode for organising and marketing Everest ascents throughout the 1980s and the end of the Cold War.

The critique of commercialisation

Everest expeditions in the 1970s had many of the features that are often associated with the later critique of commercialisation since the 1990s. Consider these examples:

- In 1973, an Italian Everest expedition led by the climber and polar explorer Guido Monzino, scion of a supermarket fortune, included a huge team of 60 members and more than 100 Sherpas, lavish accommodations, and helicopters that took gear above the icefall.[23]
- In 1975, Barclays Bank was principal sponsor of the British expedition to the Southwest Face of Everest. Expedition tents, rather than climber's parkas, had Barclays' logos since the climbers did not want to look like race car drivers. Barclays donated £141,000 but recouped most of its investment through book royalties and selling other rights, so its net outlay was only £20,000.[24]
- Also 1975, Junko Tabei, first woman to climb Everest, was sponsored by a Tokyo newspaper and Japanese television network. Known as the "Everest mother," she said the attention and responsibility were overwhelming. After the ascent, she did not seek corporate funding again. "If I accept sponsorship, then climbing the mountain is not my own experience," she said later. "It's like working for the company."[25]
- In 1976, the American Bicentennial Expedition was launched by a group of lawyers, doctors, and professors, along with several professional climbers. Their budget was over $200,000 and funded mostly by CBS television.[26]
- Messner paid for his place on an Austrian expedition in 1978 and had multiple sponsorship deals. After his Everest ascents without oxygen in 1978 and alone in 1980, his endorsements and royalties from books and merchandise funded a successful career as a professional mountaineer and explorer.[27]
- The Chinese-Japanese expedition on the Chinese side of Everest in 1980 included 60 climbers and a dozen reporters and had an estimated cost over £800,000.[28]

The income earned by Messner and a few others was exceptional and only possible because Everest appealed to a mass-market audience. In later years, few climbers could hope to earn similar amounts from climbing. In 1988, a spokesman for Rolex explained their sponsorship strategy by noting the "disappearance" of potentially important discoveries and "there is only one Everest."[29]

The expansion of access and reduction in reputational as well as financial rewards since the 1990s have been felt keenly as a loss by some climbers. At a forum on Everest in 2014, the prominent American climber Conrad Anker said that as a young man, he was in awe of Doug Scott's ascent of Everest's Southwest Face: "Now, [when] I go to Yosemite, they're like, 'dude, you've climbed Everest, you're not worthy anymore.' So, it is like this big change around, where it has become far more commercial."[30]

Controversies over commercial expeditions and deaths on Everest in the 1990s and 2000s are well known and related in articles, films, television, and books with titles like *Dark Summit*.[31] Crowds lined the ropes, climbers were left to die, and garbage piled up.[32] Climbers pay from $40,000 to $110,000 to climb on a route with camps, cooks, and fixed ropes from Base Camp to the summit. According to Messner, the prepared routes on Everest have changed the mountain fundamentally. The standard route via the South Col in Nepal was no longer "wilderness," he said, but "piste alpinism" that follows a groomed ski trail or via ferrata prepared by Sherpas.

> But piste alpinism is tourism. What is tourism? Tourism is an activity where the organizer is preparing your stay in a way that is quite safe and secure. . . . But alpinism, classical, traditional alpinism is beginning where tourism is finishing.[33]

The twenty-first-century Everest

Climbers often place alpinism and tourism in opposition, but this rhetorical move once again obscures the connections between alpinism and adventure tourism and mystifies the claims that climbers make for their own modernity through mountaineering.[34] Not even the earliest Everest climbers arrived in an uninhabited, pristine wilderness outside of time and history. From a longer perspective, the trouble with "traditional alpinism" is also the trouble with wilderness: "it reproduces the very values its devotees seek to reject."[35] Alpinism on Everest and elsewhere was and is a form of tourism that cannot disentangle climbers from the relationships they bring with them or the societies they encounter. For Messner, though, climbing Everest has become banal and has nothing to do with alpinism. "People don't climb Hillary's Everest or my Everest. They climb another mountain, even if it is geologically the same."[36]

By the first quarter of the twenty-first century, nostalgia for this earlier Everest ("Hillary's Everest or my Everest") is being challenged by Sherpas and others in Nepal who balance the risk of death with the income from climbing differently than some visitors.[37] Though western perspectives on Everest have been challenged for years in the Himalayas and elsewhere,[38] the demands of Sherpas and Nepalis have become increasingly vocal in the last decade, especially during the "Everest brawl" of 2013, an icefall avalanche in 2014, the Nepal earthquake in

2015, and the repeated closures of the mountain after some of these events and the coronavirus pandemic.

The so-called "Everest brawl" broke out after three European climbers insulted a group of high-altitude workers fixing ropes on Everest. The European climbers, led by Simone Moro, asserted a right to roam freely in the mountains, calling their effort the "NO(2) Limits Everest Expedition." These climbers "feel that Everest – just like every mountain – should be open to all, anytime."[39] While climbing on the regular Everest route to acclimatise, they literally and figuratively stepped over the line, cursing at the Sherpas who were preparing fixed ropes, which led to a violent scuffle in a climbing camp.[40] Though the "brawl" should have demonstrated that mountains are *not* spaces without limits, where anyone can do as they please, the global media coverage fell into colonial stereotypes and critiques of commercialisation. Yet the conflict was not a clash between commercial Sherpas and "adventure" climbers unencumbered by commerce but rather an encounter of multiple forms of commercial mountaineering that are mutually interdependent.

After years of quiet suffering and deference helping visitors to achieve glorious first ascents, Nepalis complained in 2013 that they were tired of the disrespect and arrogance of western climbers and guides. "As a Nepali-owned outfitter," wrote Sumit Joshi of Himalayan Ascent, "we often hear our western outfitter friends acknowledge that the skilled Sherpa climbers deserve more. But what are they actually willing to give more of? More money? More benefits? More fame? Perhaps they should start with more respect."[41] Tashi Sherpa, a member of the rope-fixing team in the altercation, complained that Sherpas risked their lives but did not get any credit. "Even in documentary films like *Into Thin Air* and *Everest*, you don't get to see Sherpas. We have been left out." Sherpas benefited from mountaineering, but so had "whites" and the Nepali government. Relations were still good, "but this incident was waiting to happen, and it will happen again as long as Sherpas are humiliated."[42]

On 18 April 2014, a block of ice detached from the West Shoulder of Everest, and an avalanche fell on the climbing route in the Khumbu Icefall just above Everest Base Camp. The avalanche killed 16 Nepali high-altitude workers, then Everest's deadliest single disaster. After rescues of the injured and recovery of the dead, three victims remained buried in the ice. Sherpas refused to climb over the bodies of their colleagues and demanded better insurance, higher compensation for victim's families, and more respect from expedition operators and the Nepali government. Film crews that had planned to broadcast stunts on the mountain instead recorded these debates. The documentary *Sherpa* follows Phurba Tashi, a 21-time Everest summitteer and climbing leader for Himalayan Experience, a European expedition operator, back to his village where his family fears for his safety and anguishes over his return to the mountain. While watching his sons, Phurba remarks: "There are no other opportunities for Sherpas. Mountaineering is where we can make the most money. Everyone needs money, so we go on pretending that it's safe."[43]

A year later, a 7.8 magnitude earthquake on 25 April 2015, caused the deaths of almost 9,000 people in Nepal. The earthquake set off an avalanche that swept directly into Everest Base Camp with the force of an enormous bomb, killing at least 21 people.[44] Climbing was cancelled without protest. The 2015 earthquake opened the eyes of some climbers to the precarity of everyday life in Nepal. The first-world bubble around Everest was recognised after the earthquake with awkwardness, as if for the first time: "Even as we have been climbing their mountains, we've been living in a different world."[45] Disparities of wealth had been visible for years, but the earthquake ruptured a complacency that looked upward toward the summits but lacked the peripheral vision to see the conditions of life in Nepal.

Crowds returned to Everest within a few years, with nearly 700 ascents in 2017, more than 800 in 2018, and almost 900 in 2019, from both sides of the mountain. "2019 will go down as the year Everest finally broke," declared one commentator, reflecting on 11 deaths, accusations of fraud, and large crowds of climbers.[46] Guiding companies multiplied on Everest, and Nepali outfitters offered cheaper options. In 2019, about 80% of the climbers were with Nepali firms and 20% with foreign expedition operators, a reversal of the ratio only five years earlier.[47] Indians outnumbered Americans as the largest nationality for Everest climbers and were represented disproportionately among recent deaths.[48] Some established operators complained that local firms were targeting the Indian and Chinese markets with low-priced ascents. In 2019, unsettled weather created a brief period of several days to reach the top, and the scene of climbers waiting back-to-back in lines on the summit ridge was captured in a viral photograph.[49]

The climber who photographed these lines heading for the summit was Nirmal Purja Pun Magar, a Nepali climber and former soldier in the Gurkhas and UK special forces. Nirmal Purja was climbing Everest for *Project Possible*, an effort to ascend all the world's 14 highest peaks in less than seven months. "Securing the financial partners was clearly going to be an additional mountain to climb," his website noted. A UK-based GoFundMe page raised £121,000, and he mortgaged his house and potentially his future. After early successes, Bremont, a British maker of luxury watches founded in 2002, acquired the naming rights to the project. Others like Red Bull signed Purja to sponsorships with further success.

The closure of Everest during the coronavirus pandemic once again emphasised Nepal's dependence on mountaineering and other forms of adventure tourism.[50] Policies requiring experience on other peaks and other technical changes to the Everest industry will not end debates over commercialisation. The intensity of these debates in recent years has less to do with climbing policies than with the extremes of wealth and poverty and contests for control over Everest and how these have become politically relevant.

The day Nirmal Purja summitted and photographed the line on Everest – 22 May 2019 – a total of 222 climbers reached the summit, including 133 from Nepal, 27 from India, 27 from China, and 35 from all other countries combined.[51] That year Nepalis made 57% of all ascents of Everest. Incentives to reach the summit are considerable. High-altitude workers earn more in two months on Everest than the average income in Nepal for a year, yet their earnings remain a fraction of what western guides are paid for the same work. By contrast, western guides and climbers are from some of the wealthiest countries in the world, even if they are not the wealthiest clients paying the highest fees. Recently, some Indian climbers on Everest came from families of modest means.[52] Disparities of wealth between climbers and guides, including those from India and China, are common in Himalayan mountaineering.

These disparities gained salience as Nepalis have asserted control over climbing on Everest. They have asserted control because the prosperity and well-being of their communities depends on Everest's continued commercialisation. If commercialisation has a long history on Everest, so too does the avoidance of calling it by name, a reluctance once associated with imperial or nationalist points of view. Disparities of wealth did not start with globalisation, and they will not be reduced or overcome by pretending that the Himalayas are simply the Alps with higher elevations. There is no going back to an age that never was, no position "outside" the continuum of commercialisation on Everest or elsewhere.

Everest and the world's highest peaks remain climbers' challenges as well as commercial ventures. "THE IMPOSSIBLE IS MADE POSSIBLE" read the headline of Nirmal Purja's announcement that an all-Nepali team of ten climbers made the first winter ascent of K2 in January 2021. This ascent was heralded as completion of one of the "last" great climbing challenges. This all-caps headline could be transformed into an historical explanation by appending the phrase ". . . BY THE COMMERCIALIZATION OF MOUNT EVEREST." Nine of the ten Nepali climbers were Sherpas who had started their climbing careers as porters, developing and honing their climbing skills to an elite level on Everest. Their collective achievement on K2 was the culmination of developments on Everest and other peaks across the long twentieth century. These climbers were aware of the significance of this moment in a longer history. When they neared the top, "the whole team waited 10m below the summit to form a group then stepped onto the summit together whilst singing our Nepalese National Anthem."[53]

Notes

1 The author is grateful for the support of the Durham University Institute of Advanced Study and for comments at Durham's Hatfield College and the conference on geographical exploration in Milan.
2 I. Rowan, "A Summit Bathed in Publicity", *Daily Telegraph Magazine*, 16 April 1971.
3 John H.C. Hunt and Christopher Brasher, *The Red Snows: An Account of the British Caucasus Expedition, 1958* (London: Hutchinson, 1960); Carolin F. Roeder, *European Mountaineers between East and West: A Transnational History of Alpinism in the Twentieth Century* (Doctoral dissertation, Harvard University, Graduate School of Arts & Sciences, 2017); Ilaria Scaglia, *The Emotions of Internationalism: Feeling International Cooperation in the Alps in the Interwar Period* (New York: Oxford University Press, 2020).
4 Maurice Isserman and Stewart A. Weaver, *Fallen Giants: A History of Himalayan Mountaineering from the Age of Empire to the Age of Extremes* (New Haven: Yale University Press, 2010), 435.
5 Richard Salisbury, *The Himalayan Database* (2020), www.himalayandatabase.com/, last access 10 December 2021.
6 Julie Rak, *False Summit: Gender in Mountaineering Nonfiction* (Montreal: McGill-Queen's University Press, 2021).

154 *Peter H. Hansen*

7 Mark Liechty, *Far Out: Countercultural Seekers and the Tourist Encounter in Nepal* (Chicago: University of Chicago Press, 2017); Sherry B. Ortner, *Life and Death on Mt. Everest: Sherpas and Himalayan Mountaineering* (Princeton: Princeton University Press, 2001).
8 Esther Bott, "Big Mountain, Big Name: Globalised Relations of Risk in Himalayan Mountaineering", *Journal of Tourism and Cultural Change* 7, no. 4 (2009): 287–301. doi:10.1080/14766820903521785.
9 Peter H. Hansen, *The Summits of Modern Man: Mountaineering after the Enlightenment* (Cambridge: Harvard University Press, 2013).
10 Ben Anderson, *Cities, Mountains and Being Modern in Fin-de-Siècle England and Germany* (London: Palgrave Macmillan, 2020); Peter H. Hansen, "Partners: Guides and Sherpas in the Alps and Himalayas, 1850s-1950s", in *Voyages and Visions: Towards a Cultural History of Travel*, eds. Jás Elsner and Joan-Pau Rubiés (London: Reaktion, 1999), 210–231; Tait Keller, *Apostles of the Alps: Mountaineering and Nation Building in Germany and Austria, 1860–1939* (Chapel Hill: University of North Carolina Press, 2016).
11 Sidney Gerald Burrard, *Mount Everest and Its Tibetan Names: A Review of Sir Sven Hedin's Book* (Dehra Dun: Geodetic Branch Office, Survey of India, 1931); Sven A. Hedin, *Mount Everest Och Andra Asiatiska Problem* (Stockholm: A. Bonner, 1922).
12 Sunil S. Amrith, *Unruly Waters: How Mountain Rivers and Monsoons Have Shaped South Asia's History* (New York: Basic Books, 2018); Philip J. Stern, *The Company-State: Corporate Sovereignty and the Early Modern Foundations of the British Empire in India* (New York: Oxford University Press, 2011); Matthew H. Edney, *Mapping an Empire: The Geographical Construction of British India, 1765–1843* (Chicago: University of Chicago Press, 1997); Bernard S. Cohn, *Colonialism and Its Forms of Knowledge: The British in India* (Princeton: Princeton University Press, 1996).
13 Peter H. Hansen, "The Dancing Lamas of Everest: Cinema, Orientalism, and Anglo-Tibetan Relations in the 1920s", *The American Historical Review the American Historical Review* 101, no. 3 (1996): 712. doi:10.1086/ahr/101.3.712.
14 Peter Gillman and Leni Gillman, *The Wildest Dream: Mallory, His Life and Conflicting Passions* (London: Headline, 2001), 171.
15 "Climbing Mount Everest Is Work for Supermen", *New York Times*, 18 March 1923.
16 Rachel S. Gross, "Logos on Everest: Commercial Sponsorship of American Expeditions, 1950–2000", *Enterprise & Society* (2020): 1–36. doi:10.1017/eso.2020.31.
17 Benedict Anderson, *Imagined Communities: Reflections on the Origin and Spread of Nationalism* (London and New York: Verso, 1991); Peter H. Hansen, "Confetti of Empire: The Conquest of Everest in Nepal, India, Britain, and New Zealand", *Comparative Studies in Society and History* 42, no. 2 (2000): 307–332. doi:10.1017/S0010417500002486.
18 T. Barcham, *The Modernisation of Elite British Mountaineering: Entrepreneurship, Commercialisation and the Career Climber, 1953–2000* (Doctoral dissertation, De Montfort University, 2018), http://hdl.handle.net/2086/16546.
19 Bob Edwards and Ugo Corte, "Commercialization and Lifestyle Sport: Lessons from 20 Years of Freestyle BMX in Pro-Town, USA", *Sport in Society Sport in Society* 13, no. 7–8 (2010): 1135–1151. doi:10.1080/17430431003780070.
20 Joseph E. Taylor, *Pilgrims of the Vertical: Yosemite Rock Climbers and Nature at Risk* (Cambridge: Harvard University Press, 2011).
21 Harvey Manning, *REI: 50 Years of Climbing together: The REI Story* ([Seattle]: REI, 1988).
22 Philip W. Clements, *Science in an Extreme Environment: The 1963 American Mount Everest Expedition* (Pittsburgh: University of Pittsburgh Press, 2018); Vanessa Heggie, *Higher and Colder: A History of Extreme Physiology and Exploration* (Chicago: University of Chicago Press, 2019).

23 Walt Unsworth, *Everest: The Mountaineering History* (Seattle, WA and London: Mountaineers; Bâton Wicks, 2001).
24 Thomas Barcham, "Commercial Sponsorship in Mountaineering: A Case Study of the 1975 British Everest Expedition", *Sport in History* 33, no. 3 (2013): 333–352. doi:10.1080/17460263.2013.826435.
25 Junko Tabei and Helen Y. Rolfe, *Honouring High Places: The Mountain Life of Junko Tabei*, trans. Y. Hiraki and R. Holtved (Victoria: Rocky Mountain Books, 2017); Robert Horn, "No Mountain Too High for Her: Junko Tabei Defied Japanese Views of Women to Become an Expert Climber", *Sports Illustrated* (29 April 1996), https://vault.si.com/vault/1996/04/29/no-mountain-too-high-for-her-junko-tabei-defied-japanese-views-of-women-to-become-an-expert-climber, last access 10 December 2021.
26 Rick Ridgeway, *The Boldest Dream: The Story of Twelve Who Climbed Mount Everest* (New York: Harcourt Brace Jovanovich, 1979).
27 Ronald Faux, *High Ambition: A Biography of Reinhold Messner* (London: Gollancz, 1982).
28 Unsworth, *Everest*.
29 Gross, "Logos on Everest"; M. Cannell, "Pitching the Big Trip: Explorers Spend More Time Raising Money Than Spending It", *New York Times Magazine*, 12 June 1988.
30 Sustainable Summits, dir., "Everest Knot Panel Discussion", in *Sustainable Summits Initiative* (2014), https://youtu.be/DgbKAl4C3rI, last access 10 December 2021.
31 Nick Heil, *Dark Summit: The True Story of Everest's Most Controversial Season* (New York: Henry Holt, 2008); Jon Krakauer, *Into Thin Air: A Personal Account of the Mount Everest Disaster* (New York: Villard, 1997).
32 Elizabeth Mazzolini, *The Everest Effect: Nature, Culture, Ideology* (Tuscaloosa: University of Alabama Press, 2016).
33 Luke Bauer, *Reinhold Messner Speaks at Outdoor Retailer* (2012), https://web.archive.org/web/20160824232148/http://inclined.americanalpineclub.org/2012/02/reinhold-messner-at-outdoor-retailer/, last access 10 December 2021.
34 Hansen, *The Summit of Modern Man*; Paul A. Beedie and Simon Hudson, "Emergence of Mountain-Based Adventure Tourism", *Annals of Tourism Research* 30, no. 3 (2003): 625–643. doi:10.1016/S0160-7383(03)00043-4.
35 William Cronon, "The Trouble with Wilderness", *New York Times Magazine*, 13 August 1995, www.nytimes.com/1995/08/13/magazine/the-trouble-with-wilderness.html, last access 10 December 2021.
36 Stefan Nestler, "Messner: 'First Ascent a Magic Moment of Mountaineering'", 29 May 2013, www.dw.com/en/messner-first-ascent-a-magic-moment-of-mountaineering/a-16844185, last access 10 December 2021.
37 Young Hoon Oh, "Dying Differently: Sherpa and Korean Mountaineers on Everest", *Minnesota Review* 90 (2018): 100–113. doi:10.1215/00265667-4391560.
38 Peter H. Hansen, "Tenzing's Two Wrist-Watches: The Conquest of Everest and Late Imperial Culture in Britain 1921–1953", *Past & Present* 157 (1997): 159–177. doi:10.1093/past/157.1.159.
39 Freddie Wilkinson, "Attack on Mount Everest", *Men's Journal*, 4 June 2013, www.mensjournal.com/features/attack-on-mount-everest-20130614/, last access 10 December 2021.
40 *Machtkampf am Everest Sherpas, Bergsteiger und die blutige Eskalation eines Konflikts* (Malik, 2013).
41 S. Joshi, *A Comment on the Brawl Incident* (5 May 2013, 10 AM), https://web.archive.org/web/20140216131937/https://himalayanascent.com/live-blog/140-a-comment-on-the-brawl-incident-05-05-13-10am-.html, last access 10 December 2021.
42 Deepak Adhikari, "The Everest Brawl: A Sherpa's Tale", *Outside Online* (13 August 2012), www.outsideonline.com/1929351/everest-brawl-sherpas-tale?page=all, last access 10 December 2021.

43 Jennifer Peedom, dir., "Sherpa: Trouble on Everest", in *Australia: Screen Australia* (Australia: Universal Sony Pictures Home Entertainment, 2015).
44 Dave Hahn and J.J. Justman, "Mt. Everest Expedition: Dave Hahn Details the Days Events as the Team Arrives Base Camp", *RMI Expeditions* (27 April 2015), www.rmiguides.com/blog/2015/04/27/mt._everest_expedition_dave_hahn_details_the_days_events_as_the_team_arrive, last access 10 December 2021.
45 Freddie Wilkinson, "Who Controls Nepal's Helicopters?", *Foreign Policy* (2 May 2015), https://foreignpolicy.com/2015/05/02/nepal-helicopters-earthquake-relief-everest/, last access 10 December 2021.
46 Alan Arnette, "Everest 2019: Season Summary the Year Everest Broke" (2019), www.alanarnette.com/blog/2019/06/07/everest-2019-season-summary-the-year-everest-broke/, last access 10 December.
47 Abhirup Roy and Gopal Sharma, "Summit Fever: Everest's Budget Climbing Boom Puts Indians Most at Risk", *Reuters* (31 May 2019), www.reuters.com/article/us-nepal-everest-indians-idUSKCN1T10OD, last access 10 December 2021.
48 J. Branch, "Deliverance from 27,000 Feet", *New York Times*, 19 December 2017, www.nytimes.com/interactive/2017/12/18/sports/everest-deaths.html, last access 10 December 2021; Rajan Pokhrel, "Congestion Didn't Cause Everest Deaths", *Himalayan Times*, 5 June 2019, https://thehimalayantimes.com/nepal/congestion-didnt-cause-everest-deaths/, last access 10 December 2021.
49 Svati Kristen Narula, "Yes, This Photo from Everest Is Real", *Outside Online* (23 May 2019), www.outsideonline.com/2397164/everest-summit-traffic-jam, last access 10 December 2021.
50 Sanjay K. Nepal, "Adventure Travel and Tourism after COVID-19: Business as Usual or Opportunity to Reset?", *Tourism Geographies* 22, no. 3 (2020): 646–650. doi:10.1080/14616688.2020.1760926.
51 Salisbury, *The Himalayan Database*.
52 Branch, "Deliverance from 27,000 Feet".
53 Nirmal Purja [nimsdai], "The Impossible Is Made Possible!", #K2winter: History Made for Mankind, History Made for Nepal! [Instagram], 16 January 2021, accessed 19 January 2021, www.instagram.com/p/CKGyyPDBNL-/, last access 10 December 2021.

10 Geographical exploration via the environmental humanities

Decolonising approaches to space

Roberta Biasillo

Encounters, not discoveries

> I got detoured. Took a wrong turn and ironically went upon Columbus Street, you know? And I said to my wife: 'Isn't it ironic that I am on the street that they changed from Delaware Avenue, which is what the English called my people and here we are wandering lost on Columbus Street'? And based upon the way folks tell the story, until today we were lost here on this continent and we didn't know we were here until Columbus came and told us where we were.
> (Rev. Dr. John Norwood, New Jersey, 2015)[1]

We have so much to rewrite about the past, and we have so much to recast about the present. The previous extract introduces two aspects that this chapter would like to discuss: how past and present are interconnected and how they interconnect in specific places. Myths of discovery and a sense of otherness recur in all the geographical expeditions analysed earlier in this volume. Contributors historicise expeditions and show rationales, aspirations, gazes, and appropriation practices via political, scientific and commercial means. That said, places and peoples under scrutiny disclose their own agency and challenge their avowed marginality.

Research on exploration and discoveries of hostile, extreme, exotic, sublime, obscure, and peripheral environments enriches our historical, anthropological, ecological, and geographical knowledge, as in the case of the present volume. At the same time, it appears apt to create thorny ethical and value issues around the concept of otherness rather than solving them.

The concept of otherness – the very foundation of European superiority and colonialism – has been questioned extensively in recent decades in scholarly debates and the public sphere. In the late 1980s, Gayatri Chakravorty Spivak noticed that European scholars offered a self-contained version of the West by ignoring the imperialist project and relying on a "geographical (geopolitical) discontinuity" that produced "a miniature version" of European imperialism.[2] In the early 2000s, Dipesh Chakrabarty demonstrated that scholars embarking on the reconstruction of the history of any country "outside of the Western capitalist democracies of the world" deemed social science and historicising approaches

DOI: 10.4324/9781003095965-11

inadequate to "think through the various life practices that constitute the political and the historical" – the way in which Europe could be "provincialised" was to chronologically and theoretically break the unidirectional perspective from the West towards the rest of the world, now perceived as the Global North and the Global South.[3] These two influential reflections exposed the social sciences and humanities to a decolonising process by means of a call for a condition in which subalterns could speak for themselves, be heard, and be subaltern no longer.[4]

Decolonisation and postcolonial studies in the 1960s had already inspired new interpretations of exploration and discoveries, with scholars starting to include different points of view within a wider picture. Exploration and discoveries studies thus made progress towards a "global history of the encounter".[5] Today, the interpretation of the past through narratives of discovery appears extremely controversial because they reassert a human universal and re-present a core process of Western imperialism.[6]

In the attempt to let academic disciplines and their conceptual tools unlearn imperialism,[7] scholars must interrogate what they prioritise in their analyses. In "Decolonization Is Not a Metaphor", Eve Tuck and K. Wayne Yang argue for looking into land appropriation and land-use dynamics and advocate for "questions of landedness, racial categories, and settlement".[8]

An underlying theme unites postcolonial and exploration scholarship, the case studies explored earlier in this volume, and this chapter's epigraph from Reverend Norwood. Their directions of travel empower citizens and scholars to draw out different networks, spaces, and articulations of geographical areas and open up practices of re-writing territories and worlds. Geography, in its etymological sense of writing and determining the texture of a space, seems to be the pivotal tool with which to understand local and global orders; to unsettle different scales of inequality; and to tie disciplinary, non-disciplinary, embodied, and community-based framing efforts to the environment or the landscape.

In the following sections, the reader will encounter ongoing socially inclusive and environmentally conscious models for actively approaching and framing urban environments without silencing social and climate injustices. Then, the reader will enter the academic realm and get to know ways in which the humanities have shifted their paradigms and how the global environmental crisis triggered what I called the "decolonial turn". The final section will offer fruitful additional areas for reflection based on spatial narratives drawn from environmental humanities (EH) scholarship.

The "spatiality of decolonization"[9]

Drawing on decolonial thinkers such as Walter Mignolo and Franz Fanon, Daniel Clayton and M. Satish Kumar show that decolonisation is simultaneously a history-making and space-making endeavour in ways that bring out the complex relationship between geographical study and the process of post-war

Geographical exploration via EH 159

decolonisation, with a focus on "critical and contextual historical geography"[10] in relation to a combination of different temporalities embedded in space.

The theorist Edward Said, along with the geographers Susan Hanson and Richard Phillips, started "de-mapping the Empire" in the 1990s, recovering territories geographically and culturally through the acknowledgment that every map depicts a biased human perspective and that the evolution of maps does not necessarily follow a linear progression in the knowledge of a place.[11] Landscape – the key unit of geographical analysis – was still widely assumed to be colonial in the early 2000s. Indeed, colonialism had been naturalised as part of landscapes to the extent that it was not possible to recognise its characteristics and related phenomena. According to Andrew Sluyter, "despite the magnitude and continuing consequences of that transformation, geographers have not produced a meaningful conceptual framework for understanding the relationships between colonization and landscape transformation".[12]

In the past few years, a new phase has begun, in which native and long-term sustainable agroecologies are valued as valid economic and ecological alternatives to Western orthodox development. Postcolonial geography is making room for multiple knowledge systems on the part of native peoples, too. Here, another element emerges: "critiques of science and the plurality of knowledges" have featured prominently in decolonial approaches to postcolonial worlds in recent decades.[13] In contrast to generalised knowledge, native knowledges have been rooted for many generations in places.[14]

Rural landscapes are being richly explored,[15] as are cities, with overviews of urban decolonial experiments highlighting intersecting issues of colonial planning.[16] Processes of returning and reclaiming land are also generating radical epistemologies and producing place-, community-, and gender-based accounts for cities that involve more respectful relationships with their diversities.[17]

A repertoire of geographical skills, strategies and networks, which long served colonial rule,[18] proves instrumental to subverting spatial patterns.[19] If the making of maps of protest or to protest was once a rather rare occurrence, modern-day maps bear a close connection with expressions of dissent. They are a powerful medium that can move the needle in political action and are produced to account for how social movements and social protests claim space.[20] As textual and visual representations of power relationships, maps play a significant role within postcolonial theory and the postcolonial novel. Activists and scholars are mapping postcolonial spaces through action-research methodologies and bottom-up initiatives enabling previously subaltern groups and marginal areas to draw their own textual and visual narratives and previously invisible human and non-human actors to speak for themselves. Martine Drozdz terms these practices "emancipatory mapping" or "maptivism", a portmanteau of *map* and *activism*.[21] Maptivism is a tool not only for social and political protest but also for experimental and creative methodologies. Let us now examine three examples.

Chiaiano

Maps of the Chiaiano district in the metropolitan area of Naples tend to reinforce "toxic narratives", that is, contaminating and contaminated public discourses imposing official truths while dismissing any alternative point of view.[22] In mainstream maps, Chiaiano appears as a peripheral metro station in the inefficient Neapolitan public transport system and in geo-referred diagrams of the regional criminal organisation system. In addition, maps of Chiaiano often convey a massive contaminated area due to the presence of two landfills. Marco Armiero's wide-ranging research on waste and struggles for environmental justice in Campania – the administrative region where Naples is located – offers a more nuanced image, elaborated upon in 2018 with a team of informed activists and committed researchers (Figure 10.1). In their map, we see two landfills (Chiaiano and Pianura), but we also see a forest (confiscated from the mafia), a social farm, places of individual and collective memories, and the Insurgencia community centre that has long been active in local social and environmental struggles. To make sense of this territory, there is a need for a multi-disciplinary approach that can capture relationships connecting space, time, emotions, memories, and practices.[23]

Marrickville

In Australia, we encounter the Mapping Edges transdisciplinary research studio, directed by Ilaria Vanni and Alexandra Crosby. The studio aims to "experiment with edges as transition zones between different ecosystems; interfaces between mediums, projects and processes on the margin of activities where it is possible to cross-pollinate, tinker and develop alternatives".[24] Marrickville is a suburb on Gadigal and Wangal land, also known as Sydney's Inner West, one of these zones where different knowledges have co-developed as a result of shifting demographics, including significant migrations of Greeks and Vietnamese, and where climate change is adding a challenging level of transformation.

The project by Mapping Edges entails a map of Marrickville following three types of flora: bananas, papayas, and dragon fruit (Figure 10.2). Although these plants are commonly considered "tropical", Sydney is classified as a subtropical climate zone. This botanical abundance suggests a shift that can be called "not yet tropical". Based on a counter-cartography of plants, (self-)guided walks, and interviews with gardeners, Marrickville Walks invites participants to connect to the suburb's ecologies by following the maps and adding their own discoveries.

Walking along the flora-determined itineraries, engaging in conversation with gardeners, and documenting in real time are the ingredients for discovering the ecologies of the land of Bulanaming – as it is known to First Peoples – in terms of past, present, and future. The presence of bananas, papayas, and dragon fruit reveals how the urban landscape is altering due to rising temperatures and how neighbours develop social relations through those plants. Maps are thus also an invitation to look at the interstices of human-made environments.[25]

Geographical exploration via EH 161

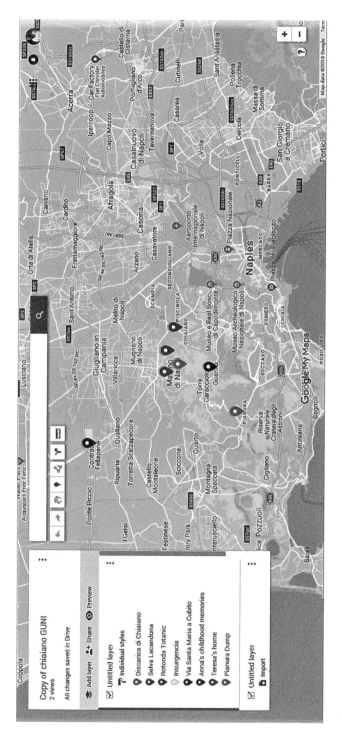

Figure 10.1 Chiaiano Neighbourhood, Naples (Italy), Global University Network for Innovation (2019), courtesy of the authors Marco Armiero and activists from Chiaiano. Available at www.guninetwork.org/files/download_full_report_heiw7.pdf, last access 10 December 2021.

162 Roberta Biasillo

Figure 10.2 Marrickville Maps: Tropical Imaginaries of Abundance (2018) by Mapping Edges Studio, creative commons.

New York City

New York is a tremendous decolonial laboratory. The Center for the Humanities at City University of New York's Graduate Center serves as a hub of many initiatives in public engagement and collaborative research.[26] One of these, the Climate Action Lab, aims to generate a toolkit organised around popular responses to climate change.[27] The artist, educator, and urban planner Aurash Khawarzad has produced a book, *The Upper Manhatta(n) Project*, as an outcome of collaborative mapping workshops.[28] Energy, emergencies, heat, food, waste, social hubs, green infrastructure, governance, housing, waterfronts and social inequality are mapped, with the benefits of climate resilience planning presented in each category. In terms of a decolonial perspective on instrumental maps of New York,[29] perhaps the best example is Khawarzad's *New York City Climate Change Displacement Map* (Figure 10.3). This map provides information about displacements

Geographical exploration via EH   163

Figure 10.3 New York City Climate Change Displacement Map (2020) by Aurash Khawarzad, courtesy of the author. Available at www.aurashkhawarzad.com/displacementmap, last access 10 December 2021.

of communities in NYC caused by climate change, institutional racism and gentrification. An innovative feature of the map is the iconography used to connect bygone displacements of indigenous communities and people of colour with what is happening today.[30]

In summary, these examples of geographical representations are indicative of a fruitful reorientation of critical urban studies. It is clear that recent literature has called into question the roles, functions and shapes of urban areas where accepted understandings derive from Euro-American contexts.[31] Another *fil rouge* of these examples is the conundrum of environmental injustice that global warming is making more prominent. Urban encounters with nature, as much as infrastructural presences in the countryside, are blurring entrenched dichotomies of urban/rural and natural/artefact.[32] The humanities and social sciences are thus embracing new methodologies, collaborations and vocabulary spurred by postcolonial theory and climate change.[33]

The environmental humanities: the "decolonial turn"

The past decade has seen the rise of new kinds of humanities, including a wave of hybrid fields: digital humanities, energy humanities, global humanities, urban humanities, blue humanities, food humanities, medical humanities, legal humanities, public humanities and environmental humanities. These new amalgams emphasise interactions with disciplines beyond the traditional scope of the humanities, particularly professional fields and STEM, that is, science, technology, engineering and maths. At the intersection of societal and academic concerns, EH has spawned centres, initiatives, networks, and programmes, including undergraduate majors.[34]

EH seems to offer the most suitable academic home for decolonising perspectives on place – on land and landscapes – because it addresses material and non-material domains that are not epistemically severed from colonial specificities.[35] Indeed, EH has been defined as a postcolonial field that applies cultural frameworks to material environments.[36] It does not carry a burden of historicism and complicity in imperial constructions, since it has been shaped by postcolonial and feminist scholars, including several working outside Europe and the United States. It also rejects the notion that Western cultures are superior and recognises that much knowledge is place specific. Furthermore, it puts value on a plurality of human experiences by drawing on theoretical developments from new materialism, Indigenous and postcolonial criticism, animal studies and queer ecology.[37]

In stressing the legacy of colonialism in the environment as part of a "decolonial turn", postcolonial approaches have always negotiated between scales of analysis. Research oriented towards a global dimension has engaged with epistemologies of climate change, the Anthropocene, worlding and world ecology, globalisation and globality, the planetary and planetarity and gaps between the Global North and Global South.[38] Elsewhere, scholars have reframed multifaceted worldwide enterprises through engagements with local places and cultural traditions.[39] Others, moved by the ethical practice of "becoming-witness", have called for a very personal attentiveness to the more-than-human world and highlighted the role of feelings and the senses in the EH epistemic project.[40] Indeed, this last strand of inquiry is becoming more and more prominent. The intrinsic decolonial character of EH is thus opening a window of opportunity to redefine the humanities from within, particularly history and geography, including their objects of inquiry.

I am going to explore two major ways in which EH scholarship avoids the acute sense of "colonial *déjà vu*",[41] calling for an anti-colonial relationship with land and a radically inclusive epistemology of space – a new frame for the contemporary age and a new premise for landscape research.

Decolonising the Anthropocene

Climate change is pervading every aspect of human and non-human lives,[42] and human beings have been recognised as a geological force.[43] The environment, conceived as a historical formation of human and non-human elements,[44] is thus an inescapable category. In view of the pressures raised by ecological and social crises, there is increasing consensus about defining the current epoch as the "Ecocene" (from a human perspective)[45] or the "Anthropocene" (from an Earth-centred perspective). The notion of the Anthropocene has gained traction beyond the natural sciences, with its use now widespread in the social sciences, the humanities, and public discourse. The most common formulation of the Anthropocene – an epoch defined by human transformations of all life on Earth – has been criticised as an overly simplistic and globalised view of human agency. To provide a more context-dependent, localised, and social understanding of such a powerful frame, scholars have engaged in a sort of diffraction experiment with the term.[46] They show how the notion of the Anthropocene is being used increasingly by different communities in a variety of contexts, and they unpack injustices and colonial legacies.

Differences of opinion have arisen over the Anthropocene's beginning. Some date its emergence to 1610–1620, when the colonisation of the Americas produced unequal power relations between different groups of people based on capitalist accumulation that led to globalised trade and fossil-fuel dependency. Others date it to circa 1800 at the onset of Europe's industrial revolution, whose long-term impacts have intensified since 1945 during the so-called Great Acceleration. A third hypothesis sets its beginning between the Trinity nuclear test in 1945 and 1964, when the rhetoric of economic and social progress intertwined with a growth in militarisation in the Cold War.[47] Each of these beginnings is rooted in colonialism and/or colonial appropriation.

It is crucial to complement a data-driven definition of the Anthropocene with an acknowledgement of continuities and ruptures in the human-environment relationship, especially in association with the colonial era. By accepting the early seventeenth century as a starting point that links the Anthropocene with colonisation, attention is drawn to violence at the core of the epoch. Indigenous philosophies and processes of Indigenous self-governance can thus be considered a necessary political corrective.[48] The capitalist and colonialist logic at the root of the Anthropocene translates into an all-encompassing top-down technocratic project[49] that has been defined as "Capitalocene"[50] or "Developmentocene".[51] When atomic blasts and nuclear tests are set as the beginning of the human-dominated age, the colonial spectre rears its head. Joint projects between academics, scientists, and Indigenous artists have framed the appropriation of the Pacific Ocean and Islands for military tests as "nuclear colonialism" that eventually created "radiation ecologies" and a "Nuclear Pacific".[52]

The concept of the Anthropocene *qua* climate change has made visible the "collateral of history", the by-products of industrial development, and the very *telos* of the colonial project.[53] To be sure, it is more than a rise in temperature. In the words of Donna Haraway, it is the intersection of many long-lasting inequalities that are simultaneously "Anthropocene, Capitalocene, Plantationocene, Chthulucene" – "extraordinary burdens of toxic chemistry, mining, depletion of lakes and rivers under and above ground, ecosystem simplification, vast genocides of people and other critters, etc, etc".[54] The Anthropocene is also a stimulus to broaden the scope of history and its agents,[55] as well as an invitation to communities to take seriously the moral, political, and ethical implication of human-planet relationships.[56]

Decolonising -scapes

Within the expanding literature on space and history, little has been said about the role that emptiness serves or the process by which it is produced. Similarly, little research explores the social and cultural practices used to create or maintain conditions of emptiness.[57] Nevertheless, literature on colonialism has dealt with the use of empty spaces in the construction of historical narratives and the contextualisation of myths and illusions of emptiness.[58] Indeed, processes of colonial inscription of emptiness have been shown to begin even before the arrival of the explorers who end up preparing maps with a view to for settlement in ways that utterly disregard people and ecologies on the ground.[59] The immaterial conceptualisation and material representation of empty expanses literally made room for colonialism.

However, emptiness alone is unable to explain seemingly contradictory aspects of colonial phenomena, in particular the connection with a mythical past.[60] As geographer Noam Leshem argues, material decay and ruination trigger ideologically driven processes of spatial transformation by increasing the *status* of an allegedly empty space so that it becomes prone to de-signification and re-signification.[61] Myths of emptiness and ruination established colonial land-, urban-, and sea-scapes as Year Zero, with mapping acting as "a technology in the service of empire and as a metaphor for the colonial project of mastery through knowledge accumulation and control".[62]

- Colonialism in the countryside (Maurits Ertsen):

    o The farming community was expected (and often forced) to cultivate exactly what the colonial management prescribed. The factory resemblance is also reflected in the mathematical layout of the systems where possible: canals are straight, and plots are square. Not only was the farming community to act according to prescription; the landscape had to be changed into a new, modern, and particularly geometric form. In the same way as they could transform the landscape, the colonial powers could also force peasants to grow certain crops, or organise the management of facilities, as they considered best.[63]

- Colonialism in the urban space (Mia Fuller) (Figure 10.4):

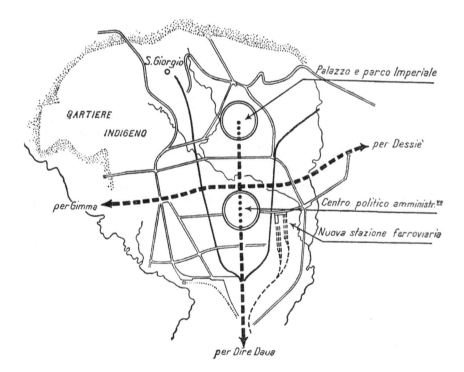

Figure 10.4 First plan of Addis Ababa as capital of the Italian Empire (1938), public domain. Available at https://it.wikipedia.org/w/index.php?curid=2404950, last access 10 December 2021.

The first Italian plan for Addis Ababa, showing St George's Church, the old imperial compound (*vecchio ghebi*), and the proposed site for the new Italian imperial compound (*nuovo ghebi*). The planners intended to use existing green surfaces (*zone verdi*) along the riverbeds to maintain divisions between the native 'quarter' (*quartiere indigeno*), the commercial 'quarter' (*quartiere commerciale*), and the Italian and political 'centres' (*quartiere italiano* and *centro politico*).[64]

- Colonialism across the ocean (William Sherman):
  - Claims for English sea-sovereignty explicitly rested on the sophisticated legal distinction between "Limits Absolute" and "Limits Respective". The former term applied whenever a body of water was flanked by lands belonging to a single country. In this case, the ocean simply became the jurisdiction of that country's monarch. The latter term applied whenever a body of water separated the territories of two or more monarchs. In this case, the sea jurisdiction would be determined either by the conventional one-hundred mile limit or by a line drawn midway between the coasts in question.[65]

Historical and historiographical narratives of emptiness and ruination, as well as geographical representations of empires, cannot present colonial projects as historical transformative projects inscribed in space and time, as exemplified previously. Historicising colonialism assumes that a pre-colonial environment existed. Adopting a political ecology approach leads to an interpretation of the colonial environment as a site of conflicts among different ontologies, rationales and epistemic systems. Multiplicities of peoples, plants, animals, soils, cultures and practices are what got lost in these imperial translation strategies. They erased the "marks of the natives" that preceded the arrival of the colonisers, co-existed with them, and resisted them.[66]

Questioning emptiness is the starting point of an EH approach. Land and space are key elements in unveiling the prospect of long indigenous ontologies. "There is no outer settler space. There is only *someone else's country*" – in order to make a case for this assumption, anthropology needs to be rethought as political ecology, and cultural heritage needs to be rethought as ethics.[67] Work in EH challenges amnesia concerning sacrifice zones,[68] especially the small islands of Austronesia and Taiwan, the Caribbean, Scotland and the Pacific. Interdisciplinary methods that combine politics and ecologies are allowing scholars and activists to read the effects of global capital and fantasies of racial superiority in countless "twilight islands", that is, mostly nonhuman-inhabited small spaces and biodiversity hotspots.[69] Research is making visible the traces of imperialism and its aftermath as concealed in the sea.[70] Undersea cables and oil rigs, islands of plastic particles, thousands of drowned slaves across the Atlantic – all these appear in decolonial histories of oceanic space that provide new approaches to aesthetic understandings of water, contributing to an oceanic humanities appropriate to the Global South.[71]

Ruination is another crucial aspect in EH. Climate change, resource depletion, long-term pollutants, food and water insecurity and extinctions have all fuelled ethical responses to earth's damaged environments and ecosystems. Models emerging from capitalist ruins, particularly in the wake of racial and epistemological violence, challenge classical western frameworks based on the impossibility of a relation between humans and nature outside of an extractivist metabolism.[72] In lexical terms, "encounter" is replacing "discovery", and "repair" is taking the place of the European modernist tendency to emphasise the creative capacity of humans to make something "new" by manipulating material resources, organising information, or delineating space. Indeed, repair is "the expression of care, and therefore a way of making ethical decisions about design within complex and traumatized ecological systems".[73]

EH is a decolonial and multispecies assemblage of perspectives and influences. It is a space where multitudes of lively agents "bring one another into being through entangled relations that include, but always also exceed, dynamics of predator and prey, parasite and host, researcher and researched, symbiotic partner, or indifferent neighbour".[74] It questions naturalisations and presumptions of innocence that perpetuate forms of ecological and social injustice. It embraces local and global complexities of economic and social practices and political discourses through narrative, history, critical thinking, cultural analysis, ethics, and aesthetics.[75]

Concluding considerations

Geography and history have been remarkably effective "producers of otherness" by way of the construction and maintaining of certain spatial patterns. To this end, a critical and reflexive perspective necessarily implies identifying and deconstructing the disciplinary bedrock for oppression.[76] This process raises awareness about epistemic colonial automatisms. Moreover, it is increasingly clear that climate change is accentuating pre-existing inequalities and causing disadvantaged groups to suffer disproportionately.[77] Conversely, climate change is drawing attention to alternative voices[78] and epistemic paradigms, such as EH.

EH has been particularly adept at showing how expeditions and places should be reframed. Michael Davis examines episodes in the collaborative engagement between voyagers and First Peoples during the expedition of the British ship *HMS Rattlesnake*, which, during 1847–1849, led an expedition to survey Australia's tropical northeast coasts, islands and reefs. According to Davis's thinking within EH, forms of integrated knowledge emerged in this scenario, even though the goal was to assess the suitability of the newly encountered land for British settlement. Indeed, records of the expedition describe First Peoples as collaborators, companions, and experts regarding the environment. The encounter between British explorers and First Peoples is an example of the practice of "walking together", that is, moments in which humans of different backgrounds met in the common purpose of knowing local human and nonhuman species.[79] Of course, violence does not disappear from this reconstruction.

170 *Roberta Biasillo*

Serenella Iovino's *Ecocriticism and Italy: Ecology, Resistance, and Liberation* (2016) explores places across the Italian peninsula. Her places "are at once territory and map, individual sites and cognitive instruments" – she aims to "sketch a map (one among the innumerable possible ones) of the landscapes of bodies and imagination through which a specific place becomes 'all the places'".[80] Iovino listens to past, present and future places; collects stories of death, violence and possibility; and interprets spaces through the filter of "material ecocriticism".[81] After all, thoughts and words constitute places as much as geographical circumstances. Emerging work on geography and memory shows how legacies of the past and emotions shape imagined environments. In a wider sense of "non-representational geography", ecologies of memories and feelings form "interlinkages between individuals, various social collectives, materialities, texts, and past/present/future timespaces".[82] In effect, *-scapes* are "palimpsests"[83] or material texts: just as humanists are equipped to interpret a text, environmental humanists look to read environments as texts.

Ultimately, the explorations addressed earlier in this volume span a late phase of colonial expansion and an under-researched period of post-war decolonisation. In line with recent scholarship focusing on space, this collection explores the impact of non-western forces on European gazes; re-examines nineteenth- and twentieth-century exploration; and argues that the contribution of non-western cultural, political, and social forces to expeditionary literature, reports, and administrative files was far greater than studies have suggested.[84] If, dear reader, you felt that these essays displaced you and took you on detours, our purpose has been fulfilled. We should all get lost on Delaware Street sooner rather than later.

Notes

1 "American Myths Symposium #1: Re-Thinking the Meaning of Christopher Columbus" (7 October 2015), accessed 12 October 2020, https://davidkrueger.org/events/american-myths/myth-of-discovery. Reverend Doctor John Norwood is involved in America Indian tribe leadership in New Jersey and at the federal level.
2 Gayatri Chakravorty Spivak, "Can the Subaltern Speak?", in *Colonial Discourse and Post-Colonial Theory*, eds. Patrick Williams and Laura Chrisman (New York: Columbia University Press, 1994), 84–87. Originally published in *Marxism and the Interpretation of Culture*, eds. Cary Nelson and Lawrence Grossberg (Basingstoke: Macmillan Education, 1988), 271–313.
3 Dipesh Chakrabarty, *Provincializing Europe: Postcolonial Thought and Historical Difference* (Princeton: Princeton University Press, [2000] 2007), 6–7.
4 Subaltern studies as a field of enquiry emerged in the 1960s. For an overview of the field, see: Gayatri Chakravorty Spivak, "Subaltern Studies: Deconstructing Historiography", in *Selected Subaltern Studies*, eds. Ranajit Guha and Gayatri Chakravorti Spivak (New York: Oxford University Press, 1988), 3–32; Gyan Prakash, "Subaltern Studies as Postcolonial Criticism", *The American Historical Review* 99, no. 5 (1994): 1475–1490. A list of resources on decolonisation has been made available by the movement *Decolonize This Place*, accessed 12 October 2020, https://decolonizethisplace.org/resources.

5 Richard Weiner, "Exploration History Scholarship: An 'Untamable Beast'", *Terrae Incognitae* 52, no. 2 (2020): 124–125. The expression "global history of the encounter" was coined by Luca Codignola in 2001, quoted from Weiner's article.
6 Matthew H. Edney, "Creating 'Discovery': The Myth of Columbus, 1777–1828", *Terrae Incognitae* 52, no. 2 (2020): 196–197.
7 Ariella Aïsha Azoulay, *Potential History: Unlearning Imperialism* (New York: Verso, 2019).
8 Eve Tuck and K. Wayne Yang, "Decolonization Is Not a Metaphor", *Decolonization: Indigeneity, Education & Society* 1, no. 1 (2012): 2–7. See also Aimee Carrillo Rowe and Eve Tuck, "Settler Colonialism and Cultural Studies: Ongoing Settlement, Cultural Production, and Resistance", *Cultural Studies ↔ Critical Methodologies* 17, no. 1 (2017): 6.
9 This expression is from Daniel Clayton and M. Satish Kumar, "Geography and Decolonisation", *Journal of Historical Geography* 66 (2019): 1–8.
10 Clayton and Kumar, "Geography and Decolonisation", 5.
11 Caroline Lee Schwenz, "Geography and Empire", *Postcolonial Studies@Emory*, accessed 12 October 2020, https://scholarblogs.emory.edu/postcolonialstudies/2014/06/20/geography-and-empire.
12 Andrew Sluyter, *Colonialism and Landscape: Postcolonial Theory and Applications* (Lanham, MD: Rowman & Littlefield, 2002), 5. Environmental history had already de-naturalised the colonial landscape thanks to two significant contributions: William Cronon, *Changes in the Land: Indians, Colonists, and the Ecology of New England* (New York: Hill and Wang, 1983) and Carolyn Merchant, *Ecological Revolutions: Nature, Gender, and Science in New England* (Chapel Hill, NC: North Carolina University Press, 1989).
13 Boaventura de Sousa Santos, João Arriscado Nunes, and Maria Paula Meneses, "Opening Up the Canon of Knowledge and Recognition of Difference", in *Another Knowledge Is Possible: Beyond Northern Epistemologies*, ed. Boaventura de Sousa Santos (New York: Verso, 2007), xix–lxii.
14 Sluyter, *Colonialism and Landscape*, 201–204.
15 Edward Karabenick, "A Postcolonial Rural Landscape: The Algiers Sahel", *Yearbook of the Association of Pacific Coast Geographers* 53 (1991): 87–108; Claiton Marcio da Silva, *De agricultor a farmer: Nelson Rockefeller e a modernização da agricultura no Brasil* (Curitiba: UFPR, 2015); Claire Mercer, "Landscapes of Extended Ruralisation: Postcolonial Suburbs in Dar es Salaam, Tanzania", *Transactions of the Institute of British Geographers* 42, no. 1 (2016): 72–83.
16 Anke Schwarz and Monika Streule, "A Transposition of Territory: Decolonized Perspectives in Current Urban Research", *Journal of Urban and Regional Research* 40, no. 5 (2016): 1000–1016; Libby Porter et al., "Indigenous Planning: From Principles to Practice . . .", *Planning Theory & Practice* 18, no. 4 (2017): 639–666.
17 Terence Tapiwa Muzorewa, Vongai Z. Nyawo, and Mark Nyandoro, "Decolonising Urban Space: Observations from History in Urban Planning in Ruwa Town, Zimbabwe, 1986–2015", *New Contree* 81 (2018): 1–23; Rebecca Kiddle, Bianca Elkington, Moana Jackson, Ocean Ripeka Mercier, Mike Ross, Jennie Smeaton, and Amanda Thomas, *Imagining Decolonisation* (Wellington, New Zealand: BWB Texts, 2020). The treaty and constitutional law expert Dr. Moana Jackson's *Imagining Decolonisation* is excerpted at *The Spinoff*, https://thespinoff.co.nz/atea/07-03-2020/where-to-next-decolonisation-and-the-stories-in-the-land/, last access 10 December 2021. In the same vein, see Leslie Kern, *Feminist City: Claiming Space in a Man-Made World* (New York: Verso, 2020).
18 Matthew H. Hedney, *Mapping an Empire: The Geographical Construction of British India, 1765–1843* (Chicago: University of Chicago Press, 1997); Peter Whitfield, *New Found Lands: Maps in the History of Exploration* (New York: Palgrave, 1998).

19 See *The Decolonial Atlas*, https://decolonialatlas.wordpress.com, last access 10 December 2021.
20 Martine Drozdz, "Maps and Protest", in *International Encyclopedia of Human Geography*, ed. Audrey Kobayashi (Amsterdam: Elsevier, 2020), 367–378.
21 Drozdz, "Maps and Protest", 374–375.
22 Marco Armiero et al., "Toxic Bios: Toxic Autobiographies: A Public Environmental Humanities Project", *Environmental Justice* 12, no. 1 (2019): 7–11.
23 Marco Armiero, "The Environmental Humanities and the Current Socioecological Crisis", *Higher Education in the World* 7 (2019): 427. See also: Marco Armiero, *Wasteocene: Stories from the Global Dump* (Cambridge: Cambridge University Press, 2021).
24 See *Mapping Edges*, www.mappingedges.org, last access 10 December 2021.
25 Ilaria Vanni and Alexandra Crosby, "The Not-Yet-Tropical: Mapping Recombinant Ecologies in a Sydney Suburb", *Visual Communication* 19, no. 3 (2020): 1–22; Alexandra Crosby, "Marrickville Maps: Tropical Imaginaries of Abundance", *Mapping Edges* (2018), www.mappingedges.org/wp-content/uploads/2018/02/mappingedges_marrickville_POUCH.pdf, last access 10 December 2021. See also Alexandra Crosby and Ilaria Vanni, *The Planty Atlas of UTS* (2019), https://opus.lib.uts.edu.au/bitstream/10453/140123/1/PlantyAtlas_SpecialEdition_Digital.pdf, last access 10 December 2021.
26 See the Center for the Humanities at City University of New York, www.centerforthehumanities.org/, last access 10 December 2021.
27 Climate Action Lab, *A People's Climate Plan for New York City?*, www.centerforthehumanities.org/programming/a-peoples-climate-action-plan-for-new-york-1, last access 10 December 2021.
28 Aurash Khawarzad, *The Upper Manhatta(n) Project* (New York: AAK PRESS, 2018). For more information, see: www.aurashkhawarzad.com/uppermanhattanproject, last access 10 December 2021.
29 Ashley Dawson and Aurash Khawarzad, "Hot City: New York City Will Never Be the Same Again – And It Shouldn't Be", *Verso*, 20 August 2020, www.versobooks.com/blogs/4829-hot-city-new-york-city-will-never-be-the-same-again-and-it-shouldn-t-be, last access 10 December 2021.
30 On the same topic, see Ashley Dawson, "How We Forgot the Sea", *Social Text*, 29 October 2013, https://socialtextjournal.org/periscope_article/how-we-forgot-the-sea/, last access 10 December 2021.
31 Garth Myers, *Rethinking Urbanism: Lessons from Postcolonialism and the Global South* (Bristol: Bristol University Press, 2020), 1–22.
32 Joseph Goddard, "Landscape and Ambience on the Urban Fringe: From Agricultural to Imagined Countryside", *Environment and History* 15, no. 4 (2009): 413–439; Mirek Dymitrow and Marie Stenseke, "Rural-Urban Blurring and the Subjectivity Within", *Rural Landscapes: Society, Environment, History* 3, no. 1 (2016): 4; Siân Moxon, "Drawing on Nature: A Vision of an Urban Residential Street Adapted for Biodiversity in Architectural Drawings", *City, Territory and Architecture* 6, no. 6 (2019), https://doi.org/10.1186/s40410-019-0105-0, last access 10 December 2021.
33 Jocelyn Thorpe, Stephanie Rutherford, and L. Anders Sandberg, eds., *Methodological Challenges in Nature-Culture and Environmental History Research* (Abingdon: Routledge, 2018).
34 Deborah Bird Rose, Thom van Dooren, Matthew Chrulew, Stuart Cooke, Matthew Kearnes, and Emily O'Gorman, "Thinking Through the Environment, Unsettling the Humanities", *Environmental Humanities* 1, no. 1 (2012): 1–5; Jeffrey J. Williams, "The New Humanities: Once-Robust Fields Are Being Broken Up and Stripped for Parts", *The Chronicle of Higher Education*, 14 November 2019, www.chronicle.com/article/the-new-humanities, last access 10 December 2021.

35 Antonio Ortega Santos and Chiara Olivieri, "Narrativas Coloniales de la Historia Ambiental: Un balance hacia la Decolonialidad como nueva epistemología", *Historia Ambiental Latinoamericana y Caribeña* 7, no. 2 (2018): 32–64; Eve Tuck and Marcia McKenzie, *Place in Research: Theory, Methodology, and Methods* (London: Routledge, 2016), 48–58.
36 David E. Nye, Linda Rugg, James Flemming, and Robert S. Emmett, *The Emergence of the Environmental Humanities* (Stockholm: Mistra, 2013); Stephanie LeMenager, "The Humanities after the Humanities", in *The Routledge Companion to the Environmental Humanities*, eds. Ursula K. Heise, Jon Christensen, and Michelle Niemann (London: Routledge, 2017), 473–481.
37 Robert S. Emmett and David E. Nye, *The Environmental Humanities: A Critical Introduction* (Cambridge, MA: MIT Press, 2017), 4–9; 139–140.
38 Joshua Mousie, "Global Environmental Justice and Postcolonial Critique", *Environmental Philosophy* 9, no. 2 (2012): 21–46; Elizabeth DeLoughrey, Jill Didur, and Anthony Carrigan, "Introduction: A Postcolonial Environmental Humanities", in *Global Ecology and the Environmental Humanities: Postcolonial Approaches*, eds. Elizabeth DeLoughrey, Jill Didur, and Anthony Carrigan (New York: Routledge, 2015), 17–25; Jennifer Wenzel, "Turning over a New Leaf: Fanonian Humanism and Environmental Justice", in *The Routledge Companion to the Environmental Humanities*, 165–173; Dipesh Chakrabarty, "The Planet: An Emergent Humanist Category", *Critical Inquiry* 46, no. 1 (2019): 1–31.
39 Libby Robin, "Global Ideas in Local Places: The Humanities in Environmental Management", *Environmental Humanities* 1, no. 1 (2012): 69–84.
40 Deborah Bird Rose and Thom van Dooren, "Encountering a More-Than-Human World: Ethos and the Arts of Witness", in *The Routledge Companion to the Environmental Humanities*, 120.
41 Kyle Powys Whyte, "Is It a Colonial *déjà vu*? Indigenous People and Climate Injustice", in *Humanities for the Environment: Integrating Knowledge, Forging New Constellations of Practice*, eds. Joni Adamson and Michael Davis (London: Routledge, 2017), 88.
42 Anna-Katharina Hornidge and Fabian Scholtes, "Climate Change and Everyday Life in Toineke Village, West Timor: Uncertainties, Knowledge and Adaptation", *Sociologus* 61, no. 2 (2011): 151; Margaret Alston, "Gender and Climate Change in Australia", *Journal of Sociology* 47, no. 1 (2010): 53–54.
43 Dipesh Chakrabarty, "The Climate of History: Four Theses", *Critical Inquiry* 35, no. 2 (2009): 197–222; Robert S. Emmett and Thomas Lekan, eds., "Whose Anthropocene? Revisiting Dipesh Chakrabarty's 'Four Theses'", *RCC Perspectives* 2 (2016).
44 Sverker Sörlin and Paul Warde, "Making the Environment Historical: An Introduction", in *Nature's End: History and the Environment*, eds. Sverker Sörlin and Paul Warde (London: Palgrave Macmillan, 2009), 2–4.
45 *Ecocene* is Cappadocia University's new journal in EH, http://ecocene.kapadokya.edu.tr/Anasayfa.aspx, last access 10 December 2021.
46 Frank Biermann et al., "Down to Earth: Contextualizing the Anthropocene", *Global Environmental Change* 39 (2016): 341–350; Michael Simpson, "The Anthropocene as Colonial Discourse", *Environment and Planning D* 38, no. 1 (2020): 53–71.
47 Tony Birch, "'The Lifting of the Sky': Life outside the Anthropocene", in *Humanities for the Environment*, 200; Rob Nixon, "The Anthropocene: The Promise and Pitfalls of an Epochal Idea", in *Future Remains: A Cabinet of Curiosities for the Anthropocene*, eds. Gregg Mitman, Marco Armiero, and Robert S. Emmett (Chicago, IL: University of Chicago Press, 2018), 1–2.
48 Heather Davis and Zoe Todd, "On the Importance of a Date, or Decolonizing the Anthropocene", *ACME* 16, no. 4 (2017): 761–780.

49 Arturo Escobar, "The Making and Unmaking of the Third World through Development", in *The Post-Development Reader*, eds. Majid Rahnema and Victoria Bawtree (London: Zed Books, 1997), 91.
50 Jason W. Moore, "The Capitalocene, Part I: On the Nature and Origins of Our Ecological Crisis", *The Journal of Peasant Studies* 44, no. 3 (2017): 594–630.
51 Latin American studies stress the issue of development, with the "Developmentocene" showing the geography of consumption and the geography of extractivism. See Marina Dantas de Figueiredo, Fábio Freitas Schilling Marquesan, and José Miguel Imas, "Anthropocene and 'Development': Intertwined Trajectories since the Beginning of the Great Acceleration", *Revista de Administração Contemporânea* 24, no. 5 (2020): 400–413.
52 Hsinya Huang and Syaman Rapongan, "Radiation Ecologies, Resistance and Survivance on Pacific Islands: Albert Wendt's *Black Rainbow* and Syaman Rapongan's *Drifting Dreams on the Ocean*", in *Humanities for the Environment*, 165–166.
53 Birch, "'The Lifting of the Sky'", 201.
54 Donna Haraway, "Anthropocene, Capitalocene, Plantationocene, Chthulucene: Making Kin", *Environmental Humanities* 6 (2015): 159–160.
55 Dipesh Chakrabarty, "History on an Expanded Canvas: The Anthropocene's Invitation", Haus der Kulturen der Welt, 13 January 2013, www.hkw.de/en/app/mediathek/video/22392, last access 10 December 2021.
56 Libby Robin, "A Future beyond Numbers", in *Welcome to the Anthropocene: The Earth in Our Hands*, eds. Nina Möllers, Christian Schwägerl, and Helmut Trischler (Munich: Deutsches Museum, 2015), 19.
57 Courtney J. Campbell, Allegra Giovine, and Jennifer Keating, "Introduction: Confronting Emptiness in History", in *Empty Spaces: Perspectives on Emptiness in Modern History*, eds. Courtney J. Campbell, Allegra Giovine, and Jennifer Keating (London: University of London Press, 2019), 3–4.
58 Katherine G. Morrissey, *Mental Territories: Mapping the Inland Empire* (Ithaca, NY: Cornell University Press, 1997); Julia Obertreis, *Imperial Desert Dreams: Cotton Growing and Irrigation in Central Asia, 1860–1991* (Göttingen: V & R Unipress, 2017); Andrew C. Isenberg, Katherine G. Morrissey, and Louis S. Warren, eds., "Deserts in Environmental History", *Global Environment* 12, no. 1 (2019).
59 Simon Ryan, "Inscribing the Emptiness: Cartography, Exploration and the Construction of Australia", in *De-Scribing Empire: Post Colonialism and Textuality*, eds. Chris Tiffin and Alan Lawson (London: Routledge, 1994), 115–130.
60 Alexander De Grand, "Mussolini's Follies: Fascism in Its Imperial and Racist Phase, 1935–1940", *Contemporary European History* 13, no. 2 (2004): 128–129; Diana K. Davis, *Resurrecting the Granary of Rome: Environmental History and French Colonial Expansion in North Africa* (Athens: Ohio University Press, 2007).
61 Noam Leshem, "Repopulating the Emptiness: A Spatial Critique of Ruination in Israel/Palestine", *Environment and Planning D* 31, no. 3 (2013): 525.
62 Lauren Benton, "Spatial Histories of Empire", *Itinerario* 30, no. 3 (2006): 19–34.
63 Maurits W. Ertsen, "Colonial Irrigation: Myths of Emptiness", *Landscape Research* 31, no. 2 (2006): 165.
64 Mia Fuller, *Moderns Abroad: Architecture, Cities and Italian Imperialism* (London: Routledge, 2007), 198.
65 William H. Sherman, "Putting the British Seas on the Map: Johan Dee's Imperial Cartography", *Cartographica* 35, no. 3/4 (1998): 8.
66 John Noyes, *Colonial Space: Spatiality in the Discourse of German South-West Africa, 1884–1915* (London: Routledge, 1992), 242–251.
67 Stephen Turner and Timothy Neale, "First Law and the Force of Water: Law, Water, Entitlement", *Settler Colonial Studies* 5, no. 4 (2015): 389.
68 Rob Nixon, *Slow Violence and the Environmentalism of the Poor* (Cambridge, MA: Harvard University Press, 2011), 7–8.

69 Karen N. Salt, "Twilight Islands and Environmental Crisis: Re-Writing a History of the Caribbean and Pacific Regions through the Islands Existing in Their Shadows", in *Humanities for the Environment*, 58–61.
70 Isabel Hofmeyr, "Oceans as Empty Spaces? Redrafting Our Knowledge by Dropping the Colonial Lens", *The Conversation*, 6 September 2018. https://theconversation.com/oceans-as-empty-spaces-redrafting-our-knowledge-by-dropping-the-colonial-lens-102778, last access 10 December 2021.
71 Stacy Alaimo, "The Anthropocene at Sea: Temporality, Paradox, Compression", in *The Routledge Companion to the Environmental Humanities*, 153–161. See also the project "Oceanic Humanities for the Global South", www.oceanichumanities.com, last access 10 December 2021.
72 Anna Lowenhaupt Tsing, *The Mushroom at the End of the World: On the Possibility of Life in Capitalist Ruins* (Princeton, NJ: Princeton University Press, 2015); Alexis Shotwell, *Against Purity: Living Ethically in Compromised Times* (Minneapolis: University of Minnesota Press, 2016); Anna Lowenhaupt Tsing, Heather Anne Swanson, Elaine Gan, and Nils Bubandt, eds., *Arts of Living on a Damaged Planet: Ghosts and Monsters of the Anthropocene* (Minneapolis: University of Minnesota Press, 2017).
73 Alexandra Crosby and Jesse Adams Stein, "Repair", *Environmental Humanities* 12, no. 1 (2020): 179–181.
74 Thom van Dooren, Eben Kirksey, and Ursula Münster, "Multispecies Studies: Cultivating Arts of Attentiveness", *Environmental Humanities* 8, no. 1 (2016): 3.
75 Serpil Oppermann and Serenella Iovino, "The Environmental Humanities and the Challenges of the Anthropocene", in *Environmental Humanities: Voices from the Anthropocene*, eds. Serpil Oppermann and Serenella Iovino (London: Rowman and Littlefield, 2017), 1–2, 13.
76 Jean-François Staszak, "Other/Otherness", in *International Encyclopaedia of Human Geography*, eds. Rob Kitchin and Nigel J. Thrift, vol. 8 (Oxford: Elsevier, 2009), 43–47.
77 S. Nazrul Islam and John Winkel, "Climate Change and Social Inequality", *United Nations Department of Economic and Social Affairs Working Papers* 152 (2017), www.un.org/esa/desa/papers/2017/wp152_2017.pdf, last access 10 December 2021.
78 Mélanie Rateau and Luisa Tovar, "Formalization of Wastepickers in Bogota and Lima: Recognize, Regulate, and Then Integrate?", *EchoGéo* 47 (2019): 1–11; Rocío Silva Santisteban, ed., *Indigenous Women and Climate Change* (Copenhagen: IWGIA, 2020).
79 Michael Davis, "Walking Together into Knowledge: Aboriginal/European Collaborative Environmental Encounters in Australia's North-East, 1847–1849", in *Humanities for the Environment*, 181–182.
80 Serenella Iovino, *Ecocriticism and Italy: Ecology, Resistance, and Liberation* (London: Bloomsbury, 2016), 2–5.
81 Regarding the foundations and features of material ecocriticism, see Serenella Iovino and Serpil Oppermann, "Theorizing Material Ecocriticism: A Diptych", *Interdisciplinary Studies in Literature and Environment* 19, no. 3 (2012): 448–475; Serenella Iovino and Serpil Oppermann, "Introduction: Stories Come to Matter", in *Material Ecocriticism*, eds. Serenella Iovino and Serpil Oppermann (Bloomington: Indiana University Press, 2014), 1–17.
82 Owain Jones, "Geography, Memory and Non-Representational Geographies", *Geography Compass* 5, no. 12 (2011): 875.
83 Eugenio Turri, *Semiologia del paesaggio italiano* (Venice: Marsilio, 2014).
84 Adrian S. Wisnicki, *Fieldwork of Empire, 1840–1900: Intercultural Dynamics in the Production of British Expeditionary Literature* (Abingdon: Routledge, 2019).

Appendix
The rediscovery of two files relating to the Karakoram (1928–1929) and North Pole (1928) expeditions conserved at the Municipal Archives in Milan

Stefano Twardzik

The documentation and its origin

The Municipal Archives of Milan, today *Cittadella degli Archivi*, contains two bulky dossiers relating to the 1928–1929 Italian geographical expedition to the Karakoram led by Prince Aimone di Savoia-Aosta, Duke of Spoleto, and the 1928 expedition another to the North Pole under the command of General Umberto Nobile: nine bundles crammed with documents, covering the 1927–1932 time span, with sundry other papers up to 1935 (and some later).

Concerning the amount of information contained, this documentation, recording the events and controversies surrounding these two significant Italian expeditions, is on a par with that kept in Rome at the Italian Geographical Society. The latter is perhaps more copious but less consistent than the Milanese trove.[1]

The two expeditions were both planned in 1927[2] as the highlight in celebrations commemorating the tenth anniversary of the Italian victory in the Great War (World War I) and were warmly championed by Ernesto Belloni. In addition to being president of the Milanese section of the Italian Alpine Club, at the time, Belloni also held the important office of *podestà* of Milan. In fact, approximately a year earlier, a royal decree, issued by the Mussolini government, had replaced elected mayors with *podestà*; although this had the trappings of a royal appointment, it was essentially a governmental one.[3]

Belloni wanted to put a national but also a distinctively Milanese stamp on this initiative. Thus, having obtained the consent of the head of the government, on 18 October, he convened representatives of the city's industrial and financial institutions in Palazzo Marino, the seat of the municipal administration, and obtained their commitment to set up a funding committee. The committee's task was to come up with the substantial resources needed to carry out the two explorations – initially estimated at 3.5 million lire for the Arctic expedition and 2 million lire for that to Karakoram[4] – through fundraising from banks, industry and insurance companies.[5] However, the sums collected from Milanese business, about 1,200,000 lire, fell short of expectations,[6] and after the disaster of the airship *Italia* crash on the polar icepack (25 May 1928), which put an end to the expedition, this funding approach was replaced by a public fundraising scheme geared to paying for rescue operations.[7] Consequently, the brunt of the financial commitment fell on the city's coffers, and, regarding the ill-fated expedition to the North Pole, also on the national government. The latter, in fact, was obliged to pitch in with a special allocation to the tune of 850,000 lire (not all of which was ultimately used), subsequently noted in the budget ledgers of the Aeronautics Ministry, to cover the losses incurred by the expedition.[8]

As early as October 1927, the financing machinery of the two undertakings was centralised in Milan, while the Italian Geographical Society played a role in the organisational aspects,[9] which, in the case of the polar expedition, however, were mainly overseen by Umberto Nobile. Since it was the Municipality of Milan which made the most significant contribution to the two expeditions, chairmanship of the funding committee was entrusted to its *podestà* – later, after Belloni, Giuseppe De Capitani D'Arzago and ultimately Marcello Visconti di Modrone[10] – while bureaucratic support came naturally from the Cabinet Office and, more specifically, the *podestà*'s special secretariat. An osmosis of sorts began between the municipality and the funding committee, mainly due to the fact that the formal constitution of the latter was never officialised.[11] It remained a legally weak entity, as a diplomatic examination of the records makes clear: the committee had neither letterhead and stamp, nor its own register (*registro di protocollo*), and the *podestà* signed letters as the head of the funding body, making use of his own special secretariat's register. Even the body's headquarters was the *podestà*'s cabinet.

The fact that the matters concerning the expeditions were managed directly by the head of the municipality therefore explains the presence of these large dossiers in the Civic Archives, where they were transferred in 1935 by the General Secretariat, which formally also subsumed the cabinet.

In this regard, it is interesting to note that the two large files, in addition to documenting the numerous issues related to the two explorations, also indirectly shed light on those responsible for the settling of these papers, and sometimes even on their *modus operandi*, their personal styles. Therefore, some figures emerge, historically less well known, who worked closely with the *podestà* Belloni and De Capitani D'Arzago and played a decisive part in the management of the two journeys from a bureaucratic and financial standpoint.

I will mention just two of these here: Biagio Gabardi (1881–1941) and Arturo Andreoletti (1884–1977). The former, a long-term municipal consultant,[12] was an esteemed trustee of both *podestà* and therefore frequently tasked with handling high-level political relations. As a cotton-mill industrialist and member of the Executive Committee of the *Cassa di Risparmio delle Province Lombarde* (Savings Bank of the Lombard Provinces), in the late 1920s and throughout the 1930s, he was a pivotal figure among the private industrial and financial circles and local municipal and provincial government bodies.[13] The latter, Andreoletti, in the employ of the Milan Municipality since 1907, was promoted to officer rank after the Great War (in which he was a front-line combatant) and at the same time played a role of public importance as founder of the National Alpine Association, of which he was the first assembly chairman. In 1928, he was appointed head of Belloni's cabinet, and then – Belloni having been obliged to resign by Mussolini on September 1929 – of De Capitani D'Arzago's: a prestigious role that was however cut short in June 1929, when Andreoletti was forced to request dispensation from service on the grounds of the hostility of Giuseppe Siracusa, Milan prefect, and also because, at a higher level, he had been the target of criticism from Alpino troop instructor General Ottavio Zoppi.[14]

That archival management of these two files was the directly responsibility of the head of the *podestà*'s cabinet until the summer of 1929 can likely be inferred from the geometrically patterned decorative icons that carefully surround the titles marked on the folders of the various subfiles (see Figure 11.1), as the same decorative style appears on the folders of Andreoletti's personal archives, at least those that have survived.[15]

Implications of the Nobile expedition brought to light by the Milanese documentation

The two hefty dossiers highlight the various aspects of these events which, as is well known, had very different outcomes. The range and heterogeneity of the issues addressed by the documents frustrate any attempt at an even partially summary. I will therefore limit my focus to certain issues emerging from the papers which I deem to be of particular significance. A more systematic description of the matters dealt with will result in an analytical inventory of the two files, a work currently in progress.

The overflowing bundles relating to the North Pole expedition feature a common thread that, at times in an evident and others in a more subtle way, appears to run through the entire matter: namely the clash between the funding committee and General Umberto Nobile, which began around July–August 1928. I will deal with this later on. The documents in question, however, also point up disputes with other members of the expedition who survived the *Italia* disaster of 25 May 1928, Alfredo Viglieri and Giuseppe Biagi, who failed to comply with contractual obligations requiring payment to the committee of a share of publishing rights on books written after the expedition;[16] these differences, furthermore, were resolved without recourse to the courts. Particularly revealing in this connection is the letter exchange with publisher Arnoldo Mondadori. There are also a great many letters regarding the dispute that arose with the LUCE Institute[17] due to the latter's refusal to acknowledge the committee's claim to profits accruing from film screenings of the expedition and subsequent rescue operations: this notwithstanding the categorical opposition voiced by Finance Minister Antonio Mosconi. Many are the documents that describe the preparatory phase of the expedition and the funding strategies employed. Here, also, papers relating to the Karakoram expedition are particularly numerous. In addition, there is no dearth of records on negotiations with both the Italian and foreign press relative to exclusive rights to news releases and media articles regarding the polar undertaking. Cases in point are the contracts underwritten by crew members; the copious correspondence with

Appendix 179

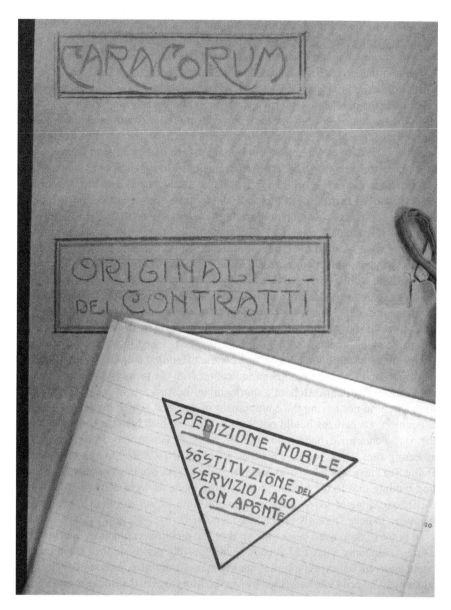

Figure 11.1 Examples of subfiles folders of the two dossiers. Courtesy of Cittadella degli Archivi.

the Italian Geographical Society relative to the settling of expedition costs; the exchange of letters with the Finance, Air and Navy Ministries; those concerning the underwritings for the rescue expedition; and records connected with the payment of insurance premiums to the families of the victims and the injured.

The fact that so much of the documentation preserved in Milan relating to the North Pole expedition – as well as the Karakoram – addresses the topic of the proceeds from the publication of articles, writings, photographs and film footage can easily be explained in terms of the stringent economic commitment undertaken for the financing of the exploration, a commitment assumed largely – as we have seen – by the City of Milan without initial costs to the state (apart from the airship concession and free labour at the Aeronautics Ministry's aircraft construction plant):[18] according to the original financial plans drawn up by *podestà* Belloni and his staff, almost two-thirds of this sum was to have been recouped through hefty exclusive rights on expedition news and subsequent reports, to be syndicated with the major Italian and foreign newspapers.[19]

This is what sparked the clash with the expedition leader: it is a story which merits further examination, especially as it has hitherto been neglected in studies dealing with Nobile and the tragic history of the airship *Italia*.

As is exhaustively documented in the Milanese papers, Nobile was well aware of the need for the financing committee to cover the high costs of the expedition, even via agreements on press and publishing rights to be worked out with the major media agencies of the time. In fact, he personally worked to persuade the members of the *Italia* crew to sign contracts binding them to the committee's mediation and consent for all communication with the press and potential future publications.[20] *Podestà* Belloni's shortcoming, however, was one of superficiality: namely in not having the commitment in question signed by the head of the expedition. Or perhaps he did not want to hurt the feelings of a man who, after the *Norge* enterprise, had acquired on his home turf enormous prestige and even an heroic aura. Thus, Nobile left Milan on 14 April 1928 for Stolp (a town on the Baltic Sea chosen as a half-way station) in the absence of any contractual obligation binding him to the funding body, whose interests were ensured only by the earlier exchange of letters between him and the *podestà* and verbal agreements that were to have "morally bound" the General.[21]

In point of fact, even before the start of the airship's exploratory journey and its tragic outcome, there had already been signs of a poorly defined situation that could undercut the expectations of the Milanese Committee, as is well evinced by a letter of 23 April 1928 addressed by Manlio Morgagni to the Hon. Ernesto Torrusio in Berlin. In this letter, the then-deputy *podestà* confided to his colleague that, before leaving Milan, he had not been able to clarify a series of issues with the General, issues "that plunge us in a state of perplexity, which is at odds with the commitments we have had to make, and which we will indeed make":

> In conversations with us, General Nobile has repeatedly stated that, during the expedition, he would write at least three articles in his own hand. This clause of the three Nobile articles is in fact an explicit part of the commitments

agreed to with the newspapers. But, in effect, the General has never given us formal assurance regarding the matter. Presently, Belloni will be writing to Nobile asking him to specify at which phases of the expedition he intends to draft the above mentioned articles; however, it would be well that you have him reiterate his assurances so as to avoid offering any pretext for invalidating contracts underwritten by the newspapers. . . . Lastly, press rights, photo-cinematographic and editorial rights regarding the expedition have naturally been allocated to the Funding Committee. Gen. Nobile, in turn, asked to be consulted before closing the deal with publishers as the matter was both of personal and direct concern to him; and Belloni – informing him that we *cannot miss* this opportunity to substantially recoup our funds – told him that he would not fail *to consult him* before closing the deal. Hence, it would be a good idea for you, using all due discretion, to get him to "expand" on the matter as much as possible.[22]

Subsequently, Morgagni asked Torrusio to go to Stolp during the General's stopover on that leg in order to get confirmation and assurances from him. Belloni, however, may well have changed his mind as to the real need for such clarification, since sending the letter, as evinced by an annotation added to its upper margin, had been "suspended by order of the Honorable Podestà". As things stood, the issues still needing to be ironed out and effectively summarised in the previous document did not fail to surface and became increasingly difficult to settle as early as the following August 1928. By then, Nobile had returned from the Svalbard Islands.

Between July and August, Nobile began to resent the men of the funding committee, because he held them responsible – through their representative in London, Carlo Camagna – for the publication in Swedish and German newspapers, between July 6 and 8, of an interview he granted *Il Popolo d'Italia* correspondent Ugo Ardemagni earlier that month. In the interview, the authenticity of which was categorically denied by the person concerned, Nobile stated that "if I had not been firmly determined to plant the Italian flag on the North Pole on 24 May, the anniversary of Italy's entry into the War, the disaster could have been averted".[23] This statement had the effect of precipitating a torrent of ill feelings toward the explorer by German-language newspapers, for whom, of course – unlike in Italy – the date in question evoked the beginning of a searing defeat. We do not know whether, as Nobile always claimed, the interview was made up, but it is very likely that – contrary to what he said – the departure time chosen did not depend simply on the weather forecast but was instead determined by his steadfast intention to reach the North Pole on that symbolic day, as indeed happened. At any rate, probably for reasons of political expediency, the interview was not published in *Il Popolo d'Italia* but relayed by the paper's editor Arnaldo Mussolini to Camagna's London office. It should be noted that Camagna represented not only the interests of the funding committee but also those of the newspaper. Nobile evidently believed that, in selling the interview to the Anglo-American press agency, along with its consequent publication in foreign newspapers, Camagna was acting on behalf of the committee, while in actual fact it was – as far as we can tell from the documents – an autonomous initiative taken in the interests of the newspaper, without the involvement of the aforementioned body.[24]

This misunderstanding, a crux that remained unsolved despite a lengthy meeting between Nobile, Gabardi and Andreoletti in Rome on 21 October 1928, during which the representatives of the Milanese Committee reiterated their non-involvement in the issue of the disputed interview,[25] further exacerbated the General's resentment towards the body that, more than any other, had contributed to the polar enterprise. On one hand, Nobile continued to postpone the delivery of the photo and film negatives of the expedition still in his possession, material whose use was covered by contractual commitments agreed on by the committee before his departure (all Nobile sent to the Milan Municipality was 113 photo-positives).[26] In addition, he refused to send the committee the three articles he had promised to draft, which appeared in the clauses of an important contract granting exclusive rights to the US publishing group Hearst Press (the contract was underwritten by the funding body via its representative Camagna).[27] Matters became so strained that, following direct intervention by the head of the government, eager to avoid the risk of an international squabble fuelled by the possibility of a trial with the powerful US publishing group, which was capable of channelling "very powerful currents of opinion" in North America,[28] Nobile ultimately decided to write the articles. Even then, however, he delivered them directly to Hearst with the explicit caveat that they had nothing to do with the agreements signed between the US company and the committee, to which he declared himself in no way bound. The failure of the US company, which was still under contract with the Milan Municipality, to pay Nobile for these articles led the General to promote a civil lawsuit at the Court of Rome in 1930, suing both the Hearst Press's Rome representative, Prince Valerio Pignatelli, and the Milan Municipality. As it turned out, court proceeding was ignored by the Italian press of the time. In any case, about two years later, the suit was dropped by the plaintiff and the matter ended in stalemate.[29]

In the same turn of years, the funding body proved incapable even of collecting the share of publishing rights due it (35,000 lire on the publication of Nobile's book *L'Italia al Polo Nord*) from publisher, Arnoldo Mondadori, because the general had warned the latter against paying this sum, and the *podestà* thought it best to forgo taking legal action against Mondadori to obtain its due.[30]

It is likely that it was this stubborn conduct, characterised by anger and resentment, this unfounded belief that he was not bound by any obligation towards the agency that had made the *Italia* expedition possible, that was one of the causes behind the hostility of the regime and Mussolini himself towards a man who, just a year earlier, had been held in high esteem. In this light, it also may be inferred that his behaviour had negative repercussions on relations between Nobile and the government to a greater extent than his alleged self-distancing from Fascism[31] and the jealousy and envy shown him by General Giuseppe Valle and undersecretary and later then-Air Force Minister Italo Balbo. Such, in fact, were the reasons Nobile gave as causes for his downfall according to the autobiographical reconstruction of events he was able to convey over the thirty years following the fall of the Fascist regime, thanks to his widely published memoirs.[32]

In point of fact, extensive delays in the sale of Nobile's articles and the photographic documentation he had assembled led to the commercial devaluation of all this material. This, together with his failure to recovery royalties on his Mondadori-published book, was a further blow to the already money-losing accounts of the North Pole expedition. The deficit from this expedition, to a much greater extent than that to Karakoram, further depleted Milan's municipal coffers. Despite underwritings designed to fund the two explorations, and two additional Milan Municipality contributions in 1928 and 1929 (for a total of 400,000 lire), and notwithstanding two special allocations granted by the government to cover liabilities (500,000 lire in December 1929 and 270,000 in June 1934),[33] on 31 December 1934, the accounts of the two expeditions still showed a shortfall of 200,567 lire. The accounts were only settled at the end of 1938 by means of a clearing entry (approximately 114,000 lire) posted to the Municipality's general budget ledger.[34]

Therefore, it can be seen how far Cesco Tomaselli was wide of the mark in a 1961 report recalling the expedition in the popular weekly magazine *La Domenica del Corriere*. The by-then-elderly special envoy who went along on Nobile's Nordic enterprise, while depicting the consultant Gabardi as an "insolvency administrator who, with icy zeal, devoted himself to recouping even the lowest financial transaction", stated that for the Milan Municipality, the 1928 adventure "was, after all, not the ruinous business deal that people had been led to believe," given that "the sum still outstanding was (only) 76,890 lire".[35]

One archival aspect of the dossier is particularly significant: it is tangibly more untidy than its Karakoram counterpart. Such disorder dates back to the years the matter was first dealt with, which is readily understandable since the *Italia* disaster, along with the lengthy dispute with Nobile, led to the drafting of additional subfiles, with the subsequent grafting of new documents onto earlier records which were reused for purposes other than those originally intended.

This relative untidiness cannot be expunged but must be maintained to some extent. In short, the going here is not at all easy: to what extent can the records be rearranged? How far can we go? It should be pointed out that it was only once the accurate description of both files had been completed that it was possible to fully grasp the state of the papers. I then noticed that, whilst there were subfiles which partially replicated the same issues, the content was almost always consistent with what was written on the original folders. Consequently, shifting documents from one subfile to another was ruled out (even if such repositioning would sometimes have allowed for a more immediate understanding of the progression of a given issue). As far as the subfiles are concerned, instead, in some cases, I changed their position in the sequence of the units, though only if and when it was clear that their collocation was extraneous to the sequential logic of the papers while the matter was still under way and that this position was due to a partial 'mix-up' which occurred several years after the two dossiers were transferred to the archives.

The Karakoram expedition papers

The state of the papers relating to the 1929 Karakoram expedition led by Aimone di Savoia-Aosta[36] is to some extent different and not only as a result of their order, although this is certainly the case. Here, too, there is an abundance of records relating to the handling of press rights (with profits optimistically overestimated) and accounting documents, but the degree of conflict that emerges from the papers is significantly lower than in the other dossier. Careful consultation of this copious dossier, moreover, suggests there is ample room for more in-depth analysis. Instances in point are: the initial entrusting of the command to geographer Giotto Dainelli and the contrasting opinions that put him at odds with mountaineer Gaetano Polvara; the careful organisation and carrying out of the preparatory voyage ahead of the actual journey, which took place between May and October 1928; the reports and travel correspondence – both dating to 1928 and 1929 – of the Duke of Spoleto's assistant, frigate captain Mario Cugia; the editing for the newspapers of the reports expedition members (which had to be authorised by the Duke); the scarce interest shown by the National Body of Cinematography in the commercial exploitation of the film documentary of the expedition shot by Massimo Terzano[37] (with negative repercussions here too in connection with film rights); the clash between Aimone di Savoia-Aosta and Umberto Balestreri in the wake of the exploration of the high Shaksgam valley (of which, however, more details are be found in the files of the Italian Geographical Society);[38] and the continual postponement of the publication of a monograph containing the scientific results of the expedition[39] because of *podestà* Visconti di Modrone's refusal to charge further sums to the municipality in addition to those it had already had to bear.

Of special interest is the photographic documentation contained in this file:[40] an almost complete series of photographs taken during the preparatory voyage made in 1928 by Captain Mario Cugia, or at any rate with the camera made available to him: over 300 negatives (numbered 1–318) on cellulose nitrate film, size 67×110 mm. However, unlike the original title that appears on the box containing these negatives – "First phase expedition 1928 / newspaper clippings and photographs by Captain Cugia" (see Figure 11.2) – there are also nearly 100 negatives (numbered 1–179)[41] of photos taken during the actual exploratory voyage between March and September 1929, also taken with this same camera and probably by Cugia himself. Overall, the negatives total 398, but there is also a selection of 127 "positives" taken from the two series of negatives.[42]

This material, for the most part hitherto unseen,[43] has been entirely digitised, put into standard containers and fully filed, albeit summarily. The Milan photographs are, in fact, different from those contained in the 'official' albums of the trip, available in Rome at the Italian Geographical Society, which consist solely of the photos taken in 1929, although they are more numerous (2,261 photos):[44] the latter are photographs taken by various members of the expedition but mostly by cameraman Terzano and by Vittorio Ponti and Ardito Desio.[45]

Figure 11.2 Cover of the box which contained negatives of the Karakoram expedition's photos. Courtesy of Cittadella degli Archivi.

Thanks to the Milanese documentation, it has been possible to trace the manner in which these albums were compiled, while we know almost nothing of the photos taken by Cugia, the only ones preserved in the dossier. The negatives of all the photos were to have been concentrated in Milan because, as we have seen, the commercial rights connected with this material were the purview of the funding committee (this is also evident from the contracts drawn up before departure with each member of the expedition).[46] As things turned out, however, some of the negatives escaped the committee's attention. Then, in 1934, the municipality waived its rights to the photographs and ceded most of the negatives to the Duke of Spoleto,[47] in view of the publication of his travelogue (but the negatives of the images taken by Cugia, mostly dating back to the preparatory phase, were not handed over, since they remained in the archive). In any event, in December 1929, the *podestà* of Milan, the Geographical Society's commissioner Nicola Vacchelli and the Duke of Spoleto agreed to create three equal photo collections from the negatives:[48] each collection was initially composed of two albums (in 1930), to which was then added a third album of only panoramic photos (in 1931). The three album collections were then handed over to the Italian Geographical Society, where they have remained; to Aimone di Savoia-Aosta; and to the City of Milan, where there appears to be no trace of them. A fourth exemplar of the panoramic photo album was then made and sent as a gift, at Aimone's request, to the Royal Geographical Society of London.[49]

While almost every page of the albums is accompanied by exhaustive captions written at the time, and obviously gleaned from information provided by the explorers themselves (the Milanese dossier contains the typewritten lists of these titles, with a corresponding numerical sequences),[50] Captain Cugia's negatives often seem to have been "voiceless", since they lack any annotation on the subjects depicted and because no list of these negatives has been found in the dossier. Admittedly, the photographic prints do bear an original title on the *verso*, but – as we have said – there are fewer of them than there are of the negatives they were taken from, and moreover they mainly relate to the real exploratory phase of 1929 (85 out of 127 photos).

Luckily, however, a small collection conserved by the Sella Foundation in Biella (Piedmont), made up of the photographs taken by Umberto Balestreri in both phases of the expedition, came to our rescue: this consists of 620 negatives on stereoscopic plates collected in 33 original boxes, of which the negatives numbered 11–282 document the 1928 journey, while the subsequent ones, numbered 293–640, are images of the following year's exploration.[51] We still don't know how these photos got to the Vittorio Sella Institute of Alpine Photography (merged into the newly instituted foundation in 1980), but the captions inked onto each plate, probably by Balestreri himself, with an indication of the precise date of each shot, have certainly proved invaluable in identifying the events and places impressed on the Mario Cugia negatives, especially regarding the 1928 voyage. In the latter, the two travelled, together with the Duke of Spoleto, through exactly the same places on the same roads and often immortalised the same subjects. Thus, in step with the various phases of the May–September 1928 journey, countrysides, mountains, villages, towns, monuments, campsites, men at work and scenes of daily life flash before our eyes, together with period views of Shimla; Rawalpindi; Srinagar; the mountain village of Gulmarg; the Deosai plateau; the villages of Skardu, Shigar, Askole; and then – on the return trip – the Indus and Dras valleys (with Parkutta, Kargil, Dras) and the Sind valley, and then the cities of Srinagar (again), Lahore, Amritsar, Benares, Agra, Jaipur and Amber, dotting territories that today lie in India and Pakistan.[52]

Digitalisation of the photos by means of a professional scanner, and their subsequent transformation into .tiff format files, has, on the one hand, afforded visitors to the Municipal Archives (Cittadella degli Archivi) easy access to high-definition, negative-to-positive images, and, on the other hand, it has reduced the risk of deterioration and subsequently of any lack of information to which nitrate films are frequently susceptible (fortunately, in this case, the film's state of preservation is good).

The archival context and description of the two dossiers

Turning now to considerations of a more archival nature, it should be noted that, their size notwithstanding, these are two 'files', not two 'fonds' (or even 'series'). Having been transferred from the General Secretariat in the mid-thirties to the Civic Archives, these files were allocated numbers 133 and 134 by archive staff. In fact, these are the numbers that appear in the 1935 file repertory (called "inventory"), compiled shortly after the arrival of these papers at what was then the Civic Administrative Archives.[53] The documentation in question was far more copious than was generally the case for the Municipality's bureaucratic files, although the customary nomenclature was maintained. Thus, in this case, the meaning of term 'file' changed from logical and physical to simply a logical unit. We are therefore dealing with two organic archival units which were arranged, in accordance with an increase of the included documents, in different bundles. Markings for "file 133/1935" and "file 134/1935" are penned in red ink on the folders of the original bundles, inverting the usual relationship between the storage unit 'bundle' (usually a higher level) and archival unit 'file' (a lower level, which is higher level here). It follows that, in order to accord with the original nomenclature, which has its own foundation in reality, the two files are split up into four and five bundles, respectively, while the bundles are in turn made up of units that I have had to call 'subfiles'.

A few words about the context of these two files. A good starting point is Milan City's new records management system, the result of new regulations by the Civic Administrative Archives that came into effect in 1928:[54] a system that worked smoothly for several decades. In fact, it cannot honestly be said that these two dossiers were not 'discovered' but rather 'rediscovered', since, although they have never been used for historical research purposes,[55] they were easy to access in the archives thanks to the finding aids of these far-off times (the 1935 inventory and the ten-year index of files).

The new records management methods introduced in 1928 included a proviso that documents related to completed transactions should be regularly and periodically delivered, "complete and already arranged in their individual *incarti*", to the Archives by the different offices. Once at the Civic Archives, the *incarti-fascicoli*, that is files, were classed by provenance by the various "large administrative divisions of the municipal offices",[56] starting with the General Secretariat, followed by all the other branches. Thus, the subdivision sequence was a classification of sorts modelled on the Municipality's bureaucratic structure. At a higher level, however, there was an entire annual series of files, which were to be transferred from the various offices year by year.

Let us now consider the multilevel structure into which these two important dossiers fit:

> *Institute with archival holdings*: Cittadella degli Archivi of the City of Milan, formerly the Civic Archives.

Fonds: General Archive of the City – from Deledda road (the main but not the only fond of the Cittadella degli Archivi)
Series: year 1935 (intended as year of transfer)
Classification code (based on internal municipality branches): General Secretariat
Files: 133/1935 ("Caracorum Expedition"), 134/1935 ("Arctic Expedition")
Bundles: 9, 10, 11, 11B (file 133/1935); 12, 13, 14, 15, 15B (file 134/1935).

Notwithstanding the 'datedness' of these papers, they are not kept in the Civic Historical Archives at Castello Sforzesco but at the Cittadella degli Archivi, a sort of municipal non-current record centre, in the northern outskirts of Milan. The Cittadella receives periodic transfers from the various civic offices in order to concentrate mainly documentation from recent decades. However, limited space at the Castello Sforzesco Archives has led to the records centre also becoming a historical archive in the long run, with huge numbers of 1930s, 1940s and 1950s files.[57]

What follows is a summary inventory of the two files, with bundle-level descriptions, bearing their original titles, where present, flanked by quotation marks. An analytical inventory, to be completed shortly, will further detail the archival units inside the bundles, that is the subfiles.

The 1935 inventory features three bundles (*cartelle*) linked to the expedition led by the Duke of Spoleto (numbered 9–11) and four bundles related to the Arctic expedition (numbered 12–15). However, when I was reordering and rearranging the records, I realised that there should be nine rather than seven bundles: meaning that two bundles were added with a "B" numeration (*bis* in Italian) to avoid altering the numerical sequence of the 157 bundles transferred to the Archives in 1935, within which these dossiers are located.

It should be noted that bundle 12 is the first to be included in file 134/1935, the Arctic expedition dossier: that it is a part of this file can be inferred from the stamp and the relative annotation on the folder, as well as on the following ones (Figure 11.3). Bundle 12, however, as can also be seen from its original title, contains records related to both expeditions, especially cost estimates and a great many reports, which highlight the links between the two dossiers since the outset, especially in financial terms. The staff who archived the two dossiers in 1935 wanted to warn of internal correspondences and therefore added the following annotation to the previous folders in file 133, which contain the Karakoram documents: "See also Arctic expedition. General Secretariat, file 134/1935 bundle n. 12", a clear reference to this initial unit of file 134.

Appendix 189

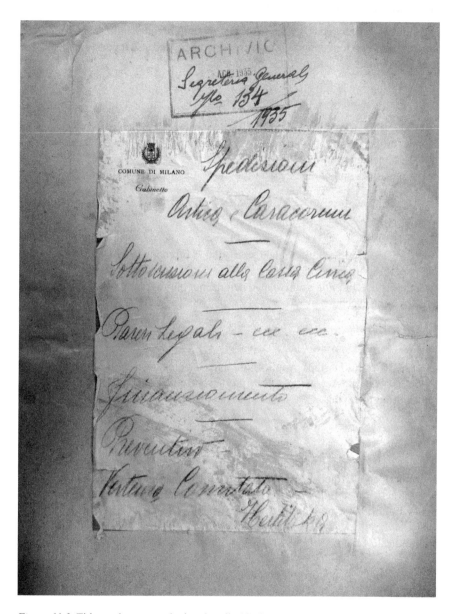

Figure 11.3 Titles and notes marked on bundle 12. Courtesy of Cittadella degli Archivi.

Summary inventory of the two files (1927–1935)

The number in brackets after the numbers of some bundles indicates a catalogue number that is no longer current but is reported here because it constituted a reference for scholars consulting these documents in 2019.

    Bundle 9   1927–1934

"File 133/1935. Caracorum. Correspondence with H.R.H. Duke of Spoleto. *Idem* with R. Italian Geographic Society. Newspapers and magazines. Photographs and movies. Cinematography".

The negatives and photos, but not the films, are also present (currently in separate boxes).

    Bundle 10   1927–1929

"File 133/1935. Expedition to the Caracorum. Correspondence pertinent to press and photographic material".

Contains lists of photos and related details, not photographs; also contains press releases and speeches.

    Bundle 11   1927–1930, with papers relating to 1934–1935

File 133/1935. Initial steps. Applications and participants. Report of the first phase of the expedition. Accounting from the second phase. Insurance. Milan City's contribution to expenses. Publication of the official expedition report.

    Bundle 11B (12)   1928–1931, with papers until 1933

"File 133/1935. Correspondence: De Filippi – Tomaselli – Ponti – Desio – Bron – di Caporiacco – Croux – Chiardola – Cugia – Terzano – diversi – Aragozzini".

Contracts, disciplinary agreements and warranties. Management of exclusive rights. Reports by Commander Cugia. Payments.

    Bundle 12 (13)   1927–1932, with papers 1935–1939

"File 134/1935. Arctic expedition and Caracorum. Civic coffers underwritings. Legal opinions, etc. etc. Funding. Cost estimates. Committee-Herliztka dispute".

Also contains statements and account closures on the two expeditions.

    Bundle 13 (14)   1927–1930, with papers until 1932

"File 134/1935. Cost estimates – Offers of material and various contributions. Various procedures. 'Il Popolo d'Italia' – Press rights. Correspondence with the Ministry of Finance and Aeronautics. Funding. Copies of correspondence between the Committee and Camagna [missing]. Polar expedition management by R.S.G.I. [Nobile's] Cost estimate. Italcable reports. Residual material. Insurance contracts with participants. Relations with the Royal Italian Geographical Society. Contracts with the expedition individual members and related correspondence".

Bundle 14 (13B)   1928–1930, with papers until 1933

"File 134/1935. Unitas-Tommaselli controversy. Italian press rights. Viglieri's correspondence. Luce Institute: negotiations and agreements. Cinematography and photographs. Editorial rights Treves Hoepli. Photographs to be published. 'I segreti di Nobile' [Nobile's Secrets]. Sums given to the Italian Royal Geographic Society. Press rights – photographs. Foreign press rights [missing, see bundle 15]".

Bundle 15   1927–1932, with papers until 1934.

"File 134/1935. Editorial press rights. Ministry of Aeronautics agreement. Meeting in Rome 21-10-1928 between Gen. Nobile and Gr. Uff. Gabardi. Press contracts. 'Nulla osta del Duce' [Go-ahead from Mussolini]. Mondadori. 'Corriere della Sera'. Non-subscription newspapers. 'Italia' wreck and rescue – etc."
Also contains "dispute with Nobile".

Bundle 15B   (14B) 1928–1929

File 134/1935. Telegrams. Justification of expenses incurred by the Italian Geographical Society. Proof of expenses presented by Nobile. "S.E. Senni account. Colonel Fier account".

Notes

1 The documentation on the Karakoram and North Pole expeditions held in the archives of the Italian Geographical Society (hereafter SGI) has been split up into two artificial fonds, "historical fonds" and "administrative fonds". Moreover, the present files and their 'objects' do not correspond to the original ones. Some references to the SGI archives are to be found in Agostina Trovato, ed., *Guida ai fondi dell'Archivio storico della Società geografica italiana* (Roma, 2019), http://societageografica.net/wp/wp-content/uploads/2016/08/GUIDA-AI-FONDI-DELLARCHIVIO-STORICO-1.pdf, last access 10 December 2021.
2 But, as Stefano Morosini has noted in his chapter in this volume, the idea of mountaineering exploration aimed at conquering K2 had already been mooted in Milan's Alpine circles for some years.
3 By the royal decree (r.d.) of 3 September 1926, no. 1910, city councils and mayors (the mayor being chosen by majority council vote) were removed from all municipalities of the Italian Kingdom and replaced with *podestà* and supporting limited adjunct council (the Municipal *Consulta*).
4 According to the current monetary indexes, the two amounts correspond to approximately €2,736,000 and €1,824,000.

5 Municipal Archives of Milan-Cittadella degli Archivi, General Archive (hereafter ACCM, GA), 1935, file 134, bundle 15, subfile 44, stenographic account of the meeting held at Palazzo Marino on 18 October 1927; ibid., file 134, bundle 12, subfile 1 "Finanziamento spedizioni".
6 The total obtained from the underwriting, 2,100,000 lire, also included the amounts paid by public bodies: ACCM, GA, 1935, file 134, bundle 12, subfile 8 "Spedizioni. Situazioni introiti e spese al 1° dicembre 1928".
7 On the reasons for the airship's crash and the conclusions of the subsequent Italian Navy Ministry Commission of Inquiry (chaired by Admiral Cagni), see Gregg A. Bendrick and Sergio Alessandrini, "No Second-in-Command: Human Fatigue and the Crash of Airship *Italia* Revisited", *Polar Research*, 38 (2019), https://polarresearch.net/index.php/polar/article/view/3467; for a documented re-examination of the *Italia* expedition and Nobile's political biography, see the recent book by Claudio Sicolo, *Umberto Nobile e l'Italia al Polo Nord. Politica e storia nelle carte inedite, 1928–1978* (Canterano: Aracne, 2020); further bibliographic references can be found in the chapters by Steinar Aas and Luciano Zani in this volume.
8 Regarding state financial aid, see ACCM, GA, 1935, file 134, bundle 13, subfile 26 "Spedizione Artica. Ministero Finanze e Aeronautica", and subfile 27 "Rapporti con la R. Società Geografica Italiana".
9 In general, on the role of SGI in promoting and sponsoring Italian exploration, see Claudio Cerreti, *Della Società geografica italiana e della sua vicenda storica, 1867–1997* (Roma: Società geografica italiana, 2000); Sandro Rinauro, "La conoscenza del territorio nazionale", in *Storia d'Italia, Annali 26, Scienze e cultura dell'Italia unita* (Torino: Einaudi, 2011), 497–523.
10 These are the periods of office of the three *podestà* in chronological order, December 1926–September 1928; September 1928–November 1929; November 1929–November 1935.
11 ACCM, GA, 1935, file 134, bundle 13, subfile 26 "Spedizione Artica. Ministero Finanze e Aeronautica", Visconti di Modrone to the Geographical Society's commissioner, December 7 and December 13, 1929.
12 The *Consulta Municipale*, the *podestà*'s auxiliary body, had replaced the city council by virtue of the aforementioned r.d. 1910 of 1926.
13 See the commemorative pamphlet *In memoria del N.H. Cav. Di Gr. Cr. Biagio Gabardi* (Milano: Cassa di Risparmio delle Province Lombarde, 1941).
14 Andreoletti's personal file is missing from the Milan Cittadella degli Archivi; from a confidential letter by him sent to the special commissioner of the SGI, Nicola Vacchelli, it is possible, however, to place the moment of his resignation as head of the cabinet to mid-June 1929: SGI, Historical Archives, administrative fonds, bundle 68, file 7/a, Andreoletti to Vacchelli, 17 June 1929. For additional background on these hostilities, see Saverio Almini, ed., *Arturo Andreoletti, 1884–1977* (Milano: Nomos edizioni, 2018), 124–133, 156.
15 I am indebted for this information to Saverio Almini, who was able to see these files before Andreoletti's personal archive was acquired by the National Alpine Association, in Milan, where it is now held at the Documentation Centre but not yet available for consultation.
16 Books by Alfredo Viglieri, *48 Days on the Pack*, and by Giuseppe Biagi, *Biagi racconta. I miracoli della radio nella tragedia polare* (both by: Milan: Mondadori, 1929).
17 The public corporate body in charge of circulating film material for information and propaganda purposes, set up in 1925 after absorbing the previous joint-stock company LUCE (L'Unione Cinematografica Educativa).
18 SGI, Historical Archives, historical fonds, bundle 83/a, file 14, agreement between the Ministry of Aeronautics and the Italian Geographical Society, 6 December 1927.

Appendix 193

19 ACCM, GA, 1935, file 134, bundle 12, subfile 1 "Finanziamento spedizioni"; the idea of funding polar exploration using exclusive contracts was suggested in confidence by Cesco Tomaselli to Andreoletti on October 21, 1927: ibid., file 134, bundle 14, subfile 29 "Piani cessione diritti stampa etc.".

20 ACCM, GA, 1935, file 134, bundle 15, subfile 58 "New York Times"; ibid., subfile 64 "Diritti giornalistici"; subfile 67 "Convenzione con Ministero dell'Aeronautica e impegni verso R. Società Geografica".

21 The expression is used by Eugenio Muggiani, the Municipality's lawyer, on p. 8 of his closing statement on 13 April 1931 presented to the Court of Rome, in the case Nobile v. Hearst Press and Milan Municipality: ACCM, GA, 1935, file 134, bundle 15, subfile 65 "Diritti editoriali".

22 Ibid., file 134, bundle 15, subfile 64 "Diritti giornalistici", Morgagni to Torrusio, April 23, 1928; the italics in the quoted extract correspond to underscores in the document. The author translated this text from Italian to English.

23 The quoted paragraph is contained in Umberto Nobile, *Posso dire la verità: Storia inedita della spedizione polare dell'"Italia"* (Roma: Mondadori, 1945), 39–40, 257–260, and corresponds to the translation of the final part of an article published on 6 July 1928 in the newspaper *Dagens Nyheter* in Stockholm.

24 See ACCM, GA, 1935, file 134, bundle 15, subfile 67 "Convenzione con Ministero dell'Aeronautica e impegni verso la R. Società Geografica", Camagna to Andreoletti, December 8 1928, January 6 and 7, February 12 1929; Nobile to De Capitani D'Arzago, January 5, 1929; De Capitani D'Arzago to Balbo, 6, 7 and 10 January 1929; SGI, Historical Archives, historical fonds, bundle 84, file 1, Andreoletti to Camagna, 9 January 1929.

25 ACCM, GA, 1935, file 134, bundle 15, subfile 62 "Riunione a Roma 21-X-1928", drafts of the minutes of the meeting on October 21, 1928 prepared respectively by the Financing Committee and General Nobile, with notes in the margin; ibid., subfile 67, De Capitani D'Arzago to Balbo, 6 January 1929.

26 ACCM, GA, 1935, file 134, bundle 14, subfile 32 "Fotografie e cinematografie": "fotografie della spedizione Nobile occorrenti al Comitato finanziatore di Milano", October–November 1928.

27 The full name of the joint-stock company was Hearst Newspapers Universal Service, known as Hearst Press.

28 The expression appears in a memorandum by Camagna to the Italian Ambassador in London on October 3, 1928, in Archivio Centrale dello Stato (hereafter ACS), Presidenza del Consiglio dei Ministri (hereafter PCM), Gabinetto – Affari Generali, 1928–1930, file 3.2.4. 1830, subfile 9.

29 ACCM, GA, 1935, file 134, bundle 15, subfile 65 "Diritti editoriali"; ibid., subfile 66 "Vertenza Nobile"; of this case, the closing statements by the defendant, Milan Municipality, but not by the plaintiff, are kept in the two subfiles indicated.

30 See ACS, PCM, Gabinetto – Affari Generali, 1931–1933, file 3.2.4. 9942, letters from the Minister of Finance Guido Jung to the Presidency of the Council of Ministers, 23 September 1932 and 29 May 1933, and "notes" for the head of the Government of 14 October 1932 and 15 June 1933; Arnoldo and Alberto Mondadori Foundation, Milan, Arnoldo Mondadori Editore archive, Arnoldo correspondence, file "Podestà di Milano", Arnoldo Mondadori to Visconti di Modrone, August 21, 1930; ibid., file "Nobile", advice on "pratica generale Nobile", 29 September 1930.

31 Actually, until at least the outbreak of the war, Nobile always presented himself as a Mussolini stalwart, as emerges, among other things, from his letters in the 1930s sent to the head of the government, kept in ACS, Segreteria Particolare del Duce, Carteggio riservato, bundle 59, file 278/R, subfile 4 "Atti diversi", and from an interesting personal letter from Andreoletti to Nicola Vacchelli, January 27 1930, in SGI,

Historical Archives, administrative fonds, bundle 68, file 7/a. See also Luciano Zani, "Between Two Totalitarian Regimes: Umberto Nobile and the Soviet Union (1931–36)", *Totalitarian Movements and Political Religions* 4, no. 2 (2003): 63–112, 99.

32 See, in particular, Nobile, *Posso dire la verità*, 10–13, 19–27; Umberto Nobile, *La tenda rossa: Memorie di neve e di fuoco* (Milano: Mondadori, 1969), 130–134, 242–288; Umberto Nobile, *La verità in fondo al pozzo* (Milano: Mondadori, 1978), 17–20, 131–136, 144–149. This edifying autobiographical rendering of events has also influenced historians, some of whom have accepted Nobile's theses without the necessary critical scrutiny: see, for instance, Francesco Surdich, "Umberto Nobile", in *Dizionario Biografico degli Italiani*, vol. 78 (Roma: Istituto della Enciclopedia Italiana Giovanni Treccani, 2013), *ad vocem*.

33 But the total expenses charged to the state deriving from the Nobile expedition, including rescue operation expenses, totalled almost 15 million lire: ACS, PCM, Gabinetto – Affari Generali, 1931–1933, file 3.2.4. 9942, Minister of Finance Mosconi to the Presidency of the Council of Ministers, 16 July 1929; a total of just under 13 million was, instead, the amount to be paid by the state as presented by the undersecretary of the Navy Giuseppe Sirianni to the Chamber of Deputies as an estimate of expenditure by the Ministry of the Navy for 1929–1930: *Atti Parlamentari, XXVIII Legislatura*, Chamber of Deputies, 30 May 1929 session, 527.

34 ACCM, GA, 1935, file 134, bundle 12, subfile 12, expedition account updated to January 1, 1935, with follow-ups in 1936–1938.

35 Cesco Tomaselli, "Una spedizione nata male", *La Domenica del Corriere* 63, no. 4 (22 January 1961), 14–15.

36 Regarding the progress of this expedition, see, among others, Luca Alessandri, "Karakorum 1929: una spedizione italiana tra aspettative e traguardi", *Geostorie* 19, no. 1–3 (2011): 41–109, www.cisge.it/ojs/index.php/geostorie/article/view/58; there is no comprehensive biographical study on Aimone di Savoia-Aosta; however, a recent doctoral dissertation partially makes up for this (with a chapter on the 1928–29 expedition too): Alberto Cauli, *Italian Pioneers: Colonial Propaganda and Geographic Explorations* (Auckland: The University of Auckland, New Zealand, 2019), 137–187, https://researchspace.auckland.ac.nz/bitstream/handle/2292/46375/whole.pdf?sequence=2&isAllowed=y, last access 10 December 2021.

37 This is the documentary: *Karakorum: Diario della spedizione italiana guidata da S.A.R. il Duca di Spoleto. Impressioni cinematografiche dell'operatore Massimo Terzano*, 1929, which, however, had limited circulation. A copy of the film is today preserved by the National Mountain Museum in Turin.

38 I must point out a significant outcome of this clash: the *Carta topografica del territorio visitato dalla spedizione comandata da S.A.R. il Duca di Spoleto*, in three sheets 1:75,000 scale (Firenze: Istituto Geografico Militare, 1932), attributes exclusive merit to Ardito Desio for the "expeditious surveys" of large parts of the territory, which, however, were explored jointly by Balestreri and Desio. A copy of this map is kept in SGI, Cartoteca, folder B9/IIIa, position R 11-XII.

39 Aimone di Savoia-Aosta (Duca di Spoleto) and Ardito Desio, *La spedizione geografica italiana al Karakoram (1929-VII E.F.): Storia del viaggio e risultati geografici* (Milano-Roma: Bertarelli, 1936).

40 Credit for the discovery, in 2017, goes to Francesco Martelli, director of the Cittadella degli Archivi, and Marco Cuzzi, professor of contemporary history at the University of Milan.

41 And therefore with several gaps, as can be deduced from breaks in the numerical sequence of the negatives.

42 For the negatives see ACCM, GA, 1935, file 133, bundle 9, subfile 4, boxes 4.1–4.2 and 4.3–4.4; for the "positives", ibid., subfile 4, box 4.5, and subfile 6 "Spedizione Karakorum. Fotografie".

Appendix 195

43 A tiny selection of these photos was reproduced for an exhibition held in December 2018 at the University of Milan: *Orme di italiani sul Karakorum. Immagini e documenti dalla spedizione di Aimone Savoia-Aosta, duca di Spoleto, in Karakorum (1927–1936)*, edited by Maura Dettoni, Stefano Morosini and Stefano Twardzik.

44 The three albums are listed as AF/276/IV in the general catalogue of the SGI Photographic Archives: Maria Mancini, ed., *Obiettivo sul mondo: Viaggi ed esplorazioni nelle immagini dell'Archivio fotografico della Società geografica italiana, 1866–1956* (Roma: Società geografica italiana, 1996), 87.

45 The chronology of the journey phases of the 1929 expedition has been carefully reconstructed by Luca Alessandri, who has also tried to identify an author and a more or less precise date for the photos in the Italian Geographical Society albums: see *Cronologia degli spostamenti della spedizione geografica italiana del 1929 al Karakorum*, online on the SGI website, www.archiviofotografico.societageografica.it/index.php?it/195/spedizione-geografica-duca-di-spoleto-al-karakorum-1929.

46 ACCM, GA, 1935, file 133, bundle 11bis, subfile 21 "Originali dei contratti", and subfile 22 "Convenzione e patto disciplinare con i partecipanti".

47 Ibid., file 133, bundle 9, sub-file 1 "Corrispondenza con S.A.R. il Duca di Spoleto", Visconti di Modrone to Aimone di Savoia-Aosta, August 25, 1934.

48 Ibid., file 133, bundle 10, subfile 10, "promemoria delle deliberazioni prese nella riunione tenutasi a Milano il 1° dicembre 1929".

49 For this reconstruction, see ACCM, GA, 1935, file 133, bundle 9, subfile 1 and subfile 2 "Rapporti con la R. Società Geografica Italiana". In all likelihood the three albums delivered to the Duke of Spoleto followed the prince into exile after the referendum of 2 June 1946, which sanctioned the end of the monarchy in Italy.

50 ACCM, GA, 1935, file 133, bundle 10, subfile 10, "Elenco delle fotografie per album".

51 Sella Foundation, Biella, Balestreri collection: each plate measures about 60×130 mm; in addition to these negatives, there are 288 contact sheets (collected into a later packaged album), which provide a broad selection of the aforementioned. For an overview of the fonds and collections in this institute, see Andrea Pivotto, "Le memorie fotografiche della Fondazione Sella", in *Beni fotografici: Archivi e collezioni in Piemonte e in Italia*, ed. Dimitri Brunetti (Torino: Regione Piemonte – Centro Studi Piemontesi, 2012), 133–144.

52 These 1928 images are of remarkable historical interest also because some of the cities photographed by Mario Cugia, such as Rawalpindi and Amritsar, suffered destruction and bloody ethnic massacres accompanying the partitioning of Punjab between India and Pakistan in 1947: see Ian Talbot and Gurharpal Singh, *The Partition of India* (Cambridge: Cambridge University Press, 2009).

53 ACCM, AG, Annual Repertories of files, "Inventario dei fascicoli 1935".

54 Comune di Milano, *Regolamento per l'Archivio civico amministrativo* (Milano: Tipografia Stucchi e Cerretti, 1927), www.comune.milano.it/comune/statuto-regolamenti-patrocini/regolamenti/ab/archivio-civico, last access 10 December 2021.

55 As far as I know, the North Pole expedition dossier (not that of the expedition to the Karakoram), was consulted, apart from by Municipal staff, only in January 1961 by a *La Domenica del Corriere* staff member, who, at the request of Dino Buzzati (in turn so authorised by the mayor of the time), proceeded to photocopy two letters (including Mussolini's official go-ahead for the enterprise), which were then published in the aforementioned retrospective account by Tomaselli dating to 22 January 1961.

56 Comune di Milano, *Regolamento per l'Archivio civico amministrativo*, 8 (Article 33).

57 A few references in the respective websites of the Archivio storico civico e Biblioteca Trivulziana, and of Cittadella degli Archivi, https://trivulziana.milanocastello.it/it and www.comune.milano.it/comune/cittadella-degli-archivi, last access 10 December 2021.

Index of names and places

Abetti, Giorgio 128
Abrahm, Erich 136, 141n47, 142n59
Abyssinia (Ethiopia) 79
Aconcagua (mount) 126
Adamson, Joni 173
Addis Ababa (Ethiopia) 167
Adhikari, Deepak 155n42
Aix-les-Bains (France) 10
Alessandri, Camillo 128
Alessio, Alberto 128
Alexandria (Egypt) 128
Afghanistan 29
Africa 22–23, 73–74, 77–79, 83–84, 87, 126, 174
Aftenposten (Norwegian newspaper) 37, 49, 51
Agra (India) 186
Akron (airship) 62
Alagna Valsesia (Italy) 125
Alaimo, Stacy 175n71
Alaska (USA) 5, 40, 43, 92–93, 95, 141n53; Alaska Highway 93
Albania 73–77, 82
Allegri, Gino 129, 130
Almagià Clara 85n11
Almagià Clelia 85n11
Almagià Clotilde 85n11
Almagià, Corrado 73
Almagià David 85n11
Almagià, Guido 73
Almagià, Roberto 5, 72–89
Almagià Saul 85n11
Almagià, Vito 73
Alps 3–10, 13, 15–18, 21, 76, 91, 108, 111–112, 121, 139, 146, 153–154
Alston, Margaret 173n42
Amannullah Khan 29
Amat Pietro, di San Filippo 23, 31n6
Amber (India) 186

Amrith, Sunil S. 154n12
Amritsar (India) 186
Amsterdam 81
Amundsen, Roald 5, 34–36, 38–51 53–55, 57–59; Roald Amundsen Memorial Fund 45
Ancona (Italy) 73, 85n11
Anderson, Ben 154n10
Anderson, Benedict 154n17
Andes 109–111, 114, 118, 119, 122n23
Andøy Avis (Norwegian newspaper) 45
Andreoletti, Arturo 177–178, 182, 192n14, 193n24, 193n31
Anfossi, Angelo 129
Angelino, Ugo 136, 141n53
Angst, Richard 132
Anker, Conrad 150
Annapurna 148
Annecy (France) 10
Anselmi, Sergio 85n11
Antarctica 1, 95, 110, 119
Anthropocene 1, 7, 164–166
Antonsich, Marco 88n53
Aosta (Italy) 16, 125, 139n7, 142n68; Valle d'Aosta 124, 125, 136, 137
Aquarone, Alberto 87n34
Aragozzini, nameless 190
Ararat (mount) 101
Arbeidet (Norwegian newspaper) 40, 47
Archangel (Russia) 59
Arctic 1, 4–5, 7, 27–28, 34–35, 38, 50, 59–60, 68, 92, 102–104, 140, 176, 188, 190; Alaskan Arctic 121; Arctic Circle 36; Arctic Institute of North America (AINA) 5, 90, 92, 94–96, 98–100, 102–105; Arctic Ocean 40, 45, 47; Arctic Siberia 1
Ardemagni, Ugo 181
Argentina 76

Index of names and places

Arizona (USA) 94
Armiero, Marco 1, 7n4, 8n15, 160–161, 172nn22–23, 173n47
Arnette, Alan 156n46
Asia 3, 5, 7, 23, 26, 28–29, 91, 139, 174
Askole (Pakistan) 129, 130, 186
Ata Ullah 137
Atkinson, David 84n1
Atlantic 168
Attolico, Bernardo 62
Aust-Agder Blad (Norwegian newspaper) 47
Australia 46, 160, 169
Austria 3, 10
Austronesia 168
Azoulay, Ariella Aïsha 171n7

Badalà, Carlo 89n67
Baghdad (Iraq) 30
Baird, nameless 103n24, 103n26
Balbo, Italo 26, 31n24, 63, 67, 182
Balestreri, Umberto 129, 130, 184, 186, 194n38, 195n51
Balkans 73–74, 77, 79, 81, 83
Baltistan 128
Baltoro (glacier) 125, 126, 129, 130, 132, 134
Baltoro Kangri (mount) 132
Barcelona (Spain) 13
Barcham, Thomas 154n18, 155n24
Barcroft, Joseph 111, 122n23
Barents (sea) 59
Bassignana, Pier Luigi 69n28
Bastiansen, Henrik G. 52n18
Bareux, Ernest 127
Barmasse, Luigi 141n47
Barucci, Piero 88n60
Basel (Switzerland) 80
Bates, Robert H. 91–92, 97, 102n13, 104n46, 140n36
Bauer, Luke 155n33
Bauerkämper, Arnd 32n27
Bavaria (Germany) 37
Bawtree, Victoria 174n49
Bay of Tranquillity (Arctic) 59
Belgium 20n30
Bell, Morag 84n1
Benares (India) 186
Ben-Ghiat, Ruth 84n1
Berner Oberland (Switzerland) 125
Bear Island (Norway) 35
Beattie, Andrew 18n1
Beedie, Paul A. 155n34

Běhounek, František 50, 55n91
Belajeff, James 132
Belgrade 13
Belloni, Ernesto 176–178, 180–181
Benjey, Bill 99, 105n67
Benton, Lauren 174n62
Berg, Roald 52n14
Bergen (Norway) 47
Berlin (Germany) 63, 180
Bert, Paul 109, 121nn11–13
Berti, Mario 87n30
Bhaumik, G. 123n43
Biafo (glacier) 126
Biagi, Giuseppe 178, 192n16
Biancani, Robusto 66–67
Biasillo, Roberta 1, 6, 18, 157
Biasutti, Renato 83, 130–131
Biella (Italy) 186
Biermann, Frank 173n46
Bigazzi, Francesco 70n56
Binda, Alfredo 26
Birch, Tony 173n47
Bird Rose, Deborah 172n34, 173n40
Bishop, Barry 96–97
Bissolati, Leonida 76
Bled (Slovenia) 13
Blum, Hester 7n8
Bodø (Norway) 51
Boffa Ballaran, Felice 30, 33n47
Bogota (Colombia) 175n78
Bogra, Muhammad Ali 134
Bolinder, Anders 140n31
Bollini, Maria Grazia 84n9
Bomann-Larsen, Tor 41, 44, 52n12, 53n30, 53n40, 53nn43–44, 53n46, 53n52, 53n54, 54n55
Bonatti, Walter 133, 136, 138, 140nn33–34, 141n47, 141n53, 142n56, 143nn70–74
Bonazzoli, Viviana 85n11
Boonstra, Rudy 105n73
Borghese, Scipione 126
Borgogni, Massimo 84n9
Borsalino, Giuseppe 126
Bothwell, Robert 104n55
Bott, Esther 154n8
Botta, Erminio 127, 139n16
Bottai, Giuseppe 83
Bourrit, Marc-Théodore 146
Boutin, Stan 105n73
Bouvet island (Norwegian island) 35
Bozzoli Parasacchi, Elvezio 143n69
Braldo (glacier) 126, 130

Index of names and places

Branch, J. 156n48
Brasher, Christopher 144, 145, 153n3
Breitenbach, Jake 112
Brescia (Italy) 135
Britannia (swiss hut) 16
British Columbia (Canada) 99
Broad Peak (mount) 128
Brocherel, Alexis 127
Brocherel, Emile 127
Brocherel, Henri 127
Bron, Leone 129, 130, 190
Brown, Joe 144
Bruers, Antonio 27, 32n32
Bubandt, Nils 175n72
Budapest 10
Bulle (Germany) 16
Bullock, Fanny 126, 127, 139n12
Burrard, Sidney Gerald 154n11
Burtscher, Martin 122n24
Butlin, Robin 84n1

Caccavale, Romolo 70n56
Caciolli, Stefano 138n1
Cadorna, Luigi 26
Calchi Novati, Gian Paolo 87n34
Calciati, Cesare 126, 139n12
Caldo, Costantino 73, 84n8
Calgary (Canada) 100
Camagna, Carlo 181–182, 191, 193n24
Cameron, Garth 68n4
Campania (Italian region) 160
Campbell, Claire 102n18
Campbell, Courtney J. 174n57
Camperio, Manfredo 23
Camp Hale (USA) 92
Canada 5, 90, 92–93, 97–100, 102, 104;
 Canali Paolo (pseudonym Adstans) 134, 135, 141n39
Canella, Maria 31n22
Cannell, M. 155n29
Cappadocia 173n45
Caprotti, Federico 31n20
Capuzzo, Ester 30n3
Carducci, Giosuè 22
Caribbean 168
Carrigan, Anthony 173n38
Caron, David D. 7n1
Carter, Adams (member of Harvard five) 91, 142n58
Capitalocene 1, 7, 166
Cappon, Massimo 140n33
Capristo, Annalisa 85n67
Carazzi, Maria 84n10
Carrel, Luigi 141n47

Carter, Hubert Adams 142n58
Casella, Antonio 85n15
Cassi, Laura 139n14
Cassin, Riccardo 133, 134, 136, 141n47, 142n54
Cassin Guido 141n53
Caucasus 125, 139n6, 153n3
Cavazzani, Francesco 139n4
Cecchini, Marcella 68n7
Cecioni, Enrico Alfonso 132
Ceirano 1500 (car) 26
Cerreti, Claudio 84n10, 192n9
Chabod, Renato 142n68
Chakrabarty, Dipesh 157, 170n3, 173n38, 174n55
Chakravorti, Gayatri 170n2, 170n4
Chamonix (France) 10, 13–14, 146
Chenoz, Cesare 126
Chiaiano (Italy) 160, 161
Chiardola, Giuseppe 129, 130, 190
Chiavolini, Alessandro 80
Chicago 96
Chile 109
China 96–98, 108, 116, 145–146, 152–153; Chinese Turkmenistan 128; Xinjang (region) 128
Chogolisa (or Bride Peak, mount) 127
Chomolungma (mount) see Everest
Cho Oyu (mount) 110
Chowri Kang (mount) 116, 123n43
Chrisman, Laura 170n2
Christensen, Jon 173n36
Christopher Columbus 83, 137, 157, 170n1, 171n6
Chrulew, Matthew 172n34
Ciocca, Gaetano 57, 68n9
Clayton, Daniel 158
Clarke, Garry K.C. 102n1, 103n22
Clarke, J. Calvitt 68n6
Clavin, Patricia 19n4
Clayton, Daniel 171n9
Clements, Philip W. 7n8, 111, 112, 121n8, 122nn25–26, 122n39, 123n55, 123n57, 154n22
Coates, Kenneth 104n61
Cohn, Bernard S. 154n12
Collotti, Enzo 26, 31n25
Colombo, Cristoforo see Christopher Columbus
Colorado (USA) 92, 118
Comintern 37
Compagnoni, Achille 133, 136–138, 141n47, 142n59
Conboy, Kenneth 104n44

Index of names and places 199

Concordia circus (Pakistan) 126, 130
Conefrey, Mick 140n34
Conway, William Martin 126
Cooke, Stuart 172n34
Copenhagen (Denmark) 46
Corbi, Gianni 70n56
Corna Pellegrini, Giacomo 84n7
Corneli, Dante 70n56
Corradini, Enrico 24, 31n15
Corriere della Sera (Italian newspaper) 24, 191
Corte, Ugo 154n19
Cortina d'Ampezzo (Italy) 13–14, 86
Costa, Amedeo 142n68, 143n69
Costantini, Ezio 141n47
Costa Pinto, Antonio 32n27
Cotes, John 116, 122n40
Courmayeur (Italy) 16, 126–127, 129
Croce, Benedetto 75–76, 80, 82–83, 86n25
Cronon, William 155n35, 171n12
Crosby, Alexandra 160, 172n25, 175n73
Cross, Wilburn 69n12
Croux, Evaristo 129, 130, 190
Cruikshank, Julie 93, 103n21
Cuaz, Marco 142n68
Cueto, Marcos 122n19, 123n58
Cugia, Mario 129, 184–186, 190, 195n52
Cupini, Ranieri 31n24
Cuzzi, Marco 5, 31n8, 32n27, 194n40
Cyrenaica (Libya) 25, 78
Czechoslovakia 13, 20n30

D'Acunzo, Benedetto 137
Dagbladet (Norwegian newspaper) 44
Dag Jølle, Harald 36, 52n2, 52nn6–7, 52n9
Dag og Tid (Norwegian newspapaer) 49
Dahlgaard, Henning 7n1
Daily Telegraph (British magazine) 144, 145, 153n2
Dainelli, Giotto 68n4, 78, 83–84, 87n39, 89n68, 124, 128–129, 131–133, 140nn28–30, 184
D'Albertis, Enrico Alberto 23
Dal Piaz, Giorgio 86n24
Danby, Ryan K. 102
D'Annunzio, Gabriele 31n16, 78
Danube (river) 27
D'Arcis, Charles Egmond 10–14, 20nn21–28
Darjeeling (India) 29
Da Polenza, Agostino 140n33
Da Roit, Armando 136, 141n47
da Silva, Claiton Marcio 171n15
da Silva, Garcia 19n6

Dass, D. 123n43
Daulton, Harry L 122n39
David, Robert G, 68n4
Davis, Diana K. 174n60
Davis, Heather 173n48
Davis, Michael 169, 173n41, 175n79
Dawson, Ashley 172nn29–30
Dean, Michele 84n7
De Bernardi, Mario 26
De Capitani d'Arzago, Giuseppe 140n20, 177–178, 193n24
Dee, Johan 174n65
De Felice, Renzo 31n21, 82, 88n59
de Figueiredo, Marina Dantas 174n51
De Filippi, Filippo 124, 127, 128, 133, 139nn15–16, 190
De Gasperi, Alcide 134, 135, 140n35, 141n39
De Grand, Alexander 174n60
de la Barre, nameless 105n67, 105n69, 105n71
Del Boca, Angelo 87n34
Deledda (Milan road) 188
De Lollis, Cesare 75
DeLoughrey, Elizabeth 173n38
Del Prete, Carlo 26
Denali (or McKinley, mount) 141n53
Deosai (Pakistanian plateu) 186
de Saussure, Horace-Bénédict 107, 146
Desio, Ardito 19n15, 89n68, 124, 129, 130, 132–138, 140nn22–23, 140nn25–26, 142n59, 184, 190, 194nn38–39
de Sousa Santos, Boaventura 171n13
De Stefani, Alberto 82, 88n60
De Toni, Antonio 86n24
Dettelbach, Michael 121n9
Diaz, Armando 26
Di Bernardino, Natale 63
di Caporiacco, Lodovico 28, 129, 190
Dick, William W. 103n42
Didur, Jill 173n38
Diesen, Jan Anders 52n13
Di Giorgio, Anita 136
di Nucci, Loreto 69n28
di Savoia-Aosta, Aimone (Duke of Spoleto) 23, 25, 124, 128–131, 140n22, 176, 184, 186, 194n36, 195n47
di Savoia-Aosta, Luigi Amedeo (Duke of Abruzzi) 28, 124, 127, 139n14
di Vallepiana, Ugo 12–13, 20nn24–26
Doel, Ronald E. 96, 103n39
Dogliani, Patrizia 32n26

Index of names and places

Dole, Minto 122n
Dolgaprudnaja (Russia) 62, 66, 70n56
Donzel, Maurice 47
Doria, Giacomo 23
Dras (India) 186
Drivenes, Einar-Arne 36, 52n2, 52nn6–9
Driver, Felix 121n9
Drozdz, Martine 159, 160, 172nn20–21
Ducci, Roberto 27, 32n29
Dundovich, Elena 70n57
Dunning, Eric 31n9
Durham 153n1
Durig, Arnold 111, 122n
Dyhrenfurth, Norman Gunther Oskar 111, 123n49, 124, 132, 140
Dymitrow, Mirek 172n32

Edney, Matthew H. 154n12, 171n6
Edwards, Bob 154n19
Egidi, Silvio 74
Eidsiva (Norwegian newspaper) 45
Einaudi, Luigi 137
Elbrus (mount) 125
Elias, Norbert 31n9
Elkington, Bianca 171n17
Ellis, Reuben 9, 18n2
Ellsworth, Lincoln 39, 41, 43, 49, 53
Elsner, Jás 154n10
Elvestad, Sven 37–39, 53
Emerson, Richard M. 111, 112
Emmett, Robert S. 173nn36–37
England 10, 28, 40, 154
Eriksen, Anne 36, 44–45, 52, 53n45, 54nn56–61
Eritrea 74, 79
Ertl, Hans 132
Ertsen, Maurits W. 167, 174n63
Escarra jean 10, 14
Escobar, Arturo 174n49
Ethiopia 67, 73, 78–79
Europe ix, 17, 23, 26, 28, 32n27, 74, 79, 109, 110, 115, 125, 126, 146, 158, 164
Everest (mount) 2, 6–7, 91, 96, 104, 110–115, 117–123, 144–156; American Mount Everest Expedition 7, 112, 115, 120, 121n8, 148, 154n22; Mount Everest Foundation 148

Fabre, Giorgio 70n56
Fallani, Fabrizio 138n1
Fanon, Franz 158
Fantin, Mario 136, 138n1, 139n7, 142n59
Farinacci, Roberto 26
Faulhorn (mount) 112

Faux, Ronald 155n27
Faylor, Robert 96–97, 103nn34–35; Ferraiolo, Carlotta 60, 63, 69n14, 69n22, 69nn32–33, 70n36
Felsch, Philipp 121n5
Ferraresi, Alessandra 85n15
Ferrari, Virgilio 137
Ferrarin, Arturo 26
Ferreri, Eugenio. 11–12, 19n15, 20nn21–23
Fiat (italian car producer) 57, 61
Fick, Adolph Eugen 112
Figari, Bartolomeo 13, 20n28
Finchelstein, Federico 32n27
1ste Mai (Norwegian newspaper) 40
Fisher, David 99, 104n63
FitzGerald, Edward Arthur 126
Flemming, James 173n36
Floreanini, Cirillo 136, 141n47, 142n59
Florence (Italy) 84; University of Florence 128, 130, 142n59
Flores, Marcello 69n28
Florentin, L. 15
France 10, 13, 20n30, 24, 26, 47
Franchey, Ernesto 141n47
Franz Joseph Land (Russian Arctic archipelago) 59
Freitas Schilling Marquesan, Fábio 174n51
Fremover (Norwegian newspaper) 45
Frevert, Ute 19n7
Fribourg (Germany) 16
Friheten (Norwegian newspaper) 46
Frisinghelli, Vittorio 11–12, 19n15
Friuli (Italian region) 136
Fogelson, Nancy 68n4
Folkets Avis (Norwegian paper) 46
Forgacs, David 3–4, 8n16
Formichi, Carlo 29, 32n42
Fortunato Formiggini, Angelo 75–76, 85n22
Foscari, Pietro 27, 32n33
Fosheim Lund, Maria 52n13
Frachey, Ernesto 136
Frachey, Oliviero 136
Fugazza, Mariachiara 31n7
Fuller, Mia 84n1, 167, 174n64
Fure, Odd-Bjørn 52nn3–5
Furet, François 56, 67n3
Furre, Berge 52n15

Gabardi, Biagio 140n20, 177, 182, 183, 191, 192n13
Gabrielli, Gianluca 85n17
Gabrielsen, Tor 49–51, 54n82, 54n84

Gadigal and Wangal (Australia) 160
Gaffuri, Luigi 84n10, 87n32
Gallotti, Pino 136, 141n47
Gambi, Lucio 72–73, 84nn2–6
Gan, Elaine 175n72
Garibaldi, Giuseppe 73
Garutti, Giacomo 63
Garzilli, Enrica 32n40
Gasherbrum IV (mount) 141n53
Gaspard, Ferdinando 141n47
Gaspard, Giuseppe 139n16
Geneva (Switzerland) 10, 13- 17, 126
Genoa (Italy) 129, 137, 142n59
Gentile, Emilio 23, 31n11, 67nn1–2
Gentile, Giovanni 24, 31n16, 75, 80, 82–83, 85n12, 85n20, 86n22, 86n24, 88n61, 89n70
Geopolitica (Italian journal) 79, 84–85n10, 88n53
Germany 10, 37, 40, 47, 50, 62–63, 132
Ghedina, Luigi 141n47
Ghiglione, Piero 124, 132, 133, 140n32
Giannini, Amedeo 79, 83, 85n20, 89n67
Gianoli, L. 16
Gilbert, Daniel L. 121n10
Gilchrist, Paul 122n29
Gilkey, Arthur Karr 134
Gillman, Leni 154n14
Gillman, Peter 154n14
Giolitti, Giovanni 139n15
Giovine, Allegra 174n57
Giuliani, Giuseppe 85n15
Giuntini, Sergio 31n22
Glérey, Emilio 126
Gobbi, Antonio 141n47
Goddard, Joseph 172n32
Godwin-Austen, Henry Haversham 137; Godwin-Austen glacier 127
Goodstein, Judith R. 85n13
Gould, Lawrence 93
Graf von Hardenberg, Wilko 8n14
Gramsci, Antonio 25
Granatstein, Jack 93, 102n16
Grandi, Dino 29
Grand St. Bernard (Italy-Switzerland Pass) 16
Grange, D. 87n34
Grant, M. W. 113, 122n30
Graziani, Rodolfo 25
Graziosi, Paolo 142n59
Great Britain 24, 26, 30, 133, 147
Greece 20n30, 26
Greenland 35, 91, 95
Grenoble-Uriage 10

Gressoney Saint-Jean (Italy) 125, 139n7
Griffin, Roger 32n27
Gross, Rachel S. 154n16, 155n29
Grossberg, Lawrence 170n2
Gruyère (Switzerland) 16
Grzywacz, Tomasz 7n10
Gsteigwiler (Switzerland) 125
Guha, Ranajit 170n4
Gulmarg (India) 186
Gund (Pakistan) 130

Habeler, Peter 115
Hackett, Peter 119
Hahn, Dave 156n44
Haldane, John Burdon Sanderson 114, 118, 123n47
Hamar Arbeiderblad (Norwegian newspaper) 38
Hansen, Peter H. 6, 7n8, 124, 139n2, 144, 154nn9–10, 154n13, 154n17, 155n38
Hanson, Susan 159
Haraway, Donna 7n3, 166, 174n54
Harm, Henry 45, 54n62, 54nn64–65
Harrer, Heinrich 30, 32n46
Harris, David E. 104n48
Hartmann, Hans 122n28
Harvard University 91
Hashmatullah Kahn 132
Hedin, Sven A. 154n11
Hedney, Matthew H. 171n18
Heeney, Arnold 93
Heffernan, Michael 84n1
Heggie, Vanessa 5, 7n8, 104n45, 104n49, 106, 121nn2–3, 121n6, 121n8, 122n27, 122n31, 122n35, 123nn44–45, 123n53, 123nn57–58, 154n22
Heil, Nick 155n31
Heise, Ursula K. 173n36
Hepp, Günter 122n28
Heymann, Harriet Paolina 132
Hidden Peak, or Gasherbrum I (mount) 132
Hik, David S. 102n1
Hillary, Edmund 110, 119, 147, 148, 150
Himalaya 1, 4, 90–91, 96–98, 104, 108–110, 112, 114, 119, 123, 125, 139nn10–11, 141n53, 144–146, 148, 150, 153–154; *Der Dämon des Himalaya* (film) 132; Hispar (glacier) 126; Hitchcock, Fred A. 121n13; Hitchcock, Mary Alice 121n13;
Hitler, Adolf 37–38
Hobsbawn, Eric 30n2, 31n9
Höchl, Albrecht 132

202 *Index of names and places*

Hodgson, Foresta 94
Hoefs, Manfred 99, 105n64
Hoel, Adolf 47, 50–51, 54n76, 54n87, 55nn95–98
Hofe, Elisabeth Kalau von 132
Hofmeyr, Isabel 175n70
Hohtürli (swiss hut) 16
Holland, Clive 68n4
Hollander, Paul 61, 69n25
Honnørbrygga (Norway) 42
Hornbein, Tom 115, 116, 118, 122n38, 123n49
Hornidge, Anna-Katharina 173n42
Horscroft, James A. 123n56
Horvath, Elizabeth C. 121n17
Horvath, Steven M. 121n17
Houston, Charles 91–92, 97, 100, 104n46, 104n48, 134, 140n36
Howe, Joshua P. 102n12
Howkin, Adrians 7n8
Huang, Hsinya 174n52
Hudson, Simon 155n34
Humboldt, Alexander von 107–109
Hungary 20n30
Hunt, John H.C. 123n50, 153n3

Il Popolo d'Italia (Italian newspaper) 26, 31n18, 181, 190
Il Tricolore (Italian newspaper) 24
Imas, José Miguel 174n51
India 28–30, 81, 96, 98, 128, 133, 146–147, 152–153, 186; East India Company 146; Great Trigonometrical Survey of India 146; Survey of India 137
Indochina 81
Indonesia 81
Indus (river) 134, 141n38, 186
Interlaken (Switzerland) 16
Iovino, Serenella 170, 175n75
Iraq 29
Irvine, Andrew 91, 113, 119, 147
Isenberg, Andrew C. 174n58
Islamabad (Pakistan) 133, 134, 140n37
Isnenghi, Mario 86n24
Isserman, Maurice 2, 7n7, 9, 18n2, 102n3, 139n1, 153n4
Italy (or Italia) 3, 5–6, 8, 11, 13, 17, 19–20, 22–24, 26–31, 33–34, 37 45, 57–58, 60–61, 63–64, 67–68, 71–75, 76–79, 81–85, 87–89, 124–135, 137–138, 142, 161, 170, 175, 181, 183, 191, 195; Italia (pass in Karakoram) 132; L'Italia che scrive (Italian newspaper) 75; Tour of Italy 26

Ivrea (Italy) 10
Jackson, Mark 121n8
Jackson, Moana 171n17
Jacomoni, Francesco 87n30
Jaipur (India) 186
Jan Mayen (Norwegian island) 35
Japan 81
Jemolo, Arturo Carlo 83
Jesus, Christ 45, 67
Jiliani, Shahzeb 142n62
Johnson, Mary Jane 101
Jolly, Margaret 7n1
Jones, Max 121n4
Jones, Owain 175n82
Joshi, Sumit 151, 155n41
Jourdanet, Denis 109, 121n14
Journal de Geneve (Swiss newspaper) 15
Judas 45
Justman, J.J. 156n44

K2 (mount) 2, 6, 7, 97, 102, 104, 124–128, 133–135, 137–143, 153, 191
Kabul (Afghanistan) 29–30
Kaika, Maria 31n20
Kallis, Aristotele 32n27
Kanchenjunga (mount) 148
Kang-xi 146
Karabenick, Edward 171n15
Karachi (Pakistan) 134; Caracorum(italian toponym of Karakoram) 188, 190; Karakoram (massif) 6, 23, 25, 28 124–129, 130–134, 139n4, 140n20, 141n53, 142n59, 176, 178, 180, 183–185, 188, 191, 194–195; Karakorum (italian toponym of Karakoram) 27, 30, 139n4, 140n20, 141n53, 142n59, 194–195
Kargil (India) 186
Kaskawulsh (glacier) 95
Kazbek (mount) 125
Kearnes, Matthew 172n34
Keating, Jennifer 174n57
Keenleyside, Hugh 93, 97, 104n53
Kellas, Alexander Mitchell 119
Keller, Tait 8n2, 9, 18n2, 154n10
Kelly, Matthew 8n14
Kennedy, John F. 98
Kennedy, Robert F. 98
Kern, Leslie 171n17
Keys, Ancel 110, 120, 121nn17–18
Khawarzad, Aurash 162, 163, 172nn28–29
Kiddle, Rebecca 171n17
Kirksey, Eben 175n74
Kitchin, Rob 175n76

Index of names and places 203

Kjellen, Rudolf 81
Klinkhammer, Lutz 71n60
Kluane (Canadian lake and region) 90–93, 95–97, 99–102
Kohli, Mohan S. 104n44
Kooperatøren (Norwegian newspapaer) 50, 54–55
Korolevskij, Cirillo 87n30
Koser Gunge (mount) 126
Krakauer, Jon 144, 155n31
Krebs, Charles J. 100, 105n73; Kristiania (Norway) 36
Kristensen, Monica 68n4
Kumar, M. Satish 158, 171n9
Kun (mount) 139n16
Kurz, Marcel 132
Kuthiah (valley and glacier) 134
Kvam Jr, Ragnar 53n33

Labanca, Nicola 87n34
Lacedelli, Lino 133, 136, 141n47, 142n59
Ladakh (India) 29, 128
La Domenica del Corriere (Italian newspaper) 183
Lahore (Pakistan) 186
Lainema, Matti 7n6
Lal, Shib 128
Land, Alexandra 59
Lando, Fabio 87n32
Lanzarotta, Tess 121n7
Larson, Edward J. 7n8, 139n1
La Suisse (Swiss newspaper) 15
Latini, Alessandro 132
La Tribune de Genève (Swiss newspaper) 16, 21
Launay, Guy 69n26
Lawson, Alan 174n59
Leal, Claudia 8n14
Lecco (Italy) 136, 141n47
Ledda, Antonio 67
Lee Schwenz, Caroline 171n11
Lehner, Giancarlo 70n56
Lekan, Thomas 173n43
LeMenager, Stephanie 173n36
Leningrad 40, 69n33; Petrograd 40
Lercoz, Roberto 124, 125, 139n6
Les Alpes (Swiss journal) 16
Leshem, Noam 166, 174n61
Lester, James T. 111
Leonardi, Sandra 85n14
Leonardo (Italian newspaper) 75
Lewis- Jones, Huw 68n4
Lhotze (mount) 141n53
L'Humanité (French newspaper) 46

Libya 5, 78, 81
Liebig, Justus von 112
Liechty, Mark 145, 154n7
Lima (Peru) 175n78
Linguerri, Sandra 85n15
Livak, Leonid 54n71
Logan (mount) 97–98
Lloyd, Peter 102n4, 104n53
Lombardi, Francesco 134, 142n59
Lombardi, Vittorio 135, 141n45, 142n56
London 46, 125, 146–147, 181
Lop Nur (China) 96
Lorenzi, Arrigo 75
Love, Herbert 104n56, 105n72
Lovejoy, Derek 140n37
Louisiana (USA) 92
Lowenhaupt Tsing, Anna 175n72
Luca institute 178, 191
Lucania (Canada mount) 92, 94
Ludwig, Emil 68n8
Luft, Ulrich Cameron 122n22
Lundborg, Einar 50, 54n86, 55n91, 58
Luzzana Caraci, Ilaria 84n10

Macugnaga (Italy) 125, 126
Maestri, Cesare 136, 141n47, 142n55
Magnar Syversen, Odd 53n25
Magrini, Giovanni 74
Mahdi (or Mehdi), Amir 133, 137, 142n62
Makalu (mount) 110, 119
Mallet, Robert 32n27
Mallory, George 91, 113–114, 119, 147
Malmgren, Finn 46
Manaresi, Angelo 11–12, 19n15, 20n17, 20n20, 20n22, 132
Manganiello, Raffaele 84
Manicardi, Nanzia 86n23
Manning, Harvey 154n21
Manservigi, Lino 66, 67
Mantovani, Roberto 140n33
Maraini, Fosco 7n11, 133
Maranelli, Carlo 75–76
Marchetti, Ada Gigli 31n7
Marcolin, Gaetano 66
Marconi, Guglielmo 79
Mariano, nameless 47
Marinelli, Olinto 84n10, 128
Marocco, Secondo 57
Marrickville (Australia) 160, 162, 172n25
Marshall, Robert 140n33
Martelloni, Francesco 84n9
Martin-Nielsen, Richard 101
Martins, Luciana 121n9
Marosz, Michail 7n10

Index of names and places

Marton, Endre (alias Andrew) 132
Marussi, Antonio 142n59
Massi, Ernesto 81, 89n68
Mastropietro, Nico 7n11
Mathieu, Jon 18n1
Matterhorn (mount) 16
Matthey-Claudet, W. 21n41
Mauri, Carlo 141n47
May Creek (USA) 96–97
Mazzitelli, G. 85n20
Mazzolini, Elizabeth 155n32
McCandless, Robert G. 103n18
McDonald, Bernadette 97, 104n45, 104n47
McKenzie, Marcia 173n35
McKinley *see* Denali
McNaught Davis, Ian 144
McTaggart-Cowan, Ian 99–100
Mediterranean (sea) 26, 27, 73; Melgara, Pierangelo 143n73
Meliga, Ferdinando 126
Menotti, Mario 66
Mercarelli, Iginio 31n23
Mercer, Claire 171n15
Merchant, Carolyn 171n12
Mercier, Ocean Ripeka 171n17
Meneses, Maria Paula 171n13
Messner, Reinhold 115, 145, 148–150, 155n27, 155n33
Mettelhorn (mount) 16
Meyer, Willy 54n86
Mezzetti, Ottorino 25
Micelli, Francesco 86n26
Michel, John 16
Middle East 23, 74
Miège, Jean-Louis 87n34
Migliorini, nameless 83
Mignolo, Walter 158
Milan 13, 25, 67–68, 135, 137–138, 140, 153n1, 176–178, 180, 182–187, 190, 192, 193
Milanini Kemeny, Anna 84n10, 87n34
Milan Municipal Archives (Cittadella degli Archivi) 6, 129, 176, 187–188, 192
Milledge, James S. 122n21
Misiani, Simone 88n60
Mitman, Gregg 173n47
Modena (Italy) 75
Mondadori, Arnoldo 178, 182–183, 191, 193n23
Monge Medrano, Carlos 110
Monina, Giancarlo 87n34
Monte Rosa (massif) 125–126
Monticone, Alberto 133
Monza (Italy) 141n47

Monzino, Guido 149
Moore, Jason W. 174n50
Moore, Martin D. 121n8
Moore, Terris 91
Morgagni, Manlio 180–181, 193n22
Mori, Assunto 75
Mori, Attilio 78, 87n39
Moro, Aldo x
Moro, Simone 151
Morosini, Stefano 1, 6, 18, 31n10, 124, 142n56, 191n2, 195n43
Morrison, William R. 104n61
Morrissey, Katherine G. 174n58
Mosca, Manuela 88n60
Moscati, Ruggero 32n39
Mosconi, Antonio 178, 194n33
Moscow (Russia) 57, 62–63, 65, 67
Mosse, George L. 31n9
Mousie, Joshua 173n38
Moxon, Siân 172n32
Mulgrew, Peter 119
Müller, Jakob 125
Mumbai (India) 28, 129–130
Munksgaard, Odd 54n72
Münster, Ursula 175n74
Mussolini, Arnaldo 31n18, 32n37, 181
Mussolini, Benito 11, 24–29, 31n17, 37–38, 42, 46, 52n21, 57–58, 62–64, 67, 77, 80–81, 128–129, 140n20, 174, 176, 178, 182, 191
Mustagh (pass in Karakoam) 130
Muzorewa, Terence Tapiwa 171n17
Myers, Garth 172n31
Myhre, Jan Eivind 52n20

Naczyk, Marta 7n10
N*adir* Shah, Mohammed 29
Nalesini, Oscar 33n47
Nanda Devi (mount) 96
Nanga Parbat (mount) 122n28, 139n7
Nansen, Fridtjof 35–36, 43–45
Naples (Italy) 49, 57, 130, 160–161
Narula, Svati Kristen 156n49
Narvik in Nordland (Norway) 45
Natili, Daniele 84n10
Naville, Paul 21n39
Nazrul Islam, S. 175n77
Neale, Timothy 174n67
Negrotto, Federico 127
Nelson, Cary 170n2
Nencioni, Giuseppe 68n4
Nepal 29, 30, 112, 145, 147, 150–152, 154n17
Nepal, Sanjay K. 156n50

Index of names and places 205

Nestler, Stefan 155n36
Netherlands i, 20n30
Neufeld, David 93, 99, 101, 102n18, 103n20, 105n68, 105n75
Neveu, Pie Eugène 62
New York (USA) 24, 162–163
New York Times (American newspaper) 36, 97, 101, 147
New Zealand 126, 154n17
Nice, nameless 83
Niemann, Michelle 173n36
Nixon, Rob 173n47, 174n68
Nobile, Maria 62–64
Nobile, Umberto 5, 23, 25, 28, 34, 38–51, 56–67, 68n4, 68nn10–11, 69nn14–24, 69n26, 69nn30–34, 70nn36–56, 129, 135, 176–178, 180–183, 191, 193–194nn31–33
Noel, John 146
Nordlandposten (Norwegian newspaper) 51
Nordlys (Norwegian newspaper) 40
Norsk Kommunistblad (Norwegian newspaper) 40
North Africa 126
North America x, 26, 92, 94, 109, 110, 182
North Pole 2, 6, 25, 40, 43, 56–58, 63, 67, 128–129, 135, 176–178, 180–181, 183
Norway 34–38, 40–47, 49–55
Norwegian Aviation Club 39
Norwood, John 157, 158, 170n1
Novello, Elisabetta 31n20
Noyce, Wilfred 123n51
Noyes, John 174n66
Nun (mount) 139n16
Nunes, João Arriscado 171n13
Nurminen, Juha 7n6
Nutt, nameless 103n28
Nyandoro, Mark 171n17
Nyawo, Vongai Z. 171n17
Nye, David E. 173nn36–37

Oberto, Giuseppe 141n47
Obertreis, Julia 174n58
Odell, Noel Ewart 91, 94, 102n4
Oestreich, Johann Wilhelm Karl 126, 139n10
Officer, Charles 68n4
Oggioni, Luigi 141n47
O'Gorman, Emily 172n34
Oh, Young Hoon 155n37
Olivieri, Chiara 173n35
Omberg, Asbjørn 49, 54n80
Omodeo, Angelo 57

Oppermann, Serpil 175n75
Oreskes, Naomi 103n40
Oriani, Alfredo 23, 31n5
Ortega Santos, Antonio 173n35
Ortner, Sherry B. 123n54, 145, 154n7
Oslo (Norway) 38, 42, 45
Oslo Aftenavis (Norwegian newspaper) 39
Østbye, Jan 54n83
Østlendingen (Norwegian newspaper) 47
Otranto (Mediterrenean Canal) 73, 77
Ottawa 92–93, 101
Ottosen, Rune 52nn17–18, 53n24, 53n31
Ottoz, Arturo 136, 141n47

Padua (Italy) 142n59
Pagani, Guido 136, 141n47, 142n59
Page, Jake 68n4
Pakistan 129, 133, 134, 136, 140n37, 142n62, 186, 195n52
Pala, Augusto 141n47
Panmah (glacier) 130
Papa, Emilio Raffaele 86n24
Paris (France) 13, 46
Parijanine, Maurice (alias Maurice Donzel) 47
Parkutta (Pakistan) 186
Parvanova, Deyna 30n2
Pastore, Alessandro 11, 19n3, 20n20, 142n55
Pastorelli, Pietro 27, 32n31, 84n9
Pavolini, Paolo Emilio 87n30
Peak XV (mount) 146
Peedom, Jennifer 156n43
Pella, Giuseppe 135
Pelissier, Camillo 141n47
Penzo, Vittorio 136, 141n47
Perrone, Andrea 84n10, 88n53
Persia 29
Pershad, Jamna 128
Peru 109, 116, 122n19, 123n58
Peter I (Antarctica Island) 35
Peterkin, Grant 126
Petigax, Joseph 126–128
Petigax, Laurent 126, 127
Petit St. Bernard (Italy-France Pass) 16
Petracchi, Giorgio 68nn5–6
Phillips, Richard 159
Piacenza (Italy) 126
Piacenza, Mario 139n16, 140n16
Pianura (Italy) 160
Piccin, Antonio 61, 69nn28–29
Pigliasco, Guido Carlo 31n8
Pignatelli, Valerio 182
Pikes Peak (mount) 118

Index of names and places

Pini, Giorgio 27, 32n30
Pioneer Peak (mount) 126
Piramide Vincent (mount) 125
Pirijanin, Maurice 54n74
Pisa (Italy) 58
Pizzo, Chris 119
Plantationocene 1, 166
Plint, Michael 139n12
Point Nemo (South Pacific Ocean) 1
Pokhrel, Rajan 156n48
Poland 10, 20n30, 63
Polvara, Gaetano 184
Ponta, Angelo 140n33
Ponti, Gio 134
Ponti, Vittorio 129, 130, 184, 190
Pontresina (Switzerland) 13
Porter, Libby 171n16
Port Said (Egypt) 128
Pozzi, Mario 22, 30n1
Prague (Czech Republic) 13
Prakash, Gyan 170n4
Prezzolini, Giuseppe 75, 85n20
Prudhoe Bay (Alaska) 102n15
Puchoz, Mario 136, 137, 141n47
Pugh, Lewis Griffith Cresswell Evans 110, 111, 113, 118, 121n3, 122n30, 123n48
Pulham (UK) 40
Punta Zumstein (mount) 125
Purja Pun Magar, Nirmal 152, 156n53

Quaisier, Simeone 126
Queen Maud Land (Antartica) 35

Ragle, Dick 95
Rahnema, Majid 174n49
Rainero, Romain H. 32n31
Rak, Julie 153
Rambert, Eugène 17
Rapongan, Syaman 174n52
Rateau, Mélanie 175n78
Ratzel, Friedrich 81, 131
Rawalpindi (Pakistan) 186
Redaelli, Daniele 141n53
Reddy, William M. 19n8
Red Sea 128
Reed, John 95, 103nn29–30, 103n36
Reichenbach im Kandertal (Switzerland) 16
Reichwein, PearlAnn 9, 104n57, 104n60
Reihard, Wolfang 30n2
Revelli, Paolo 75
Rey, Adolphe 126
Rey, Enrico 141n47
Rey, Henry 126

Rey Ubaldo 136, 141n47, 142n59
Riccardi, Andrea 89n67
Ricchieri, Giuseppe 75–76, 86nn25–26
Richalet, Jean-Paul 121n14
Ridgeway, Rick 155n26
Rigano, Anna Rita 88n60
Rima (glacier) 128
Rimu (glacier) 132
Rinauro, Sandro 5, 72, 84n10, 192n9
Risør (Norway) 47
Rivista Coloniale (Italian magazine) 78
Robert, E. A. 20n34
Roberts, David 92, 102n6, 104n59
Roberts, Peder 5, 7n8, 90
Robin, Libby 173n39, 174n56
Robinson, L.H. 105n67
Rocco, Alfredo 81
Roch, Andrè 132
Rodway, George W. 121n15
Roeder, Carolin F. 153n3
Rogoschin, Wladimir (alias Gustav Diessel) 132
Roletto, Giorgio 81, 89n68
Rolfe, Helen Y. 155n25
Romania 26, 128
Rome x, 12, 13, 27–30, 30n4, 32n27, 39, 40, 43, 57, 58, 63, 64, 66, 70n35, 73, 77, 78, 80, 81, 83, 85n12, 86n26, 88nn48–50, 88nn64–65, 89n66, 134, 136, 137, 174n60, 176, 182, 184, 191, 193n21
Roots, Fred 98, 104n58
Roselli, Alessandro 84n9
Ross, Mike 171n17
Roussy, Albert 16, 20n34
Rovereto (Italy) 142n68
Rowan, I. 153n2
Rowe, Carrillo 171n8
Rowell, Galen 140n36
Roy, Abhirup 156n47
Rubiés, Joan-Pau 154n10
Ruby, Robert 68n4
Rugg, Linda 173n36
Russia 60–64, 66, 69n14, 70n41, 108, 128
Rutherford, Stephanie 172n33
Ryan, Simon 174n59
Ryon, Eugenio 141n47

Saglio, Silvio 142n67
Said, Edward 159
Salerno (Italy) 66
Salisbury, Richard 153n5, 156n51
Salt, J. D. 103n24
Salt, Karen N. 175n69

Index of names and places 207

Salvemini, Gaetano 75–76, 79–80, 86n25
Samoilovitch, Rudolph L. 58
Sandberg, L. Anders 172n33
Santoro, Stefano 89n67
Sapolsky, Harvey 103n40
Saragat, Giuseppe 135
Sarpo-Lago (glacier) 130
Savio, Andrea 141n45
Savoia (pass on K2 north-west ridge) 127
Savoye, Albert 127
Savoye, Cyprien 126, 139n16
Sawicka, Magdalena 7n10
Saxon, Wolfgang 105n74
Scaglia, Ilaria 4, 7n8, 9, 18, 19nn5–6, 153n3
Schama, Simon 139n3
Schaumann, Caroline 121n5
Scheffler, Robin Wolfe 121n16
Scheiber, Harry N. 7n1
Schmatz, Hannelore 119
Scholtes, Fabian 173n42
Schwarz, Anke 171n16
Scola-Camerini, Zanetto 134
Scotland 168
Scott, Doug 150
Scott, James C. 3, 7n12
Scott, Robert Falcon 121n4
Seattle 41- 42, 44
Selassié, Hailé 79
Sella, Vittorio 127, 139n14, 186
Sella foundation 186
Senatori, Luciano 19n3
Seville (Spain) 82
Seward (glacier) 93
Sforza, Carlo 29
Shaksgam (valley) 129, 130, 184
Sharma, Bharda 7n9
Sharma, Gopal 156n47
Sharp, Bob 93–94
Sherman, William 168, 174n65
Shigar (valley) 126, 129, 186
Shimla (India) 186
Shipton, Eric 144
Shkumbini (Albanian river) 77
Shotwell, Alexis 175n72
Siàcen (valley) 132
Sia Kangri (massif) 132
Sias, Jose 100
Sicolo, Claudio 68n12, 69n13, 71n58, 192n7
Signori, Elisa 85n15
Silva Santisteban, Rocío 175n78
Simmons, George 68n4
Simpson, Michael 173n46
Sind (Indian valley) 186
Singhiè (glacier) 130
Sion (Switzerland) 16
Siracusa, Giuseppe 178
Siri, Will 112
Skardu (Pakistan) 130, 186
Skolnick, Adam 7n9
Skyang Kangri (mount) 127
Slovenia 13
Sluga, Glenda 19n4
Sluyter, Andrew 159, 171n12, 171n14
Smeaton, Jennie 171n17
Smiraglia, Claudio 142n59
Smith, Albert 139n2
Soldà, Gino 136, 141n48, 142n59
Somalia 79
Somervell, Thomas H. 117, 123n46
Sørensen, Gert 32n27
Sori, Ercole 85n11
Sörlin, Sverker 7n5, 173n44
South America 26, 109, 116, 123n58, 126
South Pole 2, 36, 44
South Tyrol (Italy) 145
Spain 10, 13, 26
Spampanato, Bruno 26
Spitsbergen (Norwegian island) 40, 46, 50
Spivak, Gayatri Chakravorty 157, 170n2, 170n4
Spørck, A. 53n51
Spranger, John Alfred 128
Spufford, Francis 68n4
Srinagar (India) 129–130, 133, 186
Stak (valley) 134
Stalin, Josef 47, 64–66
Staszak, Jean-François 175n76
Stavanger (Norway) 46–47
Steele (mount) 92
Stein, Jesse Adams 175n73
Steinar, Aas 5, 34, 53–55, 68, 140nn18–19, 192
St Elias (massif) 5, 90–91, 95–96, 98, 101
Stenseke, Marie 172n32
Stern, Philip J. 154n12
Stettler, Peter 139n9
Stirone, Shannon 8n17
Stolp (Germany) 40, 180–181
Streule, Monika 171n16
Studi Albanesi (Journal) 79, 87n46
Sturani, Enrico 136
Soviet Union 5, 26, 30, 40, 57, 60–61, 63–66, 68–70, 194
Svalbard (Norwegian Arctic archipelago) 34–35, 40, 43–44, 46, 53, 129, 181

208 Index of names and places

Svendsen, Georg 50, 54nn89–90, 55n94, 55n101
Swanson, Heather Anne 175n72
Switzerland ix, xii, 10, 13, 17, 20n30, 31, 112, 126, 132
Sydney (Australia) 160, 172n25
Szymczak, Robert K. 7n10

Tabei, Junko 149, 155n25
Tagliavini, Carlo 87n30
Takeda, Pete 104n44
Tandberg, Rolf S. 51, 55n99
Tarbela (dam) 134, 141n38
Tashi, Phurba 151
Taylor, Joseph E. 154n20
Taiwan 168
Teheran (Iran) 30
Telemark Arbeiderblad (Norwegian newspaper) 45
Teller (Alaska) 40
Tenderini, Mirella 142n54
Tenzing, Norgay 118, 147, 148, 155n38
Terzano, Massimo 129, 184, 190, 194n37
The Daily Mail (British Newspaper) 46
Thrift, Nigel J. 175n76
Tien Shan (massif) 126
Tiffin, Chris 174n59
Thomas, Amanda 171n17
Thommesen, Rolf 39–40, 43
Thompson, Gerry 105n72
Thorpe, Jocelyn 172n33
Tibet 29–30, 32–33, 125, 146–147
Tidens Tegn (Norwegian newspaper) 35, 38 40, 43
Tissi, Attilio 135
Todd, Zoe 173n48
Togliatti, Palmiro 66–67
Tollardo, Elisabetta 19n13
Tomaselli, Cesco 183, 190, 193n19, 194n35, 195n55
Tonella (nameless) 20nn30–33
Torino (Italy) *see* Turin
Torrusio, Ernesto 180–181, 193n22
Tortorelli, Gianfranco 86n86
Toscanini, Antonio 24
Tovar, Luisa 175n78
Tracy, Sarah W. 110, 121nn17–18, 123n56
Trentino (Italian region) 136
Trevisan, Luca 141n45
Trieste (Italy) 142n59
Tripolitania (Libya) 25, 78
Trojani, Felice 62, 70n56
Tromsø (Norway) 45
Trondheim (Norway) 39

Trotter, William R. 102n11
Tucci, Giuseppe 29–30, 32n40
Tuck, Eve 158, 171n8, 173n35
Tuckey, Harriet 121n3
Turati, Augusto 28
Turi, Gabriele 85n21, 86nn23–24, 89n70
Turin (Italy) 20, 24, 125, 129, 132, 136, 139n7, 142n37, 194
Turkey 26, 29
Turner, Stephen 174n67
Turri, Eugenio 175n83
Twardzik, Stefano 6, 140n17, 176, 195
Tyndall, John 107

Ugolini, Luigi 87n30
Ungaro, Mario 32n44
United Nations 147
United Stated of America 10, 42, 44, 57, 62, 86, 92, 94–98, 110, 125, 147, 164
University of Milan 73, 129, 135, 194–195
Unsworth, Walt 122n41, 155n23
Upton, Phil 95, 97, 100
Urdok (glacier) 130
Urdukas (Pakistan) 130

Vacchelli, Nicola 185, 192n14, 193n31
Vacek, Jarmila 132
Vadsø (Norway) 38
Vale do Javari (Brasil) 1
Valle, Giuseppe 182
Valle d'Aosta see Aosta
Vancouver (Canada Mount) 94
van der Watt, Lize-Marié 7n8, 101
van Dooren, Thom 172n34, 173n40, 175n74
Vanni, Ilaria 160, 172n25
Vanoli, Luigi 66
Vatican 5, 25, 66, 83
Venier, Elio 89n67
Vento, Andrea 32n43, 32n45
Venturi Ginori, Nello 128
Vermont (USA) 92, 97
Verne, Jules 23
Vernet, C. 17
Viault, François-Gilbert 109
Vietnam 96–97
Villa, Attilio 63
Vincent, Johann Nicolaus 125
Vinci, Anna Maria 85n10, 88n53
Viola, Eric 140n34
Viotto, Sergio 136, 141n47, 142n59
Visconti di Modrone, Marcello 177, 184
Vittorio Emanuele III 25
Volterra, Vito 73–75, 79, 83

Wahl, H.E. 104n51
Wakild, Emily 8n14
Wall Street Journal (American newspaper) 148
Ward, John R. 30n2
Warde, Paul 7n5, 173n44
Ward Hunt (Artic Canada ice shelf) 95
Warren, Louis S. 174n58
Washburn, Bradford 91–92
Washburn, Lincoln 93, 103n25
Washington 96, 137
Weaver, Stewart 2, 7n7, 9, 18n2, 139n1, 153n4
Weiner, Richard 171n5
Wendt, Albert 174n52
Wenzel, Jennifer 173n38
West, John B. 118, 121n1, 121n14, 122n36, 123n43, 123n52
Whillans, Don 144
Whittaker, Jim 148
Whyte, Kyle Powys 173n41
Wiese, Vladimir Julevich 59
Wiessner, Fritz 102n9
Wilkinson, Freddie 155n39, 156n45
Williams, Andrew 102n1
Williams, Andy 100, 105n70
Williams, Jeffrey J. 172n34
Williams, Patrick 170n2
Windsor, Jeremy S. 121n15
Winkel, John 175n77
Winzeler, Hans 132
Wislicenus, Johannes 112
Wisnicki, Adrian S. 175n84
Wolff, Eric 7n1

Wolford, Wendy 7n2
Wood, Henry 128
Wood Abbott, Harrison 94
Wood Abbott, Valerie 94
Wood Abbott, Walter 5, 90–105
Workman, William Hunter 126, 127, 139n12
Wormbs, Nina 7n5

Yang, K. Wayne 158, 171n8
Yarcand (river) 128
Yugoslavia 20n30, 77
Yukon (Canada) 5, 90, 99, 102–104

Z3 (mount) 139n16
Zahir Shah, Mohammed 29
Zakopane (Poland) 10
Zanetti, Bruno 142n59
Zani, Luciano 5, 56, 68–71, 140nn18–19, 192, 194
Zannini, Andrea 19n3
Zanskar (valley) 139n16
Zanzi, Luigi 133, 140n33
Zappfe, Peter Wessel 45
Zappi, Filippo 47, 54n73
Zeman, Ellen J. 104n48
Zermatt (Switzerland) 11–13, 16
Zog, Ahmet Lekë Bej 77
Zoji La (pass in Karakoram) 130
Zoli, Corrado 78, 87n39
Zomia (massif) 3
Zoppi, Ottavio 178
Zurbriggen, Matthias 125, 126, 139n8
Zürich (Switzerland) 80, 91, 118

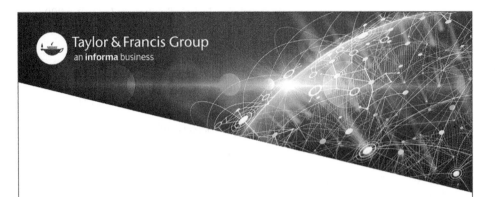